Communications in Computer and Information Science 1447

More information about this series at http://www.springer.com/series/7899

Marten van Sinderen · Leszek A. Maciaszek ·
Hans-Georg Fill (Eds.)

Software Technologies

15th International Conference, ICSOFT 2020
Online Event, July 7–9, 2020
Revised Selected Papers

Editors
Marten van Sinderen
Information Systems Group
Enschede, The Netherlands

Hans-Georg Fill
Universität Fribourg
Fribourg, Switzerland

Leszek A. Maciaszek
Wrocław University of Economics Institute
of Business Informatics
Wrocław, Poland

Macquarie University
Sydney, Australia

ISSN 1865-0929 ISSN 1865-0937 (electronic)
Communications in Computer and Information Science
ISBN 978-3-030-83006-9 ISBN 978-3-030-83007-6 (eBook)
https://doi.org/10.1007/978-3-030-83007-6

This Springer imprint is published by the registered company Springer Nature Switzerland AG
The registered company address is: Gewerbestrasse 11, 6330 Cham, Switzerland

Preface

The present book includes extended and revised versions of a set of selected papers from the 15th International Conference on Software Technologies (ICSOFT 2020), exceptionally held as a web-based event, due to the COVID-19 pandemic, during July 7–9, 2020.

ICSOFT 2020 received 95 paper submissions from 36 countries, of which 19 were accepted and presented as full papers at the conference. After the conference, the authors of a selection of the presented full papers were invited to submit a revised and extended version of their paper, having at least 30% new material. This resulted in 12 revised and extended papers (i.e., 13% of the original 95 submissions) that were included in this book.

The papers were selected by the event chairs and their selection was based on a number of criteria that included the classifications and comments provided by the Program Committee members, the session chairs' assessment, and the verification of the papers' revisions and extensions by the program and conference chairs.

The purpose of the ICSOFT conference series, which started in 2006, is to bring together researchers, engineers, and practitioners interested in software technologies. The conference areas are "Software Engineering and Systems Development", "Software Systems and Applications", and "Foundational and Trigger Technologies".

The topics of the extended and revised papers cover a wide range of some of the most recent and highly relevant software technologies ranging from model-based approaches for cyber-physical systems and internet-of-things systems, and machine learning algorithms for software testing, to semantic methods for cloud and data applications and formal verification approaches.

We would like to thank all the authors for their contributions and the reviewers who have helped ensure the quality of this publication.

July 2020

Hans-Georg Fill
Marten van Sinderen
Leszek Maciaszek

Organization

Conference Chair

Leszek Maciaszek	Wroclaw University of Economics and Business, Poland, and Macquarie University, Sydney, Australia

Program Co-chairs

Marten van Sinderen	University of Twente, The Netherlands
Hans-Georg Fill	University of Fribourg, Switzerland

Program Committee

Peter Amthor	Technische Universität Ilmenau, Germany
Vincent Aranega	University of Lille, France
Pasquale Ardimento	University of Bari Aldo Moro, Italy
Ethem Arkin	Hacettepe University, Turkey
Soumyadip Bandyopadhyay	BITS Pilani K K Birla Goa Campus, India, and Hasso Plattner Institute, Germany
Davide Basile	University of Florence, Italy
Yann Ben Maissa	INPT, Morocco
Jorge Bernardino	Polytechnic of Coimbra - ISEC, Portugal
Mario Berón	Universidad Nacional de San Luis, Argentina
Marcello Bersani	Politecnico di Milano, Italy
Dominique Blouin	Telecom Paris, France
Antonio Bucchiarone	Fondazione Bruno Kessler, Italy
Thomas Buchmann	University of Bayreuth, Germany
Jonas Bulegon Gassen	Antonio Meneghetti Faculdade, Brazil
Andrea Burattin	University of Innsbruck, Austria
Fergal Caffery	Dundalk Institute of Technology, Ireland
Alejandro Calderón	University of Cádiz, Spain
Ana Castillo	Universidad de Alcalá, Spain
Ana Cavalli	Telecom SudParis, France
Alexandru Cicortas	West University of Timisoara, Romania
Lidia López Cuesta	Universitat Politècnica de Catalunya, Spain
Sergiu Dascalu	University of Nevada, Reno, USA
Cléver Ricardo de Farias	University of São Paulo, Brazil
Martina De Sanctis	Gran Sasso Science Institute, Italy
Steven Demurjian	University of Connecticut, USA
Chiara Di Francescomarino	FBK-IRST, Italy
Amleto Di Salle	University of L'Aquila, Italy

Francisco Domínguez Mayo	University of Seville, Spain
German-Lenin Dugarte-Peña	Universidad Carlos III de Madrid, Spain
Gencer Erdogan	SINTEF, Norway
Morgan Ericsson	Linnaeus University, Sweden
Anne Etien	Université Lille 1, France
João Faria	University of Porto, Portugal
Estrela Ferreira Cruz	Instituto Politécnico de Viana do Castelo, Portugal
Felix Garcia Clemente	University of Murcia, Spain
Alejandra Garrido	Universidad Nacional de La Plata and CONICET, Argentina
Aritra Ghosh	Florida Atlantic University, USA
Paola Giannini	University of Piemonte Orientale, Italy
John Gibson	Telecom SudParis, France
Ana-Belén Gil-González	University of Salamanca, Spain
Gorkem Giray	Independent Researcher, Turkey
Ricardo Giuliani Martini	Universidade Franciscana, Brazil
Jose Gonzalez	University of Seville, Spain
Gregor Grambow	Hochschule Aalen, Germany
Christiane Gresse von Wangenheim	Federal University of Santa Catarina, Brazil
Hatim Hafiddi	INPT, Morocco
Ludovic Hamon	Le Mans Université, France
Jean Hauck	Universidade Federal de Santa Catarina, Brazil
Pedro Henriques	University of Minho, Portugal
Jose Herrera	Universidad del Cauca, Colombia
Mercedes Hidalgo-Herrero	Universidad Complutense de Madrid, Spain
Jose R. Hilera	University of Alcala, Spain
Ralph Hoch	TU Wien, Austria
Andreas Holzinger	Medical University Graz, Austria
Jang-Eui Hong	Chungbuk National University, South Korea
Miloslav Hub	University of Pardubice, Czech Republic
Zbigniew Huzar	Wroclaw University of Science and Technology, Poland
Ivan Ivanov	SUNY Empire State College, USA
Judit Jasz	University of Szeged, Hungary
Maria Jose Escalona	University of Seville, Spain
Hermann Kaindl	TU Wien, Austria
Carlos Kavka	ESTECO SpA, Italy
Dean Kelley	Minnesota State University, USA
Jun Kong	North Dakota State University, USA
Rob Kusters	Open Universiteit Nederland, The Netherlands
Wing Kwong	Hofstra University, USA
Pierre Laforcade	Lium, France
Giuseppe Lami	ISTI-CNR, Italy
Yu Lei	The University of Texas at Arlington, USA

Pierre Leone	University of Geneva, Switzerland
Letitia Li	BAE Systems, USA
David Lorenz	Open University, Israel
Daniel Lucrédio	Federal University of São Carlos, Brazil
Ivan Lukovic	University of Novi Sad, Serbia
Stephane Maag	Telecom SudParis, France
Ivano Malavolta	Vrije Universiteit Amsterdam, The Netherlands
Eda Marchetti	ISTI-CNR, Italy
Manuel Mazzara	Innopolis University, Russia
Hamid Mcheick	University of Quebec at Chicoutimi, Canada
Andreas Meier	Zurich University of Applied Sciences, Switzerland
Francesco Mercaldo	IIT-CNR, Italy
Antoni Mesquida Calafat	Universitat de les Illes Balears, Spain
Gergely Mezei	Budapest University of Technology and Economics, Hungary
Cristian Mihaescu	University of Craiova, Romania
Antao Moura	Federal Universisty of Campina Grande, Brazil
Christian Muck	University of Vienna, Austria
Antonio Muñoz	University of Malaga, Spain
Takako Nakatani	The Open University of Japan, Japan
Elena Navarro	University of Castilla-La Mancha, Spain
Joan Navarro	La Salle - Universitat Ramon Llull, Spain
Viorel Negru	West University of Timisoara, Romania
Paolo Nesi	University of Florence, Italy
Claus Pahl	Free University of Bozen-Bolzano, Italy
Marcos Palacios	University of Oviedo, Spain
Asier Perallos	University of Deusto, Spain
Jennifer Pérez	Universidad Politécnica de Madrid, Spain
Dana Petcu	West University of Timisoara, Romania
Dietmar Pfahl	University of Tartu, Estonia
Giuseppe Polese	Università Degli Studi di Salerno, Italy
Mohammad Mehdi Pourhashem Kallehbasti	University of Science and Technology of Mazandaran, Iran
Rosario Pugliese	Universita' di Firenze, Italy
Stefano Quer	Politecnico di Torino, Italy
Traian Rebedea	University Politehnica of Bucharest, Romania
Werner Retschitzegger	Johannes Kepler University, Austria
Marcela Xavier Ribeiro	Federal University of São Carlos, Brazil
Andres Rodriguez	Universidad Nacional de La Plata, Argentina
Colette Rolland	Université Paris 1 Panthèon Sorbonne, France
António Rosado da Cruz	Instituto Politécnico de Viana do Castelo, Portugal
Gustavo Rossi	Universidad Nacional de La Plata, Argentina
Matteo Rossi	Politecnico di Milano, Italy
Stuart Rubin	University of California, San Diego, USA
Gunter Saake	Institute of Technical and Business Information Systems, Germany

Maria-Isabel Sanchez-Segura	Carlos III University of Madrid, Spain
Nickolas Sapidis	University of Western Macedonia, Greece
Santonu Sarkar	BITS Pilani K K Birla Goa Campus, India
Elad Schiller	Chalmers University of Technology, Sweden
Peter Schneider-Kamp	University of Southern Denmark, Denmark
Eva-Maria Schoen	HAW Hamburg, Germany
Istvan Siket	Hungarian Academy of Science, Hungary
Kuldeep Singh	Carnegie Mellon University, USA
Harvey Siy	University of Nebraska at Omaha, USA
Cosmin Stoica	Romania
Ketil Stolen	SINTEF, Norway
Hiroki Suguri	Miyagi University, Japan
Selma Suloglu	Rochester Institute of Technology, USA
Claudine Toffolon	Université du Maine, France
Michael Vassilakopoulos	University of Thessaly, Greece
László Vidács	University of Szeged, Hungary
Yan Wang	Google, USA
Dietmar Winkler	Vienna University of Technology, Austria
Jinhui Yao	Xerox Research, USA
Murat Yilmaz	Dublin City University, Ireland
Fatiha Zaidi	Université Paris-Saclay, France
Zheying Zhang	Tampere University, Finland

Additional Reviewers

Jaganmohan Chandrasekaran	University of Texas at Arlington, USA
Franck Chauvel	SINTEF, Norway
Alexandru Cicortas	West University of Timisoara, Romania
Enrique Garcia-Ceja	SINTEF, Norway
Hana Mkaouar	Telecom Paris, France
Mounira Msahli	Telecom Paris, France
Nikola Obrenović	University of Novi Sad, Serbia

Invited Speakers

Dominik Slezak	University of Warsaw, Poland
Wil van der Aalst	RWTH Aachen University, Germany
Frank Buschmann	Siemens AG, Germany

Contents

Shared Autonomous Mobility on Demand: A Fuzzy-Based Approach and Its Performance in the Presence of Uncertainty

Rihab Khemiri(✉), Mohamed Naija, and Ernesto Exposito

Univ. Pau & Pays Adour, E2S UPPA, LIUPPA, EA3000, 64600 Anglet, France
ernesto.exposito@univ-pau.fr

Abstract. Ride-sharing Autonomous Mobility-on-Demand system (RAMoD), whereby self-driving vehicles provide coordinated travel services on-demand and potentially allowing multiple passengers to share a trip, has recently emerged as a promising solution to cope with several problems such as low vehicle utilization rates, pollution, and parking spaces. The expected uncertain travel demand on such systems and its resulting imbalance and insufficient charging resources require an efficient fleet management strategy. This paper focuses on designing and testing an integrated strategy for dispatching, rebalancing, and charging by accounting for the uncertain travel demands. Specifically, we first devise a novel multi-objective possibilistic (MILP) model, which contemplates the variability and uncertainty affecting travel demands in the RAMOD systems. The main target is to centralize the various decisions in order to keep vehicle availabilities balanced over the planning horizon and the transportation network so that travel requests are satisfied at a minimum cost. Second, leveraging appropriate strategies, we transform this fuzzy formulation into an equivalent auxiliary crisp multi-objective model. Due to the conflicting nature of the considered objectives, a goal programming approach with specific weights for each goal is used to compute an efficient compromise solution. Results show the applicability and usefulness of the proposed fuzzy approach as well as its merits compared to other schemes.

Keywords: Autonomous mobility-on-demand systems · Ride-sharing · Dispatching · Rebalancing · Charging · Fuzzy logic

1 Introduction

Personal-vehicles contribute significantly to increasing levels of pollution, traffic congestion, and in several instances the under-utilization of vehicles. Explicitly, in 2015 the utilization rate of owned automobiles in the U.S. is about 5% [1], certainly unsustainable practice for the years to come. The urgent need to deal with these trends spurred the conception of efficient, cost-competitive, and more sustainable transportation systems such as ride-sharing (e.g. Lyft and Uber) and car-sharing (e.g. Car2Go and Zipcar).

M. van Sinderen et al. (Eds.): ICSOFT 2020, CCIS 1447, pp. 1–24, 2021.
https://doi.org/10.1007/978-3-030-83007-6_1

Nevertheless, without efficient fleet management, these emerging transportation systems will inevitably lead to a problem of vehicle imbalances: due to the asymmetry between travel destinations and origins, vehicles rapidly depleted in some stations while becoming accumulated in others, affecting the quality of service.

Autonomous vehicles have the particular advantage of being capable of rebalancing themselves, in addition to the enhancement of system-wide coordination, cost reduction, convenience, and potentially rise safety of not needing a human driver.

Accordingly, these distinctive advantages has spurred the device of strategies that entail to optimally rebalance Autonomous Mobility on Demand (AMoD) systems by repositioning empty vehicles.

A Specific focus is also given to the development of dispatching strategies that attempt to optimally assign the customers to self-driving vehicles, in order to satisfy the customer's request at each time period. However, as we will show in the literature review section, most of the proposed strategies either assume deterministic customer requests or do not integrate operational constraints such as parking capacities and electric vehicle charging, which restricts their practical application.

In particular, while customer request is relatively predictable, it is subject to considerable uncertainties due to various external factors such as traffic conditions and weather. Thus, successful rebalancing and dispatching strategies must deal with these uncertainties. Although some recent research works have been developed to address this key challenge, these studies consider the uncertainty of demand approximately by using probability concepts. A probability distribution is generally derived from historical data. Nevertheless, when there is a lack of such information, the standard probabilistic approaches are not appropriate. In particular, in several practical situations, the uncertain parameters can be obtained subjectively based on the experience and managerial judgment. For example, the uncertain customer request may be more suitably expressed either in imprecise terms (e.g. approximately 500 demand per hour) or in linguistic terms (e.g. 'low', 'high' 'moderate'). However, such vagueness in the critical data cannot be captured in a stochastic or deterministic formulation, and thus the associated optimal results may not accomplish the real objective of modeling. Zadeh [2] introduced the Fuzzy Set Theory and the Possibility Theory to handle the epistemic uncertainty of this type.

To the best of the authors' knowledge, the only paper exploring the potential of fuzzy set theory to deal with uncertainty in AMOD systems is the preliminary version of this article appeared as [3].

This extended version includes as additional contributions: (i) integration of the charging process, (ii) integration of a number of real-world constraints such as parking space limitations, charging stations capacities, and charging duration, which extend the practical application of the proposed approach, (iii) additional simulation results and corresponding discussion, and (iv) proofs of all results.

More specifically, the purpose of this article is to develop and test an integrated strategy for dispatching, rebalancing, and charging decisions for Ridesharing Autonomous Electric Mobility On-Demand systems. In this regard, we design a three-phase approach, which starts with introducing a new Multi-Objective Possibilistic Linear Programming model that handles the uncertainty affecting future travel demand. The goal is to reduce transportation costs and improve customer satisfaction. In the second phase, the fuzzy model is converted into an auxiliary crisp MOLP model by applying a combination of appropriate strategies. Then, the well-known GP approach is exploited to find an efficient compromise solution for the multi-objective problem.

The rest of this article is organized as follows. In the next section, we review some well-known existing works and outline their limitations. Section 3 provides some basic notions regarding the fuzzy set theory and the goal programming method. Then, we detail the model of the RAMoD system in the presence of uncertain travel demand and formulate the integrated dispatching, rebalancing, and charging problem. Section 5 proposes a three-phase fuzzy strategy to deal with the issue under consideration. In Sect. 6, computational results are reported to highlight the feasibility of our proposed approach in practice. The last section concludes this work together with some future direction of research.

2 Literature Review

The last decade has been marked by the rapid expansion and the promising development of AMOD and RAMOD systems. Its multiple strengths have spurred a number of companies and researchers to aggressively pursue the design and analysis of these emerging transportation systems. Previous work can be categorized into three major areas: simulation-based models, model predictive control (MPC) algorithms and queuing-theoretical models.

In [4], the authors introduce the "Expand and Target" algorithm that has been integrated with scheduling strategies to automatically dispatch self-driving vehicles. They implement an agent-based simulation framework and evaluate the effectiveness of the proposed approach based on the New York City taxi data. The results show that the algorithm greatly enhances the performance of the AMOD systems: increases the travel success rate by around 8% and decreases the average waiting time for passengers by around 30%.

Another study conducted in New York City [5] addressed both the problems of assigning travel requests to vehicles and finding optimal routes for the vehicle fleet while varying passenger capacities. The results show that a fleet of 3000 vehicles with a four-passenger capacity or even 2000 vehicles with a ten-passenger capacity can serve 98% of the travel demands, currently supported by more than 13,000 single-occupant vehicles. However, specificities of the model (for instance, the algorithms employed to represent the traffic flow) are still unexplained, and only very little information has been reported in this regard.

Another study [6] conducted in a similar context of ride-sharing systems for a case study conducted in Austin implemented a simulation framework in Java. The authors suggested that shared AMoD systems without introducing dynamic ride-sharing can increase congestion levels and travel times.

Melbourne, Australia is another city for which the performance of AMoD systems has been explored using an agent-based simulation tool [7]. This work also has discovered a quadratic relationship between Vehicle-Kilometres Travelled and AMoD fleet size. The findings of this simulation model showed that an AMoD system under demand uncertainty, which provides either ridesharing or car-sharing service could decrease the fleet size by 84%. This, however, can increase the current Vehicle-Kilometres Travelled by up to 77% while car-sharing is allowed, and 29% in the ride-sharing systems.

On the other hand, the queueing-theoretical approach is commonly used for the modeling and analysis of AMoD systems. Zhang and Pavone [8], for instance, implemented this method to conduct a real-world case study of New York City. They first cast the transportation system within a Jackson network model with the concept of "passenger loss" (i.e. if there are no vehicles parked at a station, instead of waiting, the passengers will immediately exit the system). Second, the theoretical insights have been leveraged to design a real-time rebalancing algorithm, where the objective is to reduce the number of rebalancing self-driving vehicles on the roads, while still maintaining a balance throughout the transportation network.

An extended and revised version of this paper appeared as [9] by extending the proposed Jackson network approach by adopting a Baskett–Chandy–Muntz–Palacios (BCMP) queuing-theoretical framework [10, 11]. Such a BCMP framework allows capturing vehicle routing, stochastic customer arrivals, battery charging-discharging for electric vehicles as well as traffic congestion.

The significance of the results in these papers could be in providing a rigorous approach to the problem of rebalancing and routing as well as a rapid determination of the corresponding performance metrics. However, both of the studies fail to address the case where several passengers may share the same vehicle that each person travels alone. Moreover, these works consider a static instead of a dynamic number of travelers since they only change pick-up location without leaving the system.

In [12], a fog based-architecture was proposed to handle charging and dispatching problems. The fog-based design delivers the micro-management of electric vehicles to the fog controller of each zone that is near the passengers, thus minimizing communications and computation delays. Using a queuing model, this paper focuses on representing multi-class dispatching and charging processes and finding the optimal number of required vehicles (i.e. vehicle dimensioning) for each zone in order to ensure a bounded response time. Decisions on the relative proportions of vehicles of the different classes to directly serve passengers or to fully/partially charge are also optimized so as to minimize the overall number of vehicles in-flow to a given area. While the proposed dispatching and charging architecture seems promising, the model assume a certain customer request, fail to address the critical issue of vehicle imbalance and do not leverage the emerging paradigm of ride-sharing service.

Due to their capacity to accommodate complex constraints and their simplicity, a number of previous studies on the control of AMoD and RAMoD systems use a network flow framework to model the transportation system.

For instance, Rossi et al. [13] investigate the problem of rebalancing and routing a shared fleet of self-driving vehicles offering on-demand mobility services for a capacitated road network, where congestion is susceptible to disrupt throughput. Within the proposed network flow model, empty rebalancing and customer-carrying vehicles are represented as flows over the capacitated network. Using the real road network of Manhattan, the authors show the efficiency and the superior performance of the proposed rebalancing and routing algorithm compared to state-of-the-art algorithms. Despite these significant findings, it was interesting for the authors to investigate other approaches to reduce congestion, such as ride sharing services. Moreover, the paper fails to explore the interaction between the power network and such electric fleets and assume that travel demands are known with certainty.

Salazar et al. [14] devise a multi-commodity network flow optimization approach that captures the interaction between public transit and AMoD systems. This model aims to maximize social welfare by minimizing the operational costs generated by the intermodal AMoD system together with customers' travel time. Real-world case studies were undertaken in the transportation networks of Berlin and New York, which allowed to assess of the significant benefits of intermodal systems such as reducing the total number of vehicles, travel times, overall costs, and pollutant emissions. However, the proposed model considers only single-occupant vehicles and fails to capture the uncertainty effects such as variable travel demand, time-varying traffic congestion, and transportation delays.

MPC algorithms are amenable to achieve efficient performance and allow for the incorporation of complex and constrained systems. Accordingly, they have been widely employed in problems ranging from control to analyze AMoD and RAMoD systems. MPC algorithm (also called receding horizon control) is an iterative control technique by which an optimization problem is solved at each stage to produce a series of control actions up to a given fixed horizon, and the first action is implemented [15].

In [15], a linear discrete-time model to optimize vehicle scheduling and routing in an AMoD system was proposed allowing the easy inclusion of several real-world constraints such as vehicle charging constraints. Then, leveraging this formulation an MPC algorithm was devised for the optimal coordination of the self-driving vehicles in the transportation network. At each time step, the optimization problem is solved as a mixed-integer linear program, with the objective of avoiding unnecessary vehicle rebalancing and servicing passengers as quickly as possible. Although numerical results demonstrate that the proposed approach outperforms previous strategies, these real-world data were run for moderately-sized systems and without considering ride-sharing services.

A time-expanded network has been exploited in [16] to model the AMoD system. Such a model allows simultaneously finding the minimum fleet size and the optimal rebalancing policy. This formulation was adopted to devise an MPC algorithm to operate the AMoD system in real-time by taking into account short-term forecasts of travel demand. For this purpose, the authors use a forecasting model trained based on historical data and neural networks. The complexity of the proposed approach does not depend on the number of passengers or the number of vehicles. Thus it can be implemented to control large-scale transportation systems. However, the authors did not indicate if the proposed MPC algorithm can be employed to effectively control ridesharing systems.

To address the stochasticity of travel demand, [17] introduces a stochastic MPC algorithm leveraging the uncertainty of demand forecasts for dispatching and rebalancing self-driving vehicles in an AMoD system. To generate the forecasts, The Long Short Term Memory (LSTM) neural network was used to estimate the mean of future travel demand. The proposed algorithm was tested using real data, and it has been exhibited that the latter outperforms state-of-the-art non-stochastic approaches. However, the authors did not discuss if the proposed algorithm can achieve similar gains by predicting stochastic future demand in the context of ride-sharing systems.

This will be the subject of the paper appeared as [18], which focuses on devising an MPC approach for RAMoD systems based on the present and future customer request. The goal of this MPC algorithm is to minimize the weighted combination of the operational costs and the total travel time (i.e. maximize the social welfare). Despite the fact that this model was developed to respond to travel requests in a ride-sharing context, the authors choose to focus only on double-occupancy vehicles and they avoid investigating high-occupancy models given computational complexity.

To position our research work in the extended domain of AMoD systems, we use four criteria, namely the decision processes handled, the modeling approach used, the source of uncertainty that the problem deals with, and whether the ride-sharing service has been addressed. Table 1 shows a summary of the related works analyzed above in accordance with these four dimensions. The majority of these studies are fairly recent because AMoD and RAMoD systems are emerging transportation systems. As mentioned before, the majority of these studies fall into three specific groups: simulation-based models, queuing-theoretical models, and MPC algorithms.

Simulation models are based on the interaction of complex choice models and microscopic interactions and are a very interesting modeling approach that allows to accurately capture transportation systems. Although such a modeling approach has shown its effectiveness to deal with real transport networks, it fails to find an optimal solution for the problem of controlling AMoD systems.

Queueing-theoretical models are amenable to efficient capture the uncertainty of the travel demands, which can be adapted to an efficient control synthesis [19]. Such modeling approaches have been built upon the "Jackson network" concept [20], in which all road segments are modeled as queues of vehicles waiting to cross an intersection. According to the Jackson network concept, the new arrivals at each queuing station occur following the random Poisson process, assuming constant rates of occurrence for a given random variable. For example, if the random variable is passenger arrival times, constant rates of occurrence will assume that passengers will arrive at a constant rate at a station for a specified period of time. This means that this concept fails to reflect the time-variant nature of the passenger arrival rates that occurs in the real world, and thereby reduces realism. Thus, although queuing models can lead to a tractable solution to the complex challenges of AMoD systems, the outlined drawback restrict the ability of transport modelers to provide a realistic view of these systems.

Despite the advantage of efficiently implementing time-varying travel demand compared to the previously discussed approaches, the most current MPC algorithms assume a deterministic future travel demand. Moreover, the limited number of models that address uncertainty to forecast travel requests mainly suggest the use of stochastic programming. Whenever historical data is unavailable or even unreliable, reasoning probabilistic approaches may not be the best option. Thus, the Fuzzy set theory [21] and the possibility theory [2] are adequate to handle such problems with a lack of data knowledge. Subsequently, it has been successfully adopted for modeling and dealing with uncertainties in a variety of disciplines such as supply chain planning [22], image processing [23], Business Process modelling [24], web services [25], etc. Despite these advents, the

Table 1. Summary of the analysis of the literature according to four criteria.

Paper	Process	Method	Uncertainty	RideSharing
[4]	Dispatching	Simulation	–	–
[5]	Dispatching and routing	Simulation	–	–
[6]	Dispatching and routing	Simulation	–	X
[7]	Rebalancing	Simulation	Demand	X
[8]	Routing and rebalancing	Queuing model	–	–
[9]	Routing, rebalancing and charging	BCMP queuing network model	Demand	–
[12]	charging and dispatching	Queuing model	–	–
[13]	Routing and rebalancing	Network flow model	–	–
[14]	Routing and rebalancing	Network flow model	–	–
[15]	Dispatching, routing and rebalancing	MPC algorithm	–	–
[16]	Dispatching and rebalancing	MPC algorithm	–	–
[17]	Dispatching and rebalancing	MPC algorithm	Demand	–
[18]	Dispatching, routing and rebalancing	MPC algorithm	–	X
[3]	Dispatching and rebalancing	Fuzzy logic	Demand	X
This paper	dispatching, rebalancing, and charging	Fuzzy logic	Demand	X

only research work exploring the potential of the fuzzy logic to deal with uncertainties in AMoD systems is our previous work appeared as [3]. As mentioned in Table 1, the major technical difference is that in this research work we address the integrated problem for dispatching, rebalancing, and charging for RAMoD systems, rather than the dispatching and the rebalancing problem.

In the following section, the basic concepts of the fuzzy set theory and the possibility theory are summarized.

3 Basic Concepts

This section briefly outlines the fuzzy set theory, the triangular fuzzy numbers and the goal programming method used in this paper.

3.1 Fuzzy Set Theory

Fuzzy set theory was first suggested by Zadeh [21] to model and handle information pervaded by uncertainty and imprecision. Moreover, it allows easy integration of subjective experts' judgments. From a mathematical perspective, a fuzzy set is a class of elements characterized by a membership function. Unlike classical logic, the attachment of an element to a class is not anymore binary but rather a matter of degree ranging from zero to one. There are various kinds of fuzzy numbers. Among these different shapes, Triangular Fuzzy Numbers and Trapezoidal Fuzzy Numbers (illustrated respectively in Figs. 1 and 2) are the most popular ones.

3.2 Triangular Fuzzy Numbers

In this paper, the pattern of triangular fuzzy numbers (TFN) is adopted to model the imprecise travel demands. Due to its various advantages, this kind of fuzzy numbers has been widely adopted in the literature. Among others, the simplicity of collecting the required information, intuitiveness (i.e., a decision-maker usually finds it significantly easier to identify the most pessimistic, optimistic, and likely values of a given business process), and efficiency in related computations are the key advantages. These benefits were our principal motivation for adopting the TFNs pattern for representing the imprecise information in our problem. For more detailed theoretical justifications of TFN, we refer the reader to [26, 27].

As depicted in Fig. 1, a TFN $\tilde{N} = (n1, n2, n3)$ where *n1, n2, n3* are receptively the most pessimistic, the most possible and the most optimistic value of $\tilde{N}$ evaluated by the decision-maker.

Definition 1: The TFN $\tilde{N}$ can be defined by the following membership function:

$$\mu_{\tilde{N}}(x) = \begin{cases} 0, & x \le n_1 \\ \frac{x - n_1}{n_2 - n_1}, & n_1 < x \le n_2 \\ \frac{n_3 - x}{n_3 - n_2}, & n_2 < x \le n_3 \\ 0, & x > n_3 \end{cases} \tag{1}$$

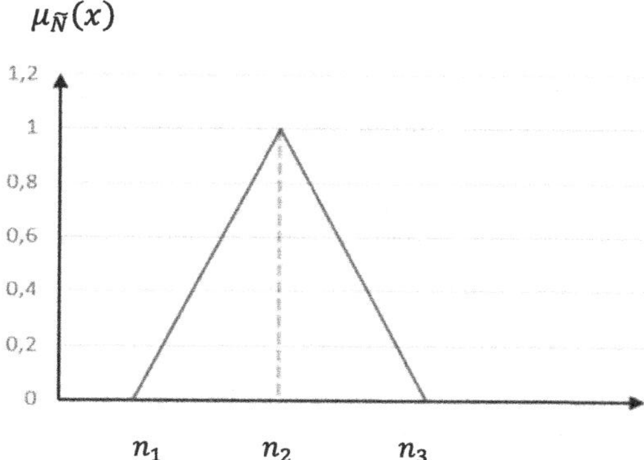

Fig. 1. The triangular possibility distribution of $\tilde{N}$.

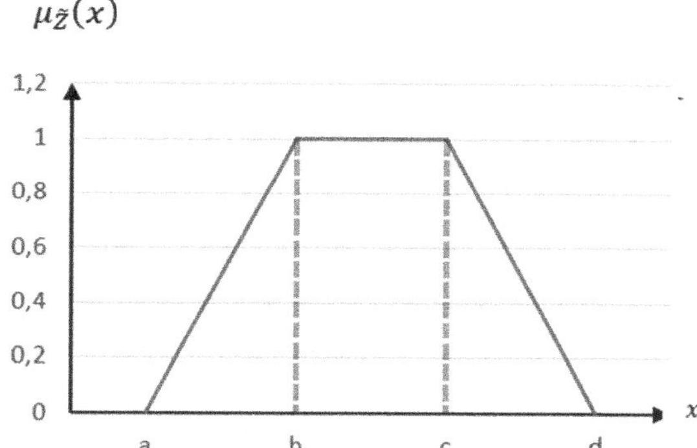

Fig. 2. The trapezoidal possibility distribution of $\tilde{Z}$.

Definition 2: Let A and B two triangular fuzzy numbers defined as $N = (n_1, n_2, n_3)$, $M = (m_1, m_2, m_3)$. The main operations on these fuzzy numbers can be summarized as follows:

$$\tilde{N}_1 \oplus \tilde{M}_2 = (n_1 + m_1,\ n_2 + m_2,\ n_3 + m_3) \tag{2}$$

$$\tilde{N}_1 \Theta \tilde{M}_2 = (n_1 - m_1,\ n_2 - m_2,\ n_3 - m_3) \tag{3}$$

$$\tilde{N}_1 \otimes \tilde{N}_2 = (n_1 \times m_1,\ n_2 \times m_2,\ n_3 \times m_3) \tag{4}$$

$$\tilde{N}_1 \otimes k = (n_1 \times k,\ n_2 \times k,\ n_3 \times k), \text{ for each } k\ \in \mathbb{R} \tag{5}$$

$$\frac{\tilde{N}_1}{\tilde{N}_2} = \left(\frac{n_1}{m_3}, \frac{n_2}{m_2}, \frac{n_3}{m_1}\right) \tag{6}$$

$$\left(\tilde{N}_1\right)^{-1} = \left(\frac{1}{n_3}, \frac{1}{n_2}, \frac{1}{n_1}\right) \tag{7}$$

3.3 Goal Programming

There are a number of multi-objective decision-making approaches in the scientific literature. Among them, goal programming which is one of the most powerful techniques for processing multi-objective models in concrete decision-making. This technique was originally proposed by Charnes et al. [28] and successfully implemented in several issues [29, 30]. The popularity of the GP approach is based, among others, on its robustness, its mathematical flexibility, and its accuracy.

The formulation of the GP approach is based on introducing for each criterion an expected goal to be achieved and identifying the best solution that minimizes the sum of the deviations from these objectives. However, the application of the GP method in practical decision-making problems can face a significant challenge, namely the integration of decision-makers' preferences. In such a situation, the use the Weighted Goal Programming (WGP) method comes in handy.

The basic form of WGP can be written as:

$$\underset{x \in A}{Min} \sum_{i=1}^{n} \left(w_i^+ \delta_i^+ + w_i^- \delta_i^- \right) \tag{8}$$

$$\begin{gathered}
\text{Subject to :} \\
C_k(x) \leq 0, \quad l = 1, 2, .., L \\
F_i(x) - \delta_i^+ + \delta_i^- = g_i, \quad i = 1, 2, .., n \\
\delta_i^+, \delta_i^- \geq 0
\end{gathered}$$

Where:

- $C_k(x)$ is the kth constraint.
- $\mathbf{g_i}$ is the target value of the objective function i.
- $F_i(x)$ is the evaluation of the solution x with respect to criterion i.
- w_i^+ is the weight attached to the positive deviation.
- w_i^- is the weight attached to the negative deviation.
- δ_i^+ is the positive deviation from the goal g_i.
- δ_i^- is negative deviation from the goal g_i.

4 The Problem Setting

As depicted in the literature review section, significant progress has been achieved in recent years to control and analyze AMoD and RAMoD systems. However, these various initiatives are conducted in urban areas and do not address the specificities of low-density where travel solutions are scarcer.

The problem considered in this paper is motivated by the Tornado Mobility research project [31], aiming to study the interaction between connected infrastructures for mobility services and autonomous vehicles in a low-density environment.

For this propose, we consider a transportation network partitioned into multiple stations and served by self-driving vehicles offering on-demand mobility services. All autonomous vehicles in this transportation network are multiple-occupancy, i.e. they can serve several customers at any given time without exceeding their carrying capacity.

The considered fleet of self-driving vehicles is endowed with a high level of heterogeneity, i.e. transportation costs, carrying capacity, and speeds can be very different from one vehicle to another.

In the specific context of the Tornado project, passengers can request transportation to and from in the predefined road network via a mobile application. If there are available cars, one of them will be assigned to carry this customer towards its destination. Otherwise, the customer will leave the system immediately without any waiting time. This is because we adopt in our RAMoD system the customer model referred to as a "passenger loss" model [8, 9]. A consequence of this model is that the number of passengers at each station is always zero (since users either leave the system or depart immediately with a car). Such an assumption is well suited for AMoD and RAMoD systems where a high-quality service is desired [9].

By the trip's end, the vehicle could either assigned to provide other on-demand mobility or rebalance itself throughout the transportation network. It could also park in the drop-off station or even recharge its battery at a charging station.

Each station in the transportation network has a limited number of parking spaces and charging resources.

Note that the time is measured in discrete and ordered intervals.

The proposed model differs from other traditional approaches, as we do not assume perfect knowledge of future travel requests; Instead, it was assumed that such critical information is evaluated by the decision-maker using fuzzy numbers.

5 A Solution Procedure for the Dispatching, Rebalancing and Charging Problem

To address the challenging problem detailed in the previous section, we propose a three-phase framework, where the main stages are illustrated in Fig. 3 and detailed in the following sub-sections.

5.1 Phase I: Formulation of the Dispatching, Rebalancing and Charging Problem

- Notation

  Below are the indices, decision variables and parameters used in the formulation of the problem.

  - *Indices*

    t index of time periods ($t = 1, 2..., T$).
    v index of vehicles ($v = 1, 2..., V$).
    s index of stations ($s = 1, 2, ..., S$).

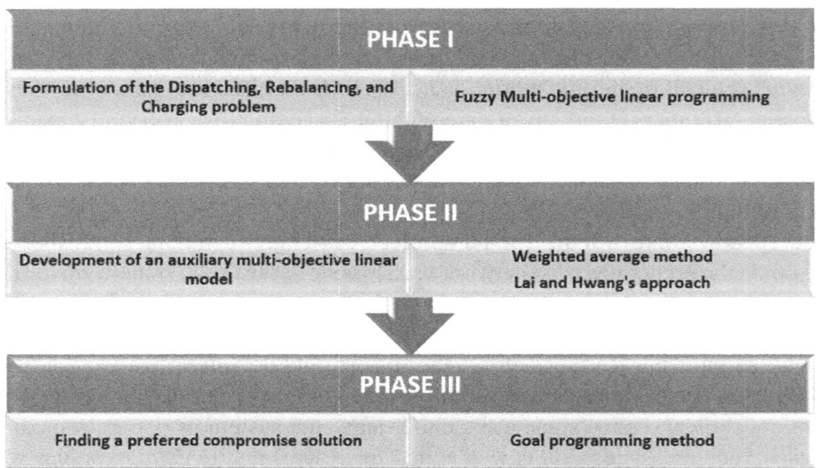

Fig. 3. A solution procedure for the Dispatching, Rebalancing and Charging problem.

– *Parameters*

$\tilde{Cr}_{t,s1,s2}$	number of travel requests from station *s1* to station *s2* in period *t*.
$D_{s1,s2}$	distance separating the stations *s1* and *s2*.
SP_v	sailing speed of the autonomous vehicle *v*.
Cap_v	carrying capacity of the autonomous vehicle *v*.
$init_{v,s}$	indicates the availability of the autonomous vehicle *v* at station *s* in the first period. i.e. if vehicle *v* is initially available at station *s*, $init_{v,s} = 1$ and *0* otherwise.
RC_v	rate of charge of the autonomous vehicle *v* at a charging station.
RD_v	rate of discharge of the autonomous vehicle *v* while driving.
$Park\_cap_s$	number of parking space at the station *s*.
Ch_cap_s	number of charging station at the station *s*.

– *Decision Variables*

$Park_{v,t,s}$	binary variable specifying if the autonomous vehicle *v* is parked in station *s* during the period *t*.
$Ch_{v,t,s}$	binary variable indicating if the autonomous vehicle *v* is charging in station *s* during the period *t*.
$Wait_{v,t,s}$	binary variable indicating if the autonomous vehicle *v* is waiting in station *s* during the period *t*.
$Miss_{v,t}$	binary variable specifying if the autonomous vehicle *v* is on mission during the period *t*.
$Miss\_T_{v,s1,s2,t1,t2}$	binary variable specifying if the autonomous vehicle *v* is on a transport mission from the station *s1* to the station *s2* starting at period *t1* and arriving at period *t2*.

$\boldsymbol{Miss\_R_{v,s1,s2,t1,t2}}$	binary variable specifying if the autonomous vehicle v is on a rebalancing mission from the station $s1$ to the station $s2$ starting at period $t1$ and arriving at period $t2$.
$\boldsymbol{Soc_{v,t}}$	shows the state of charge of the autonomous vehicle v over time. i.e. a value $Soc_{v,t}= 1$ means that the battery of the vehicle v is fully charged at the end of the period t while $Soc_{v,t}= 0$ means that the battery of v is depleted at the end of t.
$\boldsymbol{S\_Cr_{t,s1,s2}}$	The number of satisfied travel demands from station $s1$ to station $s2$ starting at the period t.

- Mathematical Model
  Using the notation of the previous sub-section, a multi-objective possibilistic linear programming model can be written as:

  – *Objective Functions*
  We consider two major and conflicting goals in our integrated dispatching, rebalancing, and charging problem: the total cost (TC) and the level of customer satisfaction ((L$\tilde{C}$r)).

  Objective 1: Minimizing the total cost.

$$Minimize\ TC = \sum_{t1,t2=1}^{T} \sum_{s1,s2=1}^{S} \sum_{v=1}^{V} RD_v * Dist_{s1,\ s} * (Miss\_T_{v,s1,s2,t1,t2} + Miss\_R_{v,s1,s2,t1,t2}) \tag{9}$$

  Objective 2: Improving the level of customer satisfaction through minimizing the number of lost travel demands.

$$Minimize\ L\tilde{C}r = \sum_{t=1}^{T} \sum_{s1,s2=1}^{S} C\tilde{r}_{t,s1,s2} - S\_Cr_{t,s1,s2} \tag{10}$$

  – *Model Constraints*

$$Park_{v,t,s},\ Ch_{v,t,s},\ Wait_{v,t,s},\ Miss_{v,t},\ Miss\_R_{v,s1,s2,t1,t2},\ Miss\_T_{v,s1,s2,t1,t2} \in \{0,1\}\quad t,\ t1,\ t2,\ s,\ s1,\ s2,\ v \tag{11}$$

$$Soc_{v,t} \in [0,1]\quad \forall v, t \tag{12}$$

$$S\_Cr_{t,\ s1,\ s2} \geq 0\ and\ integer\quad \forall s1,\ s2,\ t \tag{13}$$

The limitation of the decision variables is presented by the Eqs. (11), (12), and (13): $S\_Cr_{t,s1,s2}$*is an integer,* $Soc_{v,t}$ is ranging from zero to one, while other variables are binary.

$$\sum_{s=1}^{S} Miss_{v,t} + Park_{v,t,s}\quad \forall v,\ t \tag{14}$$

Constraints (14) presents the two possible states that an autonomous vehicle can take, i.e. parking in a station and being on a mission. On the other hand, this equation ensures that a vehicle can have just one state at any given time.

$$Park_{v,t,s} = Ch_{v,t,s} + Wait_{v,t,s} \quad \forall v,\ t,\ s \tag{15}$$

When a vehicle is parked in a station, two different actions can be achieved: it can charge at a charging point or wait for customers. This is specified using the constraint (15), which also means that the vehicle can perform just one action at any given time.

$$Miss_{v,t} = \sum\nolimits_{s1,s2=1}^{S} \sum\nolimits_{t1,t2\le t} Miss\_R_{v,s1,s2,t1,t2} + Miss\_T_{v,s1,s2,t1,t2} \quad \forall v,\ t \tag{16}$$

Similarly, when a self-driving vehicle is on a mission, two different actions can be performed (i) transport one or several passengers from one station to another, and (ii) travel without passengers to rebalance the RAMoD system. These constraints are specified using the Eq. (16), which also implies that a self-driving vehicle can perform only one action at any given time.

$$\begin{gathered} init_{v,s} \ge Miss\_R_{v,s,s2,t,t2} + Miss\_T_{v,s,s1,t,t1} + Park_{v,t,s} \\ \forall v,\ s,\ t = 1,\ s1,\ s2,\ t1 = t + (D_{s,s1}/SP_v) \end{gathered} \tag{17}$$

Equation (17) states that a vehicle cannot be parked at a station s during the first period if, and only if, it is initially available at this station. Similarly, a self-driving vehicle v may only travel on a passenger(s) transport mission or a rebalancing mission from a station s during the first period if, and only if, it is initially available at this station.

$$\begin{gathered} Park_{v,t,s} \le \sum\nolimits_{s1\ne s} Miss\_R_{v,s1,s,t1,t-1} + \sum\nolimits_{s2\ne s} Miss\_T_{v,s2,s,t2,t-1} + Park_{v,t-1,s} \\ \forall v,\ s,\ t > 1,\ t1 = t - (D_{s1,s}/SP_v) - 1,\ t2 = t + (D_{s2,s}/SP_v) - 1 \end{gathered} \tag{18}$$

Equation (18) ensures that if a self-driving vehicle v is parked at a station s during a time period t, it must be physically located in s at the beginning of t.

$$\begin{gathered} Miss\_T_{v,s1,s2,t1,t2} \le \sum\nolimits_{s3\ne s1} Miss\_R_{v,s3,s1,t3,t1-1} + \sum\nolimits_{s4\ne s1} Miss\_T_{v,s4,s1,t4,t1-1} + Park_{v,t1-1,s1} \\ \forall\, v,\ s1,\ s2,\ t1 > 1,\ t2 = t1 + (D_{s1,s2}/SP_v), \\ t3 = t1 - (D_{s3,s1}/SP_v) - 1,\ t4 = t1 - (D_{s4,s1}/SP_v) - 1 \end{gathered} \tag{19}$$

$$\begin{gathered} Miss\_R_{v,s1,s2,t1,t2} \le \sum\nolimits_{s3\ne s1} Miss\_R_{v,s3,s1,t3,t1-1} + \sum\nolimits_{s4\ne s1} Miss\_T_{v,s4,s1,t4,t1-1} + Park_{v,t1-1,s1} \\ \forall\, v,\ s1,\ s2,\ t1 > 1,\ t2 = t1 + (D_{s1,s2}/SP_v), \\ t3 = t1 - (D_{s3,s1}/SP_v) - 1,\ t4 = t1 - (D_{s4,s1}/SP_v) - 1 \end{gathered} \tag{20}$$

When a self-driving vehicle v is on a mission from station *s1* to station $s2$ beginning at *t1*, v must be physically located in *s1* at the beginning of *t1*. It means, either the vehicle v i) parked at *s1* during the last period (i.e. $\text{Park}_{v,t-1,s1} = 1$) or ii) arrived at *s1* during the last period (i.e. $\text{Miss\_T}_{v,s3,s1,t3,t1-1} = 1$ Or $\text{Miss\_R}_{v,s4,s1,t4,t1-1} = 1$). The constraints (19) and (20) ensure that this rule is respected respectively for passenger transport missions and rebalancing missions.

$$\sum\nolimits_{v=1}^{V} Park_{v,t,s} \le Park\_cap_s \quad \forall t,\ s \tag{21}$$

Constraint (21) represents the parking capacity limitation for all time. This means that the overall number of vehicles parked at a station s during the time period t *(i.e.* $\sum_{v=1}^{V} Park_{v,t,s}$*)* must not exceed the parking space limitation at the station s (i.e. $Park\_cap_s$).

$$\sum\nolimits_{v=1}^{V} Ch_{v,t,s} \leq Ch\_cap_s \quad \forall t,\ s \tag{22}$$

Equation (22) indicates the charging capabilities at each station for all time.

$$S\_Cr_{t,s1,s2} \leq \tilde{C}r_{t,s1,s2} \quad \forall t,\ s1,\ s2 \tag{23}$$

Constraint (23) assures that self-driving vehicles dispatched to transport customer(s) from one station to another cannot serve more customers than requested.

$$S\_Cr_{t1,s1,s2} \leq \sum\nolimits_{v=1}^{V} Cap_v * Miss\_T_{v,s1,s2,t1,t2} \quad \forall\, t1,\ t2 = t1 + (D_{s1,s2}/SP_v),\ s1,\ s2 \tag{24}$$

Constraint (24) guarantees that the number of satisfied travel demands from station *s1* to station *s2* starting at the period *t1* cannot exceed the overall capacity of the vehicles dispatched to transport passengers from *s1* to *s2* starting at *t1*.

$$Soc_{v,t} \geq Min(Soc_{v,t-1} + \sum\nolimits_{s=1}^{S} Ch_{v,t,s} * RC_v,\ 1) - RD_v * Miss_{v,t} \quad \forall v,\ t > 1 \tag{25}$$

$$Soc_{v,1} \geq Min(1 + \sum\nolimits_{s=1}^{S} Ch_{v,1,s} * RC_v,\ 1) - RD_v * Miss_{v,1} \quad \forall v \tag{26}$$

Equations (25) and (26) model the evolution of each vehicle's charge while assuming that the batteries are fully charged at the beginning of the first period.

$$\begin{gathered} Soc_{v,t1} \geq Miss\_R_{v,s1,s2,t1,t2} * RD_v * (D_{s1,s2}/SP_v) \\ \forall v,\ s1,\ s2,\ t1,\ t2 = t1 + (D_{s1,s2}/SP_v) \end{gathered} \tag{27}$$

$$\begin{gathered} Soc_{v,t1} \geq Miss\_T_{v,s1,s2,t1,t2} * RD_v * (D_{s1,s2}/SP_v) \\ \forall v,\ s1,\ s2,\ t1,\ t2 = t1 + \left(D_{s1,s2}/SP_v\right) \end{gathered} \tag{28}$$

Equations (27) and (28) are the charge constraints to ensure that each self-driving vehicle has sufficient charge to accomplish its trip. Specifically, Eq. (27) guarantees enough charge for rebalancing trips, and Eq. (28) guarantees enough charge for passengers' trips.

5.2 Phase II: Development of an Axillary Multi-objective Linear Model

In this paper, we adopt the TFNs pattern for representing the imprecise travel request in the customer satisfaction objective function and constraint (23). As outlined below, triangular possibility distribution $\widetilde{Cr}$ can be presented by the triplet $(Cr^p,\ Cr^m,\ Cr^o)$ where Cr^p, Cr^m *and* Cr^o are the most pessimistic value of $\widetilde{Cr}$, the most possible value of $\widetilde{Cr}$, and the most optimistic value of $\widetilde{Cr}$.

The main goal of this second phase is to treat such fuzzy parameter and transform the proposed fuzzy formulation into an equivalent auxiliary crisp multi-objective model.

- Treating the Soft Constraint
  To treat the fuzzy travel request in the right-hand side of Eq. (23), the well-known weighted average method is implemented for the defuzzification process and transforming the $\widetilde{Cr}$ parameter into an equivalent crisp number.

This method was first developed by Lai and Hwang [33] and has been successfully implemented in several research studies [34–36] due to its efficiency and simplicity. In order to do so, we must first identify a minimal acceptable possibility degree of occurrence for the fuzzy parameter, α. The original fuzzy constraint (23) can then be represented by a new crisp equation as described below:

$$S\_Cr_{t,s1,s2} \leq w_1 Cr^p_{t,s1,s2,\alpha} + w_2 Cr^m_{t,s1,s2,\alpha} + w_3 Cr^o_{t,s1,s2,\alpha} \quad \forall t,\ s1,\ s2 \tag{29}$$

Where and w_1, w_2, and w_3 designate respectively the weight of the most pessimistic, the weight of the most possible, and the weight of the most optimistic of the fuzzy travel and verifying the following equation:

$$w_1 + w_2 + w_3 = 1. \tag{30}$$

In practice, these weights, as well as the minimum acceptable degree of possibility α, can be subjectively specified on the basis of the decision maker's knowledge and experience.

In our framework, we use the concept of most likely values, which is extensively adopted in the literature [33]. In accordance with this concept, the most optimistic and pessimistic values should be given a lower weight than the most possible value. Therefore, similarly to [33], we fix these parameters as follows:

$$w_1 = w_3 = 1/6;\ w_2 = 4/6\ \textit{and}\ \ \alpha = 0.5. \tag{31}$$

- Treating the Imprecise Customer Satisfaction Objective Function
  Due to the inaccuracy of the travel request parameter in the customer satisfaction objective function, it is typically not possible to identify an optimal solution to the problem defined by the Eqs. (9)–(28).

In the academic literature, various approaches are suggested to find compromise solutions [33, 37–40]. As stated by Hsu and Wang [41], the first four strategies are predicated on restrictive assumptions and are usually hard to implement in practice, we, therefore, adopt Lai and Hwang's approach [33, 35].

Since the imprecise travel request $\tilde{C}r$ is modeled using a triangular-shaped possibility distribution, the customer satisfaction objective function $L\tilde{C}r$ could also be represented by a triangular possibility distribution. This imprecise goal is geometrically presented by the three main points $(LCr^p, 0)$, $(LCr^m, 1)$, and $(LCr^o, 0)$. It is consequently possible to minimize the fuzzy goal by pushing these critical points towards the left.

According to Lai and Hwang's approach, resolving this problem consists of minimizing LCr^m, maximizing $(LCr^m - LCr^p)$, and minimizing $(LCr^o - LCr^m)$. Thus, our imprecise customer satisfaction objective function can be converted into three crisp objectives as described below:

$$Min\ Z_1 = LCr^m = \sum_{t=1}^{T} \sum_{s1,s2=1}^{S} Cr^m_{t,s1,s2} - S\_Cr_{t,s1,s2} \quad (32)$$

$$Max\ Z_2 = LCr^m - LCr^p = \sum_{t=1}^{T} \sum_{s1,s2=1}^{S} (Cr^m_{t,s1,s2} - Cr^p_{t,s1,s2}) - S\_Cr_{t,s1,s2} \quad (33)$$

$$Min\ Z_3 = LCr^o - LCr^m = \sum_{t=1}^{T} \sum_{s1,s2=1}^{S} (Cr^o_{t,s1,s2} - Cr^m_{t,s1,s2}) - S\_Cr_{t,s1,s2} \quad (34)$$

5.3 Phase III: Finding a Preferred Compromise Solution

In the previous phase, the proposed multi-objective possibilistic model has been transformed into an equivalent auxiliary crisp multi-objective model. In this third phase, we adopt the Weighted Goal Programming method, incorporating specific weights for each criterion, allowing us to treat this multi-objective model.

Therefore, we can reformulate our problem as below:

$$1.\ \text{Min}\ F_{GP} = W_{TC} * \delta^+_{TC} + W_{Z1} * \delta^+_1 + W_{Z2} * \delta^-_2 + W_{Z3} * \delta^+_3 \quad (35)$$

$$Subject\ to:\ (11) - (22),\ (24) - (29)$$

$$TC - \delta^+_{TC} = TC^* \quad (36)$$

$$Z_1 - \delta^+_1 = Z^*_1 \quad (37)$$

$$Z_2 + \delta^-_2 = Z^*_2 \quad (38)$$

$$Z_3 - \delta^+_3 = Z^*_3 \quad (38)$$

Where:

- TC^* is the goal calculated based on the mathematical model with *the total cost* objective function (9) subject to constraints (11)-(22), (24)–(29), and δ^+_{TC} is the positive deviation from this goal.
- Z^*_1 is the goal calculated using the mathematical model with the objective function (32) subject to the constraints (11)–(22), (24)–(29), and δ^+_1 is the positive deviation from this goal.
- Z^*_2 is the goal calculated using the mathematical model with the objective function (33) subject to the constraints (11)–(22), (24)–(29), and δ^-_2 is the negative deviation from this goal.
- Z^*_3 is the goal calculated using the mathematical model, with the objective function (34) subject to the constraints (11)–(22), (24)–(29), and δ^+_3 is the positive deviation from this goal.
- W_{TC}, W_{Z1}, W_{Z2} and W_{Z3} are the importance weights of the various goals such that $W_{TC} + W_{Z1} + W_{Z2} + W_{Z3} = 1$.

6 Numerical Experiments

In this section, we present numerical experiments to demonstrate the validity and applicability of our integrated strategy for dispatching, rebalancing, and charging decisions, especially in the presence of imprecise travel demands. Then, we explore the performance of the newly suggested strategy, in comparison with other dispatch strategies by varying travel demand over the forecast horizon.

For all experiments, we consider five stations and a fleet size of 20 self-driving vehicles.

The forecast horizon is decomposed into ten time periods. Such periods correspond to 10 different predicted travel demands with TFNs.

At the beginning of the first period, the self-driving vehicles were distributed equally over the road network, i.e. six vehicles for each station.

The carrying capacity of the vehicles is characterized by a high level of heterogeneity, which varies from a single capacity to a ten-passenger capacity.

For simplification purposes, we assume that the travel time between two given stations is a one-time step. Moreover, we consider that the importance weight of the various goals is the same (i.e. $W_{TC} = W_{Z1} = W_{Z2} = W_{Z3} = 1/4$).

For all numerical experiments, the suggested approach has been implemented using the LINGO optimization package.

6.1 Detailed Results

Figure 4 illustrates the results generated by the suggested approach by specifying the status of self-drive vehicles over the planning horizon.

We remind that a self-driving vehicle can be on a rebalancing mission, be on a customer(s) transport mission, and be waiting or charging in a station.

These different decisions are constrained by the criteria of minimizing overall costs and maximizing customer satisfaction in each period of the forecast horizon.

It has been found that the increased cost of transporting a vehicle leads to not using it if the travel request can be met by vehicles with lower costs. For instance, during the first period, travel requests were met with the various stations. Especially for S2, this fuzzy travel demand has been met by using the V5 and V6 with the use of ride-sharing, while the V7 and V8 remain parked in S2 due to their significantly higher transportation costs. Similarly, in the second period, V10 and V11 remain parked in S3 as travel demand was met by self-driving vehicles with lower transportation costs (i.e. V2, V6, and V17). With the increasing travel demands in the third and fourth periods and directed by the maximization of customer satisfaction, all vehicles in the fleet were launched on missions, including the most costly ones.

Nevertheless, beyond the 5th time period, the mobilization of all the fleet's vehicles becomes insufficient to meet travel request, especially when certain stations are more popular than others, at the end of the journey, vehicles tend to accumulate in these stations and deplete in others. This justifies the need to integrate rebalancing decisions from overloaded stations to under loaded ones as a solution to the problem of vehicle imbalances. Such decisions are also driven by the cost-minimization criterion. In fact, the least costly vehicles will be assigned in the first place to rebalancing missions.

6.2 Performance Analysis

To explore the performance of the proposed strategy (called "D-R-C-RAMoD-Fuzzy" in this section), we conducted numerical experiments comparing it against other strategies. Specifically, these dispatching strategies are three different variants of the newly suggested approach.

D-C-RAMoD-Fuzzy: This version is exclusively dedicated to the problem of dispatching and recharging, and vehicles do not rebalance in any circumstances.
D-R-C-AMoD-Fuzzy: This version uses the same model outlined in the previous section for single-capacity vehicles (i.e. without the use of ride-sharing service).
D-R-C-RAMoD-Perfect: This is the integrated strategy for dispatching, rebalancing, and charging proposed in the previous section based on exact travel demand as it appears in the data set as a forecast for the next ten periods. It is an effective approach to finding the optimal dispatching, rebalancing, and charging policies in the situation where the customer's demand is already known in advance. In this way, it can be leveraged to deliver upper bounds of system performance.

The results of this comparative analysis are summarized in Fig. 5, which provides an illustration of the number of lost travel requests for each strategy over time.

As intended, the approach with precise travel demands is undoubtedly the most powerful strategy, with reduced transport costs and a minimum number of lost travel requests.

The "D-R-C-AMoD-Fuzzy" strategy has by far the most poor performance, with mean lost travel demands sixfold than that of the "D-R-C-RAMoD-Perfect" approach and multiplied by four compared to that of our suggested strategy (i.e. D-R-C-RAMoD-Fuzzy". That is not unexpected, because here the single-capacity policy is compared to ride-sharing schemes, where the maximum allowable capacity of vehicles is increased to ten.

The significant difference in performance between the "D-R-C-RAMoD-Perfect" strategy and the "D-C-RAMoD-Fuzzy" strategy can also be observed from Fig. 5, illustrating the number of lost travel requests over the planning horizon. Specifically, this strategy has caused a significant increase in the number of lost travel demands over the planning horizon, with an average of lost travel demands multiplied by three compared to the "D-R-C-RAMoD-Fuzzy" strategy and multiplied by four compared to the "D-R-C-RAMoD-Perfect" strategy. This is also not surprising, as we can achieve significant performance gains by integrating rebalancing trips to ensure a balance between the number of available vehicles at each station and travel demands.

Vehicles	T1	T2	T3	T4	T5	T6	T7	T8	T9	T10
V1	S1→S5	S5→S1	S1→S2	S2→S1	S1→S2	S2→S3	S3	S3→S5	S5→S1	S1→S2
V2	S1→S3	S3→S1	S1→S3	S3→S1	S1→S3	S3→S1	S1	S1→S2	S2→S5	S5→S1
V3	S1→S4	S4	S4→S1	S1→S2	S2→S3	S3→S1	S1→S2	S2	S2→S3	S3→S1
V4	S1	S1	S1→S2	S2→S1	S1→S4	S4→S3	S3→S5	S5→S1	S1	S1→S2
V5	S2→S1	S1→S2	S2→S3	S3→S1	S1→S4	S4→S5	S5→S1	S1→S3	S3→S1	S1→S3
V6	S2→S3	S3→S1	S1→S3	S3→S5	S5→S4	S4→S1	S1→S3	S3	S3→S2	S2→S1
V7	S2	S2→S5	S5→S1	S1→S5	S5→S2	S2→S3	S3→S2	S2	S2→S4	S4→S1
V8	S2	S2→S4	S4→S2	S2→S4	S4→S2	S2→S1	S1→S4	S4	S4→S1	S1→S4
V9	S3→S4	S4→S3	S3→S4	S4→S2	S2→S5	S5→S1	S1	S1→S4	S4→S2	S2→S3
V10	S3	S3	S3→S4	S4→S1	S1	S1→S3	S3→S1	S1	S1→S2	S2→S4
V11	S3	S3	S3→S1	S1→S3	S3	S3→S2	S2→S1	S1	S1→S3	S3→S2
V12	S3→S5	S5→S2	S2→S4	S4→S3	S3→S5	S5→S2	S2	S2→S3	S3→S4	S4→S3
V13	S4→S1	S1→S3	S3→S4	S4→S5	S5→S2	S2→S4	S4→S3	S3→S1	S1	S1→S5
V14	S4→S1	S1→S2	S2→S5	S5→S2	S2→S4	S4→S2	S2→S5	S5→S2	S2→S1	S1
V15	S4	S4	S4→S3	S3→S1	S1	S1→S5	S5	S5→S2	S2	S2→S5
V16	S4	S4→S2	S2→S5	S5→S2	S2→S3	S3→S5	S5→S2	S2→S3	S3→S4	S4
V17	S5→S3	S3→S1	S1→S2	S2→S3	S3→S5	S5→S3	S3→S4	S4→S1	S1	S1→S5
V18	S5	S5	S5→S3	S3→S1	S1→S4	S4→S5	S5→S3	S3→S4	S4→S3	S3→S4
V19	S5	S5	S5→S3	S3→S4	S4→S2	S2→S5	S5→S4	S4→S3	S3→S5	S5→S3
V20	S5	S5	S5→S4	S4→S5	S5	S5→S4	S4→S2	S2	S2→S4	S4→S5

$S_i \to S_j$	The vehicle is on a customer(s) transport mission from S_i to S_j
$S_i \to S_j$	The vehicle is on a rebalancing mission from S_i to S_j
S_i	vehicle is parked in a station S_i
S_i	vehicle is charging in a station S_i

Fig. 4. Vehicle scheduling as a function of time.

A considerable performance gain is attributed to the integration of rebalancing policies as part of the "D-C-RAMoD-Fuzzy" strategy and the fact that several passengers can share the same trip. Indeed, it can be seen that out of ten different experiments, the proposed strategy produces an optimal design for six experiments. It also generates solutions that are very close to the optimal plan for the other time periods, with a variance of 35%. These findings demonstrate the robustness of the proposed strategy for managing the fleet and meeting customer needs, even when travel demand forecasts are tainted by ambiguity.

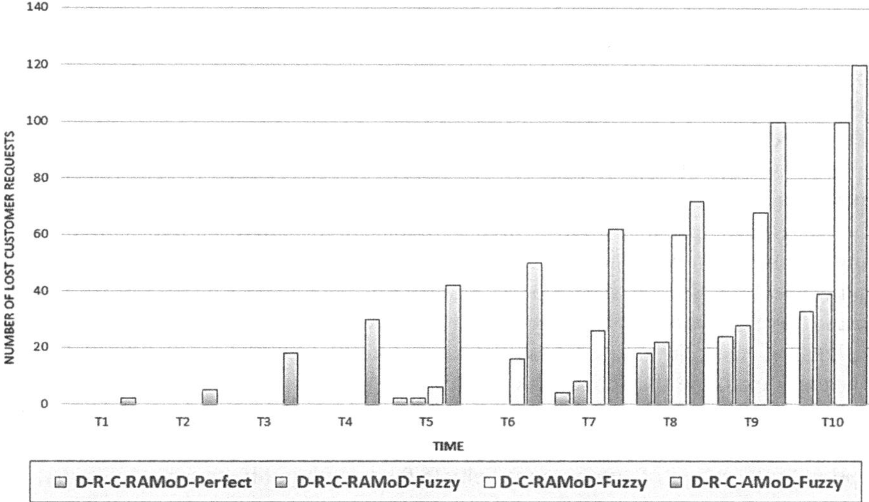

Fig. 5. The number of lost travel requests for each strategy as a function of time.

7 Conclusion

Despite the significant progress achieved in vehicle electrification and automation, the next decade's aspirations for large-scale deployments of AMoD and RAMoD services in metropolitan cities are still threatened by two significant bottlenecks. First, due to several externalities, the travel demand forecasts are subject to significant uncertainties, thus resulting in excessive, if not prohibitive, delays for customers if dispatching and rebalancing decisions fail to address uncertainty on the travel forecasts. Moreover, the requirement to make additional trips for recharging electric vehicles and in some cases, a vehicle may need to wait to charge instead of transporting waiting customers can significantly affect the convenience of AMOD systems and reduce its impact in resolving urban congestion problems.

In order to target travel demand uncertainty, we suggest the exploitation of the fuzzy set theory. Indeed, while deterministic or stochastic formulations remain unable to capture vagueness in the critical data, fuzzy logic is widely agreed to be a key framework for describing and treating uncertainty. To address the second limitation, the paper suggests the integration of a smart charging process with dispatching and rebalancing decisions. The optimal coordination of such decisions proves its efficiency to establish optimal schedules for electric vehicles charging given travel demand forecasts.

Specifically, the problem is first formulated as a multi-objective possibilistic linear programming model incorporating two important conflicting goals simultaneously: minimizing transportation costs and improving customer satisfaction. The proposed Fuzzy model is then transformed into an equivalent multi-objective integer linear programming model by combining two appropriate strategies. In order to guarantee the obtaining of an efficient compromise solution, the weighted goal programming model is being exploited reducing the initial problem to a scalar formulation and allowing the decision-maker to define an aspiration level for each objective. Numerical experiments demonstrate that the proposed approach is tractable and practical to deal with real-sized problems and provides an effective tool for managing dispatching, rebalancing, and charging decisions in RAMoD systems.

This paper opens the field for numerous important directions for further research. First, it is of great interest to study the inclusion of routing policies by designing a comprehensive road network with finite capacity (currently, the road network is modeled with infinite capacity). This research axis can also address congestion effects, thus leaving an important extension open to study the impact of the proposed strategies on overall congestion. Second, the proposed framework can be extended to address not only uncertain travel demand but also fluctuations of several other critical parameters such as transportation costs, the state of charge electric vehicles, vehicle availability, etc. Third, we currently examine the RAMoD system independently of other transportation systems, whereas, in practice, travel demand depends on the different transportation modes. Future studies will investigate the effect of RAMoD systems on passenger behavior and the optimal integration of autonomous vehicle fleets with public transport. Finally, it is of interest to investigate the couplings that could occur between the electric grid and the charging strategies of an electric-powered RAMoD fleet.

Acknowledgment. This work is financed by national funds FUI 23 under the French TORNADO project focused on the interactions between autonomous vehicles and infrastructures for mobility services in low-density areas. Further details of the project are available at https://www.tornado-mobility.com/.

References

1. Could self-driving cars spell the end of ownership. http://www.wsj.com. Accessed 09 Oct 2020
2. Zadeh, L.A.: Fuzzy sets as a basis for a theory of possibility. Fuzzy Sets Syst. **1**(1), 3–28 (1978)
3. Khemiri, R., Expósito, E.: Fuzzy multi-objective optimization for ride-sharing autonomous mobility-on-demand systems. In: 15th International Conference on Software and Data Technologies, pp. 284–294. Lieusaint, Paris (2020)
4. Shen, W., Lopes, C.: Managing autonomous mobility on demand systems for better passenger experience. In: Chen, Q., Torroni, P., Villata, S., Hsu, J., Omicini, A. (eds.) PRIMA 2015. LNCS (LNAI), vol. 9387, pp. 20–35. Springer, Cham (2015). https://doi.org/10.1007/978-3-319-25524-8_2
5. Alonso-Mora, J., Samaranayake, S., Wallar, A., Frazzoli, E., Rus, D.: On-demand high-capacity ride-sharing via dynamic trip-vehicle assignment. Proc. Natl. Acad. Sci. **114**(3), 462–467 (2017)
6. Levin, M.W., Kockelman, K.M., Boyles, S.D., Li, T.: A general framework for modeling shared autonomous vehicles with dynamic network-loading and dynamic ride-sharing application. Comput. Environ. Urban Syst. **64**, 373–383 (2017)
7. Javanshour, F., Dia, H., Duncan, G.: Exploring the performance of autonomous mobility on-demand systems under demand uncertainty. Transportmetrica A Transp. Sci. **15**(2), 698–721 (2019)

8. Zhang, R., Pavone, M.: Control of robotic mobility-on-demand systems: a queueing-theoretical perspective. Int. J. Robot. Res. **35**(1–3), 186–203 (2016)
9. Iglesias, R., Rossi, F., Zhang, R., Pavone, M.: A BCMP network approach to modeling and controlling autonomous mobility-on-demand systems. Int. J. Robot. Res. **38**(2–3), 357–374 (2019)
10. Baskett, F., Chandy, K.M., Muntz, R.R., Palacios, F.G.: Open, closed, and mixed networks of queues with different classes of customers. J. ACM **22**(2), 248–260 (1975)
11. Kobayashi, H., Gerla, M.: Optimal routing in closed queueing networks. ACM SIGCOMM Comput. Commun. Rev. **13**(2), 26 (1983)
12. Belakaria, S., Ammous, M., Sorour, S., Abdel-Rahim, A.: Optimal vehicle dimensioning for multi-class autonomous electric mobility on-demand systems. In: IEEE International Conference on Communications Workshops, pp. 1–6. IEEE, Kansas City (2018)
13. Rossi, F., Zhang, R., Hindy, Y., Pavone, M.: Routing autonomous vehicles in congested transportation networks: structural properties and coordination algorithms. Auton. Robot. **42**(7), 1427–1442 (2018)
14. Salazar, M., Lanzetti, N., Rossi, F., Schiffer, M., Pavone, M.: Intermodal autonomous mobility-on-demand. IEEE Trans. Intell. Transp. Syst. **21**(9), 3946–3960 (2019)
15. Zhang, R., Rossi, F., Pavone, M.: Model predictive control of autonomous mobility-on-demand systems. In: IEEE International Conference on Robotics and Automation (ICRA), pp. 1382–1389. IEEE, Stockholm (2016)
16. Iglesias, R., Rossi, F., Wang, K., Hallac, D., Leskovec, J., Pavone, M.: Data-driven model predictive control of autonomous mobility-on-demand systems. In: IEEE International Conference on Robotics and Automation (ICRA), pp. 1–7. IEEE, Brisbane (2018)
17. Tsao, M., Iglesias, R., Pavone, M.: Stochastic model predictive control for autonomous mobility on demand. In: 21st International Conference on Intelligent Transportation Systems (ITSC), pp. 3941–3948. IEEE, Hawaii (2018)
18. Tsao, M., Milojevic, D., Ruch, C., Salazar, M., Frazzoli, E., Pavone, M.: Model predictive control of ride-sharing autonomous mobility-on-demand systems. In: International Conference on Robotics and Automation (ICRA), pp. 6665–6671. IEEE, Montreal (2019)
19. Salazar, M., Rossi, F., Schiffer, M., Onder, C.H., Pavone, M.: On the interaction between autonomous mobility-on-demand and public transportation systems. In: 21st International Conference on Intelligent Transportation Systems (ITSC), pp. 2262–2269. IEEE, Maui (2018)
20. Jackson, J.R.: Networks of waiting lines. Oper. Res. **5**(4), 518–521 (1957)
21. Zadeh, L.A.: Fuzzy sets. Inf. Control **8**(3), 338–353 (1965)
22. Khemiri, R., Elbedoui-Maktouf, K., Grabot, B., Zouari, B.: A fuzzy multi-criteria decision-making approach for managing performance and risk in integrated procurement–production planning. Int. J. Prod. Res. **55**(18), 5305–5329 (2017)
23. Ali, M.A.H., Lun, A.K.: A cascading fuzzy logic with image processing algorithm–based defect detection for automatic visual inspection of industrial cylindrical object's surface. Int. J. Adv. Manuf. Technol. **102**(1–4), 81–94 (2018). https://doi.org/10.1007/s00170-018-3171-7
24. Sarno, R., Sinaga, F., Sungkono, K.R.: Anomaly detection in business processes using process mining and fuzzy association rule learning. J. Big Data **7**(1), 1–19 (2020). https://doi.org/10.1186/s40537-019-0277-1
25. Bagga, P., Joshi, A., Hans, R.: QoS based web service selection and multi-criteria decision making methods. Int. J. Interact. Multimedia Artif. Intell. **5**(4), 113–121 (2019)
26. Pedrycz, W.: Why triangular membership functions? Fuzzy Sets Syst. **64**(1), 21–30 (1994)
27. Dubois, D., Foulloy, L., Mauris, G., Prade, H.: Probability-possibility transformations, triangular fuzzy sets, and probabilistic inequalities. Reliable Comput. **10**(4), 273–297 (2004)
28. Charnes, A., Cooper, W.W., Ferguson, R.O.: Optimal estimation of executive compensation by linear programming. Manag. Sci. **1**(2), 138–151 (1955)

29. Kaucic, M., Barbini, F., Camerota Verdù, F.J.: Polynomial goal programming and particle swarm optimization for enhanced indexation. Soft. Comput. **24**(12), 8535–8551 (2019). https://doi.org/10.1007/s00500-019-04378-5
30. Bakhtavar, E., Prabatha, T., Karunathilake, H., Sadiq, R., Hewage, K.: Assessment of renewable energy-based strategies for net-zero energy communities: a planning model using multi-objective goal programming. J. Clean. Prod. **272**, 122886 (2020)
31. Ruben, C., Dhulipala, S.C., Bretas, A.S., Guan, Y., Bretas, N.G.: Multi-objective MILP model for PMU allocation considering enhanced gross error detection: a weighted goal programming framework. Electr. Pow. Syst. Res. **182**, 106235 (2020)
32. Tornado Mobility-Fui Project. https://www.tornado-mobility.com/index.php/en/home-2/. Accessed 10 Nov 2020
33. Lai, Y.J., Hwang, C.L.: A new approach to some possibilistic linear programming problems. Fuzzy Sets Syst. **49**(2), 121–133 (1992)
34. Wang, R.C., Liang, T.F.: Applying possibilistic linear programming to aggregate production planning. Int. J. Prod. Econ. **98**(3), 328–341 (2005)
35. Liang, T.F.: Distribution planning decisions using interactive fuzzy multi-objective linear programming. Fuzzy Sets Syst. **157**, 1303–1316 (2006)
36. Khemiri, R., Elbedoui-Maktouf, K., Grabot, B., Zouari, B.: Integrating fuzzy TOPSIS and goal programming for multiple objective integrated procurement-production planning. In: 22nd IEEE International Conference on Emerging Technologies and Factory Automation, pp. 1–8. IEEE, Limassol (2017)
37. Luhandjula, M.K.: Fuzzy optimization: an appraisal. Fuzzy Sets Syst. **30**(3), 257–282 (1989)
38. Sakawa, M., Yano, H.: An interactive fuzzy satisficing method for multiobjective nonlinear programming problems with fuzzy parameters. Fuzzy Sets Syst. **30**(3), 221–238 (1989)
39. Tanaka, H., Asai, K.: Fuzzy linear programming problems with fuzzy numbers. Fuzzy Sets Syst. **13**(1), 1–10 (1984)
40. Tanaka, H., Ichihashi, H., Asai, K.: A formulation of linear programming problems based on comparison of fuzzy numbers. Control Cybern. **13**, 185–194 (1984)
41. Hsu, H.M., Wang, W.P.: Possibilistic programming in production planning of assemble-to-order environments. Fuzzy Sets Syst. **119**(1), 59–70 (2001)

Efficient Scheduling of Periodic, Aperiodic, and Sporadic Real-Time Tasks with Deadline Constraints

Aicha Goubaa[1,2,3](✉), Mohamed Kahlgui[2,3], Frey Georg[1], and Zhiwu Li[4,5]

[1] Automation and Energy Systems, Saarland University, 66123 Saarbrucken, Germany

[2] School of Electrical and Information Engineering, Jinan University, (Zhuhai Campus), Zhuhai 519070, China

[3] National Institute of Applied Sciences and Technology (INSAT), University of Carthage, 1080 Tunis, Tunisia

[4] Institute of Systems Engineering, Macau University of Science and Technology, Taipa, Macau 999078, China

[5] School of Electro-Mechanical Engineering, Xidian University, Xi'an 710071, China

Abstract. A real-time system is an operating system that guarantees a certain functionality within a specified time constraint. Such system is composed of tasks of various types: periodic, sporadic and aperiodic. These tasks can be subjected to a variety of temporal constraints, the most important one is the deadline. Thus, a reaction occurring too late may be useless or even dangerous. In this context, the main problem of this study is how to configure feasible real-time system having both periodic, aperiodic and sporadic tasks. This paper shows an approach for computing deadlines in uniprocessor real-time systems to guarantee real-time feasibility for hard-deadline periodic and sporadic tasks and provide good responsiveness for soft-deadline aperiodic tasks. An application to a case study and performance evaluation show the effectiveness of the proposed approach.

Keywords: Real-time feasibility · Periodic task · Sporadic task · Aeriodic task · Hard deadline · Soft deadline

Nomenclature

Π	Real-time system;
$\mathcal{P}$	Set of periodic tasks in Π;
$\mathcal{S}$	Set of sporadic tasks in Π;
$\mathcal{A}$	Set of aperiodic tasks in Π;
n	Number of periodic tasks in Π;
m	Number of sporadic tasks in Π;
k	Number of aperiodic tasks in Π;

M. van Sinderen et al. (Eds.): ICSOFT 2020, CCIS 1447, pp. 25–43, 2021.
https://doi.org/10.1007/978-3-030-83007-6_2

τ_i^0	Periodic task;
τ_{ij}^0	The jth job of τ_i^0;
τ_e^1	Sporadic task;
τ_{ef}^1	The fth job of τ_e^0;
τ_o^2	Aperiodic task;
R_i^0	Release time of τ_i^0;
r_{ij}^0	Release time of the jth job of τ_i^0;
C_i^0	Worst-case execution time of τ_i^0;
P_i^0	Period of τ_i^0;
D_i^0	Hard relative deadline of τ_i^0 to be determined;
d_{ij}^0	Relative deadline of τ_{ij}^0 to be determined;
ϕ_i^0	Degree of criticality of τ_i^0;
E_{ij}^0	End execution time of τ_{ij}^0;
R_e^1	Release time of τ_e^1;
r_{ef}^1	Release time of the fth job of τ_e^1;
C_e^1	Worst-case execution time of τ_e^1;
P_e^1	Minimum interval between the arrival of two successive instances of τ_e^1;
D_e^1	Hard relative deadline of τ_e^1 to be determined;
d_{ef}^1	Relative deadline of τ_{ef}^1 to be determined;
ϕ_e^1	Degree of criticality of τ_e^1;
E_{ef}^1	End execution time of τ_{ef}^1;
C_o^2	WCET of τ_o^2;
D_o^2	Soft deadline of τ_o^2 to be determined;
ϕ_o^2	Degree of criticality of τ_o^2;
C^s	Capacity of the NPS server;
P^s	Period of the NPS server;
HP	Hyper-period;
OC	Maximum number of aperiodic tasks' occurrences estimated on HP;
Q	Maximum cumulative execution time requested by periodic and sporadic jobs on HP;
τ_{i_1}	Periodic or sporadic task;
$\tau_{i_1 j_1}$	The j_1th job of $\tau_{i_1 j_1}$;
$\Delta_{i_1 j_1}$	Maximum cumulative execution time requested by periodic and sporadic jobs that have to be executed before $\tau_{i_1 j_1}$;
$\beta_l^{i_1 j_1}$	Number of jobs produced by a periodic or sporadic task τ_l to be executed before $\tau_{i_1 j_1}$.

1 Introduction

Nowadays, computer systems, to control real-time functions, are considered among the most challenging systems. As a consequence, real-time systems have become the focus of much study [4–6]. A real-time system is any system which has to respond to externally generated input stimuli within a finite and specified delay. The development of real-time systems is not a trivial task because a failure can be critical for the safety of human beings [1–3]. Such system must react to events from the controlled environment while executing specific tasks that can be periodic, aperiodic or sporadic. A periodic task is activated on a regular cycle and must adhere to its hard deadline. It is characterized by its arrival time, worst-case execution time (WCET), period, relative deadline, and a degree of criticality that defines its applicative importance. The degree of criticality is defined as the functional and operational importance of a task. A sporadic task can arrive to the system at arbitrary points in time, but with defined minimum inter-arrival time between two consecutive invocations. It is characterized by its worst-case execution time, minimum inter-arrival time, relative deadline, and a degree of criticality that defines its applicative importance. These attributes are known before system execution. Additional information available on-line, is its arrival time and its absolute deadline. An aperiodic task is activated at random time to cope with external interruptions, and it is based upon soft deadline. Its arrival time is unknown at design time. It is characterized by its worst-case execution time, relative deadline, and a degree of criticality that defines its applicative importance.

Real-time scheduling has been extensively studied in the last three decades. These studies propose several Feasibility Conditions for the dimensioning of real-time systems. These conditions are defined to enable a designer to grant that timeliness constraints associated with an application are always met for all possible configurations. In this paper, Two main classical scheduling are generally used in real-time embedded systems: RM and EDF. EDF is a dynamic scheduling algorithm used in real-time operating systems [8]. EDF is an optimal scheduling algorithm on preemptive uniprocessors, in the following sense: if a collection of independent jobs (each one characterized by an arrival time, an execution requirement, and a deadline) can be scheduled (by any algorithm) such that all the jobs complete by their deadlines, then the EDF will schedule this collection of jobs such that all of them complete by their deadlines. On the other hand, if a set of tasks is not schedulable under EDF, then no other scheduling algorithm can feasibly schedule this task set. Rate Monotonic (RM) for fixed priorities and Earliest, it was defined by Liu and Layland [7] where the priority of tasks is inversely proportional to their periods.

Enforcing timeliness constraints is necessary to maintain correctness of a real-time system. In order to ensure a required real-time performance, the designer should predict the behavior of a real-time system by ensuring that all tasks meet their hard deadlines. Furthermore, scheduling both periodic, sporadic and aperiodic tasks in real-time systems is much more difficult than scheduling a single type of tasks. Thus, the development of real-time systems is not a trivial task because a failure can be critical for the safety of human beings [19]. In this context, the considered problem is how to calculate the effective deadlines (hard and soft) of the different mixed tasks to guarantee that all tasks will always meet their deadlines while improving response times for aperiodic tasks.

The major contribution of this work is a methodology defined in the context of dynamic priority preemptive uniprocessor scheduling to achieve real-time feasibility of a software system. Differently from earlier work [22], which is based on maximum deadlines, the deadline calculation in the current work is based on the degree of criticality of tasks and on their periods. In fact, as the degree of criticality is defined as the functional and operational importance of a task, we consider that an important task must be executed ahead, i.e., that its relative deadline must be well defined to reinforce its execution while using the EDF scheduling algorithm. The calculation of deadlines is done off-line on the hyper-period which is the lowest common multiple (LCM) of the periodic tasks' periods [20]. We suppose that the maximum number of occurrences of aperiodic tasks in a given interval of time is a random variable with a Poisson distribution which is a discrete probability distribution that expresses the probability of a given number of events occurring in a fixed interval of time. This proposed approach consists of two phases. The first one defines the NPS server which serves periodically aperiodic tasks. In fact, the server can be accounted for in periodic task schedulability analysis, it has (i) a period which is calculated in such a way that the periodic execution of the server is repeated as many times as the maximum number of aperiodic tasks occurrences in the hyper-period, and (ii) a capacity which is the allowed computing time in each period and it is calculated based on unused processing time by a given set of periodic and sporadic tasks in the hyper-period in a such way aperiodic task execution should not jeopardize schedulability of periodic and sporadic tasks. Then, this approach calculates aperiodic tasks soft deadlines while supposing that an aperiodic task, with highest degree of criticality, gets the highest priority to be executed. The second one calculates hard deadlines of periodic and sporadic tasks ensuring real-time system feasibility while considering the invocation of aperiodic task execution, i.e., while considering the maximum cumulative execution time requested by aperiodic tasks that may occur before periodic and sporadic jobs on the hyper-period. Thus, at runtime, even if an aperiodic task occurs, the periodic and sporadic tasks will certainly respect their deadlines and the response time of aperiodic task is improved. For each periodic or sporadic task, the maximum among its calculated jobs deadlines will be its relative deadline. Thus, at runtime, even if an aperiodic task occurs, the periodic and sporadic tasks will certainly respect their deadlines and the response time of aperiodic task is improved as the invocation of aperiodic task execution is considered when calculating hard deadlines.

The remainder of the paper is organized as follows. Section 2 discusses the related studies. Section 3 presents a computational model, assumptions, and problem formulation. Section 4 gives the proposed scheduling method. Section 5 presents a case study for evaluating our method. Finally, Sect. 6 summarizes this paper with our future work.

2 Related Studies

In this section, we present the related works that deal with real-time systems and scheduling policies.

Several works deal with the synthesis problem of real-time systems. The correctness of such systems depends both on the logical result of the computation and the time when the results are produced. Thus enforcing timeliness constraints is necessary to maintain correctness of a real-time system. In this context, many approaches have been carried out in the area of schedulability analysis for meeting real-time requirement [9–14,26]. Some of them [11–13] work on real-time schedulability without considering the deadlines analysis. Some other [9,10] seek to schedule tasks to respect energy constraints and consider that deadlines are given beforehand. Pillai and Shin [26] propose an optimal algorithm for computing the minimal speed that can make a task set schedulable. Furthermore, these researches does not consider mixed tasks set. Moreover, techniques to calculate tasks' deadlines are seldom presented. For this reason, the studies that address this problem are few. The work reported in [15] presents a method that minimizes deadlines of periodic tasks only. The research in [18] calculates new deadlines for control tasks in order to guarantee close loop stability of real-time control systems. On the other hand, several related works, such as in [16,17] have chosen to manage the tasks of a real-time system by modifying either their periods or worst-case execution times (WCET). This orientation affects the performance of the system, since increasing the periods degrades the quality of the offered services, and decreasing the WCET increases the energy consumption.

Furthermore, the research works reported in [23–25] take into account the energy requirements without considering the deadlines analysis, as long as they are given beforehand. Indeed, in these researches, the authors seek to schedule tasks to respect energy constraints. In addition, it is done online, which can be heavy and expensive.

We note that most of existing studies working on real-time schedulability, address separately periodic, sporadic or aperiodic tasks but not together. Thus, the originality of this work compared with related studies is that it

- deals with real-time tasks of various types and constraints simultaneously,
- parameterizes periodic server to execute aperiodic tasks,
- calculates soft deadlines of aperiodic tasks,
- calculates periodic and sporadic tasks hard deadlines which will be certainly respected online,
- improves response times of aperiodic tasks which can lead to a significant improvement of the system performance.

3 Assumptions and System Formalization

3.1 System Model

It is assumed in this work that a real-time system Π deals with a combination of mixed sets of tasks and constraints: periodic and sporadic tasks with hard constraints, and soft aperiodic tasks. Thus, Π is defined as having three task sets as presented in Fig. 1.

We assume that all periodic tasks are simultaneously activated at time $t = 0$;

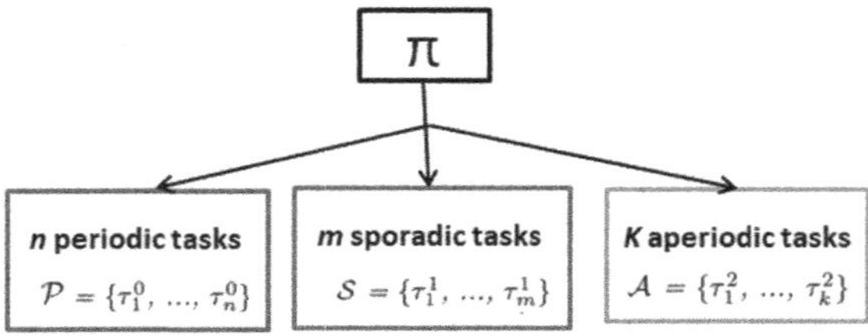

Fig. 1. *Π*'s tasks sets.

3.2 Periodic Task Model

Each periodic task τ_i^0, $i \in [1, ..., n]$, in $\mathcal{P}$ is characterized by: (i) a release time R_i^0 which is the time at which a task becomes ready for execution [27], (ii) a worst-case execution time (WCET) C_i^0, (iii) a period P_i^0, (iv) a relative deadline D_i^0 to be calculated, and (v) a degree of criticality phi_i^0. Figure 2 depicts the task parameters:

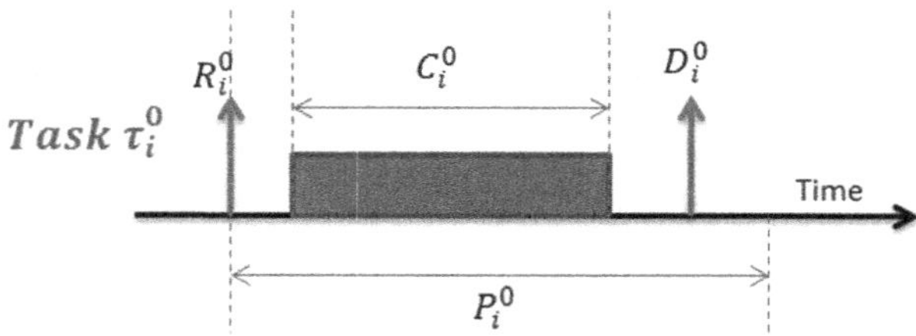

Fig. 2. Periodic task parameters.

Each periodic task τ_i^0 produces an infinite sequence of identical activities called jobs τ_{ij}^0 [27], where j is a positive integer. Each job τ_{ij}^0 is described by: (i) a release time r_{ij}^0, (ii) a relative deadline d_{ij}^0, and (iii) an end execution time E_{ij}^0. We note that

$$D_i^0 = max\{d_{ij}^0\} \tag{1}$$

where $i \in [1, ..., n]$.

Finally, we denote by HP the hyper-period which is the lowest common multiple (LCM) of the periodic tasks' periods.

$$HP = LCM\{P_i^0\} \tag{2}$$

where $i \in [1, ..., n]$.

3.3 Sporadic Task Model

Each sporadic task τ_e^1, $e \in [1, ..., m]$, is defined by: (i) a release time R_e^1, (ii) a worst-case execution time C_e^1, (iii) a relative deadline D_e^1, (iv) a period P_e^1 which measures the minimum interval between the arrival of two successive instances of a task τ_e^1, and (v) a degree of criticality phi_e^1

Each sporadic task τ_e^1 produces an infinite sequence of jobs τ_{ef}^1, where f is a positive integer. Each job τ_{ef}^1 is described by: (i) a release time r_{ef}^1, (ii) a relative deadline d_{ef}^1, and (iii) end execution time E_{ef}^1. Figure 3 depicts the sporadic task's jobs parameters:

$$D_e^1 = max\{d_{ef}^1\} \tag{3}$$

where $e \in [1, ..., m]$.

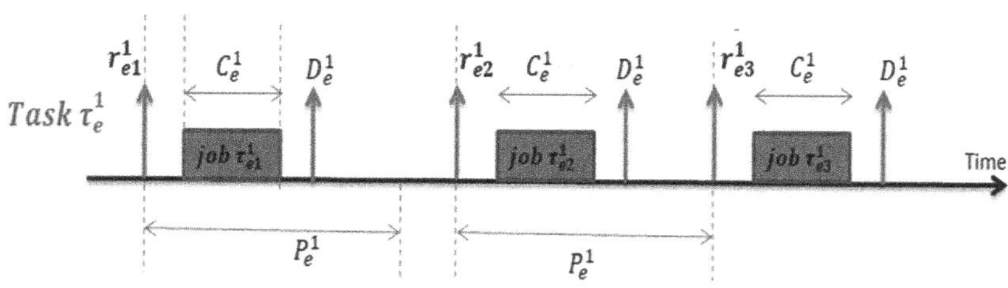

Fig. 3. Sporadic task parameters.

3.4 Aperiodic Task Model

Each aperiodic task τ_o^2, $o \in [1, ..., k]$, is defined by: (i) a worst-case execution time C_o^2, (ii) a relative soft deadline D_o^2, and (iii) a degree of criticality phi_o^2. An aperiodic task can arrive in a completely random way. Thus, we model this number by the Poisson distribution with a parameter λ. We note by OC the maximum number of aperiodic tasks' occurrences estimated on the hyper-period.

Let NPS be a periodic server that behaves much like a periodic task, but created to execute aperiodic tasks. It is defined by: (i) a period P^s, and (ii) a capacity C^s. These parameters will be calculated to meet time requirements of aperiodic tasks.

3.5 Problem: Feasible Scheduling of Real-Time Tasks with Various Types

We undertake a real-time system which is composed of mixed tasks sets with various constraints. Thus, the considered problem is how to configure feasible scheduling of software tasks of various types (periodic, sporadic and aperiodic) and constraints (hard and soft) in the context of dynamic priority, preemptive, uniprocessor scheduling. To ensure that this system runs correctly, it is necessary to check whether it respects the following constraints:

- the execution of aperiodic tasks must occur during the unused processing time by a given set of periodic and sporadic tasks in the hyper-period in such way aperiodic task execution should not jeopardize schedulability of periodic and sporadic tasks. This constraint is given by

$$C^s \leq HP - Q$$

  where, C^s is the capacity of the NPS server and Q is the maximum cumulative execution time requested by periodic and sporadic jobs on the hyper-period HP.
- During each hyper-period, each periodic or sporadic job has to be completed before the absolute deadline using the EDF scheduling algorithm even if an aperiodic task is executed. In fact, the cumulative execution time requested by aperiodic tasks must be token into consideration when calculating the tasks' deadlines. Thus, s an aperiodic task will be executed as soon as possible of its activation, and periodic and sporadic tasks will meet their deadlines. This constraint is given by
  - For periodic jobs:

$$\forall i \in \{1, ..., n\}, \text{ and } j \in \{1, ..., \frac{HP}{P_i^0}], E_{ij}^0 \leq r_{ij}^0 + D_i^0 \tag{4}$$

  - For sporadic jobs:

$$\forall e \in \{1, ..., m\}, \text{ and } f \in \{1, ..., \left\lceil \frac{HP}{P_e^1} \right\rceil], E_{ef}^1 \leq r_{ef}^1 + D_e^1 \tag{5}$$

In what follows, it is always considered that $i \in [1...n]$, $e \in [1...m]$, $o \in [1...k]$, $j \in [1...\frac{HP}{P_i^0}]$, where $\frac{HP}{P_i^0}$ denotes the number of jobs produced by task τ_i on hyper-period HP and $f \in [1...\lceil\frac{HP}{P_i^0}\rceil]$. In addition, we suppose that a ztask lower its value, higher the criticality.

4 Contribution: New Solution for Deadlines Calculation

4.1 Motivation

The proposed methodology deals with real-time tasks of various types and constraints simultaneously. This approach is divided into two phases as presented in Fig. 4:

- **First Phase:** consists on parameterizing the NPS server which is a service task, with a period P^s and a capacity C^s, invoked periodically to execute aperiodic tasks. Then, this approach calculates soft deadlines of aperiodic tasks while supposing that an aperiodic task, with highest degree of criticality, gets the highest priority. The NPS can provide a substantial reduction in the average response time of the aperiodic tasks.
- **Second Phase:** starts by calculating jobs'deadlines. In fact, for each periodic/sporadic task, it calculates the deadlines of its jobs that occur on the hyper-period based on the maximum cumulative execution time requested by i) other periodic/sporadic jobs that will occur before the considered periodic/sporadic job on the hyperperiod based on the degree of criticality, and ii) aperiodic tasks that may occur before periodic/sporadic job on the hyperperiod. Then, for each periodic/sporadic task, its deadline will be equal to the maximum of its jobs' deadlines. Thus, at runtime, even if an aperiodic task occurs, this methodology ensures certainly real-time system feasibility of periodic and sporadic tasks.

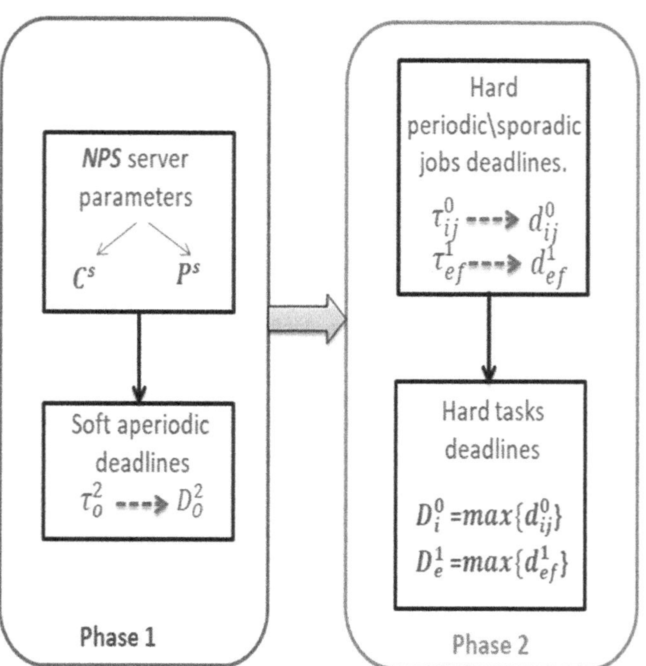

Fig. 4. New methodology of deadlines calculation.

4.2 Proposed Approach

In this section, we present the solution that we propose to extend. This solution is mainly based on the calculation of effective deadlines of mixed tasks set in order to ensure that the system will run correctly and to satisfy the real-time feasibility.

Parameterizing Aperiodic Tasks: As mentioned previously, aperiodic tasks will be run periodically by the periodic server NPS (P^s, C^s). As, OC is the maximum number of aperiodic tasks' occurrences estimated on the hyper-period, then, NPS must be activated OC times to serve all possible activations of aperiodic tasks that may occur. Thus, its period is calculated as below

$$P^s = \lfloor \frac{HP}{OC} \rfloor \tag{6}$$

Moreover, aperiodic tasks are scheduled by utilizing unused processing time by a given set of periodic and spordic tasks in the hyper-period. Thus, the capacity of server is calculated as follows: first, we calculate the unused time by subtracting the maximum cumulative execution time requested by periodic and sporadic jobs from HP, and second we divide the obtained result by OC, i.e., the possible activation number, to affirm that in each period the same amount of execution time will be executed, hence the server capacity value.

$$C^s = \lceil \frac{HP - Q}{OC} \rceil \tag{7}$$

where, Q is the maximum cumulative execution time requested by periodic and sporadic jobs on the hyper-period HP.

$$Q = (\sum_{\tau_i^0 \in \mathcal{P}} (C_i^0 \times \frac{HP}{P_i^0})) + (\sum_{\tau_e^1 \in \mathcal{S}} (C_e^1 \times \lceil \frac{HP}{P_e^1} \rceil)) \tag{8}$$

By assuming that the aperiodic task with the highest degree of criticality,i.e., the smallest value of ϕ_o^2, gets the highest priority, we calculate the deadlines D_o^2 as following

$$D_o^2 = \sum_{x=1}^{x=k} C_x^2 \times \alpha_x \tag{9}$$

where,

$$\alpha_x = \begin{cases} 1 \text{ if } (\phi_o^2 \geq \phi_x^2), \\ 0 \text{ else.} \end{cases} \tag{10}$$

Parameterizing Periodic and Sporadic Tasks: At the peak of activity, a sporadic task τ_e runs at each P_e^1. In this case, we can estimate the value r_{ef}^1 of each job τ_{ef}^1. Therefore, to calculate the deadline of a sporadic task, we follow the same procedure of a periodic task deadline calculation. For that, we unify the notation of periodic and sporadic tasks by $\tau_{i_1}(R_{i_1}, C_{i_1}, P_{i_1}, D_{i_1}, \phi_{i_1})$, where i_1 $in[1, ..., n+m]$, also for these parameters. For example, let's consider a system with two tasks: a periodic task $\tau_1^0(R_1^0, C_1^0, P_1^0, D_1^0, \phi_1^0)$ and a sporadic task $\tau_1^1(R_1^1, C_1^1, P_1^1, D_1^1, \phi_1^1)$, then they becomes $\tau_1(R_1, C_1, P_1, D_1, \phi_1)$ and $\tau_2(R_2, C_2, P_2, D_2, \phi_2)$.

This solution allows the calculation of deadlines of a task τ_{i_1}. We denote by $\Delta_{i_1 j_1}$ the job quantity, coming from periodic and sporadic jobs, to be executed before the job $\tau_{i_1 j_1}$. In other words, $\Delta_{i_1 j_1}$ is the maximum cumulative execution time requested by jobs that have to be executed before each job $\tau_{i_1 j_1}$.

$\Delta_{i_1 j_1}$ is given by

$$\Delta_{i_1 j_1} = (j_1 - 1) \times C_{i_1} + \sum_{\tau_l^{\in} \mathcal{P} \cup \mathcal{S} and l \neq i} (\lfloor \frac{j_1 \times P_{i_1}}{P_l} \rfloor - \beta_l^{i_1 j_1}) \times C_l \quad (11)$$

where $(j_1 - 1) \times C_{i_1}$ represents the cumulative execution time requested by the previous instances of τ_{i_1}, i.e., if we are working on the j_1th instance, then we are sure that there are $(j_1 - 1)$ instances that have already been executed, and $\sum_{\tau_l^{\in} \in \mathcal{P} \cup \mathcal{S} and l \neq i} (\lfloor \frac{j_1 \times P_{i_1}}{P_l} \rfloor - \beta_l^{i_1 j_1}) \times C_l$ represents the cumulative execution time requested by the other tasks' jobs, where $\beta_l^{i_1 j_1}$ is an integer given by

$$\beta_l^{i_1 j_1} = \begin{cases} 0 \text{ if } (\lfloor \frac{j_1 \times P_{i_1}}{P_l} \rfloor \times P_l < j_1 \times P_{i_1}) \text{ or } (\lfloor \frac{j_1 \times P_{i_1}}{P_l} \rfloor \times P_l = j_1 \times P_{i_1} \text{ and } \phi_{i_1} > \phi_l) \\ 1 \text{ if } (\lfloor \frac{j_1 \times P_{i_1}}{P_l} \rfloor \times P_l > j_1 \times P_{i_1}) \text{ or } (\lfloor \frac{j_1 \times P_{i_1}}{P_l} \rfloor \times P_l = j_1 \times P_{i_1} \text{ and } \phi_{i_1} < \phi_l) \end{cases} \quad (12)$$

The value $d_{i_1 j_1}$ that guarantees the feasibility of this job takes the form

$$d_{i_1 j_1} = \begin{cases} \sum_{\tau_l^2 \in \mathcal{A}} (C_l^2 \times \lceil \frac{P_{i_1}}{P^s} \rceil) + C_{i_1} + \Delta_{i_1 j_1} - r_{i_1 j_1} \\ \text{if } \Delta_{i_1 j_1} > r_{i_1 j_1}, \\ \sum_{\tau_l^2 \in \mathcal{A}} (C_l^2 \times \lceil \frac{P_{i_1}}{P^s} \rceil) + C_{i_1} \text{ else.} \end{cases} \quad (13)$$

The deadline D_{i_1} of task τ_{i_1} is expressed by

$$D_{i_1} = max\{d_{i_1 j_1}\} \quad (14)$$

Finally, D_{i_1} is the fixed deadline for τ_{i_1}.

New Solution for Deadline Calculation of Periodic, Sporadic and Aperiodic Real-Time Tasks: We can implement our approach by the algorithm below with complexity O(n).

We use the following functions: $NPS\_Parameters(HP, OC)$ which is a function that returns the NPS server parameters, and $H\_Dead\_Calc(\mathcal{P}, \mathcal{S})$ which a function that returns the periodic and sporadic hard deadlines. This function starts by computing jobs deadlines and then for each periodic/sporadic task, it calculates its fixed deadline to be equal to the maximum of its jobs' deadlines.

Algorithm 1. New method for deadline calculation.

Require: $\mathcal{P}$, $\mathcal{S}$,$\mathcal{A}$, OC
Ensure: D_i^0, D_e^1, D_o^2
function $NPS\_Parameters(HP, OC)$
  $P^s = \lfloor \frac{HP}{OC} \rfloor$
  $Q = (\sum_{\tau_i^0 \in \mathcal{P}}(C_i^0 \times \frac{HP}{P_i^0})) + (\sum_{\tau_e^1 \in \mathcal{S}}(C_e^1 \times \lceil \frac{HP}{P_e^1} \rceil))$
  $C^s = \lceil \frac{HP - Q}{OC} \rceil$
end function
for all $\tau_o^2 \in \mathcal{A}$ **do**
  $D_o^2 = \sum_{x=1}^{x=k} C_x^2 \times \alpha_x$
end for
function $H\_Dead\_Calc(\mathcal{P}, \mathcal{S})$
  for all $\tau_l \in \mathcal{P} \cup \mathcal{S}$ **do**
    $\Delta_{i_1 j_1} = \sum_{\tau_l \in \mathcal{P} \cup \mathcal{S}}(C_l \times \beta_l^{i_1 j_1})$
    if $\Delta_{i_1 j_1} > r_{i_1 j_1}$ **then**
      $d_{i_1 j_1} = \sum_{\tau_l^2 \in \mathcal{A}}(C_l^2 \times \lceil \frac{Pi_1}{P^s} \rceil) + C_{i_1} + \Delta_{i_1 j_1} - r_{i_1 j_1}$
    else
      $d_{i_1 j_1} = \sum_{\tau_l^2 \in \mathcal{A}}(C_l^2 \times \lceil \frac{Pi_1}{P^s} \rceil) + C_{i_1}$
    end if
  end for
  $D_{i_1} = max\{d_{i_1 j_1}\}$
end function

5 Implementation

5.1 Case Study

We present in this section a simple example of an electric oven whose temperature we want to keep constant after in interruption that may disturb the temperature stability. For example, we want to keep it at 180 °C after a sudden opening of the oven's door as presented in Fig. 5. The oven is heated by an electrical resistance, the intensity of which can vary. Inside the oven there is also a temperature probe, which allows to measure and monitor the temperature in the oven.

This system is implemented by three sets: $\mathcal{P} = \{\tau_1^0, \tau_2^0\}$, $\mathcal{S} = \{\tau_1^1\}$ and $\mathcal{A} = \{\tau_1^2\}$. The tasks are presented in Table 1:

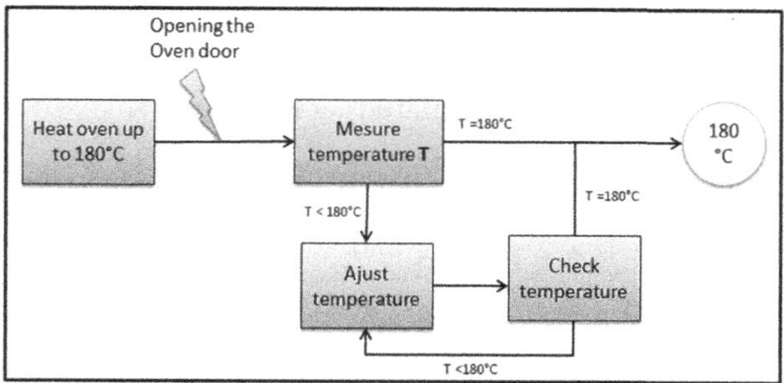

Fig. 5. Electric oven modelisation.

Table 1. System tasks.

Task	Fonction	WCET	Period	Degree of criticality
τ_1^0	Mesures temperature	2	8	1
τ_2^0	Heats the oven	2	16	3
τ_1^1	Checks temperature value	2	16	2
τ_1^2	Adjusts temperature	2		5

We have, $HP = LCM\{8, 16\} = 16s$.

Let's suppose that the parameter λ of the Poisson distribution is equal to 0.5 occurrences in 10 s. Thus, in the hyper-period we have $\frac{HP}{10} \times \lambda = \frac{16}{10} \times 0.5 = 1.6$, i.e., $OC = 2$ occurrences.

The first step is to configure the periodic server.

The periodic server parameters P^s and C^s are computed respectively as following:

According to Eq. (6), $P^s = \lfloor \frac{16}{2} \rfloor = 8$

According to Eq. (8), $Q = 2 \times 2 + 2 \times 1 = 6$

According to Eq. (7), $C^s = \lfloor \frac{16-6}{2} \rfloor = 5$

After that, we calculate the soft deadline of the aperiodic task τ_1^2. According to Eq. (9)

$$D_1^2 = C_1^2 \times \alpha_1 = 2 \times 1 = 2$$

Second step is the calculation of periodic and sporadic tasks' deadlines. As mentioned previously, we unify the notation of periodic and sporadic tasks as following: τ_1^0 becomes τ_1, τ_2^0 becomes τ_2, and τ_1^1 becomes τ_3.

As an example, we take the calculation of deadline D_1^0 for task τ_1^0, i.e., D_1 for the task τ_1. The number of jobs of task τ_1 in the hyper-period HP is $\frac{HP}{P_3} = \frac{16}{8} = 2$ jobs.

Job τ_{11}:

First of all, we calculate the job quantity Δ_{11}. According to Eq. (11), we have to calculate β_2^{11} and β_3^{11} as indicated Eq. (12).

We have $\lfloor\frac{1\times8}{16}\rfloor\times16<1\times8$, i.e., $0<8$, then we conclude that $\beta_2^{11}=0$. In the same way, we have $\beta_3^{11}=0$

According to Eq. (11), Δ_{11} is calculated as following

$$\begin{aligned}\Delta_{11}&=(1-1)\times2+\lfloor\frac{1\times8}{16}\rfloor-0)\times2+\lfloor\frac{1\times8}{16}\rfloor-0)\times2\\&=0\times2+0\times2+0\times2=0\end{aligned}$$

We have $r_{11}=0$, so $\Delta_{11}=r_{11}$. Thus, according to Eq. (13),

$$\begin{aligned}d_{11}&=\sum_{\tau_l^2\in\mathcal{A}}(C_l^2\times\lceil\frac{Pi_1}{P^s}\rceil)+C_1\\&=2+2=4\end{aligned}$$

Job τ_{12}:
First of all, we calculate the job quantity Δ_{12}. According to Eq. (11), we have to calculate β_2^{12}, and β_3^{12} as indicated in Eq. (12). We have $\lfloor\frac{2\times8}{16}\rfloor\times16<2\times8$, i.e., $16=16$, and $\phi_1<\phi_2$ then we conclude that $\beta_2^{12}=1$. In the same way, wa have $\beta_3^{11}=1$

According to Eq. (11), Δ_{12} is calculated as following

$$\begin{aligned}\Delta_{12}&=(2-1)\times2+\lfloor\frac{2\times8}{16}\rfloor-1)\times2+\lfloor\frac{2\times8}{16}\rfloor-1)\times2\\&=1\times2+0\times2+0\times2=2\end{aligned}$$

We have $r_{12}=8$, then $\Delta_{12}<r_{12}$ and we have

$$\sum_{\tau_l^2\in\mathcal{A}}(C_l^2\times\lceil\frac{Pi_1}{P^s}\rceil)=2$$

Thus, according to Eq. (13),

$$d_{12}=\sum_{\tau_l^2\in\mathcal{A}}(C_l^2\times\lceil\frac{Pi_1}{P^s}\rceil)+C_1=2+2=4$$

Finally, we calculate the deadline D_1 of the task τ_1 as bellow

$$D_1=max\{d_{11},d_{12}\}=max\{4,4\}=4$$

After completing the execution of the proposed approach, the calculated effective deadlines of the different tasks are given in Table 2.

Table 2. Tasks' calculated deadlines.

Task	τ_1^0	τ_2^0	τ_1^1	τ_2^2
Calculated deadline	4	10	6	2

Figure 6 shows the scheduling of tasks after the execution of the proposed approach. We note that the real-time constraints are respected by the proposed methodology, and the response time of each aperiodic task is equal to its execution time, i.e., they are executed with the best response time.

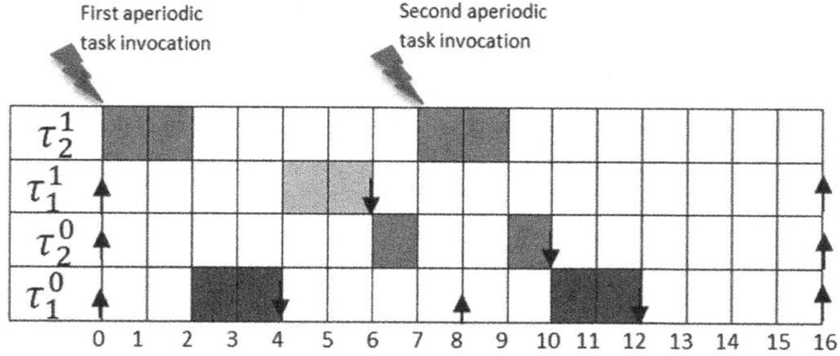

Fig. 6. Scheduling of tasks after the execution of the proposed approach.

5.2 Performance Evaluation

We have randomly generated instances with 10 to 50 periodic and sporadic tasks. We compare the proposed approach with the work reported in [15], where the critical scaling factor (CSF) algorithm is developed.

Figure 7 visualizes simulation that compares the proposed approach with the work reported in [15], where the critical scaling factor (CSF) algorithm is developed. We obtain better results in terms of decrease rate of deadlines in the proposed approach. In fact, the reduction rates of deadlines by using [15] are smaller than those by using the proposed work. The gain is more significant when increasing the number of tasks. If 10 tasks are considered, then the gain

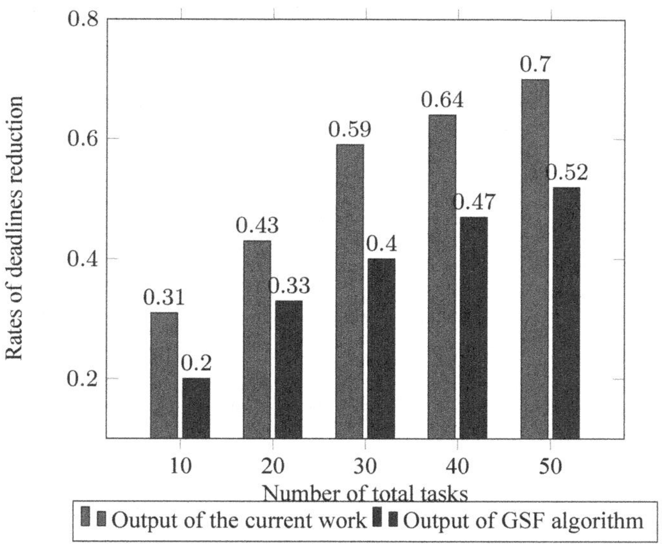

Fig. 7. Rates of deadlines reduction in the case of the proposed approach and in the case of GSF algorithm.

is equal to $(0.31 - 0.2) = 0.11$, and if 50 tasks are considered, then the gain is equal to $(0.7 - 0.52) = 0.18$.

As it was presented in [22], Fig. 8 shows that the NPS algorithm serves to improve the aperiodic response time compared to background service (BK), deferrable server (DS) and total bandwidth server (TBS).

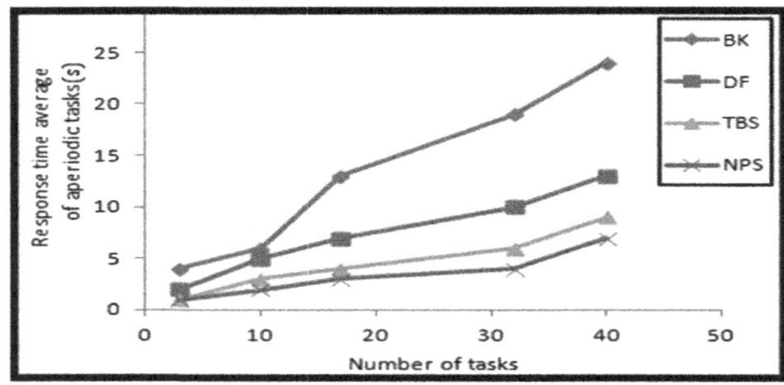

Fig. 8. The improvement of aperiodic tasks response times [22].

5.3 Comparative Study

Table 3 describes the comparison of the developed approach in this paper with some studies. The originality is manifested by treating different and independent

Table 3. Comparative study.

Work	Deadline calculation	Tasks' type	Offline/Online
[11]	This work considers periodic tasks only	It aims to ensure the system schedulability by managing the tasks of by modifying either their periods or worst-case execution time without considering the deadlines analysis. This orientation affects the performance of the system	Online: all the calculations are done online which can be expensive in case of errors
[18]	Same as [11]	It calculates new deadlines to improve the responsiveness in the context of TBS	Same as [11]
[21]	This work addresses the problem of mixed tasks	It aims to schedule mixed tasks while reducing energy consumption	Same as [11]
The proposed approach	The main objective of this work is to calculate deadlines which guarantee i) the respect of hard real-time constraints for periodic and sporadic tasks, and ii) the improvement of aperiodic tasks response time	It deals with real-time tasks of various types: periodic, sporadic and aperiodic	Offline: which is suitable for the design phase and subsequently it is not expensive in case of errors

problems together, i.e., periodic, sporadic and aperiodic tasks and hard and soft real-time constraints tasks simultaneously.

We note that the proposed approach allows to reduce the response time, to reduce the calculation time for the reason that there is no need to waste time at doing schedulability tests, to guarantee the meeting of aperiodic tasks deadlines without jeopardizing schedulability of periodic and sporadic tasks and thus improves the overall performance of the real-time system.

6 Conclusion

This paper is interested in real-time systems executing periodic, sporadic and aperiodic tasks. Our study concerns specifically the computing off effective tasks' deadlines. We propose a new approach that consists on creating the NPS server, it is a service task invoked periodically to execute aperiodic tasks after having calculated aperiodic tasks' soft deadlines. Then, this approach calculates the periodic and sporadic tasks deadlines based on the degree of criticality of tasks and while considering the invocation of aperiodic task execution. An application to a case study and performance evaluation show the effectiveness of the proposed approach and that the NPS can provide a substantial reduction in the average response time of the aperiodic tasks. In our future works, we will be interested in the implementation of the paper's contribution that will be evaluated by assuming real case studies.

References

1. Lakdhar, Z., Mzid, R., Khalgui, K., Li, Z., Frey, G., Al-Ahmari, A.: Multiobjective optimization approach for a portable development of reconfigurable real-time systems: from specification to implementation. IEEE Trans. Syst. Man Cybern. Syst. **49**(3), 623–637 (2018)
2. Anastasia, M., Jarvis, S., Todd, M.: Real-time dynamic-mode scheduling using single-integration hybrid optimization. IEEE Trans. Autom. Sci. Eng. **13**(3), 1385–1398 (2016)
3. Burns, A., Wellings, A.: Real-Time Systems and Programming Languages: Ada, Real-Time Java and C/Real-Time POSIX, 4th edn. Addison- Wesley Educational Publishers Inc., Boston (2009)
4. Ben Meskina, S., Doggaz, N., Khalgui, M., Li, Z.: Reconfiguration-based methodology for improving recovery performance of faults in smart grids. J. Inf. Sci. **454–455**, 73–95 (2018)
5. Goubaa, A., Khalgui, M., Li, Z., Frey, G., Zhou, M.: Scheduling periodic and aperiodic tasks with time, energy harvesting and precedence constraints on multicore systems. J. Inf. Sci. **520**, 86–104 (2020)
6. Ghribi, I., Ben Abdallah, R., Khalgui, M., Li, Z., Alnowibet, K., Platzne, M.: R-codesign: codesign methodology for real-time reconfigurable embedded systems under energy constraints. IEEE Access **6**, 14078–14092 (2018)
7. Liu, C., Layland, J.: Scheduling algorithms for multiprogramming in a hard-real-time environment. J. ACM (JACM) **201**, 46–61 (1973)

8. Baruah, S., Goossens, J.: Scheduling real-time tasks: algorithms and complexity. In: Handbook of Scheduling: Algorithms, Models, and Performance Analysis, vol. 3 (2004)
9. Von der Brüggen, G., Huang, W., Chen, J., Liu, C.: Uniprocessor scheduling strategies for self-suspending task systems. In: 24th International Conference on Real-Time Networks and Systems, pp. 119–128. Association for Computing Machinery, USA (2016)
10. Shanmugasundaram, M., Kumar, R., Kittur, H.: Performance analysis of preemptive based uniprocessor scheduling. Int. J. Electr. Comput. Eng. **6**(4), 1489–1498 (2016)
11. Gammoudi, A., Benzina, A., Khalgui, M., Chillet, D.: New pack oriented solutions for energy-aware feasible adaptive real-time systems. In: Fujita, H., Guizzi, G. (eds.) SoMeT 2015. CCIS, vol. 532, pp. 73–86. Springer, Cham (2015). https://doi.org/10.1007/978-3-319-22689-7_6
12. Gammoudi, A., Benzina, A., Khalgui, M., Chillet, D., Goubaa, A.: ReConf-pack: a simulator for reconfigurable battery-powered real-time systems. In: Proceedings of European Simulation and Modelling Conference (ESM), Spain, pp. 225–232 (2016)
13. Gasmi, M., Mosbahi, O., Khalgui, M., Gomes, L., Li, Z.: R-node: new pipelined approach for an effective reconfigurable wireless sensor node. IEEE Trans. Syst. Man Cybern. Syst. **486**, 892–905 (2016)
14. Wang, X., Li, Z., Wonham, W.: Dynamic multiple-period reconfiguration of real-time scheduling based on timed DES supervisory control. IEEE Trans. Industr. Inf. **121**, 101–111 (2015)
15. Balbastre, P., Ripoll, I., Crespo, A.: Minimum deadline calculation for periodic real-time tasks in dynamic priority systems. IEEE Trans. Comput. **571**, 96–109 (2007)
16. Wang, X., Khemaissia, I., Khalgui, M., Li, Z., Mosbahi, O., Zhou, M.: Dynamic low-power reconfiguration of real-time systems with periodic and probabilistic tasks. IEEE Trans. Autom. Sci. Eng. **121**, 258–271 (2014)
17. Wang, X., Khemaissia, I., Khalgui, M., Li, Z., Mosbahi, O., Zhou, M.: Dynamic multiple-period reconfiguration of real-time scheduling based on timed DES supervisory control. IEEE Trans. Industr. Inf. **121**, 101–111 (2015)
18. Cervin, A., Lincoln, B., Eker, J., Arzén, K., Buttazzo, G.: The jitter margin and its application in the design of real-time control systems. In: Proceedings of the 10th International Conference on Real-Time and Embedded Computing Systems and Applications, Sweden, pp. 1–9 (2004)
19. Wang, X., Li, Z., Wonham, W.: Optimal priority-free conditionally-preemptive real-time scheduling of periodic tasks based on DES supervisory control. IEEE Trans. Syst. Man Cybern. Syst. **477**, 1082–1098 (2016)
20. Ripoll, I., Ballester-Ripoll, R.: Period selection for minimal hyperperiod in periodic task systems. IEEE Trans. Comput. **629**, 1813–1822 (2012)
21. Yiwen, Z., Haibo, L.: Energy aware mixed tasks scheduling in real-time systems. Sustain. Comput. Inform. Syst. **23**, 38–48 (2019)
22. Goubaa, A., Khalgui, M., Frey, G., Li, Z.: New approach for deadline calculation of periodic, sporadic and aperiodic real-time software tasks. In: Proceedings of the 15th International Conference on Software Technologies (ICSOFT 2020), 452–460 (2020). ISBN 978-989-758-443-5
23. Chetto, M.: Optimal scheduling for real-time jobs in energy harvesting computing systems. IEEE Trans. Emerg. Top. Comput. **22**, 122–133 (2014)

24. Sun, Y., Yuan, Z., Liu, Y., Li, X., Wang, Y., Wei, Q., Wang, Y., Narayanan, V., Yang, H.: Maximum energy efficiency tracking circuits for converter-less energy harvesting sensor nodes. IEEE Trans. Circuits Syst. II Express Briefs **646**, 670–674 (2017)
25. Yang, J., Wu, X., Wu, J.: Optimal scheduling of collaborative sensing in energy harvesting sensor networks. IEEE J. Sel. Areas Commun. **333**, 512–523 (2015)
26. Pillai, P., Shin, K.: Real-time dynamic voltage scaling for low-power embedded operating systems. In: Proceedings of the 13th Euromicro Conference on Real-Time Systems, pp. 59–66. ACM, USA (2001)
27. Buttazzo, G.: Hard Real-Time Computing Systems: Predictable Scheduling Algorithms and Applications, vol. 24. Springer, Boston (2011). https://doi.org/10.1007/978-1-4614-0676-1

R-TNCES State Space Generation Using Ontology-Based Method on a Distributed Cloud-Based Architecture

Chams Eddine Choucha[1(✉)], Mohamed Oussama Ben Salem[2], Moahmed Khalgui[1,3], Laid Kahloul[4], and Naima Souad Ougouti[5]

[1] LISI Laboratory, National Institute of Applied Sciences and Technology (INSAT), University of Carthage, 1080 Tunis, Tunisia

[2] Team Project IMAGES-ESPACE-Dev, UMR 228 EspaceDev IRD UA UM UG UR, University of Perpignan Via Domitia, 66860 Perpignan, France

[3] School of Electrical and Information Engineering, Jinan University, (Zhuhai Campus), Zhuhai 519070, China

[4] LINFI Laboratory, Computer Science Department, Biskra University, Biskra, Algeria

[5] LSSD Laboratory, Computer Science Department, University of Science and Technology of Oran Mohamed Boudiaf, Bir El Djir, Algeria

Abstract. This paper deals with formal verification (accessibility graph generation & state space analysis) of RDECSs modeled with specified reconfigurable timed net condition/event systems (R-TNCESs) where the properties to be verified to ensure the well behave of systems are expressed by computation tree logic CTL. Reconfigurable discrete event control systems (RDECSs) are complex and critical systems, which, make their formal verification expensive in terms of complexity and memory occupation. We aim to improve model checking used for formal verification of RDECSs by proposing a new approach of state space generation that considers similarities and a parallel verification of CTL properties. In this approach, we introduce the modularity concept for verifying systems by constructing incrementally their accessibility graphs. Furthermore, we set up an ontology-based history to deal with similarities between two or several systems by reusing state spaces of similar components that are computed during previous verification. A distributed cloud-based architecture is proposed to perform the parallel computation for control verification time and memory occupation. The paper's contribution is applied to a benchmark production system. The evaluation of the proposed approach is performed by measuring the temporal complexity of several large scale system verification. The results show the relevance of this approach.

Keywords: Formal verification · Discrete-event system · Reconfiguration · Petri net · Ontology

M. van Sinderen et al. (Eds.): ICSOFT 2020, CCIS 1447, pp. 44–69, 2021.
https://doi.org/10.1007/978-3-030-83007-6_3

1 Introduction

Reconfigurable discrete event control systems (RDECSs) are the trend of future systems. RDECSs can be reconfigured in a static way (off-line) or in a dynamic way (automatically at run-time). In the latter, a reconfiguration scenario should be applied automatically and timely as a response related to dynamic environment, or user requirements. Therefore, an RDECS may go through several modes at run-time [3,9], increasing verification process complexity. Formal verification represents a reliable method to ensure the correctness of RDECSs. Usually, it consists in generating and analyzing the state spaces of studied systems. However, with the combinatorial growth, the state space size becomes too big, even with small sized systems. Hence, model-checking becomes quite challenging for industry and academia because of the state space explosion problem [19]. Several studies have been done to cope with state space explosion problems. The authors in [18] present symbolic model checking that represents the state space symbolically instead of explicitly, by exploiting the state graph regularity using boolean functions. In [6], bounded model checking (BMC) is proposed to look for a counter-example in executions whose length is limited by an integer k. If no bug is found, then k is increased until a possible bug is found. The above methods can proceed efficiently proceed to complex systems verification. However, they use an implicit representation of state spaces, which present limitation for computation of quantitative properties (e.g., state probabilities in stochastic models) [2]. With the apparition of new complex systems such as reconfigurable manufacturing systems, reconfigurable wireless networks, etc. [1], techniques and formalisms used for verification must evolve. Petri nets has been extended by many works. Reconfigurable Petri nets presented in [15], proposed for reconfigurable systems. However, although useful, being non-modular formalism, it can cause confusion to engineers for possible reusing. Timed net condition/event systems (TNCES) formalism presented in [7] as modular extension of Petri nets to deal with time constraints. TNCES is used for their particular dynamic behavior, modularity and interconnection via signals. However, dynamic behavior of reconfigurable systems is still not supported. Reconfigurable net condition/event systems (R-TNCESs) are developed as an extension of the TNCES formalism in [20], where reconfiguration and time properties with modular specification are provided in the same formalism while keeping the same semantics of TNCESs. With R-TNCES formalism, physical system processes are easily understood thanks to modular graphic representations. In addition, it can capture complex characteristics of an RDECS. Formally an R-TNCES is a multi-TNCES defined as a couple (B, R), where B is a set of TNCESs, and R is a set of reconfiguration rules [20]. A layer-by-layer verification method is proposed where similarities between TNCESs are considered. This method is improved in [7] where the authors propose a new method for accessibility graph generation with less computing time and less required memory. The previous methods improve classical ones. However, with large scale systems, their application using a unique machine (i.e., a centralized system) may be expensive in terms of time.

In this paper, we are interested in reconfigurable systems, modeled with the R-TNCES formalism where the RDECS behavior is represented by the behavior of control components (CCs) and the communication between them (synchronization) [20]. We propose a new verification method that aims to improve R-TNCES formal verification. The verification of an R-TNCES requires checking of each configuration, namely each TNCES. TNCESs which describe configurations often contain similarities called internal similarities. On another hand, some RDECSs share the same system components, so their model contains similarities called external similarities, which implies redundant calculation during checking of these systems. Thus, in order to avoid many repetitive computation due to previous problems, we propose in this paper the following contributions:

1. An ontology-based history to facilitate the detection of external similarities: Ontologies allow us to describe the RDECSs (components, work process, component relationships..., etc.) in an abstracted way than the formal model. Thus, we can efficiently detect the similarities between RDECSs with less computing time and resources, thank the ontology alignment method [13]. Each model must be accompanied by a system ontology, which describes the system to be verified. The system ontology is aligned to the ontology-based history, which contains descriptions of already verified systems. The detected similarities allow reusing state spaces computed during previous verification.
2. Incremental construction of the accessibility graphs to deal with similarities: The verification of R-TNCES requires the verification of each TNCES that composes the R-TNCES model. In order to deal with similarities that TNCESs contain (similar control components), we construct the accessibility graph in an incremental way in two steps: (i) Fragmentation: During this step, we proceed to the decomposition of the R-TNCES models into a set of CCs. Then, we generate an accessibility graph for each different CC, while preserving semantics. (ii) Accessibility graph composition: Accessibility graphs recovered thanks to ontology alignment, and those computed during the fragmentation step are composed following an established composition plan based on priority order.
3. A new method parallel CTL properties verification: The method considers the relationships that exist among properties, performs the verification in parallel way via SESA tool [16] and considers the similarity that can exist among properties.
4. An adequate distributed cloud-based architecture to perform parallel executions for formal verification: This distributed architecture is composed of computation units organized in three hierarchical levels that are: Master, workers, and sub-workers. Data storage is ensured by Amazon simple storage service S3 [11].

This paper is an extended version of our previous paper [5], presented at the 'IC-SOFT 2020' conference. The method improves by

- Improving the ontology alignment method.
- Setting up an adapted algorithm for ontology fusion.
- Integrating CTL properties parallel verification method.

The main objective of this paper is to propose a new formal verification method that improves the classical ones by controlling complexity. As a running example, we use the FESTO MPS benchmark system presented in [10], to demonstrate the relevance of the proposed contributions. The obtained results are compared with different works. The comparison shows that the sate spaces generation is improved in terms of computed states and execution time (i.e., less complexity to compute state spaces). The remainder of the paper is organized as follows. Section 2 presents some required concepts. The distributed formal verification is presented in Sect. 3. The method and the proposed algorithms are presented in Sect. 4. Section 5 presents the evaluation of the proposed method. Finally, Sect. 6 concludes this paper and gives an overview about our future work.

2 Background

In this section, we present required concepts to follow the rest of the paper.

2.1 Reconfigurable Timed Net Condition/Event System

R-TNCES represents an extension of TNCESs [17], based on Petri nets and control components CCs. R-TNCES is used for formal modeling and verification of RDECSS.

Formalization. An R-TNCES is defined in [20] as a couple $RTN = (B, R)$, where R is the control module and B is the behavior module. B is a union of multi TNCES-based CC modules, represented by

$$B = (P; T; F; W; CN; EN; DC; V; Z_0) \tag{1}$$

where, 1.P (resp, T) is a superset of places (resp, transitions), 2. $F \subseteq (P \times T) \cup (T \times P)$[1] is a superset of flow arcs. 3. W: $(P \times T) \cup (T \times P) \to \{0, 1\}$ maps a weight to a flow arc, $W(x, y) > 0$ if $(x, y) \in F$, and $W(x, y) = 0$ otherwise, where $x, y \in P \cup T$, 4. $CN \subseteq (P \times T)$ (resp, $EN \subseteq (T \times T)$) is a superset of condition signals (resp, event signals), 5. $DC : F \cap (P \times T) \to \{[l_1, h_1], .., [l_{F\cap(P\times T)}, h_{F\cap(P\times T)}]\}$ is a superset of time constraints on input arcs of transitions, where $\forall$ i$\in$ $[1, |F \cap (P \times T)|]$, l_i, $h_i \in \mathbb{N}$ and $l_i < h_i$. 6. $V : T \to \wedge, \vee$ maps an event-processing mode (AND or OR) for every transition. 7. $Z_0 = (M_0, D_0)$, where $M_0 : P \to \{0, 1\}$ is the initial marking, and $D_0 : P \to \{0\}$ is the initial clock position. R consists of a set of reconfiguration functions, formalized as follows. $R = \{r_1, .., r_n\}$ where: $r = (Cond, s, x)$ such that: 1. $Cond \to$ {true, false} is the pre-condition of r, which means specific external instructions, gusty component failures, or the arrival of certain states. 2. $s : TN(^*r) \to TN(r^*)$ is the structure modification instruction such that $TN(^*r)$(resp. $TN(r^*)$) is the original (resp. target) TNCES before (resp.

[1] Cartesian product of two sets: $A \times B = \{(a, b)|a \in A, b \in B\}$.

Table 1. Fundamental structure modification instructions of an R-TNCES.

Instruction	Symbol
Add condition signals	$Cr(cn(x, y))$
Add event signals	$Cr(ev(y, y))$
Add control component	$Cr(CC)$
Delete condition signals	$De(cn(x, y))$
Delete event signals	$De(ev(y, y))$
Delete control component	$De(CC))$

After) r application. 3. x : $last_{state}(TN(^*r))\rightarrow initial_{state}(r^*)$ is the state processing function, where $last_{state}(TN(^*r))$ (resp. $initial_{state}(TN(r^*))$) is the last (resp. the initial) state of $TN(^*r)$ (resp. $TN(r^*)$). The application of r makes a modification of the R-TNCES structure by the mean of instructions presented in Table 1. We denote by x a place, y a transition, CC a control component module, and "+" the AND of instructions to represent complex modification instructions.

R-TNCES Dynamics. The dynamics of R-TNCESs is represented by:

1. The reconfiguration between TNCESs in module behavior B, by applying a reconfiguration function r when its pre-condition is fulfilled.
2. The firing transition in each TNCES, depends on the rules of firing transitions in TNCESs and the chosen firing mode.

Reconfiguration changes the system from a configuration to another, however, the initial and the new configurations can contain similarities. In the original paper [5], we propose definition of similarities as follow:

Definition 1. *Internal similarity is the property of sharing the same physical process between different configurations of a unique RDECS. Thus, the model contains similar parts. It is caused by the fact that a reconfiguration is rarely radical.*

Definition 2. *External similarity is the property of sharing the same physical process between configurations of two or several R-TNCESs. It is caused by the fact that some systems share same components or stations.*

2.2 Production Systems: FESTO MPS and THREADING HOLE SYSTEM

This subsection presents two production systems FESTO MPS and THREADIN HOLE SYSTEM.

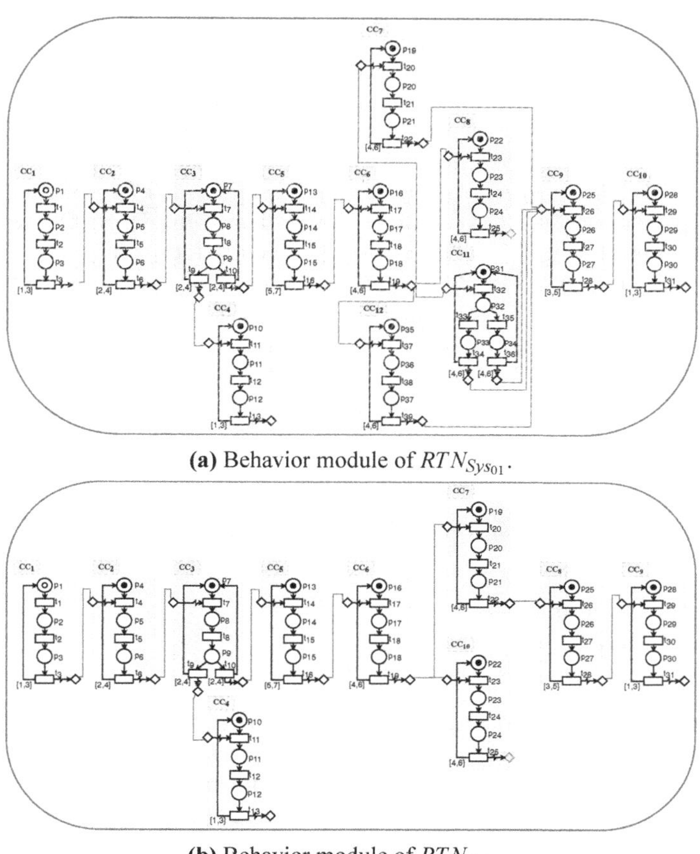

(a) Behavior module of $RTN_{Sys_{01}}$.

(b) Behavior module of $RTN_{Sys_{02}}$.

Fig. 1. Behavior module of $RTN_{Sys_{01}}$ and $RTN_{Sys_{02}}$.

FESTO MPS. FESTO MPS is a well-studied system for research and educational purposes which is defined and detailed in [7,17]. It is composed of three units. The distribution contains a pneumatic feeder and a converter. It forwards cylindrical workpieces from the stack to the testing unit. The testing unit contains the detector, the elevator and the shift out cylinder. The detection unit performs checks on workpieces for height, material type and color. Workpieces that successfully pass this check are forwarded to the processing unit. The processing unit is composed of a rotating disk, drilling machines, a checker and an evacuator. The drilling of the workpieces is performed as the primary processing of this MPS. The result of the drilling operation is then checked by the checking machine and the workpieces is forwarded for further processing to another mechanical unit. FESTO MPS performs three production modes: (i) High mode: when $Driller_1$ and $Driller_2$ are both activated and ready to work simultaneously, (ii) Medium mode: when $Driller_1$ and $Driller_2$ are both activated but work sequentially, (iii) Light mode: when only one driller is activated at once. We denote $Light_i$, when $Driller_i/i \in \{1, 2\}$ works. FESTO MPS is modeled with an R-TNCES $RT_{FESTO}\{B_{FESTO}, R_{FESTO}\}$ such that: $B_{FESTO} = \{High, Medium, Light_1, Light_2\}$ is the behavior module where the combination of CC_s describes the system modes. As shown in Fig. 1a.

$R_{FESTO} = \{r_{H,L_1}, r_{H,L_2}, r_{H,M}, r_{M,H}, r_{M,L_2}, r_{L_1,L_2}\}$ is a set of different system reconfigurations. The set of control chains describing FESTO MPS control system is presented as follows: $Cchain_1 = CC_1, CC_2, CC_3, CC_4$,
$Cchain_2 = CC_1, CC_2, CC_3, CC_5, CC_6, CC_7, CC_9, CC_{10}$,
$Cchain_3 = CC_1, CC_2, CC_3, CC_5, CC_6, CC_8, CC_9, CC_{10}$,
$Cchain_4 = CC_1, CC_2, CC_3, CC_5, CC_6, CC_{11}, CC_9, CC_{10}$,
$Cchain_5 = CC_1, CC_2, CC_3, CC_5, CC_6, CC_{12}, CC_9, CC_{10}$.

This paper uses the description and the R-TNCES model of FESTO MPS for the construction of the proposed ontology as shown in Fig. 3a.

Threading Hole System. It is modeled using R-TNCES formalism. It is composed of three units:

(i) the distribution unit,
(ii) the testing unit, and
(iii) the processing unit.

The first two units are used in FESTO MPS. The processing unit is composed of a rotating disk, threading hole machine, a checker and an evacuator perform the threading of the workpiece holes as the primary processing task of the system. The result of the threading operation is then checked by the checking machine and the workpieces are forwarded for finally further processing to another mechanical unit. Behavior module B_{THS} and ontology O_{THS} are presented in Fig. 1b and Fig. 3b respectively on page 9. such that:

$B_{THS} = \{High, Light\}$ is the behavior module shown in Fig. 1b. $R_{THS} = \{r_{H,L}, r_{H,L}\}$ is a set of different system reconfiguration.

The set of control chains describing THS control system is presented as follows:

$Cchain_1 = CC_1, CC_2, CC_3, CC_4$,
$Cchain_2 = CC_1, CC_2, CC_3, CC_5, CC_6, CC_7, CC_8, CC_9$,
$Cchain_3 = CC_1, CC_2, CC_3, CC_5, CC_6, CC_{10}, CC_8, CC_9$.

2.3 Ontology Concept

As defined in [14] an ontology is an explicit description of concepts or classes in a certain domain that constitutes a knowledge base. An ontology is defined mathematically as quadruple $O = (C, S, Re, I)$ where:

Table 2. Generic ontology which modeled RDECSs [5].

Concepts $\in C$	RDECS	Domain	Unit	Physical process	Mode
Properties $\in S$	Id: String Name: String Description: Text Synonym: String	Id: String Name: String Synonym: String	Id: String Name: String Description: Text Synonym: String	Id: String Name: String Description: Text Control chain: String Synonym: String	Id: String Name: String Description: Text Synonym: String

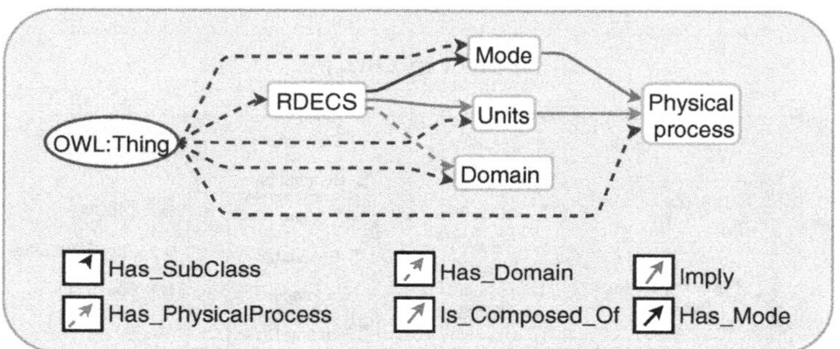

Fig. 2. Generic ontology [5].

1. $C = c_1, .., c_m$ is a set of concepts that refer to a real world objects.
2. $S = s_1, .., s_n$ is a set of properties that refer to a property of a concept, which is a value of a simple type such as Integer, String or Date.
3. $Re = Re_1, .., Re_p$ is a set of relationships defined between concepts.
4. $I = i_1, .., i_q$, where each i_w is an instance of some concept $c_x \in C$. It include a value for every property s_y associated to c_x or its ancestors.

An ontology can be presented graphically as a formed graph $O = G(C, E)$ where C is a set of concepts linked by a set of directed edges E which specifies concept relations. The function y defines the type of edges, i.e., $y : E \rightarrow T$ where T is the set of possible edge types (transitivity, symmetry and reflexivity). In [5], we define a generic ontology $Gen = (C, S, Re, I)$, which is instantiated to model the verified RDECS. Table 2 shows the defined concepts $\in C$ and their properties include in S, note that the property synonym is facultative [5]. Figure 2 shows the relations $\in Re$.

3 New State Space Generation Method

We present in this section the proposed method for state space verification during formal verification of R-TNCESs. We extend the approach proposed in [5].

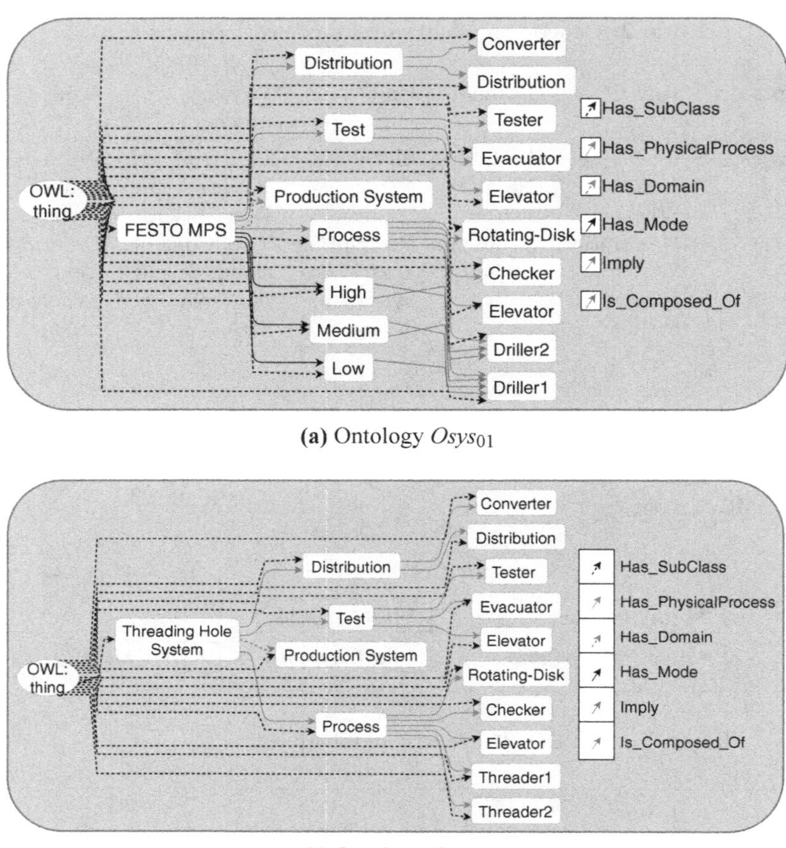

(a) Ontology $Osys_{01}$

(b) Ontology $Osys_{02}$

Fig. 3. Ontologies that describe Sys_{01} and Sys_{02}.

Thank to this approach, we minimize temporal complexity by proposing a distributed architecture on cloud server [8] for similarities detection, accessibility graph generation and CTL properties verification. Thus, we improve model-checking of reconfigurable systems and make it more efficient.

3.1 Motivation

The correctness of RDECSs can be ensured by a formal verification. The exploration of the state space is widely used for analyzing models formalized with R-TNCES, or related formalisms. The complexity of R-TNCES makes the verification task complex, because of combinatorial growth of the state space according to the model size. The verification of an R-TNCES requires the checking of each configuration, namely each TNCES. TNCESs that describe the configurations often present similarities which implies redundant calculation during

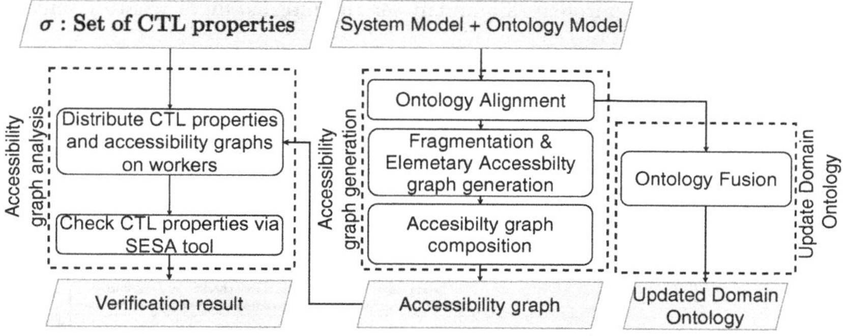

Fig. 4. Global idea for state space generation.

checking of these systems. Thus we propose an adequate approach that avoids many repetitive computations. To ensure this objective, this paper proposes a new method where verification is executed in a distributed architecture to control R-TNCESs complexity. The formal verification is performed through the following tasks: fragmentation, alignment and fusion of ontologies, accessibility graph composition. And CTL properties verification. Figure 4 presents the main steps of the proposed method and highlight the main improvement still to the original paper [5].

3.2 Formalization

In this section, we present accessibility graph generation steps according to our proposed method.

Ontology Alignment. According to the definition presented in [13], aligning two ontologies is to find a set of correspondences, where each correspondence is described by: a unique identifier Id, the concept $c_i \in O_1$, the concept $c_j \in O_2$ and σ_{ij} the degree of similarity between c_i and c_j evaluated in the interval [0,1]. Formally, it is to find $|O_1| \times |O_2|$ correspondences $(Id_{ij}, c_i, c_j, \sigma_{ij})$. A threshold τ is defined and compared with σ_{ij}. The correspondence is established only if $\sigma_{ij} > \tau$. We updates the proposed method presented in [5]. Indeed, we propose a new method for Global similarity σ_{ij} computation by considering synonyms between concepts. Therefore, σ_{ij} is computed through the following steps:

1. Compute semantic similarity by comparing concepts neighbors using Tversky measurement: $Tm_{ij} = \frac{|(n_i \cap n_j)|}{|(n_i \cap n_j)| + \alpha|(n_i - n_j) + \beta|(n_j - n_i)|}$, where:
   n_i (resp. n_j): Neighbor set of c_i (resp. c_j).
   $n_i \cap n_j$: Number of common neighbors between c_i and c_j.
   $n_i - n_j$ (resp. $n_j - n_i$): Number of neighbors that exist $\in n_i$ and $\notin n_j$ (resp. $\in n_j$ and $\notin n_i$).

Table 3. Application of ontology alignment on running example where $Concept_1 \in O_{FESTO}$ and $Concept_2 \in O_{THS}$.

Concepts \ Properties	Name	Neighbors	Descriptions	
Concept 1	Process	{Driller1, Driller2, checker, Evacuator Rotating disk}	Workpieces that pass the test unit successfully are forwarded to the rotating disk of the processing unit, where the drilling of workpieces is done. It is assumed that in this work there exist two drilling machines Drill1 and Drill2 to drill workpieces. The result of the drilling operation is next checked by a checker and finally the finished product is removed from the system by an evacuator.	
Concept 2	Process	{Threader1, Threader2, checker, Evacuator Rotating disk}	Workpieces are received by rotating disk of the process unit, where the threading of workpieces is done. It is assumed that in this work there exist one threading hole machine to thread workpieces. The result of the is next checked by a and finally the finished product is removed from the system by an evacuator.	
Similarities	$SimLex = 1$	$Tm = 0.46$	$Simdes = 0.6$	$SimLing = 0.76$ $\sigma = 0.61$

2. Compute lexical similarity, a weighted sum of *normalized Leveinstein* and *n-gram* similarities: $SimLex_{ij} = \alpha * LevNorm(i,j) + \beta * g_(i,j)$.
3. Compute semantic similarity by comparing concepts synonyms using Tversky measurement: $SimSyn_{ij} = \frac{|(n_i \cap n_j)|}{|(n_i \cap n_j)| + \alpha|(n_i - n_j) + \beta|(n_j - n_i)|}$, where:
   n_i (resp. n_j): Synonyms set of c_i (resp. c_j).
   $n_i \cap n_j$: Number of common synonyms between c_i and c_j.
   $n_i - n_j$ (resp. $n_j - n_i$): Number of synonyms that exist $\in n_i$ and $\notin n_j$ (resp. $\in n_j$ and $\notin n_i$).
   The similarity between each pair of synonyms is computed using $n - gram$ measurement. Note that this similarity is computed only if concept have synonyms.
4. Compute partial similarity of concept descriptions using the cosinus function: $SimDes_{(A,B)} = cos(\theta) = \frac{A.B}{|A||B|} = \frac{\sum A \times B}{\sqrt{\sum A^2} \times \sqrt{\sum B^2}}$.
5. Compute linguistic similarity is computed according to the comparison between lexical similarity $SimLex$ and synonyms similarity $SimSyn$ as follow:
   If $SimLex_{(i,j)} > SimSyn_{(i,j)}$, Thus, $SimLing_{(i,j)} = \alpha SimLex_{(i,j)} + \beta SimDes_{(i,j)}$.
   Otherwise, $SimLing_{(i,j)} = \alpha SimSyn_{(i,j)} + \beta SimDes_{(i,j)}$. with $\alpha = 0.4$ and $\beta = 0.6$.
6. Calculate the global similarity which is a weighted sum of linguistic and semantic similarity: $\sigma_{ij} = \alpha SimLing_{ij} + \beta Tm_{ij}$, with $\alpha = \beta = 0.5$.

Example 1. Let O_{FESTO} and O_{THD} two ontologies, which describe the production systems presented in Subsect. 2.2. Given two concepts $Process \in O_{FESTO}$ and $Process \in O_{THS}$. Table 3 shows an application of ontology alignment where, we compute:

i) lexical similarity, which concerns the concepts property "Name".
ii) semantic similarity, which concerns concepts Neighbors.
iii) description similarity, which concerns the concepts property "Description".

iv) synonyms similarity, which concerns the concepts property "synonyms".
v) linguistic similarity, which is a weighted sum of lexical/synonyms and description similarities.
vi) global similarity by combining the said similarities.

$\sigma(Process, Process) = 0.61$ (low value) and the threshold $\tau = 0.8$ (fixed). We conclude that $Process \in O_{Sys_{FESTO}}$ and $Process \in O_{Sys_{THS}}$ are non-similar. Thus, the non-similar and similar parts are efficiently distinguished and redundant calculations are avoided.

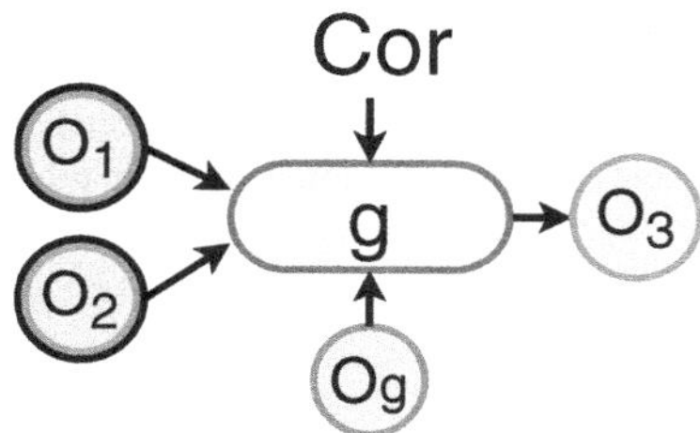

Fig. 5. Ontology fusion function (g).

Ontology Fusion. According to the definition in [12], ontology fusion is the process to detect similarities (i.e., correspondent concepts) between two ontologies and to derive from it a new ontology that brings together all the similarities and dissimilarities of concepts, while preserving semantics. Formally, ontology fusion is defined in this paper as a function g, which from two ontologies O_1, O_2, a generic ontology O_g (presented in Subsect. 2.3) and a set of correspondences Cor (computed during ontology alignment) product a new ontology O_3. The function g is illustrated in Fig. 5. Ontology fusion proceeds in three steps:

1. Enrich the concept present in the merged ontology with the name of the similar concept $\in Cor$ as a synonym property,
2. detect the class of dissimilar concepts according to the generic ontology , and
3. add the concepts according to their classes in the new ontology,

Example 2. Let apply ontology fusion on the ontologies presented in Example 1. We know that $Process \in O_{THS}$ and $Process \in O_{FESTO}$ are non-similar thank to ontology alignment. Thus, we have to add the concept $Process \in O_{FESTO}$ to O_{THS} which represent our domain ontology. Indeed, first we detect the class of concept "Process" according to the generic ontology, which is "Unit". Then, we add this concept to the domain ontology depending on its class. Figure 7 shows the result of ontology fusion (i.e., adding non-similar concepts to our domain ontology).

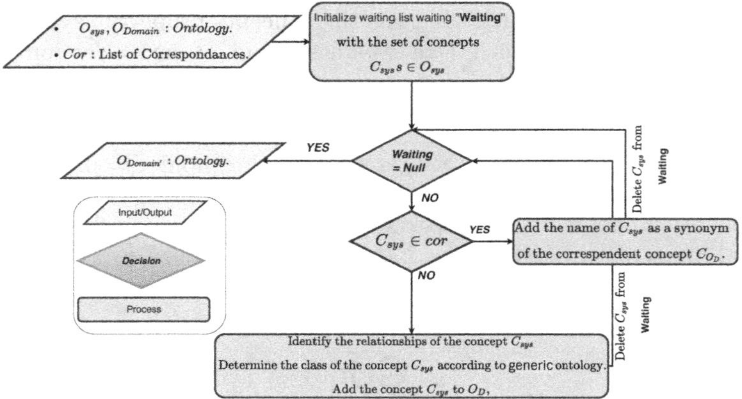

Fig. 6. Operative steps of the ontology fusion function where *Waiting* is the list of concepts $\in O_{Sys}$.

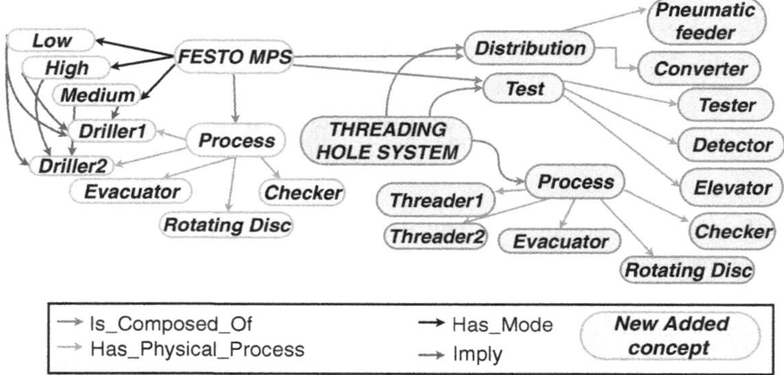

Fig. 7. Domain ontology O_D after the application of ontology fusion.

Fragmentation. Fragmentation consists on decomposing an R-TNCES into a set of CC and generating elementary accessibility graph *EAGs* for CCs that are not concerned by the correspondences computed in the previous step.

Example 3. To show the application of fragmentation, we consider production systems presented in Subsect. 2.2. They are modeled by RT_{FESTO} (to be verified) and RT_{THS} (already verified). Let *Cor* be a set of correspondences computed during alignment of O_{FESTO} and O_{THS}. Table 4 shows application of fragmentation on RT_{FESTO}. It runs in two steps: 1. decomposing RT_{FESTO} into a set of CC $f = \{CC_1, .., CC_{12}\}$, and 2. computing elementary accessibility graphs EAGs of each $CC \notin f \cap cor$. During fragmentation, CCs synchronization transitions are stored for reuse when composing the accessibility graph AG. Real RDECSs encompass millions of transitions, which increases accessibility graph generation complexity. Fragmentation allows us to control complexity. Moreover, it allows us to deal with internal similarities.

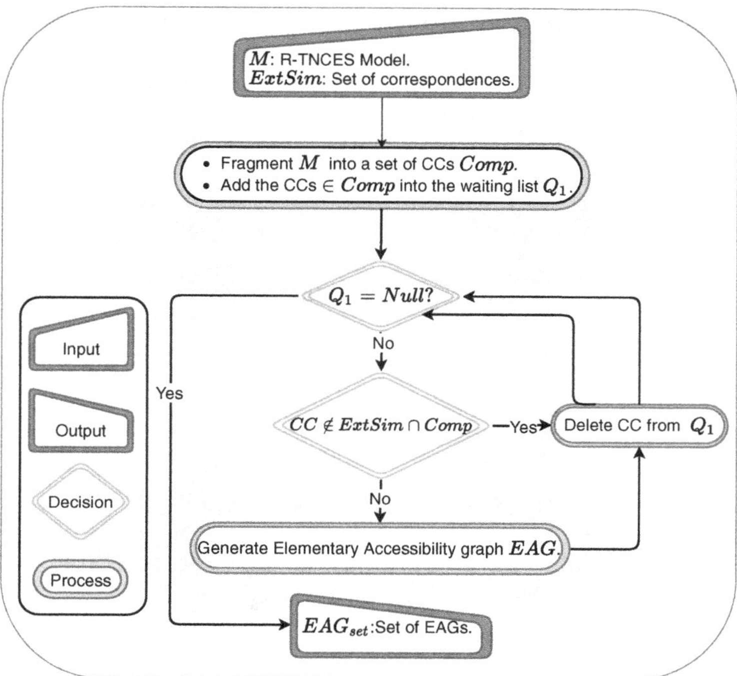

Fig. 8. Operative steps of the fragmentation function where $Waiting$ is the list of CCs to be computed.

Table 4. Application of fragmentation on FESTO MPS [5].

System	FESTO MPS
f	$\{CC_1, .., CC_{12}\}$
cor	$\{CC_1, CC_2, CC_3, CC_4, CC_5, CC_6, CC_{10}\}$
$EAGs$	EAG_{CC_7}, EAG_{CC_8}, EAG_{CC_9},$EAG_{CC_{10}}$, $EAG_{CC_{11}}$, $EAG_{CC_{12}}$

Planning. We set up a priority order for accessibility graph composition. Let RTN be a system modeled by R-TNCES and described by ontology O_{sys}. We extract from O_{sys} control chains $Cchains$. $Cchains$ are then en-queued to a queue Q depending on their length such as the smallest one is en-queued firstly.

Example 4. By using the behavior module B of RTN_{FESTO}, the composition plan to be followed for AG_{FESTO} generation for test failure case described by C_{chain_1} is presented as follows:

$$EAG_{CC_1} \times EAG_{CC_2} > PAG_{CC_{12}} \times CC_3 > PAG_{123} \times CC_4.$$

Accessibility Graph Composition. Full accessibility graph AG is computed by composing $EAGs$ computed during fragmentation step and partial accessibility graphs $PAGs$ retrieved during ontology alignment step as shown in Fig. 10. The composition is done according to the established plan.

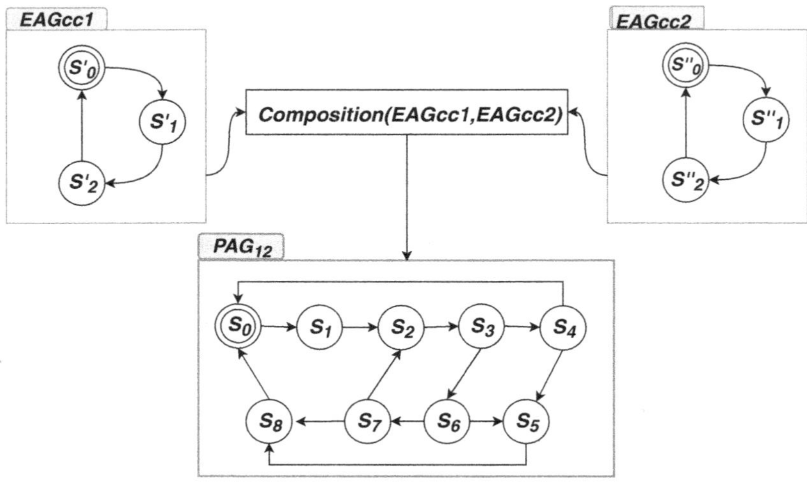

Fig. 9. Composition of EAGcc1 & EAGcc2 [5].

Example 5. During AG_{FESTO} generation, several composition of EAGs are executed. Indeed, we run $Composition(EAG_{CC_1}, EAG_{CC_2})$ function to obtain PAG_{12} shown in Fig. 9. It proceeds as follows:

1. Creates initial state S_0 by concatenating initial states S'_0 and S''_0 of both EAG_{CC_1} and EAG_{CC_2},
2. searches the set of enabled transitions from S'_0 and S''_0, and
3. checks whether the transition t is a common transition. If yes, then we create a new state S_1 by concatenating the current target states from S'_0 and S''_0. Otherwise, if t belongs only to EAG_{CC_1}, then a new state S_1 is obtained by concatenating the current state S''_0 from EAG_{CC_2} and the current target state S'_1 from EAG_{CC_1} and vice versa.

We repeat these steps for the remaining states until we get the whole state space.

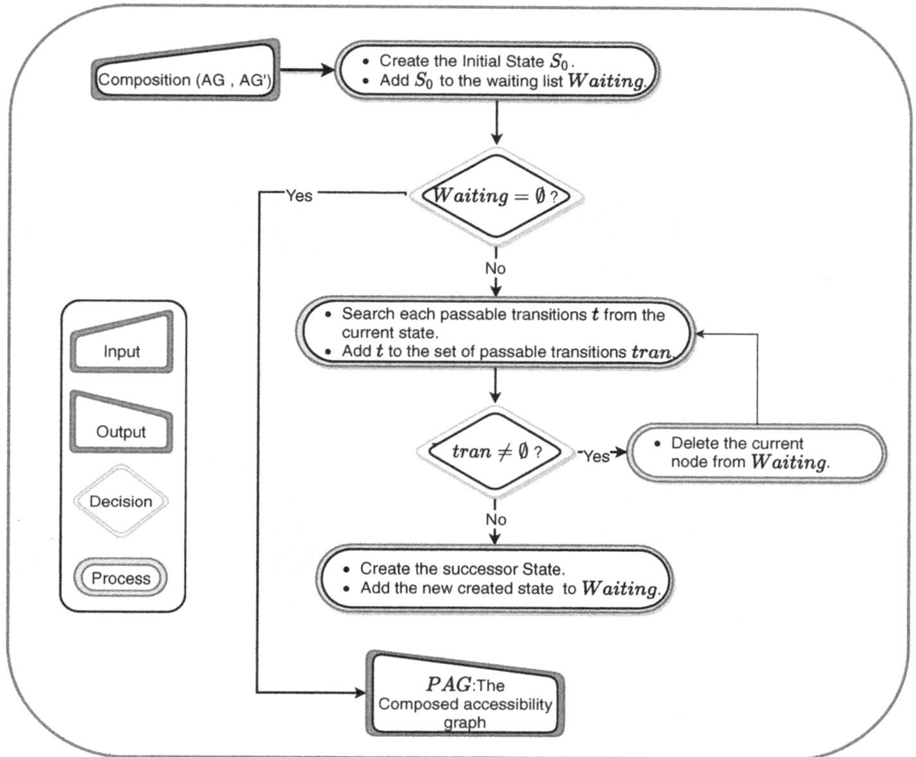

Fig. 10. Operative steps of the graph composition function, where t is the set of the fixed passable transition and $Waiting$ is the list of nodes to be computed.

Parallel CTL Properties Verification. In short-term we integrate CTL properties verification method inspired from methods proposed in [4,17]. This method consider relationships which exist among properties to be verified (Equivalence, dominance and composition) and processes the verification in parallel way. The method proposed in this paper processes as follow:

- *Step 1 (Relationships detection):* We extract different relationships that exist among CTL properties to be verified (Dominance & equivalence).
- *Step 2 (Matrix and tree parallelization generation):* First, we generate a square matrix S, where, the value of each element of S describes the nature of relationship between each pair of properties as follow: $S[i,j] = 0$ means that there is no relation between P_i & P_j and $S[i,j] = 1$ (resp. $S[i,j] = 2$) means that there is a dominance (resp. equivalence) relation between P_i & P_j. Then, we generate parallelization tree in order to coordinate the execution of properties verification. Indeed, we identify the redundancies and the factorization between properties to be verified. Each level of the tree represents the prop-

erties which can be verified simultaneously. Thus, the verification order of the CTL properties is established by exploring the parallelization tree by level.
- *Step 3 (CTL Properties verification)*: We proceed to the verification of CTL properties thanks to the SESA Tool developed in [20].

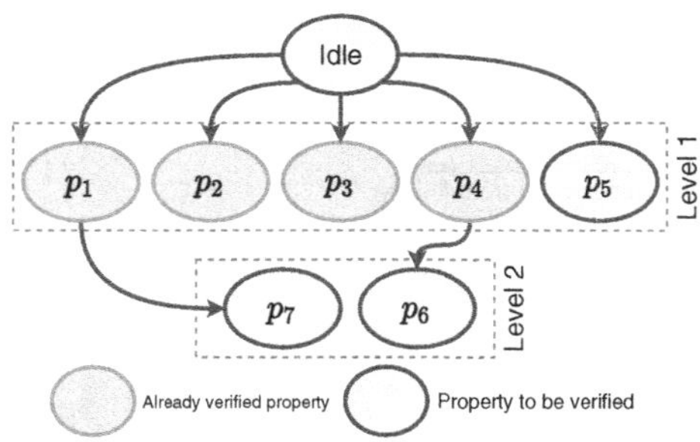

Fig. 11. Parallelization tree.

Table 5. CTL properties to be verified.

$\sigma_{F_{MPS}}$: Set of CTL properties
$P_1 : AF(p_3)$
$P_2 : AF(p_4)$
$P_3 : AF(p_9)$
$P_4 : AF(p_{18})$
$P_5 : EF(p_{33})$
$P_6 : AG(EF(p_{12}) \rightarrow AF(p_{18})$
$P_7 : AG(p_3 \rightarrow AF(p_{30}))$

Example 6. To show the application of CTL properties verification according to the proposed method, we consider a set of properties that aims to verify the safety and vivacity of Sys_{01} (FESTO MPS). Note that we consider that Sys_{02} has already been verified, indeed at this stage we have available:

1. State space generated during previous tasks.
2. Result of CTL properties verified during Sys_{02}.

Given $\sigma_{F_{MPS}}$ a set of properties to verify the safety and the vivacity of Sys_{01}. First, we proceed to the detection of relationships that exist among the properties presented in Table 5. Then, we generate the parallelization tree shown in Fig. 11, after that we check for properties already verified during Sys_{02}, in the present case it concerns the properties $p_{i/i=1,...4}$. Finally, we proceed to the verification of the remaining CTL properties using SESA tool [16].

4 Distributed Cloud-Based State Space Generation

This section presents Cloud-based distributed architecture and how to perform formal verification on it.

4.1 Distributed Architecture for State Space Generation

In this subsection, we present hierarchical and distributed architectures propose in the conference paper [5] depicted in Fig. 12. The idea that motivates the development of this architecture is to increase computation power and storage availability. It is composed of computational and storage resources. To develop the architecture shown in Fig. 12 we need the following units.

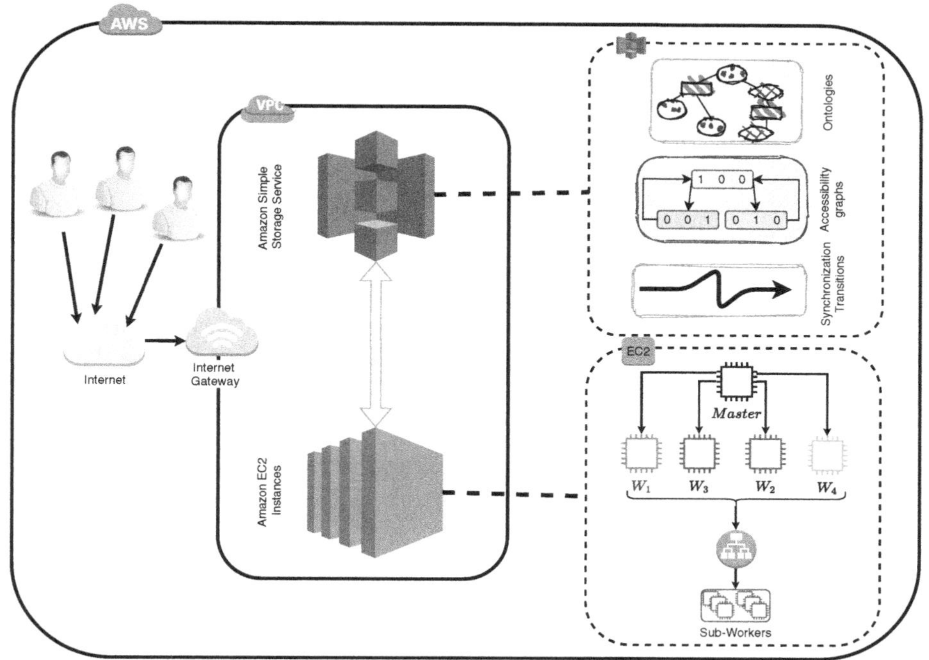

Fig. 12. Distributed architecture for formal verification.

- Computational units: Execute tasks defined in Subsect. 3.2 by means of $M+n$ machines where:
  (i) M represents the number of machines (i.e., 5 machines in our approach). The set of machines are composed of a master and four workers $W_1, ..., W_4$ that have specific tasks.
  (ii) n is the number of sub-workers that execute the high complex tasks (i.e., $EAGs$ generation and $PAGs$ composition). n depends on system size.
- Storage unit: represents the allocated cloud database that stores domain ontologies, $EAGs$ temporary and $PAGs$ permanently.

4.2 Distributed State Space Generation

This subsection presents the process of distributed Formal verification on a cloud based architecture.

Example 7. The user sends a verification request $req(R_{FESTO}$: $R\text{-}TNCES, O_{FESTO}$: $Ontology)$. The master ensures tasks coordination by receiving the verification request and sending R_{FESTO} and O_{FESTO} to workers to carry out their tasks as follows. 1. sending simultaneously ontology O_{FESTO} to workers W_1, W_4 and R_{FESTO} to worker W_2, 2. waiting signals from W_1 and W_2 and to receive the composition plan from W_4 to forward it to W_3. 3. waiting

signal from W_3 to allow beginning ontology fusion by W_1. W_1 has two main tasks: (i) Ontology alignment to extract correspondences and (ii) Ontology fusion to update domain ontology-based history, we merge O_{FESTO} AND O_D.
W_2: At the reception of R_{FESTO}, it proceeds to the fragmentation, sends CCs to sub-workers after applying a load balancer algorithm and sends a signal to master which announces the end of these two tasks: fragmentation and generation of $EAGs$.
W_3 receives the composition plan and collects the elements that it needs from the database for the AG composition. Finally, it sends a signal to master which announces the end of its task.
W_4 is responsible for planning compositional order for full accessibility graph generation. It extracts the control chains concepts from O_{FESTO}. Then the plan is sent to the master.

CTL properties presented in *Example 6* are performed in the presented architecture as follow:

- W_2: performs Relationships detection,
- W_3: performs matrix and palatalization tree generation,
- W_4: performs the exploration of the palatalization tree by level, and
- *workers* perform CTL properties verification and return the result.

4.3 Implementation

In this subsection, we present the main algorithms used in our method.

Algorithm 1. Ontology Fusion.

```
Input: O_D, O_sys: Ontology; Cor: Set of correspondences ;
Output: O'_D: Ontology;
for int i = 0 to | ∑ C_sys | do
    if ( C_sys ∈ Cor)) then
        Enrich(O_D, Co_{O_sys}.Name, Co_{O_D}.synonym);
        else
            Classe ← IdentifyRelationships(C_Sys, O_sys);
            Insert(C_sys, O_D, Classe);
        end
    end
    O'_D ← O_D;
end
return O'_D
```

Algorithm 1 describes the ontology fusion. It takes the domain ontology O_D, the system Ontology O_{sys}, and the set of correspondences Cor and returns a new updated domain ontology O'_D. It adds the dissimilar verified concepts to the domain ontology for next verification to process. The functions:

Algorithm 2. Fragmentation

```
Input: RTN: R-TNCES; TN_0: TNCES;
Output: S_EAG: Set of elementary accessibility graphs;
for int i = 0 to | ∑TN | do
  for each CC ∈ TN do
    if ( !Tagged (CC)) then
      Insert(S_EAG, Geneate_State_Space(CC)); tag(CC);
    end
  end
end
return S_EAG
```

Algorithm 3. State Space Composition.

```
Input: S_AG: Set of accessibility graphs(EAG, PAG); ∑CChain: Set of Cchains ;
Output: AG: Set Accessibility graphs;
for int i = 0 to | ∑CChain | do
  AG ← EAG_{CC_i^0};
  for int j = 0 to | ∑CC_i | do
    AG ← Compose(AG, EAG_{CC_i^j});
  end
end
return AG
```

- $Enrich(O : Ontology, C_1.Name : String, C_2.synonym : String,)$ Takes the value of the property 'Name' of the concept C_1 and add it as a value of the property 'synonym' of concept C_2 in the ontology O,
- $IdentifyRelationships(C, O)$; returns the class of a the concept C in the onotlogy O according to the generic onotlogy, and
- $Insert(C, O, Class)$ inserts the concept C in the ontology O according to his class.

Algorithm 2 describes the fragmentation task. It decomposes the R-TNCES in a set of CCs and generates their accessibility graphs EAGs. Algorithm 3 describes the steps for the full accessibility graph composition AG. It composes the accessibility graphs recovered thanks to the ontology alignment and the ones computed during fragmentation to return the full accessibility graph of the verified model.

4.4 Complexity of Distributed State Space Generation

The verification is based on three main functions: (i) the ontology alignment, (ii) the fragmentation, and (iii) the $EAG/PAGs$ composition. The ontology alignment complexity on this scale is always polynomial, thus we focus on the two other function presented respectively in Algorithm 2 and 3. As mentioned in [20], TNCES verification complexity is expressed by $\mathcal{O}(e^t)$ where t is the number of transition, in our case, we use it for each CC of the verified R-TNCES. For an R-TNCES with $TN = |B|$ the number of TNCESs composing the verified R-TNCES and C the average number of CCs that every TNCES contains, The complexity of Algorithm 2 is $\mathcal{O}(TN \times C \times e^t)$. For a composed graph with n' the number of nodes computed by the composition graph function and j the average number of the enabled transitions from each state, Algorithm 3 complexity is expressed by $(n' \times j)$. Thus, verification time complexity is: $\mathcal{O}((TN \times C \times e^t) + (n' \times j))$. Therefore, our method complexity is expressed by

$$\mathcal{O}(\max \mathcal{O}(TN \times C \times e^t), \mathcal{O}(n' \times j)) = \mathcal{O}(TN \times C \times e^t).$$

The complexity of methods presented in [7,20] is:

$$\mathcal{O}(e^m \times TN) \text{ with } m \times TN = TN \times C \times t.$$

Thus, to assert that our complexity is better, we have to prove that:

$$\mathcal{O}((TN \times C \times e^t) < \mathcal{O}((TN \times e^m),$$

which is intuitively correct.

5 Evaluation

The performance of the proposed verification method is evaluated in this section. We make a comparison between the proposed method, that uses a distributed tool to compute accessibility graphs, and the method reported in [7] that uses Rec-AG tool. Then we proceed to different evaluations in large scale systems by considering different similarities. The external similarity rate of R-TNCES R_1 with descriptive ontology O_L is given by the following formula.

$$ExternalSimilarity(R_1) = \left(\frac{AlignedConcepts(O_L)}{Concepts(O_L)}\right) \tag{2}$$

where, (i) $AlignedConcepts(O_L)$ returns the number of similar concepts between O_L and the related domain ontology O_D, (ii) $Concepts(O_L)$ returns the total number of concepts that O_L contains. The internal similarity rate is given by the adapted method used in [7] as follows.

$$InternalSimilarity(R_1) = \left(\frac{Max(\{SimCC(TN_i, TN_j)\}_{i,j \in 0\ldots(n-1)\ and\ i<j})}{Max(NumberOfCC(TN_k))}\right) \tag{3}$$

where, (i) $SimCC(TN_i, TN_j)$ is the function that returns the number of similar control components between two TNCESs, (ii) $NumberOfCC$ takes a TNCES and returns its number of control components, and (iii) Max returns the maximum among a set of natural numbers. We define three degrees of Internal Similarity (resp, External Similarity): High, Medium and low where, $InternalSimilarity$ (resp, $ExternalSimilarity$) is 50%–100%, 20%–50% and 0%–20%.

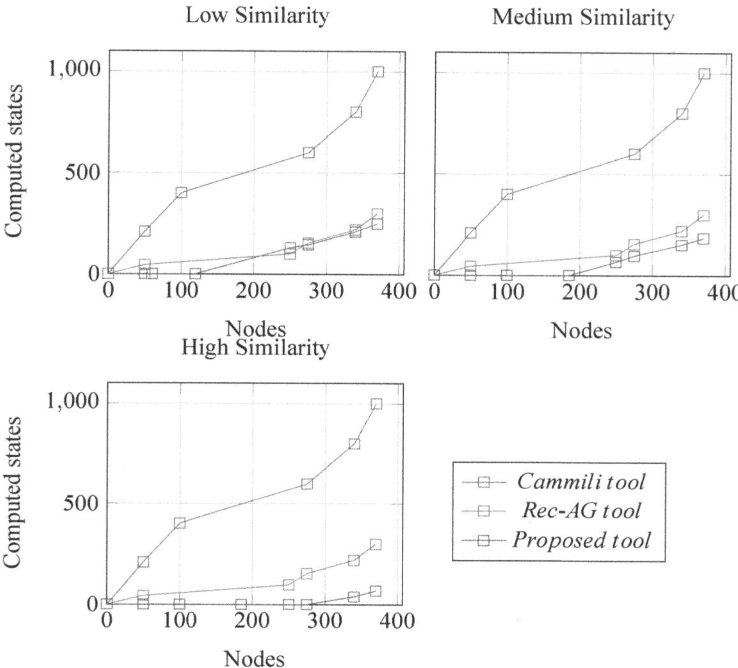

Fig. 13. Proposed verification in large scale systems considering external similarity.

5.1 Evaluation in Large Scale Systems Considering External Similarity

We apply the new proposed method on the case study used in [5]. Figure 13 describes the verification result of an R-TNCES model by considering three levels of external similarity. The model is composed of three TNCESs represented by three parallel control chains of equal length, with $Complexity(CC_{ij}) = 3$, $i \in 1...100$ and $j \in 1...3$ (i.e., each CC contains 3 nodes). By analyzing the plots in Fig. 13, we notice that: In the case of low external similarities, the number of states computed using the proposed method and the one proposed in [7] in its best case (i.e., in the case of a high internal similarity rate) becomes nearly equal with the ascent of the number of system nodes. It is explained by the fact that the difference in the number of nodes to explore is minimal and becomes non-significant when the system is larger. Nevertheless, low similarity must be exploited because it improves the results in both cases of medium and high internal similarity. In the case of high and medium external similarities: the proposed method takes advantage of those presented in [2] and [7]. It is explained by the fact that the number of nodes to explore is reduced. Thanks to the external similarity that allows us to eliminate redundancies. While in the three cases, the proposed method presents better results than the one used in

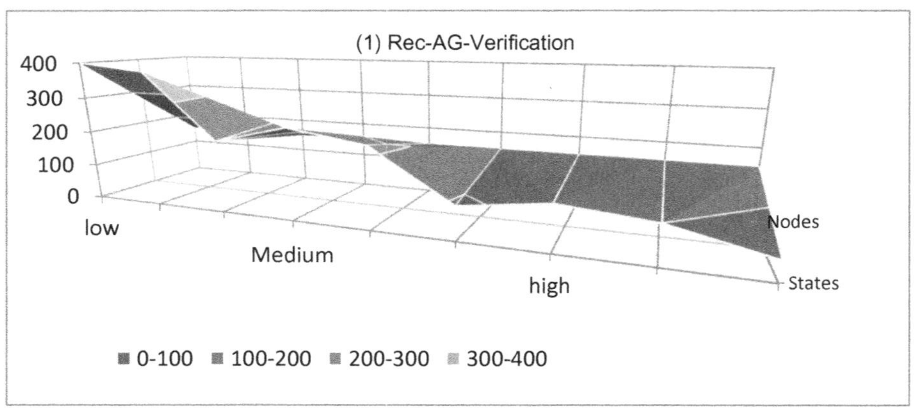

Fig. 14. Proposed verification in large scale systems considering external and internal similarities.

[2], which generates AGs via the classical methods. The proposed method can reduce calculations by more than 50%, depending on model size and similarity rates. This represents the main gain of the paper.

5.2 Evaluation in Large Scale Systems by Considering External and Internal Similarities

The surfaces in Fig. 14 describe the results of both the proposed method and the one used in [7], by using three factors: External similarities, internal similarity and nodes to be explored for a state generation. In their worst case (i.e., $InternalSimilarity = ExternalSimilarity = 0\%$) performance of both methodologies presents limits, with same results using the method reported in [20]. However, in the remaining cases, the proposed method always presents better results according to similarity rates. It performs best with: (i) Less computed states, thanks to the external source of partial graphs and elimination of internal redundancies, and (ii) less nodes to be explored for state space generation thus less complexity to generate a state, thanks to the incremental way used when composing the accessibility graph.

5.3 Evaluation of CTL Properties Verification Method Considering Similarities

Let assume we have to verify a system model with 2500 TNCESs. In order to ensure the well-behave of the system we have to verify at least 4 properties for each TNCES. Thus, we need to verify 10000 CTL properties. We assume that the similarity rate among properties: (i) *Low* in $0, 20\%$, (ii) *Medium* in $20, 60\%$, or (iii) *High* when more than 60%. The results show in Fig. 15 that the gain increases proportionally to decomposable properties rate. Thus, the gain is clearly shown when similarity rate is 'High'.

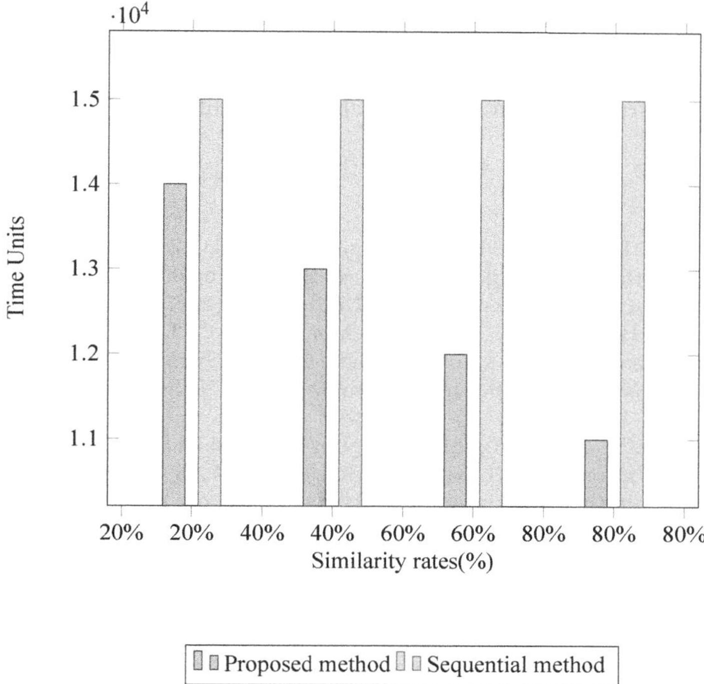

Fig. 15. Sequential method vs proposed method.

6 Conclusion

This paper deals with formal verification of RDECSs that we model with R-TNCES. The proposed method aims to improve formal verification by using a distributed architecture. We developed a distributed architecture with three hierarchical levels (Master, worker and sub-worker) and a cloud-based-storage (Amazon Simple Storage S3 [11]). It allows us to increase computational power, data availability and to perform parallel execution. For the state space generation steps, we incorporates ontologies for RDECSs verification. We set up an ontology-based history, which allows us to detect external similarities thanks to an ontology alignment. Thus, we avoid many redundant calculation. In order to deal with internal similarities, we introduce modularity concept by affecting specific tasks to each unit of our architecture, including fragmentation and accessibility graph composition, which allow us to deal with RDECSs fragment by fragment and to construct incrementally accessibility graphs. For the state space analysis, we proposed a parallel CTL properties verification, where similarities and relationships that can exist among properties are considered. An evaluation is realized and experimental results are reported. The results prove the relevance of the developed architecture and the efficiency of the proposed contribution. Future works will: 1. Deploying the distributed architecture in Amazon Elastic Compute Cloud (EC2) [11]. 2. Incorporate an automatic classification of properties thank to ontologies. 3. Extending the proposed tool to support other formalism that models RDECSs and different temporal logics.

References

1. Ben Salem, M.O., Mosbahi, O., Khalgui, M., Jlalia, Z., Frey, G., Smida, M.: Brometh: methodology to design safe reconfigurable medical robotic systems. Int. J. Med. Robot. Comput. Assist. Surg. **13**(3), e1786 (2017)
2. Camilli, M., Bellettini, C., Capra, L., Monga, M.: CTL model checking in the cloud using mapreduce. In: 2014 16th International Symposium on Symbolic and Numeric Algorithms for Scientific Computing (SYNASC), pp. 333–340. IEEE (2014)
3. Choucha., C.E., Ramdani., M., Khalgui., M., Kahloul., L.: On decomposing formal verification of CTL-based properties on IAAS cloud environment. In: Proceedings of the 15th International Conference on Software Technologies - ICSOFT, vol. 1, pp. 544–551. INSTICC, SciTePress (2020). https://doi.org/10.5220/0009972605440551
4. Choucha, C.E., Ougouti, N.S., Khalgui, M., Kahloul., L.: R-TNCES verification: distributed state space analysis performed in a cloud-based architecture. In: Proceedings of the 33rd Annual European Simulation and Modelling Conference, pp. 96–101. ETI, EUROSIS (2019)
5. Eddine, C.C., Salem, M.O.B., Khalgui, M., Kahloul, L., Ougouti, N.S.: On the improvement of R-TNCESS verification using distributed cloud-based architecture, pp. 339–349 (2020). https://doi.org/10.5220/0009836103390349
6. Gadelha, M.Y., Ismail, H.I., Cordeiro, L.C.: Handling loops in bounded model checking of c programs via k-induction. Int. J. Softw. Tools Technol. Transf. **19**(1), 97–114 (2017)
7. Hafidi, Y., Kahloul, L., Khalgui, M., Li, Z., Alnowibet, K., Qu, T.: On methodology for the verification of reconfigurable timed net condition/event systems. IEEE Trans. Syst. Man Cybern. Syst. **99**, 1–15 (2018)
8. Hayes, B.: Cloud computing. Commun. ACM **51**(7), 9–11 (2008)
9. Khalgui, M., Mosbahi, O., Li, Z., Hanisch, H.M.: Reconfiguration of distributed embedded-control systems. IEEE/ASME Trans. Mechatron. **16**(4), 684–694 (2011)
10. Koszewnik, A., Nartowicz, T., Pawłuszewicz, E.: Fractional order controller to control pump in FESTO MPS® PA compact workstation. In: 2016 17th International Carpathian Control Conference (ICCC), pp. 364–367. IEEE (2016)
11. Murty, J.: Programming Amazon Web Services: S3, EC2, SQS, FPS, and SimpleDB. O'Reilly Media, Inc., Newton (2008)
12. Noy, N.F., Musen, M.A., et al.: Algorithm and tool for automated ontology merging and alignment. In: Proceedings of the 17th National Conference on Artificial Intelligence (AAAI-2000). Available as SMI Technical report SMI-2000-0831, vol. 115. sn (2000)
13. Ougouti, N.S., Belbachir, H., Amghar, Y.: Semantic mediation in MedPeer: an ontology-based heterogeneous data sources integration system. Int. J. Inf. Technol. Web Eng. (IJITWE) **12**(1), 1–18 (2017)

14. Ougouti, N.S., Belbachir, H., Amghar, Y.: Proposition of a new ontology-based p2p system for semantic integration of heterogeneous data sources. In: Handbook of Research on Contemporary Perspectives on Web-Based Systems, pp. 240–270. IGI Global (2018)
15. Padberg, J., Kahloul, L.: Overview of reconfigurable petri nets. In: Heckel, R., Taentzer, G. (eds.) Graph Transformation, Specifications, and Nets. LNCS, vol. 10800, pp. 201–222. Springer, Cham (2018). https://doi.org/10.1007/978-3-319-75396-6_11
16. Patil, S., Vyatkin, V., Sorouri, M.: Formal verification of intelligent mechatronic systems with decentralized control logic. In: Proceedings of 2012 IEEE 17th International Conference on Emerging Technologies & Factory Automation (ETFA 2012), pp. 1–7. IEEE (2012)
17. Ramdani, M., Kahloul, L., Khalgui, M.: Automatic properties classification approach for guiding the verification of complex reconfigurable systems. In: ICSOFT, pp. 625–632 (2018)
18. Souri, A., Rahmani, A.M., Navimipour, N.J., Rezaei, R.: A symbolic model checking approach in formal verification of distributed systems. HCIS **9**(1), 4 (2019)
19. Valmari, A.: The state explosion problem. In: Reisig, W., Rozenberg, G. (eds.) ACPN 1996. LNCS, vol. 1491, pp. 429–528. Springer, Heidelberg (1996). https://doi.org/10.1007/3-540-65306-6_21
20. Zhang, J., Khalgui, M., Li, Z., Mosbahi, O., Al-Ahmari, A.M.: R-TNCES: a novel formalism for reconfigurable discrete event control systems. IEEE Trans. Syst. Man Cybern. Syst. **43**(4), 757–772 (2013)

MLCA: A Model-Learning-Checking Approach for IoT Systems

Sébastien Salva(✉) and Elliott Blot

LIMOS - UMR CNRS 6158, Clermont Auvergne University, Clermont-Ferrand, France
sebastien.salva@uca.fr, eblot@isima.fr

Abstract. The Internet of Things (IoT) is a broad concept comprising a wide ecosystem of interconnected services and devices connected to the Internet. The IoT concept holds fabulous promises, but security aspects tend to be significant barriers for the adoption of large-scale IoT deployments. This paper proposes an approach to assist companies or organisations in the security audit of IoT systems. This approach called Model Learning and Checking Approach (MLCA) combines model learning for automatically extracting models from event logs, and model checking for verifying whether security properties, given under the form of generic LTL formulas hold on models. The originality of MLCA lies in the fact that auditors do not have to craft models or to be expert LTL users. The LTL formula instantiation, which makes security properties concrete, is indeed semi-automatically performed by means of an expert system composed of inference rules. The latter encode some expert knowledge, which can be applied again to the same kind of systems with less efforts. We evaluated MLCA on 5 IoT systems with security measures provided by the European ENISA institute. We show that MLCA is very effective in detecting security issues and provides results within reasonable time.

Keywords: Model learning · Model checking · Expert system · IoT software systems

1 Introduction

Using the Internet of Things (IoT) to stimulate transformational efficiencies in several application domains among which manufacturing, automotive, health and smart cities, is an idea that holds fabulous promises. Indeed, exploiting smart and connected devices to produce real-time data and to quicker take decisions provides new ways to make businesses more efficient, and to forge links between the digital world and the real. On the other hand, after the myriad of cyberattacks on IoT systems revealed during the few past years, experts have warned that IoT could harm people if IoT is left unsecured. As many technological concepts are involved under the IoT umbrella, it is indeed not surprising to observe that IoT systems are vulnerable to a wide range of security attacks. And it is likely that this security problem will grow more complex in the future, as long as new technologies and platforms will be proposed.

Many companies or organisations have started to be aware about the importance of including cyber-security in their IoT solutions. Many of them assess the risks of their

M. van Sinderen et al. (Eds.): ICSOFT 2020, CCIS 1447, pp. 70–97, 2021.
https://doi.org/10.1007/978-3-030-83007-6_4

IoT-based services and platforms by means of security audits. There are many ways to carry out an audit depending on the scope and objectives of the audit itself and on the resources allocated by the company. But an audit process usually follows many manual steps such as Define the audit objective, Collect software usage data, or Test the systems and applications methodically. Most of these activities are time-consuming and sometimes challenging. Fortunately, some templates or documents can be used to guide auditors in these steps. For instance, the National Institute of Standards and Technology (NIST) has proposed a framework made up of several stages, which can define the audit plan [26]. The European Telecommunications Standards Institute (ETSI) has proposed a general method and activities dedicated to undertake testing and risk assessment activities for large scale, networked systems [12]. Others documents related to security measures, good practices, and threats taxonomy e.g., the reports provided by the ENISA, Cloud Security Alliance, or OWASP organisations [9, 11, 27] are proposed to help derive objectives. The standard ISO/IEC 27030 [17], due to be published in 2022, will provide guidelines for security and privacy in IoT systems. Finally, testing guides, e.g., [19, 27], along with testing tools e.g., [8, 25] may be used to conduct the review.

Despite the strong benefits brought by these approaches, the efforts required for understanding how an IoT system under audit (SUA) is structured and behaves or for generating security tests is yet tremendous. These observations motivated us to present in [29] an approach called MLCA combining model learning and model checking to assist auditors in the understanding of SUA by means of models, and in the verification of security properties on these models:

- *Model Learning:* our approach starts by recovering formal models from an event log. We use the Labelled Transition System (LTS) to express the behaviours of every component (devices, servers, etc.) of SUA. These models can be used as documentation or to comprehend the functioning of the components and their interactions;
- *Property Instantiation and Model Checking:* our approach also takes as inputs generic security properties, which can be used independently of SUA. Usually, such properties have to be adapted for every model so that they share the same alphabet. This activity is known to be difficult and time consuming. To make it easier, MLCA helps auditors make them concrete by means of an expert system composed of rules, which encode some expert knwoledge about IoT systems. Then, our approach checks whether the LTSs satisfy the security properties, and returns counterexamples when issues are detected. The counterexamples may be used to interpret the results and provide countermeasures.

Contributions: This paper presents an extension of the MLCA algorithms given in [29], which mainly aims at improving both effectiveness and performance. We indeed showed that MLCA requires a manual inspection of the generated models to detect inconsistencies. We propose to enhance MLCA with a new step for assisting auditors in this model inspection. Besides, we provide a new security property instantiation algorithm, which generates less concrete properties. Consequently, this algorithm allows to significantly save time during the model checking step. Furthermore, this paper provides more details about the generation of concrete security properties. This paper also provides an empirical evaluation, which investigates the sensitivity (ratio of true positives) and specificity (ratio of true negatives) of MLCA and its performance in terms of execution times. We also compare the MLCA of [29] with this new version. This empirical evaluation was carried out on event logs collected from 5 IoT systems. This evaluation shows that our approach allows the detection of security issues with few false positives or negatives within reasonable time delays.

Paper Organisation: The paper is organised as follows: Sect. 2 discusses related work and presents our motivations. Section 3 offers an overview of the functioning of MLCA with a real example of IoT system. The MLCA's algorithms are detailed in Sect. 4. We recall some basic definitions and describe the five steps of the approach. The next section examines experimental results and discusses about the threats to validity. Section 6 summarises our contributions and draws some perspectives for future work.

2 Related Work

2.1 IoT Audit

A plethora of surveys or papers have exposed the opportunities, challenges, requirements, threats or vulnerabilities involved in the IoT security. Among them, several approaches have been proposed to audit IoT systems. The security audit of IoT devices is carried out with check lists or threat models in [19,25]. These lists or models have been devised or extended from the recommendations published by the OWASP organisation [27]. Other works focused on the IoT device audit by decrypting the traffic sent via TLS [33] so that the TLS traffic can be verified without compromising future traffic. This king of technique could be used prior to MLCA to obtain readable event logs.

Many approaches also rely on models to analyse the security of IoT systems, because models offer the advantage of expressing systems without ambiguity. In [14], security models are devised with data collected from an IoT system. A manual security analysis is then performed to find potential attack scenarios, evaluate security metrics and assess the effectiveness of different defence strategies.

Other works introduced specialised model-based testing (MbT) methods. Some of them are said to be active, i.e. security test cases are built by hands or automatically generated from a given (formal) specification, and are later used to experiment IoT systems [1,15,22,23]. These active testing techniques could complement MLCA to get larger event logs. Other methods are said to be passive because they are based upon monitoring tools, which detect the violation of security properties by checking rule satisfiability in the long run [6,20,32].

Several papers addressed the detection of security issues in IoT systems by means of model checking. The tool IoTSAT [24] is a SMT based framework, which analyses the IoT system security. IoTSAT models the device-level interactions as in our approach, but also policy-level behaviours and network-level dependencies. SOTERIA [5] is another model checking tool for IoT software. State-models are extracted from source code, then SOTERIA checks whether concrete security properties hold on these models.

In comparison to our approach, the works [14,23] go further in the risk assessment by proposing the evaluation of metrics. IoTSAT also goes further in the modelling of the

IoT system environment. But all of these approaches require models or formal properties, which have to be manually devised. SOTERIA offers the advantage of recovering state-models on condition that the source code of every component is available. But, the concrete security properties have to be written by hands. In contrast, MLCA generates behavioural models and dependency graphs from event logs. Besides, our approach semi-automatically instantiates generic properties with an expert system. These generic properties can be reused with several IoT systems. We provide a list of generic properties derived from the security measures proposed by the ENISA institute.

2.2 Model Learning

MLCA uses a passive model learning algorithm to recover formal models from event logs. Some papers also presented model learning approaches specialised to communicating systems in the literature [3,21,30]. Mariani et al. proposed in [21] an automatic detection of failures in log files by means of model learning. The approach segments an event log with two strategies: per component or per user. The former can be used with communicating systems to generates one model for each component. CSight [3] is another tool specialised in the model learning of communicating systems. The main contribution proposed by CSight lies in the mining of invariants in logs to improve the model precision. Unfortunately, invariant mining limits the application of this algorithm to small trace sets only.

We recently proposed the model learning approach CkTail in [30] and presented a comparison of CkTail with the previous passive techniques. In summary, we showed that CkTail builds more precise models by means of its trace segmentation algorithm, which tries to recover user sessions. Besides, compared to CSight, CkTail requires less constraints. Furthermore, CkTail is the only approach that detects component dependencies and expresses them with dependency graphs. The latter are used in MLCA to instantiate security properties.

3 MLCA Overview

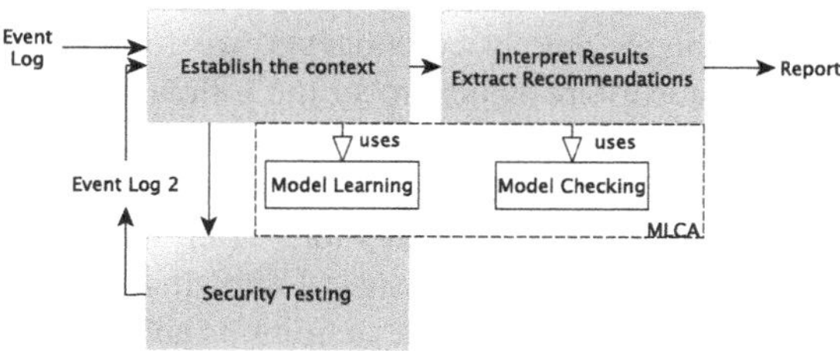

Fig. 1. Integration of MLCA with some audit stages (in grey) [29].

MLCA aims at assisting auditors to verify whether security properties hold on IoT systems with the automatic generation of behavioural models from event logs and with the generation of concrete security properties. Our approach can complement several existing security audit processes, e.g., the NIST or ETSI security audit frameworks. Figure 1 illustrates its integration. Most of the security audit processes include a step allowing auditors to understand the system context. We call it "Establish the context" in the figure. This step is often manually done by interpreting diverse documents, event logs, or by using scanning tools. With MLCA, a model learning algorithm is used instead to recover one behavioural model for every component of the IoT system from event logs. These models make the system understanding easier. They can also be given to MbT approaches for assessing the IoT system security with tests. While testing, more logs may be collected and hence new models can be re-generated to capture more behaviours.

In the meantime, these formal models can be analysed in an exhaustive manner to detect further security issues. This analysis is usually automatically performed by means of security properties modelled with formulas, which are evaluated with a model-checker. These formulas may express different security aspects, e.g., vulnerabilities. We focus in this paper on formulas expressing security measures used to protect an IoT system against threats. Several papers, e.g., [18,27,34] propose lists of recommendations dedicated to IoT systems, which can be used as security measures. We chose to consider the works proposed by the ENISA organisation as they gather the security measures suggested in several papers and works of other organisations.

3.1 The ENISA Security Measures

The ENISA organisation issued several documents exposing guidelines and security measures to implement secure IoT software systems with regard to different contexts (smart plants, hospitals, clouds, etc.). These measures correspond to high-level recommendations for developers, operators and security experts, which help improve the security level of IoT devices and communications among them.

The security measures provided by ENISA come from several other documents written by different organisations or institutes, e.g., ISO, IETF, NIST or Microsoft. We have chosen to focus on the paper related to security baselines in the context of critical information infrastructures [11]. This document gathers 57 security technical measures that should be *active* in an IoT system. As the models generated by our approach mostly express exchanges among components, we formulated the 12 security measures related to communications, which cover the following domains: Authentication, Privacy, Secure and Trusted Communications, Access Control, Secure Interfaces and Network Services, Secure Input and Output Handling, Trust and Integrity Management. These security measures are given in Table 1 (left side). We have formulated them with LTL formulas composed of predicates. Following the terminology used in [2], we call these formulas *property types*. The definitions and explanations of the LTL operators are given in Sect. 4. These property types are formulated by means of the predicates given in Table 2.

Table 1. Some ENISA security measures and LTL formulas expressing them.

GP-TM-18: the device software/firmware has the ability to update Over-The-Air (OTA), the update server is secure, the update file is transmitted via a secure connection, it does not contain sensitive data and is encrypted	$F\mathit{getUpdate}(f) \wedge (\mathrm{G}(\mathit{getUpdate}(f) \rightarrow (\mathit{encrypted}(f) \wedge \neg \mathit{sensitive}(f)))) \wedge \mathrm{G}((\mathit{begin} \wedge F\mathit{end}) \rightarrow (\neg(\mathit{getUpdate}(f) \wedge \mathit{from}(c))\,\mathrm{U}(\mathit{authenticated}(c) \vee \mathit{end})))$
GP-TM-19: offer an automatic firmware update mechanism	$F\mathit{searchUpdate} \wedge (F\mathit{searchUpdate} \rightarrow \neg(F\mathit{searchUpdate} \rightarrow (\neg \mathit{searchUpdate}\,\mathrm{U}(\mathit{input} \wedge \mathit{cmdSearchUpdate} \wedge \neg \mathit{searchUpdate}))))$
GP-TM-22: ensure that weak, null or blank passwords are not allowed	$\mathrm{G}((\mathit{Request} \wedge \mathit{from}(c1) \wedge \mathit{to}(c2) \wedge \mathit{Weakpass}(x)) \rightarrow ((\neg(\mathit{Response} \wedge \mathit{to}(c1) \wedge \mathit{from}(c2)))\,\mathrm{U}((\mathit{Response} \wedge \mathit{to}(c1) \wedge \mathit{from}(c2)) \wedge (\mathit{errorResponse} \vee (\neg \mathit{validResponse} \wedge \mathit{Response})))))$
GP-TM-24: credentials are encrypted during authentication	$\mathrm{G}((\mathit{loginAttempt}(c) \wedge \mathit{credential}(x)) \rightarrow \mathit{encrypted}(x))$
GP-TM-25: protect against abusive login attempts	$\mathrm{G}((\mathit{begin} \wedge F\mathit{end}) \rightarrow (\neg(\mathrm{G}((\mathit{begin} \wedge F(\mathit{end} \vee \mathit{authenticated}(c)) \rightarrow P(5,c))) \rightarrow (\neg \mathit{end}\,\mathrm{U}\,\mathit{lockout}(c)))\,\mathrm{U}\,\mathit{end})$ with $P(n,c) = ((\neg(\mathit{loginFail}(c)) \wedge \neg(\mathit{end} \vee \mathit{authenticated}(c)))\,\mathrm{U}(\mathit{end} \vee \mathit{authenticated}(c) \vee ((\mathit{loginFail}(c) \wedge \neg(\mathit{end} \vee \mathit{authenticated}(c)))\,\mathrm{U}(\mathit{end} \vee \mathit{authenticated}(c) \vee P(n-1,c)))))$ for $n > 0$, and $P(0,c) = (\neg(\mathit{loginFail}(c))\,\mathrm{U}(\mathit{end} \vee \mathit{authenticated}(c)))$
GP-TM-26: password recovery system does not supply an attacker with information indicating a valid account	$\mathrm{G}(\mathit{passwordRecovery} \rightarrow \neg \mathit{blackListedWord}(x))$
GP-TM-34,38: ensure a proper and effective use of cryptography	$\mathrm{G}(\mathit{sensitive}(x) \rightarrow \mathit{encrypted}(x))$
GP-TM-42: do not trust data received and always verify any interconnections	$\mathrm{G}((\neg(\mathit{validResponse} \wedge \mathit{to}(c) \wedge \neg \mathit{loginAttempt}(c))\,\mathrm{U}(\mathit{authenticated}(c))) \wedge (\neg(\mathit{Request} \wedge \mathit{to}(c) \wedge \neg \mathit{loginAttempt}(c))\,\mathrm{U}(\mathit{authenticated}(c))))$
GP-TM-48: if a single device is compromised, it does not affect the whole set	$\neg \mathrm{G}(\mathit{from}(d) \wedge \mathit{Unavailable}) \rightarrow \neg(\neg \mathit{output}\,\mathrm{U}(\mathit{output} \wedge \mathit{Unavailable})$
GP-TM-52(1): ensure a device is not susceptible to XSS	$\mathrm{G}((\mathit{Request} \wedge \mathit{from}(c1) \wedge \mathit{to}(c2) \wedge \mathit{XSS}(x)) \rightarrow \neg(\neg(\mathit{Response} \wedge \mathit{to}(c1) \wedge \mathit{from}(c2))\,\mathrm{U}(\mathit{Response} \wedge \mathit{to}(c1) \wedge \mathit{from}(c2)) \wedge (\mathit{errorResponse} \vee (\neg \mathit{validResponse} \wedge \mathit{Response}))))$
GP-TM-52(2): ensure a device is not susceptible to SQL injection	$\mathrm{G}((\mathit{Request} \wedge \mathit{from}(c1) \wedge \mathit{to}(c2) \wedge \mathit{SQLinjection}(x)) \rightarrow \neg(\neg(\mathit{Response} \wedge \mathit{to}(c1) \wedge \mathit{from}(c2))\,\mathrm{U}(\mathit{Response} \wedge \mathit{to}(c1) \wedge \mathit{from}(c2)) \wedge (\mathit{errorResponse} \vee (\neg \mathit{validResponse} \wedge \mathit{Response}))))$
GP-TM-53: avoid security issues when designing error messages	$\mathrm{G}((\mathit{errorResponse} \vee \neg \mathit{validResponse}) \rightarrow \neg \mathit{blackListedWord}(x))$

3.2 MLCA Requirements

The capability of MLCA in auditing IoT systems depends on several realistic assumptions made on a system under audit denoted SUA:

- **A1 Event Log:** we consider the components of SUA as black-boxes. We assume that each device, server, or gateway is physically secured and that we only have access to the network or user interfaces through the network. Event logs include timestamps given by a global clock. We consider having one event log;
- **A2 Message Content:** components produce events that include parameter assignments allowing to identify the source and the destination. Other parameter assignments may be used to encode data. Besides, an event is either identified as a request or a response. Many protocols, e.g. HTTP, allow to easily distinguish both of them;
- **A3 Device Collaboration:** to learn precise models, we want to recognise sessions of the system in event logs. We consider two exclusive cases:
    - **A31:** the components of SUA cannot run multiple instances; requests are processed by a component on a first-come, first served basis. Besides, the

Table 2. Predicates defined from 12 ENISA measures related to communications.

Predicate	Short Description
Begin	Beginning of a new session
End	End of a session
$From(c)$	Event coming from c
$To(c)$	Event sent to c
Request	Event is a request
Response	Event is a response
Input	Event is an input
Output	Event is an output
GetUpdate(x)	Response including an update file
CmdSearch-Update	The component received the order to search for an update
$Sensitive(x)$	Data x is sensitive
$Credential(x)$	Data x is acredential
$Encrypted(x)$	Data x is encrypted
SearchUpdate	Component requests for an update
$LoginAttempt(c)$	Authentication attempt with c
$Authenticated(c)$	Successful authentication with c
$LoginFail(c)$	Failed authentication with c
$Lockout(c)$	c is locked due to repetitive authentication failures
PasswordRecovery	Component uses a password recovery mechanism
$BlackListedWord(x)$	Message x includes black listed words
ValidResponse	Correct response with correct status
ErrorResponse	Response containing an error message
Unavailable	Component that received the request is unavailable
$XSS(x)$	Data x includes an XSS attack
$SQLinjection(x)$	Data x includes an SQL injection attack
$Weakpass(x)$	Password x is weak or blanck

components follow the request–response exchange pattern (a response is associated with one request, a request is associated with responses), or
- **A32:** the events that belong to the same session are identified by a unique parameter assignment.

The session recognition mentioned in A3 helps extract execution traces expressing complete behaviours of SUA, i.e. disjoint action sequences starting from one of its initial states and ending in one of its final states. A32 expresses that messages include an identifier allowing to observe whole collaborations among components. Usually, the session identification strongly facilitates the trace extraction. Unfortunately, we have observed that this technique is seldom adopted with IoT systems. Hence, when there is no session identifier, we restrict the functioning of SUA with A31. We have observed that this assumption can be applied with many wireless or IoT systems.

3.3 A Motivating Example

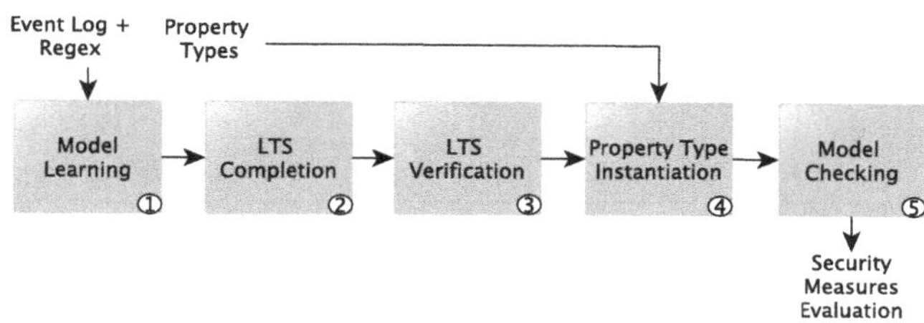

Fig. 2. The MLCA's steps.

We now present our Model-Learning-Checking approach MLCA, which aims at helping audit the security of SUA. It takes as inputs an event log, regular expressions allowing to format the event log, and generic security properties given under the form of property types. These property types have a pattern-level form, and have to be instantiated to make them concrete before being evaluated.

Figure 2 illustrates the 5 successive steps of MLCA. It starts by learning models from the event log. In short, the event log is firstly formatted by means of the regular expressions into a sequence of actions of the form $a(\alpha)$ with a a label and α some parameter assignments. In reference to A1, A2, an action $a(\alpha)$ indicates the sources and destinations of the messages with two parameters $from$ and to. The other parameter assignments capture data, e.g., acknowledgements or sensor data. Figure 3 illustrates a simple example of event log along with a regular expression allowing to format the events into actions. This expression retrieves a label (Req or Resp) and parameters in the messages (from, to and the remaining data, e.g., cmd:=auth). Figure 4 shows an example of action sequence where the first five actions are derived from the events of Fig. 3.

Then, we call the model learning algorithm CkTail to build one LTS $\mathcal{L}(c1)$ for every component $c1$ of SUA detected in the action sequence. $\mathcal{L}(c1)$ shows the behaviours of $c1$ in terms of messages exchanged with the other components. Besides, CkTail generates one dependency graph $Dg(c1)$ expressing how $c1$ interacts with the other components of SUA. The detailed functioning of our model learning algorithm is given in [30], but the auditor does not need to be aware of the details. Figures 5 and 6 illustrate the LTSs and dependency graphs obtained from our action sequence example. From these models, it becomes easier to understand that the system consists of four components: $c4$ is an application sending commands (from users), $c1$ and $c2$ are gateways and c_3 is an actuator (a smart light bulb). We can deduce from $\mathcal{L}(c1)$ and $\mathcal{L}(c2)$ that the first gateway authenticates to the second one after the receipt of commands from $c4$. Then, $c1$ sends to c_2 the state of a motion sensor, which seems to be integrated

```
Jun 08, 2019 14:16:21.521 CET;from:=c4;to:=c1 Req?cmd:=auth
Jun 08, 2019 14:16:21.758 CET;from:=c1;to:=c2 Req?login:=toto&password:=1234
Jun 08, 2019 14:16:22.136 CET;from:=c2;to:=c1 Resp response:=OK
Jun 08, 2019 14:16:22.385 CET;from:=c1;to:=c4 Resp response:=OK
Jun 08, 2019 14:16:23.287 CET;from:=c1;to:=c2 Req?presence:=1&switch:=On

Example of regular expression:
^(?<date>\w{3} \d{2}, \d{4} \d{2}:\d{2}:\d{2}.\d{3})\s(?<param1>[^;]+);
(?<param2>[\s]+)\s(?<label>[^?]+)?(?<param3>[^&]+)$
```

Fig. 3. Example of 5 HTTP messages collected from an IoT system. The regular expression retrieves a label and 3 parameters here. The label expression will be the label of the action in the action sequence *S*.

```
Req(from:=c4,to:=c1,cmd:=auth)
Req(from:=c1,to:=c2,login:=toto,password:=1234)
Resp(from:=c2,to:=c1,response:=OK)
Resp(from:=c1,to:=c4,response:=OK)
Req(from:=c1,to:=c2,presence:=1,switch:=On)
Req(from:=c4,to:=c1,cmd:=Light3min)
Resp(from:=c2,to:=c1,response:=OK)
Req(from:=c1,to:=c3,switch:=On)
Resp(from:=c3,to:=c1,response:=OK)
Req(from:=c2,to:=c3,switch:=On)
Resp(from:=c1,to:=c4,response:=OK)
Resp(from:=c3,to:=c2,response:=OK)
Req(from:=c1,to:=c3,switch:=Off)
Resp(from:=c3,to:=c1,response:=OK)
```

Fig. 4. Action sequence S.

to the gateway $c1$. According to the motion sensor state, $c2$ finally sends the command "switch:=on" to the smart light bulb $c3$.

With these models, it becomes easier to interpret the behaviours of SUA. Furthermore, as we now have formal models, different kinds of activities may be automatically or semi-automatically conducted to discover defects. In particular, the remaining steps of MLCA aims at checking whether property types hold on those LTSs. But, the LTSs and property types do not yet share the same alphabet, as the property types are generic. The auditor should re-formulate them for every LTS with the actions labelled on transitions. Instead, our approach automatically instantiates property types with the three next steps. More, precisely, given an LTS $\mathscr{L}(c1)$, the step "LTS Completion" automatically extends the LTS semantics; it analyses the LTS paths and injects new labels on transitions. These labels correspond to some predicates of the property types whose variables are assigned to concrete values. The step automates the label injection by using an expert system made up of inference rules, which encode some expert knowledge about SUA. The step produces a new LTS $\mathscr{L}'(c1)$. If we take back our example, this step completes the LTS $\mathscr{L}(c2)$ of Fig. 5 and gives the new LTS $\mathscr{L}'(c2)$ illustrated in Fig. 7. The transitions of $\mathscr{L}'(c2)$ are still labelled by the actions of the original LTS, but several new labels appeared. For instance, the expert system has detected a login attempt to $c1$ with the credentials $\{login := toto, password := 1234\}$, which are also recognised as sensitive data.

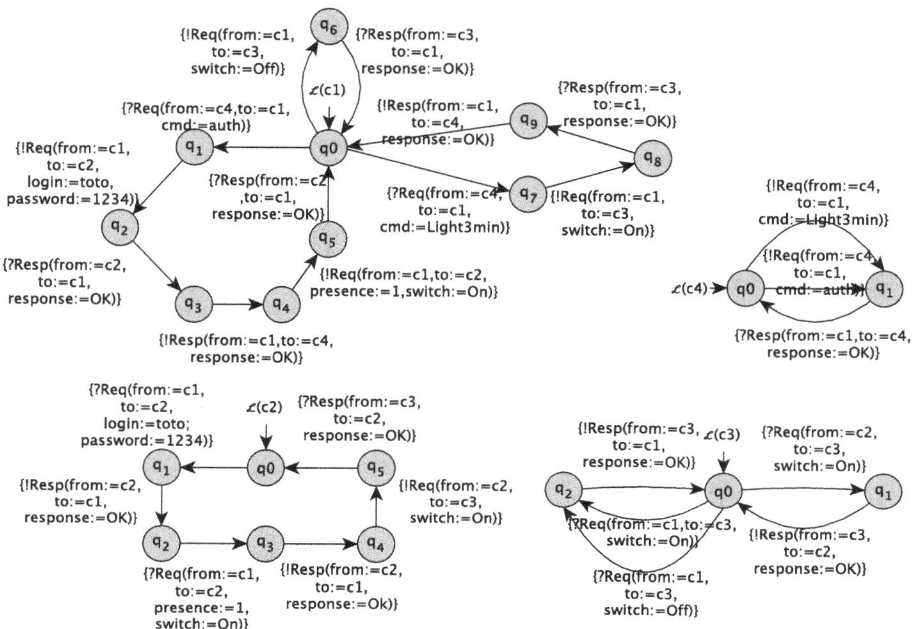

Fig. 5. LTSs generated from the action sequence of Fig. 4.

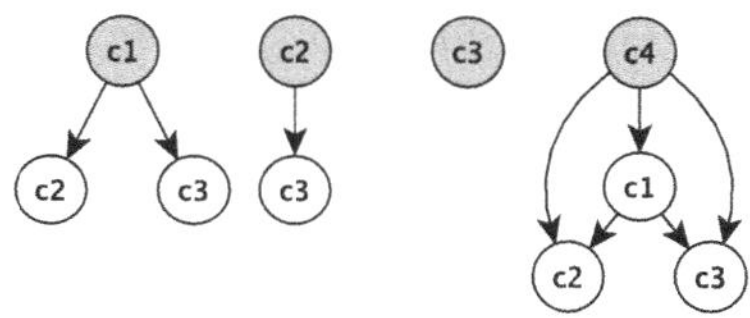

Fig. 6. Dependency graphs generated from the action sequence of Fig. 4.

The step "LTS Verification" helps auditors check the correctness of the previous step. Indeed, the expert system used to enrich the LTS transitions may suffer from the classical data acquisition problem. In other words, it may have inaccurate rules or missing ones. To help auditors check the LTS completion correctness, this step returns the list of predicates that have not been added on LTS transitions. Besides, it check the satisfiability of invariants on LTSs. These invariants allow the detection of some incorrect LTS transition completions (e.g., a transition whose action is neither a request nor a response) or missing labels (e.g., every transition must carry either an input or an output). These transitions are also retuned to auditors.

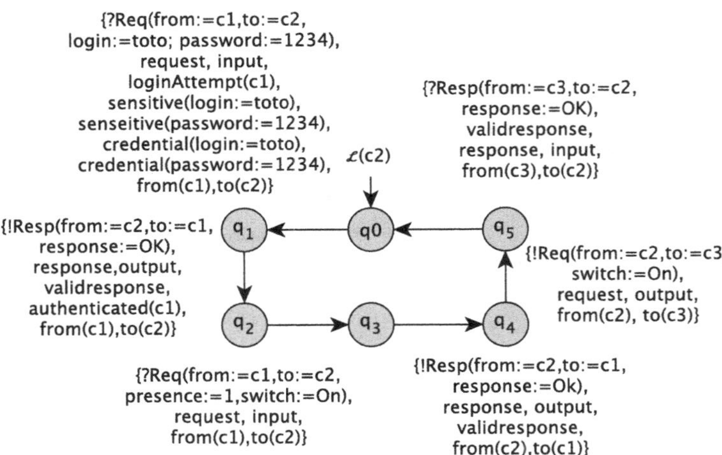

Fig. 7. Example of LTS completion. New propositions (Begin, End, Credential, Sensitive, ValidResponse, etc.) are injected on transitions.

The next step "Property type instantiation" covers every new LTS and automatically instantiates the property types. This step returns a set of LTL formulas $\mathscr{P}(\mathscr{L}'(c1))$ exclusively written with atomic propositions. We call them *property instances*. These correspond to concrete security properties. Let's illustrate this step with the LTS $\mathscr{L}'(c2)$ of Fig. 7 and the property type $\mathbf{G}((loginAttempt(c) \wedge credential(x)) \rightarrow encrypted(x))$ derived from the ENISA measure GP-TM-24. By covering the labels of $\mathscr{L}'(c2)$, we obtain $Dom(c) = \{c1\}$ and $Dom(x) = \{login := toto, password := 1234\}$. Two property instances are then derived.

The final step is more classic as it calls a model-checker to verify whether an LTS $\mathscr{L}'(c1)$ satisfies the LTL formula of $\mathscr{P}(\mathscr{L}'(c1))$. The model-checker either returns true if a property instance holds or a counterexample path that violates it. This counterexample is particularly useful to understand why a component $c1$ does not meet a security property and should help localise a problem in the LTS $\mathscr{L}'(c1)$. Figure 8 shows a example of results returned by the model-checker NuSMV [7] after having evaluated if the LTS $\mathscr{L}'(c2)$ satisfies some property instances derived from five security measures. A property instance related to GP-TM-24 does not hold because both the login and password are not encrypted. The interpretation of the counterexample helps deduce that the credentials are not encrypted (Encrypted(login:=toto), Encrypted(password:=1234) not found). Such counterexamples may be used to develop an audit report, which should include recommendations or treatments to security issues.

After this overview of MLCA, we now develop its theoretical background along with its algorithms in the next section. It is worth noting that a user does not need to be aware of these details. He/she only needs to have an event log, a list of regular expressions and our list of property types.

Applying a binding to the variables of a property type gives a property instance related to this binding. For instance, applying $\{x \rightarrow pass := "1234"\}$ to $Sensitive(x) \rightarrow Encrypted(x)$ returns the property instance $Sensitive(pass := "1234") \rightarrow Encrypted(pass := "1234")$.

The writing of property types is not a straightforward activity in the sense that it requires a good expert knowledge on LTL. This is why we provide a set of property types in Sect. 3.1. We recommend writing property types by firstly formulating general security concepts with predicates, and by applying or composing the LTL patterns given in [10] on those predicates. These patterns help structure LTL formulas with precise and correct statements that model common situations, e.g., the absence of events, or cause-effect relationships.

In order to reduce execution times, our algorithms take advantage of particular formula, which we call *conditional* property types. These will be useful to enhance the property type instantiation algorithm given in Sect. 4.5. Intuitively, a conditional property type is formed by an implication. It is worth noting that the definition given below identifies some conditional property types but is not exhaustive.

Definition 5 (Conditional Property Types).

1. *Φ is a conditional property type iff Φ is a property type of the form:* $P \rightarrow Q$, $\mathbf{G}(P \rightarrow Q)$, $\mathbf{F}(P \rightarrow Q)$, $\mathbf{G}P \rightarrow Q$, $(P \rightarrow Q) \vee \Phi_2$, $\mathbf{G}((P \rightarrow Q) \vee \Phi_2)$, $\mathbf{F}((P \rightarrow Q) \vee \Phi_2)$ *with P a predicate or a conjunction of predicates, Q a predicate or a disjunction of predicates, and Φ_2 an LTL formula;*
2. *$antecedent(\Phi)$ denotes the antecedent of the implication of Φ, which is either equal to P or $\mathbf{F}P$ here;*
3. *$consequent(\Phi) \stackrel{def}{=} Q$.*

We provide, in Sect. 3.1, 12 property types modelling the security measures of the ENISA organisation related to communications. These property types are made up of the predicates given in Table 2. For example, the security measure GP-TM-38 recommends to encrypts sensitive data, which is formulated as $\mathbf{G}(Sensitive(x) \rightarrow Encrypted(x))$. GP-TM-24 recommends encrypting authentication credentials. This measure is formulated as: $\mathbf{G}((LoginAttempt(c) \wedge Credential(x) \rightarrow Encrypted(x))$, which intuitively means that every time a component attempts to log in to another component c by using credentials x, then x must be encrypted. GP-TM-53 suggests that error messages must not expose sensitive information. This is formulated with $\mathbf{G}((ErrorResponse \vee \neg ValidResponse) \rightarrow (\neg(BlackListedWord(x)))$. This formula intuitively means that every HTTP response composed of an error message or having a status higher than 299 must not include blacklisted words. If we apply the binding $\{c \rightarrow c1, x \rightarrow login := toto\}$ on the second property type, we obtain the property instance $\mathbf{G}((LoginAttempt(c1) \wedge Credential(login := toto) \rightarrow Encrypted(login := toto))$.

4.3 MLCA Step 2: LTS Completion

Model-checkers cannot directly check the satisfiability of property types on LTSs as the properties are made up of predicate variables. This step prepares the property type instantiation by helping auditors complete the LTS transitions with some predicates of *Pred*, i.e. the predicates used to write the property types. Once this step is finished we obtain new LTSs that share the same alphabet as the property types. As an LTS encodes concrete behaviours, this step actually adds instantiated predicates of *Pred*, i.e. predicates whose variables are assigned to concrete values found in the LTS actions. Completing the LTS transitions with these instantiated predicates comes down to analysing/interpreting LTS transitions or paths and to add new labels on transitions to extend the LTS semantics. To performs this activity in an automatic manner, this step uses an expert system, made up of inference rules, which encode some expert knowledge about SUA. The expert system offers the benefits to automate the LTS transition completion and to save time by allowing to reuse it on several IoT systems.

We represent inference rules with this format: *When conditions on facts Then actions on facts* (format taken by the Drools inference engine [28]). The facts, which belong to the knowledge base of the expert system, are here the transitions of an LTS. To ensure that the transition completion is performed in a finite time and in a deterministic way, the inference rules have to meet these hypotheses:

- Finite complexity: a rule can only be applied a limited number of times on the same knowledge base,
- Soundness: the inference rules are Modus Ponens (simple implications that lead to sound facts if the original facts are true).

We devised 28 inference rules, which are available in [31]. These can be categorised as follows:

- Structural information: two rules are used to add the propositions "Begin" and "End", which describe the beginning and end of user sessions in LTS paths;
- Nature of the actions: 9 rules add information about the nature of the actions. Given a transition $q_1 \xrightarrow{\{a(\alpha)\}} q_2$, some rules analyse the parameter assignments in α and complete the transition with new propositions expressing that $a(\alpha)$ is a request or a response, an input or an output, the component that sent $a(\alpha)$, etc. Other rules analyse α to interpret if the action corresponds to an error response (analysis of the values in α to detect words like "error" or analysis of HTTP status, etc.). For instance, the first rule of Fig. 9 adds the proposition ValidResponse if the transition expresses a response whose HTTP status is between 200 and 299. The status inspection is performed by the procedure isOk();
- Security information: the other rules add predicates related to security on LTS transitions. For instance, we devised a rule that checks whether some parameters are encrypted. Other rules analyse the LTS paths to try recognise specific patterns (transition sequences containing specific words), e.g., authentication attempts, successful or failed authentications. For instance, the second rule of Fig. 9 detects a correct authentication. It adds the proposition "LoginAttempt(c)" on the transition labelled by the credentials and "Authenticated(c)" on the transition whose action encodes a correct authentication with the external component c.

```
rule "validResponse"
when
$t : Transition(isReq() == false,
isOk())
then
$t.addLabel("validResponse");
end
```

```
rule "Authentication"
when
$t1: Transition(isRequest(), contains("
login"), contains("password"))
$t2: Transition(isResponse(),isOK(),
sourceState = $t1.targetState)
then
$t1.addLabel("LoginAttempt("+
compoSender($t1) + ")");
$t2.addLabel("Authenticated("+
compoSender($t1) + ")");
end
```

Fig. 9. Inference rule examples [29].

Once the expert system has completed the LTS $\mathscr{L}(c1)$, we obtain a new LTS denoted $\mathscr{L}'(c1)$.

4.4 MLCA Step 3: LTS Verification

The notion of expert system, used in the previous step, suffers from some limitations as most of the current AI applications. One of them relates to the difficulty of knowledge acquisition. In other terms, the expert system rules may be incomplete or not adapted to SUA. For instance, the rule "Authentication" of Fig. 9 is based on the keywords "login" and "password" for recognising a successful authentication, but other keywords might be used instead. With this example, the expert system can be easily completed with new rules. But, some rules also depend of external tools, which might provide incorrect information. We observed this case for the rule dedicated to the recognition of data encryption. This rule relies on a tool, which often returns false positives or negatives, especially when the data length is short. This is why the auditors have to inspect the LTSs to assess the transition completion correctness. We propose two solutions to help auditors in this verification:

- the expert system notices and returns the names of the rules, which have not been triggered previously. The returned list of rules warns the auditor that some predicates have not been added on transitions;
- this step also automatically checks whether invariants hold on every LTS transitions. We provide a set of 7 invariants written with property types. The first 4 invariants are used to detect missing labels that have to be found on LTS transitions. The remaining ones are used to detect incorrect label completion on transitions. The predicate variables c and $c2$, which are used with some invariants, only refer to components. To make these invariants concrete, we assign both variables to the components that belong to the set C. Then, we check whether the invariants hold on the LTSs by calling a model-checker. When an invariant is not satisfied, the LTS transition is returned to the auditor, so that he/she can manually review it.

Table 3. Invariant used to verify the LTS transition completion correctness.

$Begin \wedge F End$
$G(Input \vee Output)$
$G(Request \vee (Response \wedge (ValidResponse \vee ErrorResponse)))$
$G((Request \wedge From(c) \wedge To(c2) -> F(Response \wedge To(c) \wedge From(c2))$
$G(From(c) \rightarrow \neg To(c))$
$G(\neg Input \wedge Output)$
$LoginAttempt(c) \rightarrow Request \wedge To(c)$

4.5 MLCA Step 4: Property Type Instantiation

Given an LTS $\mathscr{L}'(c1)$, this step aims at instantiating the property types of $\mathscr{P}$ to obtain a set of property instances that can be evaluated on the paths of $\mathscr{L}'(c1)$. We denote $\mathscr{P}(\mathscr{L}'(c1))$ this set of property instances. Intuitively, a property type Φ is instantiated with bindings, which assign values to the predicate variables of Φ. This step derives these bindings from the labels (instantiated predicates) added on the LTS transitions by the expert system previously.

We proposed in [29] a preliminary algorithm implementing the property type instantiation. To illustrate this algorithm, consider the property type $G(Sensitive(x) \rightarrow Encrypted\ (x))$ modelling the ENISA security measure GP-TM-38 and an LTS $\mathscr{L}'(c1)$ having the labels Sensitive(login:=toto), Encrypted(login:=toto), Encrypted(resp:=" HTTP/1.1 200 OK..."). The Property Type Instantiation algorithm builds the set $Dom(x) = \{login := toto, resp := "HTTP/1.1200OK..."\}$. Consequently, two bindings and two property instances are automatically built. Hence, despite the need for checking the LTS completion correctness, an auditor does not have to be an expert in LTL for using our approach.

We showed in [29] that the time complexity of the Property Type Instantiation algorithm is polynomial, but it is manifest that the LTS size and the number of predicate values found on the LTS transitions will increase the number of generated property instances and then negatively affect execution times, as verifying whether LTL formulas hold is usually time consuming.

From this statement, we now propose to focus on an enhancement of the algorithm given in [29] to lower the time complexity of MLCA. We indeed observed that our algorithm produces a set of pointless property instances in the sense that these formulas are always true. Consider the previous example of property type, that is $G(Sensitive(x) \rightarrow Encrypted(x))$ along with the LTS $\mathscr{L}'(c1)$ having the same labels *Sensitive(login:=toto)*, *Encrypted(login:=toto)*, *Encrypted(resp:="HTTP/1.1 200 OK...")*. The last label gives the binding $\{x \rightarrow resp := "HTTP/1.1\ 200\ OK..."\}$ and the property type $G(Sensitive(resp := "HTTP/1.1\ 200\ OK...") \rightarrow Encrypted(resp := "HTTP/1.1\ 200\ OK..."))$. The latter will always be true, as the antecedent part of the formula $Sensitive(resp := \text{"...''})$ will always be false (the predicate Sensitive(resp:="...") is not labelled on any transition of $\mathscr{L}'(c1)$). This statement can be observed with the conditional property types given in Definition 5. This is formulated by the following proposition:

Proposition 1. *Let* Φ *be a conditional property type such that there exist* $P_1(x_1, \ldots, x_k) \in antecedent(\Phi)$ *and* $P_2(x_1, \ldots, x_k) \in consequent(\Phi)$. *X' is the finite set* *of predicate variables of* Φ*. Let* $P_2(v_1,\ldots,v_k) := true$ *be an instantiated predicate of* $P_2(x_1,\ldots,x_k)$ *and* $b : X' \rightarrow Dom(X')$ *such that* $b' : \{x_1 \rightarrow v_1,\ldots,x_k \rightarrow v_k\}$ *is a restriction of b.*

The property instance $\varphi := b(\Phi)$ *resulting from the instantiation of* Φ *with b is always true.*

Sketch of Proof of Proposition 1: let us consider the conditional property type $\Phi := P \rightarrow Q$ with P a predicate or a conjunction of predicates, Q a predicate or a disjunction of predicates.

The property instance φ derived from Φ with b is denoted $\varphi := \varphi_1 \rightarrow \varphi_2$. $\varphi_2 := P_2(v_1,\ldots,v_k)$ or $\varphi_2 := P_2(v_1,\ldots,v_k) \vee \varphi_2'$ with φ_2' an LTL formula, such that $P_2(x_1,\ldots,x_k) \in SF(Q)$ and $b' : \{x_1 \rightarrow v_1,\ldots,x_k \rightarrow v_k\}$ is the restriction of b over $\{x_1,\ldots,x_k\}$.

As a consequence, as $P_2(v_1,\ldots,v_k)$ is true, φ_2 is also true. As φ_2 is true, $\varphi_1 \rightarrow \varphi_2$ is true whatever the evaluation of φ_1. Finally, $\varphi := b(\Phi)$ is always true. The same reasoning can be applied on the other conditional property types of Definition 5. ■

In reference to Proposition 1, we now provide a new implementation of the property type instantiation in Algorithm 1. The main difference between this algorithm and the previous one lies in lines 4–6. It begins by storing the predicates of the property type Φ in a set *PS*, which contains the predicates from which bindings will be computed (in contrast to the previous algorithm where all the predicates were considered). Now, if Φ is recognised as a conditional property type, if it includes two predicates $P1$, $P2$ having the same variables and if $P1$ belongs to the antecedent part of Φ whereas $P2$ belongs to the consequent part, then $P2$ is removed from *PS*. Removing $P2$ from *PS* allows to ignore the predicate values leading to pointless property type instances, as in our example. In lines 7–10, Algorithm 1 covers the LTS transitions and every label $P(v_1,\ldots,v_k)$ to generate domains of values on condition that the related predicate $P(x_1,\ldots,x_k)$ belong to *PS*. Afterwards, the property types are instantiated as before.

The time complexity of Algorithm 1 is proportional to $|\mathscr{P}|(p^2 + |\rightarrow|p + |D|)$. This complexity is higher than the one of the first algorithm, but it should return less property instances. As a consequence, MLCA should verify less property instances and hence consume less time with this algorithm. This is confirmed in our evaluation results (Sect. 5).

4.6 MLCA Step 5: Property Instance Verification

Given an LTS $\mathscr{L}'(c1)$, this step comes down to calling a model-checker for verifying whether $\mathscr{L}'(c1)$ satisfies the property instances of $\mathscr{P}(\mathscr{L}'(c1))$. If the model-checker detects a counterexample path that violates a property instance $\phi \in \mathscr{P}(\mathscr{L}'(c1))$, our approach reports the security measure related to ϕ, which is not (correctly) implemented. Our approach also returns the counterexample so that auditors may analyse it to comprehend the captured failure scenario.

Algorithm 1. Property Type Instantiation 2.

input : LTS $\mathscr{L}'(c1)$, property type set $\mathscr{P}$
output: Property instance set $\mathscr{P}(\mathscr{L}'(c1))$
Compute $Dom(deps)$ from $Dg(c1)$;
$X' := \emptyset$;
foreach $\Phi \in \mathscr{P}$ **do**
  PS set of of predicates of Φ;
  if Φ *is a conditional property type and* $\exists P1(x_1,\dots,x_k), P2(x_1,\dots,x_k) \in PS : P1(x_1,\dots,x_k) \in SF(antecedant(\Phi)) \wedge P2(x_1,\dots,x_k) \in SF(consequent(\Phi))$ **then**
    $PS := PS \setminus \{P2(x_1,\dots,x_k)\}$;
  foreach $l \in L$ *with* $s_1 \xrightarrow{L} s_2 \in \rightarrow_{\mathscr{L}'(c1)}$ **do**
    if $l = P(v_1,\dots,v_k)$ *and* $P(x_1,\dots,x_k) \in PS$ **then**
      $Dom(x_i) = Dom(x_i) \cup \{v_i\}(1 \leq i \leq k)$;
      $X' := X' \cup \{x_1,\dots,x_k\}$;
  if X' *is not equal to the set of predicate variables of* Φ **then**
    return a warning;
  else
    $D := Dom(x_1) \times \cdots \times Dom(x_n)$ with $X' = \{x_1,\dots,x_n\}$;
    foreach *binding* $b \in D^{X'}$ **do**
      $\phi := b(\Phi)$;
      $\mathscr{P}(\mathscr{L}'(c1)) = \mathscr{P}(\mathscr{L}'(c1)) \cup \{\phi\}$;

4.7 Limitations

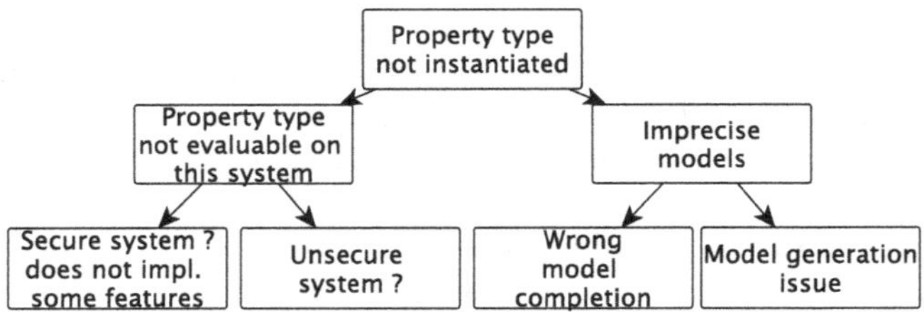

Fig. 10. Some MLCA limitations.

Our approach suffers from some limitations. The first is related to the need for formulating security measures with property types. Even though we propose a substantial set of property types, auditors might need further formulas for their own use. But, writing LTL formulas requires some expertise and experience.

The generalisation of our approach is also restricted by the requirements A1-A3. In particular, the event logs must be formatted by means of regular expressions so that the action types can be identified. Although we have observed that this task is not too difficult to carry out on HTTP messages, it is manifest that this is not generalisable to any kind of protocols, especially those encrypting some parts of the message content.

We also have showed that Algorithm 1 may return warnings showing that property types cannot be instantiated. Figure 10 summarises the main reasons. The two first ones (left side of the figure) concern SUA: it might not implement some features. Here, the auditor has to establish and decide if SUA is secure even though a security feature is missing. Additionally, a property type may not be instantiated on account of the models (right side of the figure). On the one hand, the LTSs are generated by a model learning algorithm, which may infer under-approximated (rejection of valid behaviours) or over-approximated (acceptance of invalid behaviours) models. It is worth noting that the model learning tools available in the literature tend to generate more and more precise models, which accept most of legal behaviours and reject most of anomalous ones [30]. On the other hand, the LTSs may be incorrectly completed by the second step of MLCA. As stated earlier, the resulting LTSs should be manually reviewed.

4.8 Implementation

Our approach is implemented as a tool chain, which gathers three tools: CkTail, which implements a model learning approach specialised for communicating systems, SMV-maker, which completes the LTSs produced by CkTail by means of an expert system and instantiates property types, and the model-checker NuSMV. The tools, source codes, examples of property types and traces are available in [31]. These tools were employed to evaluate our approach with several case studies.

5 Empirical Evaluation

The experiments presented in this section aim to assess the capabilities of our algorithms to verify whether security measures are active on models inferred from logs in terms of precision (exact detection of active and inactive security measures) and performance. This section supplements our preliminary evaluation proposed in [29] as we study the capabilities of our algorithms through 3 research questions and as we consider more systems. These research questions are:

- RQ1: is MLCA able to detect active security measures? RQ1 investigates the sensitivity of MLCA, that is its capability to identify the security measures related to communications that are truly implemented on IoT systems;
- RQ2: is MLCA able to detect inactive security measures? RQ2 investigates the specificity of MLCA, that is its capability to uncover the security measures that are not considered or incorrectly implemented;
- RQ3: how long does MLCA take to verify whether security measures are correctly implemented? RQ3 studies the performance of our algorithms and how they scale with the size of the event logs, and with the number of the property types.

5.1 Empirical Setup

This study was conducted on five IoT systems integrating varied devices, gateways and external cloud servers communicating over HTTP. We assembled and configured these systems using the available security options. From these systems, we collected event logs composed of HTTP messages on gateways or servers.

- **S1** is composed of 3 motion sensors that turn on a light-bulb when they detect movements. They communicate through a gateway; all of them have user interfaces, which may be used for configuration. The main purpose of this system is to focus on classical attacks (code injection, brute force, availability) and on the related security measures GP-TM 22, 25, 38, 52, 53;
- **S2** includes a motion sensor, a switch and an IP camera. The motion sensor communicates with the switch in clear-text, and with the camera with encrypted messages. The camera also communicates with external clouds requiring authentication and encryption. In this system, we mainly focus on security measures related to encryption and authentication, GP-TM 22, 24, 25, 26, 38, 42, 53;
- **S3** is composed of 3 IP cameras, which communicate with external cloud servers. Two cameras can update their software remotely. This system aims at focusing on security measures related to update mechanisms, GP-TM 18, 19, 38, 48, 53;
- **S4** is made up of a temperature sensor, which communicates with a gateway. A user can connect to the gateway for reading temperature curves. We devised this system so that the gateway is vulnerable to XSS code injections. Here, we mainly focus on security measures related to encryption, authentication, and code injection, GP-TM 22, 24, 25, 26, 38, 42, 52, 53;
- **S5** is composed of an IP camera, which interacts with a NTP, a SMTP, and an FTP server. The camera authenticates to the FTP server (with encrypted credentials), and to the SMTP server (with unencrypted credentials). A user can connect to the camera to get images or videos. With this system, we mainly focus on security measures related to encryption and authentication, GP-TM 22, 24, 26, 38, 42, 52, 53.

5.2 RQ1: Is MLCA Able to Detect Active Security Measures?

To answer RQ1, we initially experimented the above systems by hands. We gathered a first set of event logs that capture "normal behaviours" and generated first models with CkTail. From these, we identified the testable components, on which we applied a set of penetration testing tools specialised to Web applications. During this testing stage, we collected larger event logs. From them, we generated the final models used for the evaluation.

Besides, we manually analysed the source codes of the software used by the devices (sensors, gateways) when available and the event logs to list the ENISA security measures that are active and those that are not (correctly) implemented . This task allowed us to compare the results of MLCA with our observations and hence to measure the sensitivity and specificity of our approach.

For this evaluation, we considered the 12 property types given in Table 1. We ran MLCA to generate the LTSs and property instances from these property types. To not perform an unbiased evaluation, we considered two cases: the case where we did not manually completed the generated LTSs denoted "w/o modification" and the case where we manually completed them as required in the third step of the approach, denoted "w/ modifications". And finally, we called the model-checker NuSMV to check whether the property instances hold on the LTSs.

For this research question, we measured the sensitivities of MLCA (rate of correct property instances that evaluate to true) using Algorithm 1 "w/o modification" and "w/

modifications". The comparison of our previous MLCA algorithms given in [29] cannot be based on sensitivity measurements as both approaches generate different sets of property instances (in general terms, the numbers of conditional positives are different). To compare both algorithms, we measured their number of false positives FP, i.e. the number of unsatisfied property instances, which should hold.

Results:

Table 4. False positives (FP) and Sensitivity of MLCA.

IoT syst	#instantiated property types/total	FP w/o modif. MLCA of [29]	FP w/o modif. MLCA	Sensitivity w/o modif. MLCA	Sensitivity w/ modif. MLCA
S1	44/60	3	3	97.5%	98.33%
S2	14/36	0	0	100%	100%
S3	19/36	0	0	100%	100%
S4	13/24	0	0	100%	100%
S5	26/48	0	0	100%	100%

Table 4 summarises the results of our experiments. Col. 2 gives the ratio of property types that have been instantiated over the property types available for all the components of a system. For instance, S1 has 5 components, hence 5*12 property types can be used. 44 property types were instantiated for this system. None of the systems allowed to instantiate all the property types. This result was expected as none of the systems implement all the security features considered in the security measures, e.g., password recovery for S1, or authentication for some components of S2, S3. Then, Col. 3 and 4 give the number of false positives observed with MLCA of [29] and the MLCA algorithms presented in this paper. The two last columns provide the sensitivity of MLCA without or with manual modifications of the LTSs (after the third step of MLCA).

Firstly, col. 3 and 4 confirm that our new property instance algorithm (Algorithm 1) does not change the number of false positives. Col. 5 shows that the overall sensitivity of MLCA "w/o modification" is 99,5%. When we manually complete the LTSs the overall sensitivity increases up to 99,66 %. The sensitivity is below 100 % with S1. After inspection, we observed that the difference of sensitivity "w/o modification" and "w/ modifications" with S1 comes from an inference rule of the expert system, which tries to recognise whether parameters are encrypted. This rule computes the message entropy, but this technique is sometimes not precise enough to recognise encryption. Hence some LTS transitions were incorrectly completed with predicates of the form Encrypted(x). We did not find any better solution at the moment. Still with S1, the sensitivity "w/ modifications" remains below 100% on account of a false positive related to the security measure GP-TM-25. We observed that this measure is detected as active on account of an over-generalisation of the LTSs. Apart from this issue related to model learning, these results tend to show that MLCA is very effective to check whether security measures are correctly implemented since the sensitivity of MLCA is close to 100%.

Table 5. Specificity of MLCA.

IoT syst	#instantiated property types /total	Specificity w/o modif. MLCA of [29]	Specificity w/o modif. MLCA	Specificity w/ modif. MLCA
S1	44/60	99.07%	99.07%	99.07%
S2	14/36	91.66%	91.66%	91.66%
S3	19/36	92.86%	92.86%	92.86%
S4	13/24	100%	100%	100%
S5	26/48	67.57%	67.57%	89.19%

5.3 RQ2: Is MLCA Able to Detect Inactive Security Measures?

We measured the specificity of our approach, that is the rate of inactive security measures that are correctly identified by MLCA. We recall that a security measure is detected as inactive for a given system when a property instance derived from this security measure does not hold on an LTS. We considered the same models generated for RQ1 along with the same property types. In the same way, to not perform an unbiased evaluation, we considered the two cases "w/o modification" and "w/ modifications".

Results: Table 5 shows the specificity measurements of our algorithms. The number of instantiated property types and the number of property instances given in Col. 2 remain the same. Col. 3 and 4 compare the specificity of MLCA of [29] with the algorithms presented in this paper. Next, Col. 4 and 5 allow to compare the specificity without or with manual modifications of the LTSs.

The overall specificity without modification of the LTSs is 91.8% with both algorithms. Again, this confirms that the property instance optimisation used in Algorithm 1 does not modify the results of MLCA. We observe that MLCA returns some false negatives, most of them being observed with S5. After inspection, we observed that most of these false negatives come again from the expert system rule related to encryption recognition. Here, this rule has detected that many encrypted messages are not encrypted. After the manual modification of the LTSs, the specificity reaches 96,12%. The remaining false negatives come from some LTS under-approximations, i.e. rejections by the LTSs of some correct behaviours.

These results tend to show that MLCA is very effective for detecting inactive security measures since the overall specificity of MLCA is higher than 91% without modification of the models. We believe that the benefits of automatically learning models and instantiating LTL formulas exceed the drawback of having a few false negatives.

5.4 RQ3: How Long Does MLCA Take to Verify Whether Security Measures Are Correctly Implemented?

To answer RQ3, we performed three experiments. We firstly studied how the tool scales with the size of the event logs. We collected 20 new event logs from S5 by varying the number of events between 500 to 100000, then we measured execution times. We

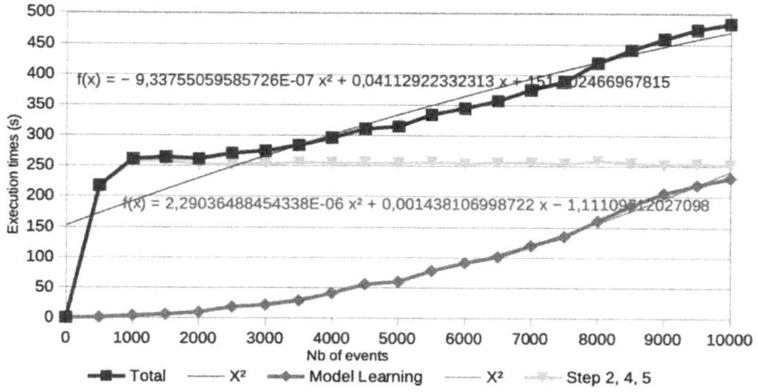

Fig. 11. Execution times vs. number of events.

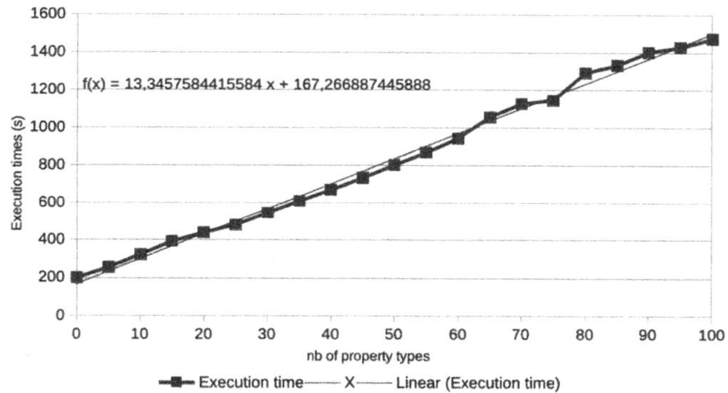

Fig. 12. Execution times vs. number of property types.

also studied how the tool scales with the number of property types. We measured the execution times of MLCA by using the event log of S5 and by increasing the property type number from 0 to 100. Finally, we measured the execution times obtained with the MLCA of [29] and the MLCA algorithms proposed in this paper on the 5 IoT systems. We also collected the number of generated property instances with both algorithms. These Experiments were carried out on a computer with 1 Intel® CPU i5-6500 @ 3.2GHz and 32GB RAM.

Results: Figure 11 depicts, with the curve Total, execution times in seconds w.r.t. the event log sizes. We observe that MLCA returns results within reasonable time even with large event logs. But, the curve follows a quadratic regression and reveals that our tool does not scale well. To understand this problem, we completed the figure with two additional curves depicting the times required to learn models and the times consumed by the other steps of the approach (Steps 2–5). These two curves clearly show that the scaling problem comes from the model learning algorithm CkTail.

Figure 12 depicts execution times in seconds w.r.t. the number of property types given as inputs. We observe that the curve follows a linear regression, showing that the tool scales well according to the number of property types. Even with 100 property types, execution times remain reasonable.

Table 6. Number of property instances and execution times measured on the 5 IoT systems.

IoT Syst	#property instance MLCA of [29]	#property instance MLCA	Execution times MLCA of [29]	Execution times Algorithm 1
$S1$	823	334	31708	4533
$S2$	37	37	509	510
$S3$	39	39	165	162
$S4$	80	68	76	60
$S5$	128	88	372	252

Table 6 compares the number of generated property instances along with execution times in seconds for the five IoT systems between the MLCA of [29] and the algorithms we proposed in this paper. In average, we observe that the new MLCA algorithms help reduce execution times by 28% thanks to the optimisations performed to reduce the set of generated property instances. With some systems (S2 and S3), we observe that both algorithms return the same amount of property instances and around the same execution times. With these systems, the property types that are instantiated are not conditional property types. In contrast, we observe that using Algorithm 1 with S1 allows to strongly reduce the set of property instances and to lower the execution time by 85%.

These results tend to show that MLCA can be used in practice even with large event logs, but it suffers from insufficient scalability, on account of the model learning step. These results also confirm that Algorithm 1 allows to save execution time.

5.5 Threat to Validity

Some threats to validity can be identified in our evaluation. The first factor, which may threaten external validity, applies to the case studies. Most of them are IoT systems using HTTP. But many communicating systems rely on other kinds of protocols, from which it may be more difficult to identify senders, receivers, requests or responses. Hence, we cannot conclude that our results are generalisable to IoT systems. This is why we deliberately avoid drawing any general conclusion. This threat is somewhat mitigated by the fact that HTTP is used by numerous communicating systems. However, the HTTP traffic should also be decipherable so that MLCA can recognise behavioural patterns and add predicates on LTS transitions. It is manifest that more experimentations are required on further kinds of systems.

There are also some threats to internal validity. The quality of the models produced by the first step of the approach strongly depends on the size and the formatting of the event logs. We showed in the evaluation that we can obtain some false positives / negatives on account of the lack of precision of the models. At the moment, none of the passive model learning tool generates "exact" models, they usually are slightly under- or over-approximated. We also mentioned that the outcomes of MLCA depend on the manual LTS verification carried out in Step 3. It is manifest that the outcomes of this step vary in accordance with the auditor knowledge and expertise. To avoid this potential threat, we considered two cases: no modification of the LTSs and manual modification. The first case gives the worst sensitivity and specificity of MLCA on the five IoT systems considered for the evaluation.

6 Conclusion

This paper has proposed the design and evaluation of an approach called MLCA (Model-Learning-Checking Approach), which combines model learning and model checking to help audit the security of IoT systems. It requires an event log along with security properties modelled with property types. The latter are generic LTL formulas, which can be used independently of the IoT system under audit. We provide 12 property types expressing some security measures provided by the ENISA organisation. MLCA automatically generates models from the event log, then it assists auditors in the generation of concrete properties by instantiating property types. This instantiation is carried out by an expert system made up of inference rules, which encode some expert knowledge about the kind of system under audit. Our evaluation, performed on 5 IoT systems, showed that MLCA is effective in detecting security issues, and that it can be used in practice on large event logs.

Nevertheless, several aspects need to be investigated in the future. The model learning approach requires some assumptions to generate precise models. We will investigate if some of them could be relaxed so that more systems under audit could be considered. Our evaluation showed that the use of an expert system offers a great potential for instantiating property types, especially when auditors are non-expert LTL users. However, this benefit strongly depends on the successful implementation of the expert system rules. We indeed observed in the experimentations that a few property types were not completely instantiated on account of the lack of precision of some rules. This is why the property type instantiation and LTS completion steps require a review to detect potential issues. Finding a way to get rid of this manual step is hence another direction for future work.

Acknowledgement. Research supported by the French Project VASOC (Auvergne-Rhône-Alpes Region) https://vasoc.limos.fr/.

References

1. Ahmad, A., Bouquet, F., Fourneret, E., Le Gall, F., Legeard, B.: Model-based testing as a service for iot platforms. In: Margaria, T., Steffen, B. (eds.) ISoLA 2016. LNCS, vol. 9953, pp. 727–742. Springer, Cham (2016). https://doi.org/10.1007/978-3-319-47169-3_55
2. Beschastnikh, I., Brun, Y., Abrahamson, J., Ernst, M.D., Krishnamurthy, A.: Using declarative specification to improve the understanding, extensibility, and comparison of model-inference algorithms. IEEE Trans. Softw. Eng. **41**(4), 408–428 (2015). https://doi.org/10.1109/TSE.2014.2369047

3. Beschastnikh, I., Brun, Y., Ernst, M.D., Krishnamurthy, A.: Inferring models of concurrent systems from logs of their behavior with Csight. In: Proceedings of the 36th International Conference on Software Engineering, pp. 468–479. ICSE 2014, ACM, New York, NY, USA (2014). https://doi.org/10.1145/2568225.2568246, http://doi.acm.org/10.1145/2568225.2568246
4. van der Bijl, M., Rensink, A., Tretmans, J.: Compositional testing with iOCO. In: Petrenko, A., Ulrich, A. (eds.) FATES 2003. LNCS, vol. 2931, pp. 86–100. Springer, Heidelberg (2004). https://doi.org/10.1007/978-3-540-24617-6_7
5. Celik, Z.B., McDaniel, P., Tan, G.: Soteria: automated iot safety and security analysis. In: 2018 USENIX Annual Technical Conference (USENIX ATC 18), pp. 147–158. USENIX Association, Boston, MA (July 2018). https://www.usenix.org/conference/atc18/presentation/celik
6. Chaabouni, N., Mosbah, M., Zemmari, A., Sauvignac, C., Faruki, P.: Network intrusion detection for iot security based on learning techniques. IEEE Commun. Surv. Tutor. **21**(3), 2671–2701 (2019). https://doi.org/10.1109/COMST.2019.2896380
7. Cimatti, A., et al.: NuSMV 2: an opensource tool for symbolic model checking. In: Brinksma, E., Larsen, K.G. (eds.) CAV 2002. LNCS, vol. 2404, pp. 359–364. Springer, Heidelberg (2002). https://doi.org/10.1007/3-540-45657-0_29
8. Costin, A., Zaddach, J.: Iot malware: Comprehensive survey, analysis framework and case studies (2018)
9. CSA: Security guidance for early adopters of the internet of things (iot), cloud security alliance, white paper (2015)
10. Dwyer, M.B., Avrunin, G.S., Corbett, J.C.: Patterns in property specifications for finite-state verification. In: Proceedings of the 1999 International Conference on Software Engineering (IEEE Cat. No.99CB37002), pp. 411–420 (May 1999). https://doi.org/10.1145/302405.302672
11. ENISA: Baseline security recommendations for iot in the context of critical information infrastructures, Technical report (2017). https://www.enisa.europa.eu/publications/baseline-security-recommendations-for-iot
12. ETSI: Methods for testing & specification; risk-based security assessment and testing methodologies, Technical report (2015). https://www.etsi.org/
13. Falcone, Y., Jaber, M., Nguyen, T.H., Bozga, M., Bensalem, S.: Runtime verification of component-based systems. In: Barthe, G., Pardo, A., Schneider, G. (eds.) SEFM 2011 - Proceedings of the 9th International Conference on Software Engineering and Formal Methods. Lecture Notes in Computer Science (LNCS), vol. 7041, pp. 204–220. Springer, Montevideo, Uruguay, November 2011. https://doi.org/10.1007/978-3-642-24690-6_15, https://hal.archives-ouvertes.fr/hal-00642969
14. Ge, M., Hong, J.B., Guttmann, W., Kim, D.S.: A framework for automating security analysis of the internet of things. J. Netw. Comput. Appl. **83**, 12–27 (2017). https://doi.org/10.1016/j.jnca.2017.01.033, http://www.sciencedirect.com/science/article/pii/S1084804517300541
15. Gutiérrez-Madroñal, L., La Blunda, L., Wagner, M.F., Medina-Bulo, I.: Test event generation for a fall-detection iot system. IEEE Internet Things J. **6**(4), 6642–6651 (2019). https://doi.org/10.1109/JIOT.2019.2909434
16. Holzmann, G.: The SPIN Model Checker: Primer and Reference Manual, 1st edn., Addison-Wesley Professional, Boston (2011)
17. ISO: Iso/iec 27030 information technology - security techniques - guidelines for security and privacy in internet of things (iot) (2019)
18. Khan, M.A., Salah, K.: Iot security: review, blockchain solutions, and open challenges. Future Gener. Comput. Syst. **82**, 395–411 (2018). https://doi.org/10.1016/j.future.2017.11.022, http://www.sciencedirect.com/science/article/pii/S0167739X17315765

19. Lally, G., Sgandurra, D.: Towards a framework for testing the security of iot devices consistently. In: Saracino, A., Mori, P. (eds.) Emerging Technologies for Authorization and Authentication, pp. 88–102. Springer International Publishing, Cham (2018)
20. Maksymyuk, T., Dumych, S., Brych, M., Satria, D., Jo, M.: An iot based monitoring framework for software defined 5g mobile networks. In: Proceedings of the 11th International Conference on Ubiquitous Information Management and Communication. IMCOM 2017, Association for Computing Machinery, New York, NY, USA (2017). https://doi.org/10.1145/3022227.3022331
21. Mariani, L., Pastore, F.: Automated identification of failure causes in system logs. In: Software Reliability Engineering, 2008. ISSRE 2008. 19th International Symposium on Software Reliability Engineering (ISSRE), pp. 117–126, November 2008. https://doi.org/10.1109/ISSRE.2008.48
22. Matheu-García, S.N., Ramos, J.L.H., Gómez-Skarmeta, A.F., Baldini, G.: Risk-based automated assessment and testing for the cybersecurity certification and labelling of iot devices. Comput. Stand. Interfaces **62**, 64–83 (2019)
23. Matheu Garcia, S.N., Hernández-Ramos, J., Skarmeta, A.: Toward a cybersecurity certification framework for the internet of things. IEEE Secur. Priv. **17**, 66–76 (2019). https://doi.org/10.1109/MSEC.2019.2904475
24. Mohsin, M., Anwar, Z., Husari, G., Al-Shaer, E., Rahman, M.A.: Iotsat: A formal framework for security analysis of the internet of things (iot). In: 2016 IEEE Conference on Communications and Network Security (CNS), pp. 180–188, October 2016. https://doi.org/10.1109/CNS.2016.7860484
25. Nadir, I., et al.: An auditing framework for vulnerability analysis of iot system, pp. 39–47 (June 2019). https://doi.org/10.1109/EuroSPW.2019.00011
26. NIST: Framework for improving critical infrastructure cybersecurity, version 1.1, standards and technology, Technical report (2018). https://doi.org/10.6028
27. OWASP: Owasp testing guide v3.0 project (2020). http://www.owasp.org/index.php/Category:OWASP_Testing_Project#OWASP_Testing_Guide_v3
28. "Red-Hat-Software": The business rule management system drools, March 2020. https://www.drools.org/
29. Salva, S., Blot, E.: Verifying the application of security measures in iot software systems with model learning. In: van Sinderen, M., Fill, H., Maciaszek, L.A. (eds.) Proceedings of the 15th International Conference on Software Technologies, pp. 350–360, ICSOFT 2020, Lieusaint, ScitePress, Paris, France, 7–9 July 2020. https://doi.org/10.5220/0009872103500360
30. Salva, S., Blot, E.: Cktail: model learning of communicating systems. In: Proceedings of the 15th International Conference on Evaluation of Novel Approaches to Software Engineering, ENASE 2020, Prague, CZECH REPUBLIC, 5–6 May 2020
31. Salva, S., Blot, E.: Verifying the application of security measures in iot software systems with model learning, companion site (2020). https://perso.limos.fr/~sesalva/tools/mlc/. Accessed Oct 2020
32. Siby, S., Maiti, R.R., Tippenhauer, N.O.: Iotscanner: Detecting and classifying privacy threats in iot neighborhoods. CoRR abs/1701.05007 (2017). http://arxiv.org/abs/1701.05007
33. Wilson, J., Wahby, R., Corrigan-Gibbs, H., Boneh, D., Levis, P., Winstein, K.: Trust but verify: Auditing the secure internet of things, pp. 464–474 (July 2017). https://doi.org/10.1145/3081333.3081342
34. Zhang, Z.K., Cho, M.C.Y., Shieh, S.: Emerging security threats and countermeasures in iot. In: Proceedings of the 10th ACM Symposium on Information, Computer and Communications Security, pp. 1–6. ASIA CCS15, Association for Computing Machinery, New York, NY, USA (2015). https://doi.org/10.1145/2714576.2737091

A Real-Time Integration of Semantic Annotations into Air Quality Monitoring Sensor Data

Besmir Sejdiu[1](✉), Florije Ismaili[1], and Lule Ahmedi[2]

[1] Contemporary Sciences and Technologies, South East European University, Tetovo, Macedonia
{bs26916,f.ismaili}@seeu.edu.mk

[2] Faculty of Electrical and Computer Engineering, University of Prishtina, Prishtinë, Kosova
lule.ahmedi@uni-pr.edu

Abstract. Nowadays, air pollution is one of the most serious problems in the world, therefore the real-time monitoring air quality is considered as necessity. Internet of Things (IoT) devices, such as sensors, enable real-time air quality monitoring, which produce sensed data continuously in the stream data, and transmit these data to a centralized server. Raw sensor stream data is useless unless properly annotated. Hence, the researchers proposed Semantic Sensor Web (SSW), which is a combination of Sensor Web and technologies of Semantic Web. However, how to advance techniques for integration of the semantic annotations in real-time is still an open issue that should be addressed. This research focuses on real-time integration of semantics into heterogeneous sensor stream data with context in the IoT. In this context, an IoT real-time air quality monitoring system and different semantic annotations are developed for sensor stream data in the format of Sensor Observation Service (SOS).

Keywords: Sensor stream data · Semantic annotations · Semantic Sensor Web (SSW) · Internet of Things (IoT)

1 Introduction

The Internet of Things (IoT) is new revolution of the Internet. It refers to the billions of physical devices around the world that are now connected to the Internet, all collecting and sharing data. Sensors are one of the main components that enable IoT, which send the observation in stream data.

Furthermore, sensor data are enabled to the web through the Sensor Web. Sensor Web by incorporating technologies of the Semantic Web creates the Semantic Sensor Web. In this way, sensor data stream can be annotated with semantics by providing machine-interpretable descriptions on what the data represents, where it originates from, how it can be related to its surroundings, who is providing it, and what are the quality, technical, and non-technical attributes [3]. The real-time integration of sensor data as dynamic data with semantics is defined as *real-time semantic annotation*, while sensor data that are

M. van Sinderen et al. (Eds.): ICSOFT 2020, CCIS 1447, pp. 98–113, 2021.
https://doi.org/10.1007/978-3-030-83007-6_5

stored in repository (data store) as static data, and then integrated with semantics is defined as *non-real-time semantic annotation* [16].

Organizations like Open Geospatial Consortium (OGC) and World Wide Web Consortium (W3C) have proposed several standards for sensor data. The OGC defines standardization for the Sensor Web named Sensor Web Enablement (SWE). It's a framework and a set of standards that allow exploitation of sensors and sets of sensors connected to a communication network. Is founded on the concept of "Web Sensor" using standard protocols and application interfaces [13].

This paper is an extended version of conference proceedings [15]. In [15], we have investigated on how to integrate semantic annotations into the sensor stream data. In particular, we have discussed the annotation techniques for real-time integration of semantics into heterogeneous sensor observation data and sensor metadata with context in the IoT. Different from conference proceedings [15], in this paper system architecture is advanced by adding new features such as archival data stream, an ontology, OGC standards, and Xlink annotated SOS. Also, implemented system is advanced as shown in Fig. 7.

The paper is organized as follows: Sect. 2 provides a discussion on literature review for semantic annotations to the sensor stream data. Section 3 is an overview of the difference between sensor streaming versus traditional streaming, semantic annotations concepts, and selection of technologies and standards for semantic annotations. An overview of the system architecture is presented in Sect. 4, while Sect. 5 represents the implemented system, including received sensor data format, integration of semantic annotations to the sensor data, and system outputs. Finally, Sect. 6 concludes the paper and identifies some of the future perspectives of the semantic integrations into the sensor stream data.

2 Literature Review

Recently, some researchers have already shown up with several investigations related to semantic enrichment of sensor stream data. Authors in [1] brought together semantic web and data mining in the context of IoT with a focus on sensors as interconnected devices, concluding that practical data mining applications can be built by usage of real world sensors ontologies, query mechanisms and linked sensor data available. SSW is described as a synthesis of sensor data and semantic metadata in [17]. It represents an approach by OGC and Semantic Web Activity of the W3C to provide meaning for sensor data. Construction of a Semantic Sensor Observation Service (SemSOS) based on the SWE standards is discussed in [7], by adding semantic annotations to sensor data and by using the ontology models to reason over sensor observations.

An extension of the SWE framework in order to support standardized access to sensor data is described in [11]. Furthermore, they list as future work the extension of SOS server with semantics, since the lack of semantically rich mechanism is seen as a significant issue, which makes it hard to explore related concepts, subgroups of sensor types, or other dependencies between the sensors and data collected.

3 Background

Currently, billions of interconnected IoT devices produce sensed data continuously in the stream data, and transmit these data to a centralized server. Due to the dramatically increase of streaming data, their management and exploitation has become increasingly important and difficult to process and integrate the semantic to sensor data stream in real time. Therefore, the selection of technologies and standards for technique development of real-time integration of semantics into heterogeneous sensor observation data and sensor metadata with context in the IoT is highly important. The proposed real-time semantic annotation system utilizes Spark Streaming[1], Apache Kafka[2], Apache Cassandra database[3], and standards like OGC Sensor Web Enablement standards, which will be discussed below.

3.1 Sensor Streaming Versus Traditional Streaming

The distinction between traditional data stream processing and sensor data stream processing is important because the sensory data stream have their own features [5]:

- The sensor data streams are only samples of entire population, while traditional streaming such as network streams, data of web logs, stock market, etc. represent the entire population of the data.
- The sensor data streams are considered noisy compared with traditional streaming data. Traditional streaming data is exact and error-free. Sometimes the environmental effect on the deployed sensor networks can also play a negative role on the sensed values. While web logs and web click streams are considered accurate values compared with data generated from sensor networks.
- The sensor data streams is typically of moderate size as compared to overwhelming storage and processing of huge data in traditional streams.

3.2 Semantic Annotations

IoT applications are enabled using heterogeneous sensors, which send observational data referred to as sensor stream data to a remote server. Raw sensor stream data is useless unless properly annotated. Therefore, the researchers proposed Semantic Sensor Web (SSW), which is a combination of Sensor Web and technologies of Semantic Web. Based on study [14], the explored publications show that major number of research are accepting the proposed industry standards, such as SWE, and techniques that can be used for annotating sensor data, such as Resource Description Framework in attributes (RDFa), XML Linking Language (Xlink), and Semantic Annotations for WSDL and XML Schema (SAWSDL), by different organizations like OGC and W3C [18]. However, how to advance techniques for integration of the semantic annotations in real-time is still an open issue that should be addressed.

[1] http://spark.apache.org.

[2] https://kafka.apache.org.

[3] http://cassandra.apache.org.

3.3 Technologies

The proposed real-time integrated semantic annotations to the sensor stream data for the IoT utilizes:

- *Spark Streaming*: Several stream data processing systems including Spark Streaming, Storm, Google Data Flow, and Flink have emerged to support real-time analytics for the streaming data sets [10]. Majority studies conclude that Spark Streaming works best with high throughput when the incoming volume is huge [6]. Therefore, we have chosen Sparking Streaming to develop our system for real-time integration of semantic annotations to sensor stream data. Spark Streaming is an extension of the Apache Spark that enables to build scalable fault-tolerant IoT applications for real-time processing sensor stream data. It can receive data from different input sources such as Apache Kafka, TCP sockets, Flume, Kinesis, Hadoop Distributed File System (HDFS), or Twitter, and can be processed using complex algorithms expressed with high-level functions like *map*, *join*, *reduce* and *window*. Finally, processed streaming data can be published in IoT real-time applications or can be pushed out to databases or file systems.
- *Apache Kafka*: Is a distributing streaming platform with capabilities to publish and subscribe to streams of records, similar to a message queue or enterprise messaging system, store streams of records in a fault-tolerant durable way, and process streams of records as they occur. Kafka is generally used for building real-time streaming data pipelines that reliably get data between systems or applications [9]. In our system Kafka is used as middleware between sensor stream data and Spark Streaming.
- *Apache Cassandra database*: Is a free and open source, distributed store for structure data that scale-out on cheap, commodity hardware or cloud infrastructure make it the perfect platform for mission-critical data. It is designed to handle large amounts of data across many commodity servers, providing high availability with no single point of failure. The Spark Streaming interacts well with Cassandra database. Therefore, in our system, the sensor stream data with their semantic annotations processed by Spark Streaming are stored in Cassandra database.

3.4 Standards

The OGC defines standardization for the Sensor Web named Sensor Web Enablement (SWE), which is divided into two parts [12]:

- *SWE Information Model*: Is comprised of conceptual language encodings that permits sensor observations visibility on the Internet. The SWE information model includes the following specifications: Sensor Model Language (SensorML), Observation and Measurement (O&M), and Transducer Model Language (TransducerML).
- *SWE Service Model*: Is a set of Web Service specifications that allow a client to search and find the required information. The SWE Service model includes the following specifications: Sensor Observation Service (SOS), Sensor Alert Service (SAS), Sensor Planning Service (SPS), and Web Notification Services (WNS).

To encode semantic annotations and data gathered by sensors, in this paper is used SOS O&M, which will be discussed in Sect. 5.2.

4 An Overview of the System Architecture

In the Fig. 1, an overview of the system architecture for real-time integration of semantics into heterogeneous sensor stream data with context in the Internet of Things is presented. As mentioned above, the proposed real-time semantic annotation system utilizes Apache Kafka, Spark Streaming, Apache Cassandra database, and SOS O&M standards.

The heterogeneous sensor stream data from the IoT-based sensor device is wirelessly transmitted to serve as the "producer" for the Kafka server. The "producer" client publishes streams of data to Kafka "topics" distributed across one or more cluster nodes/servers called "brokers". The published streams of data from Kafka are then processed by Apache Spark Streaming in parallel and real-time.

Kafka server is utilized to receive various formats of sensor data streams (e.g. text, binary, JSON, XML etc.), and to transform them in a particular format that will be processed by Spark Streaming.

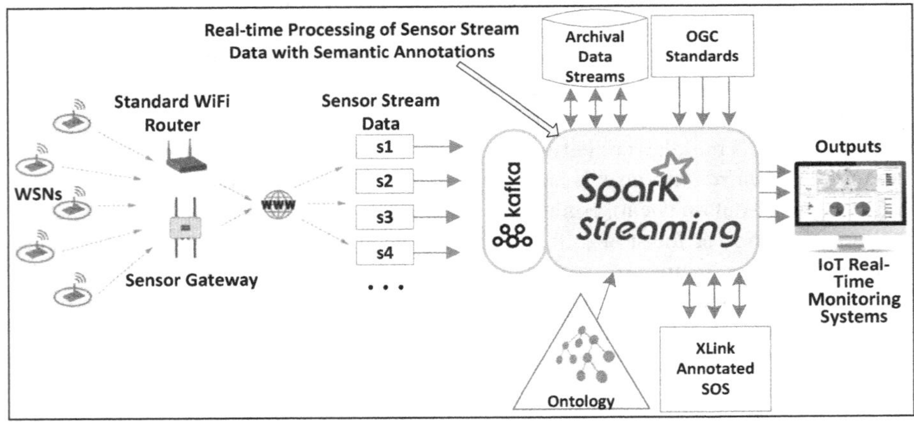

Fig. 1. An overview of the system architecture [15].

The Spark Streaming enables a real-time integration of semantics into heterogeneous sensor stream data with context in the IoT, by using sensor metadata, archival data streams, mining data streams, association rules for adding semantic annotations with concept definitions from ontologies or other semantic sources, which allows the understanding of senor data and metadata elements. The semantic annotations will be implemented into SOS O&M by using stakes, such as XLink (without including XPath) and Embedded (only a single value-scalar of semantic annotation) to add annotations in XML files. These annotations can point to extra sources of information (e.g. a file), or Uniform Resource Name (URN).

The enriched sensor stream data with the semantic annotations results will be stored in the Cassandra database, and will be displayed in IoT real-time monitoring system.

It is worth mentioning that Spark Streaming will process sensor data stream in format of OGC standards like SWE, respectively version 2.0 of the SOS standard to encode semantic annotations and data gathered by sensors [4].

The detailed description is presented in Sect. 5.2 where an example of integration of semantic annotations into the sensor stream data with context in the IoT is given.

5 System Implementation

An IoT real-time air quality monitoring system is developed to visualize sensor stream data and their semantic annotations, based on web platform. Sensor data of Hydrometeorological Institute of Kosovo (HMIK[4]) are used, through World Air Quality Index API (AQI API). The AQI API can be used for advanced programmatic integration, such as: access to more than 11000 station-level and 1000 city-level data, station name and coordinates, search station by name, geo-location query based on latitude/longitude, individual Air Quality Index (AQI) for all pollutants, current weather conditions, etc. [2].

5.1 Input Sensor Stream Data

The system receives raw sensor stream data from AQI API in JSON format, as presented in Fig. 2, which supports measuring in real-time of the following parameters:

- Carbon Monoxide (co),
- Humidity (h),
- Nitrogen Dioxyde (no2),
- Ozone (o3),
- Pressure (p),
- PM_{10} (pm10),
- PM_{25} (pm25),
- Sulphur Dioxide (so2),
- Temperature (t),
- Wind (w), and
- Water Gauge (wg).

As shown in Fig. 2, JSON data contains also attributes such as: *data* (station data: *idx* - unique id for the city monitoring station, *aqi* - real time air quality information, *time* - measurement time information, *s* - local measurement time, and *tz* - station time zone), *city* (information about the monitoring station: *name* - name of the monitoring station, *geo* - latitude/longitude of the monitoring station, and *url* - url for the attribution link), *attributions* (EPA Attribution for the station), and *iaqi* (measurement time information: *pm25* - individual AQI for the PM2.5, *v* - individual AQL for the PM2.5).

Data received by sensors every 6 min, through AQI API, are represented in corresponding numerical formats, e.g. in −3.8 (°C) for temperature parameter.

[4] http://ihmk-rks.net/.

5.2 Processing Sensor Stream Data by Integrating Semantic Annotations

In our system, an ontology name '*onto-core.owl*' is created (see Fig. 3). Here different semantic annotations for sensor stream data are developed, such as:

- #AIQ_Index,
- #Air_Pollution_Level, and
- #Health_Implications

#AIQ_Index annotation – is an index for reporting daily air quality, and tells how clean or polluted air is. United States Environmental Protection Agency (EPA[5]) calculates the AQI for five major air pollutants regulated by Clean Air Act: ground-level ozone, particle pollution (also known as particulate matter), carbon monoxide, sulfur dioxide, and nitrogen dioxide. The AQI range values is from 0 to 500.

According to EPA, the higher the AQI value, the greater the level of air pollution and the greater the health center (take the maximum of all individual AQI), as presented Eq. 1:

$$AQI = \max(AQI_{PM2.5}, AQI_{PM10}, AQI_{O3}, \ldots) \quad (1)$$

#Air_Pollution_Level annotation – based on the AQI value, its divided into six '*Air Quality Index Levels of Health Concern'* categories:

- *Good* (AQI is 0 to 50)
- *Moderate* (AQI is 51 to 100)
- Unhealthy for Sensitive Groups (101 to 150)
- *Unhealthy* (AQI is 151 to 200)
- *Very Unhealthy* (AQI is 201 to 300)
- *Hazardous* (AQI is 301 to 500)

#Health_Implications annotation – each of six categories described above, corresponds to a different level of health concert. *#Health Implications* annotation tells what they mean, for example *"Unhealthy for Sensitive Groups"* category means: 'Although general public is not likely to be affected at this AQI range, people with lung disease, older adults and children are at a greater risk from exposure to ozone, whereas persons with heart and lung disease, older adults and children are at greater risk from the presence of particles in the air.', or for *"Moderate"* category: 'Air quality is acceptable; however, for some pollutants there may be a moderate health concern for a very small number of people who are unusually sensitive to air pollution.'

The above described annotations are developed into ontology named '*ont-core'*.

After describing different types of the semantic annotations for sensor stream data, in the following is presented the process of semantic annotations.

The sensor stream data may arrive in different formats to Kafka server (JSON format - in our case), which will transform them in a specific format that will be processed by Spark Streaming. After that, through the Spark Streaming, based on measuring values, the sensor data stream will semantically be annotated and converted in SOS O&M format.

[5] https://www.epa.gov.

```
{
"status": "ok",
"data": {
  "aqi": 58,
  "idx": 12402,
  "attributions": [
    {
     "url": "http://worldweather.wmo.int",
     "name":"World Meteorological Organization - surface synoptic
observations (WMO-SYNOP)"
    },
    {
      "url": "http://ihmk-rks.net/",
      "name": "Instituti Hidrometeorologjik i Kosovës",
      "logo": "Kosovo-IHMK.png"
    },
    {
     "url": "https://waqi.info/",
     "name": "World Air Quality Index Project"
    }
  ],
  "city": {
    "geo": [ 42.648872, 21.137121 ],
    "name": "Prishtine - IHMK, Kosovo",
    "url": "https://aqicn.org/city/kosovo/prishtine-ihmk"
  },
  "dominentpol": "pm25",
  "iaqi": {
    "co": { "v": 33.3 }, "h": { "v": 76 },
    "no2": { "v": 6.2 }, "o3": { "v": 23.3 },
    "p": { "v": 1015.7 }, "pm10": { "v": 17 },
    "pm25": { "v": 58 }, "so2": { "v": 6.3 },
    "t": { "v": 1.6 },"w": { "v": 14 },
    "wg": { "v": 23 }
  },
  "time": {
    "s": "2020-03-25 20:00:00",
    "tz": "+01:00",
    "v": 1585166400
  },
  "debug": { "sync": "2020-03-26T04:17:09+09:00" }
}}
```


Fig. 2. Sensor stream data - JSON format [15].

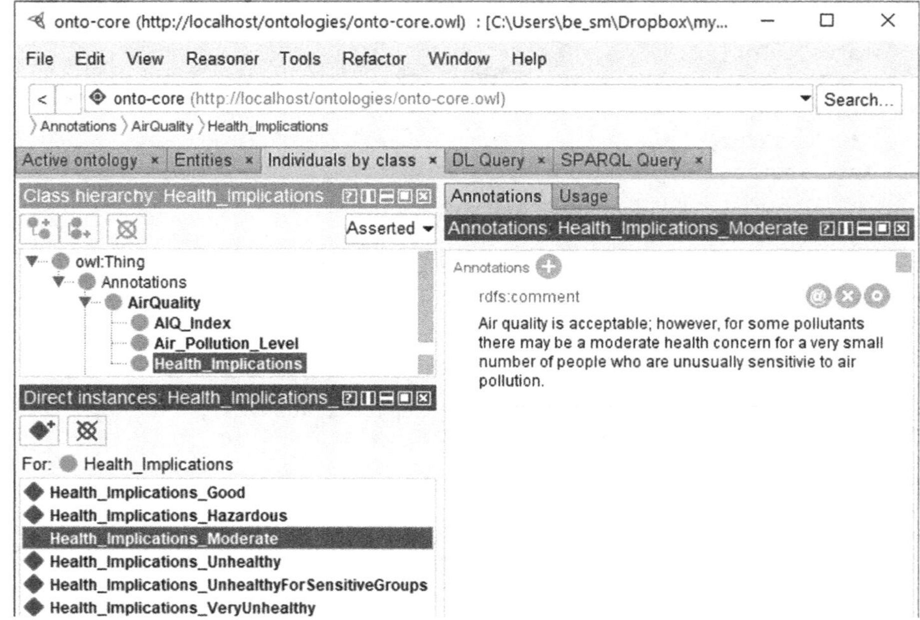

Fig. 3. 'Ont-core.owl' ontology.

A fragment of an example of integrated semantic annotations to the SOS O&M format by using stakes like XLink and Embedded, is presented in Fig. 4.

SOS O&M observation document comprise zero or multiple *observationData* entries, and each store an instance of an observation. In the following are presented common observation properties (the prefix gml indicates that this element is defined in OGC 07-033, while the prefix om indicates that the element is defined in OGC 10-025r1) [8]:

- *gml:identifier* (mandatory): identifies or refers to a specific observation.
- *om:phenomenonTime* (mandatory): describes the time instant or time period for which the observation contains sensor data.
- *om:resultTime* (mandatory): provides the time when the result became available (often this is identical to the phenomenonTime).
- *om:procedure* (mandatory): the identifier of the sensor instance that has generated the observation.
- *om:observedProperty* (mandatory): the identifier of the phenomenon that was observed.
- *om:featureOfInterest* (mandatory): an identifier of the geometric feature (e.g. sensor station) to which the observation is associated.
- *om:result* (mandatory): the observed value, the type of the result is restricted to the types shown in Table 1.

We have developed a new type of observation to add, named '*SemObservation*' with '*gml:Sem MeasureType*' result type, as shown and described in Table 2.

```
<sos:Observation ...="">
<observationData>
  <om:OM_Observation gml:id="o23525">
    <om:type xlink:href="http://www.opengis.net/def/ observationType/OGC-
OM/2.0/OM_Measurement"/>
    <om:phenomenonTime>
      <gml:TimeInstant gml:id="phenomenonTime_1">
        <gml:timePosition>2020-03-25T20:00:00+09:00</gml:timePosition>
      </gml:TimeInstant>
    </om:phenomenonTime>
    <om:resultTime xlink:href="#phenomenonTime_1"/>
    <om:procedure xlink:href="http://myserver/ontologies/ont-
core.owl#Sensor562415"/>
    <om:observedProperty xlink:href="http://myserver/ontologies/ont-
core.owl#PM25"/>
    <om:featureOfInterest xlink:href="http://myserver/ontologies/ont-
core.owl#Prishtine"/>
    <om:result xsi:type="gml:SemMeasureType" uom="pm25">
      <value>58</value>
      <sem-annotations>
        <annotation xlink:href="http://myserver/ontologies/ont-
core.owl#Air_Pollution_Level_Moderate"/>
        <annotation embedded:AIQ_Index ="58"/>
        <annotation xlink:href="http://myserver/ontologies/ont-
core.owl#Health_Implications_Moderate"/>
      </sem-annotations>
    </om:result>
  </om:OM_Observation>
</observationData>
. . .
</sos:Observation>
```

Fig. 4. An example of integrated semantic annotations to the sensor stream data [15].

For clearer explanation of semantic integration to sensor observation data, Fig. 5 illustrates (a) the concept of the O&M and relationship between the entities involved in observations, (b) data streams generated from wireless sensor networks, (c) the sensor data integrated with sensor metadata, archival data streams and the ontological knowledge, and finally, (d) the semantic annotated data with attributes: sem-annotations data, the observed value, unit, metadata, location, timestamp, result type, and gml:id of observation.

Table 1. Overview of observation types [8].

Observation type	Result type	Description	Example
Measurement	gml:MeasureType	Scalar numerical value with unit of measurement	<om:result uom="Cel">36</om:result>
Count observation	xs:integer	Count of an observed property	<om:result>12</om:result>
Truth observation	xs:boolean	Truth value (often existence) of an observed property	<om:result>true</om:result>
Category observation	gml:ReferenceType	Value from a controlled vocabulary	<om:result xlink:title="storm" xlink:href=http://en.wikipedia.org/wiki/Storm xsi:type="gml:ReferenceType"/>
Text observation	xs:string	Any kind of textual description of an observed property	<om:result>some text</om:result>
om:ComplexObservation with swe: DataArray	swe:DataArray	Compact representation of multiple observation values (e.g. time series), this observation types needs to be further restricted and enhanced by guidance in future revisions of the profile	–

5.3 System Outputs

To display the heterogeneous sensor stream data and their semantic annotations, is developed an real time IoT application in the *ASP.NET Core MVC*, a cross-platform, high-performance, open source framework for building modern, cloud-based, and Internet-connected applications. The '*DataStax C# for Apache Cassandra*' is used to read data from Apache Casandra database. It's a modern, feature-rich and highly tunable C# client

Table 2. The developed *SemObservation* observation type [15].

Observation type	Result type	Description	Example
Sem observation	*gml: Sem Measure Type*	Inside the result element, two children elements will be added: *value* and *sem-annotations*. The *value* element will contain a scalar numerical value, while the *sem-annotations* element will contain one or more annotation empty elements	*<om:result xsi:type="gml: SemMeasureType" uom="pm25"> <value>58</value> <sem-annotations> <annotation xlink:href="http://myserver/ontologies/ont-core.owl#Air_Pollution_Level_Moderate"/> <annotation embedded: AIQ_Index="58"/> <annotation xlink:href="http://myserver/ontologies/ont-core.owl#Health_Implications_Moderate"/> </sem-annotations> </om:result>*

library. To display the data in the map, is used *Leaflet*, an open-source JavaScript library for interactive web maps. *Leaflet* is designed with simplicity, performance and usability in mind. It works efficiently across all major desktop and mobile platforms out of the box, taking advantage of HTML5 and CSS3 on modern browsers while being accessible on older ones too.

As shown in Fig. 6 and Fig. 7 (map & table view), the users can observe the quality of air pollution on certain geographical points in map marked as measuring nodes. Each node (marker) has an AQI Index, to indicate air pollution. When clicking over a whatever marker, the latest measurement values obtained for that point will be shown, such as: PM2.5, PM10, O3, NO2, SO2, CO, Temperature, Pressure, Humidity, Wind, Water Gauge, and semantic annotations, such as: #AQI Index, #Air Pollution Level, and #Health Implications.

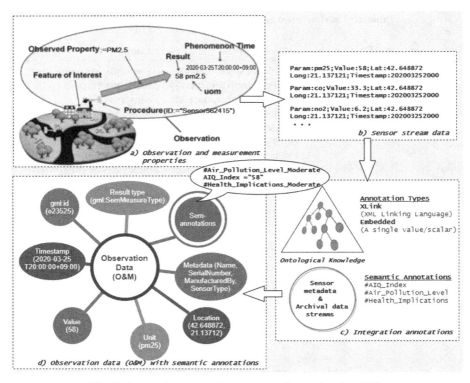

Fig. 5. Integrating semantics to sensor observation data [15].

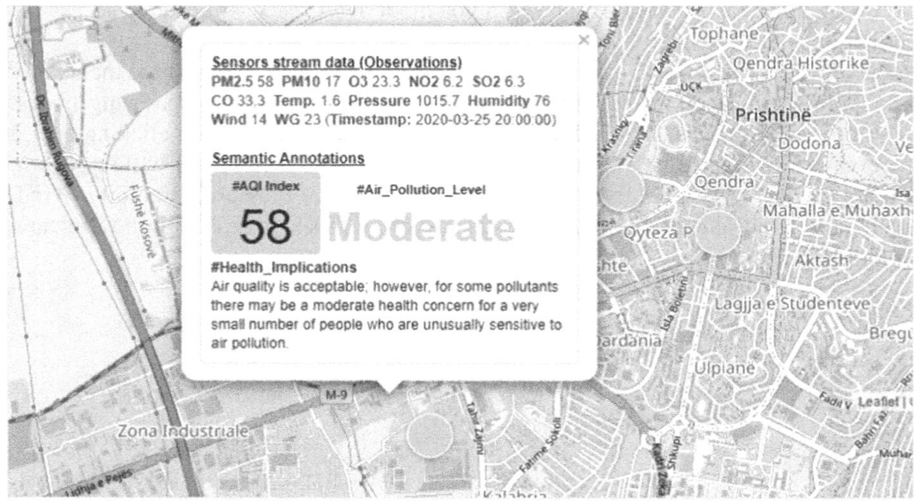

Fig. 6. System outputs: map view [15].

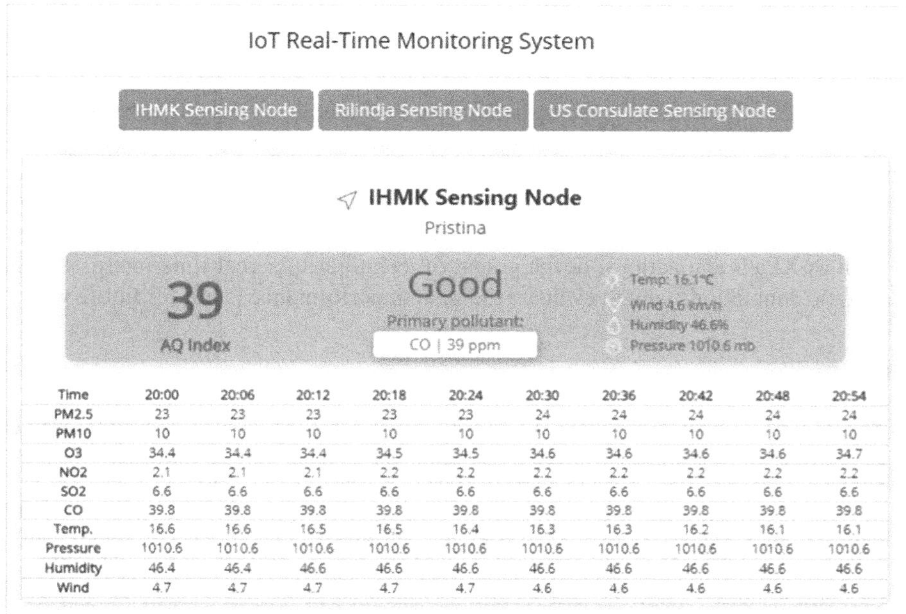

Time	20:00	20:06	20:12	20:18	20:24	20:30	20:36	20:42	20:48	20:54
PM2.5	23	23	23	23	23	24	24	24	24	24
PM10	10	10	10	10	10	10	10	10	10	10
O3	34.4	34.4	34.4	34.5	34.5	34.6	34.6	34.6	34.6	34.7
NO2	2.1	2.1	2.1	2.2	2.2	2.2	2.2	2.2	2.2	2.2
SO2	6.6	6.6	6.6	6.6	6.6	6.6	6.6	6.6	6.6	6.6
CO	39.8	39.8	39.8	39.8	39.8	39.8	39.8	39.8	39.8	39.8
Temp.	16.6	16.6	16.5	16.5	16.4	16.3	16.3	16.2	16.1	16.1
Pressure	1010.6	1010.6	1010.6	1010.6	1010.6	1010.6	1010.6	1010.6	1010.6	1010.6
Humidity	46.4	46.4	46.6	46.6	46.6	46.6	46.6	46.6	46.6	46.6
Wind	4.7	4.7	4.7	4.7	4.7	4.6	4.6	4.6	4.6	4.6

Fig. 7. System outputs: table view.

6 Conclusions and Future Work

WSNs are one of the main components of the IoT. They produce the observed data in continuous form, known as sensor stream data and transmit to the server for further processing. Raw sensor data are useless unless properly annotated. By adding semantic annotations with concept definitions from ontologies, it's possible the interpretation and understanding of sensor data streams.

First, this study provides a literature review related to the topic of the integration of semantics into sensor data for the IoT. Next, is describes the distinction between traditional data stream processing and sensor data stream processing. Then, are presents the selected technologies and standards (such as Spark Streaming, Apache Kafka, Apache Cassandra, and OGC standards) which are used to develop the proposed system. After that, an overview of the system architecture for real-time integration of semantics into heterogeneous sensor stream data with context in the Internet of Things is presented. Finally, an system implementation of an IoT real-time air quality monitoring system is presented, including:

- *input sensor stream data* in JSON format of the following measuring parameters: carbon monoxide, humidity, nitrogen dioxyde, ozone, pressure, pm10, pm25, sulphur dioxide, temperature, wind, and water gauge;
- *processing sensor stream data by integrating semantic annotations* to the sensor stream data in SOS O&M format, and a new type of observation *SemObservation* (with *gml:Sem MeasureType* result type) is developed;

- *system outputs* to display the heterogeneous sensor stream data and their semantic annotations in map and table view format.

This paper is an extended version of conference proceedings [15]. Different from this conference proceedings, in this paper system architecture is advanced by adding new features such as archival data stream, an ontology, OGC standards, and Xlink annotated SOS.

Extending the system with more advanced real-time annotation techniques of semantics such as XPath annotations, development of techniques for real-time interpretation of semantic annotations, and to evaluate the system performance is left for future work.

References

1. Aggarwal, C.C., Ashish, N., Sheth, A.: The internet of things: a survey from the data-centric perspective. In: Aggarwal, C.C. (ed.) Managing and Mining Sensor Data, pp. 383–428. Springer, Boston (2013). https://doi.org/10.1007/978-1-4614-6309-2_12
2. Aqicn: API – Air Quality Programmatic APIs. https://aqicn.org/api. Accessed 20 Feb 2020
3. Barnaghi, P., Wang, W., Henson, C., Taylor, K.: Semantics for the Internet of Things: early progress and back to the future. Int. J. Semant. Web Inf. Syst. (IJSWIS) **8**(1), 1–21 (2012)
4. Bröring, A., Stasch, C., Echterhoff, J.: OGC sensor observation service interface standard. Open Geospatial Consortium Interface Standard, 12-006 (2012)
5. Elnahrawy, E.: Research directions in sensor data streams: solutions and challenges. Rutgers University, Technical report. DCIS-TR-527 (2003)
6. Gorasiya, D.V.: Comparison of open-source data stream processing engines: spark streaming, flink and storm. Technical report (2019). https://doi.org/10.13140/RG.2.2.16747.49440
7. Henson, C.A., Pschorr, J.K., Sheth, A.P., Thirunarayan, K.: SemSOS: semantic sensor observation service. In: International Symposium on Collaborative Technologies and Systems, CTS 2009, pp. 44–53. IEEE (2009)
8. Jirka, S., Stasch, Ch., Bröring, A.: OGC Best Practice for Sensor Web Enablement, Lightweight SOS Profile for Stationary In-Situ Sensors. Open Geospatial Consortium. Version 1.0, ref. no. 11-169r1 (2014)
9. Kafka Apache: Kafka Apache – A distributed streaming platform. https://kafka.apache.org. Accessed 15 Feb 2020
10. Karimov, J., Rabl, T., Katsifodimos, A., Samarev, R., Heiskanen, H., Markl, V.: Benchmarking distributed stream data processing systems. In: Proceedings of the IEEE 34th International Conference on Data Engineering (ICDE), Paris, France (2018)
11. Lee, Y.J., Trevathan, J., Atkinson, I., Read, W.: The integration, analysis and visualization of sensor data from dispersed wireless sensor network systems using the SWE framework. J. Telecommun. Inf. Technol. **4**, 86 (2015)
12. OGC Standards: Open Geospatial Consortium (OGC). https://www.ogc.org/docs/is/. Accessed 05 Jan 2020
13. Pradilla, J., Palau, C., Esteve, M.: SOSLITE: Lightweight Sensor Observation Service (SOS) for the Internet of Things (IOT). ITU Kaleidoscope: Trust in the Information Society, Barcelona (2016)
14. Sejdiu, B., Ismaili, F., Ahmedi, L.: Integration of semantics into sensor data for the IoT - a systematic literature review. Int. J. Semant. Web Inf. Syst. (IJSWIS) **16**(4), Article 1 (2020)
15. Sejdiu, B., Ismaili, F., Ahmedi, L.: A real-time integration of semantics into heterogeneous sensor stream data with context in the Internet of Things. In: The 15th International Conference on Software Technologies (ICSOFT 2020), Lieusaint - Paris, France, 07–09 July 2020 (2020)

16. Sejdiu, B., Ismaili, F., Ahmedi, L.: A management model of real-time integrated semantic annotations to the sensor stream data for the IoT. In: The 16th International Conference on Web Information Systems and Technologies (WEBIST 2020), Budapest, Hungary, 03–05 November 2020 (2020)
17. Sheth, A., Henson, C., Sahoo, S.: Semantic sensor web. IEEE Internet Comput. **12**(4), 78–83 (2008). https://doi.org/10.1109/MIC.2008.87
18. W3C Semantic Sensor Network Incubator Group (SSN-XG): Semantic Sensor Network Ontology. https://www.w3.org/2005/Incubator/ssn/ssnx/ssn. Accessed 25 Feb 2020

On Improvement of Formal Verification of Reconfigurable Real-Time Systems Using TCTL and CTL-Based Properties on IaaS Cloud Environment

Chams Eddine Choucha[1(✉)], Mohamed Ramdani[1], Moahmed Khalgui[1,2], and Laid Kahloul[3]

[1] LISI Laboratory, National Institute of Applied Sciences and Technology (INSAT), University of Carthage, 1080 Tunis, Tunisia

[2] School of Electrical and Information Engineering, Jinan University (Zhuhai Campus), Zhuhai 519070, China

[3] LINFI Laboratory, Computer Science Department, Biskra University, Biskra, Algeria

Abstract. The verification of reconfigurable real-time systems that dynamically change their structures due to external changes in environment or user requirements continues to challenge experts which have to face new challenges such as fault tolerance, response in time, flexibility, modularity, etc. Moreover, such systems face constraints as real-time requirements, their generated state spaces are much bigger, consequently, properties to be verified are more complex, which makes the formal verification more complex. For modeling systems, in this paper, we use Reconfigurable Timed Net Condition/Event Systems (R-TNCESs) for the optimal functional and temporal specification. To control the complexity and to reduce the verification time, a new method of properties verification in a cloud-based architecture is proposed. The novelty consists of a new method for state space generation and the decomposition of the complex properties for running an efficient verification. Moreover, An algorithm is proposed for the incremental state space generation. An application of the paper's contribution is carried out on a case study to illustrate the impact of using this technique. The current results show the benefits of the paper's contribution.

Keywords: Discrete-event system · Reconfiguration · R-TNCES · Computation Tree Logic · CTL · Cloud computing · Formal verification

1 Introduction

Reconfigurable discrete event control systems (RDECSs) such as manufacturing systems [11], real time systems and intelligent control systems [10,12] are complex. RDECSs satisfy several conditions such as concurrency, control and communication. In fact, RECESs are the trend of future systems. However, ensuring the safety of these systems is crucial especially when dealing with critical situations. Formal verification is, therefore, imperative. RDECSs have flexible configurations that allow them to switch

M. van Sinderen et al. (Eds.): ICSOFT 2020, CCIS 1447, pp. 114–133, 2021.
https://doi.org/10.1007/978-3-030-83007-6_6

from a configuration to another due to user requirements or to prevent system malfunctions [6]. This verification consists of two major steps: state-space generation and state-space analysis. Mentioned steps applications are usually expensive in terms of computation time and memory occupation (i.e., huge accessibility graph to be generated and complex properties to be verified) [19]. The authors in [17] proposed to classify properties automatically and to introduce a priority order during RDECSs verification to control the high number of properties to be verified. The mentioned method improves verification by reducing the number of properties to be verified by exploiting relationships among properties (equivalence, composition and dominance). However, when the property relationship rate is low which is frequent while verifying complex RDECSs, the said method is equivalent to the classic ones. The authors in [6] proposed a method for accessibility graph generation with less computing time and less required memory, while preserving the graph semantics. They start by computing the initial TNCES accessibility graph classically, then making updates on it to compute the remaining TNCESs accessibility graphs, while considering similarities between them. Previous methods improve classical ones. However, with large scale systems, their application using a unique machine (i.e., a centralized system) may be expensive in terms of time and calculation [13]. Authors in [2] initiate the cloud-based solution for formal method problems. Authors have proposed a distributed fixed-point algorithm to check CTL properties with basic operators. The said algorithm can analyze DECS efficiently. However, RDECSs complexity forced us to move forward with big data solutions for formal method problems. To cope with RDECSs, Petri nets has been extended and developed by several works [14]. Reconfigurable Timed Net Condition/Event System (R-TNCES) is a novel formalism proposed in [18], where reconfiguration and time properties with modular specification are provided in the same formalism. This Paper deals with RDECSs modeled by R-TNCES. Authors in [2] developed a CTL Model checker in the cloud using map-reduce. The basic idea is to increase computation power and data availability to reduce time execution. They perform distributed fixed-point algorithm. However, the authors do not consider the system model similarities, which involves redundant calculations during verification. Moreover, this verification method support only simple CTL properties expressed with a restricted number of operator-quantifier combinations. Both of layer-by-layer verification proposed in [20] and the formal verification method proposed in [6] focused on the improvement of the state space generation phase, thus, they neglect state space analysis. The authors in [17] proposed automatic properties classification and introduced a priority order during RDECSs verification to control the high number of properties. The said method improves verification by reducing the number of properties by proposing an approach for exploiting relationships among them (equivalence, composition and dominance). In [16], the authors proposed Reconfigurable Computation Tree Logic R-CTL as an extension of CTL. This logic adds properties relationships management to deals redundancy caused by relationships (dominance, composition, and equivalence). RCTL improves version of CTL in terms of expressiveness, However processing RCTL properties verification on the generated space in a sequential way remains hard. Authors in [7] proposed a new method for state space generation, which extends classical accessibility graphs (AGs) to timed accessibility graphs (TAGs). The said method is efficient when dealing with reconfigurable real-time systems, it allows us to control complexity in the analysis step during verification. In our previous works, we propose a method for state space generation which, considers similarities that an R-TNCES can contain, thanks to an ontology-based history. Also, we proposed in [5] to perform CTL properties verification in a parallel way on a cloud-based architecture while considering relationships among properties. The said methods are efficient; However, the first work is only focused on state space generation, and the second one presents limits when properties are complex and properties relationship rate is low. Therefore, we propose in this paper a new work that comes to fill the limits of precedent ones. Hence, we proposed a new method that aims to improve R-TNCES formal verification. Reconfigurable Real-time systems formal verification may be expensive in terms of computation power and memory occupation, therefore, we resort to a cloud-based solution to increase computation power (resp. memory occupation) thank to the Infrastructure as a service IaaS (reps. Simple Storage Service S3) proposed by Amzon [8]. To control systems formal verification complexity we propose the following contributions:

1. Incremental timed state space generation to facilitate the access to different parts of the accessibility graph; Certain properties do not require the entire exploration of the accessibility graph in order to be validated or not, therefore, a partial exploration of the accessibility graph is sufficient. Indeed, we introduce the modularity and the time concepts to the state-space generation step, which allows us to access different parts of the accessibility graph (modules) and help us to face time constraints. This contribution allows us to proceed to a targeted verification.
2. Decomposition of CTL properties to control complexity during the state-space analysis. Due to the systems complexity, properties to be verified in order to ensure the correctness of the system behavior are more complex. Thereby, increasing the complexity of the analysis step. In order to fix the mentioned issue, we check the possibility of decomposition of the complex properties into several simple or less complex properties that can be verified in less computation time using fewer resources.
3. Development of a distributed cloud-based architecture to perform parallel computations during formal verification and to store large scale data. The huge generated state spaces, the high number of properties to be verified, and time constraints forced us to opt for a big data solution to control the complexity of reconfigurable real-time systems formal verification. Computation tasks are ensured by the master and the workers via virtual machines allocated thanks to the EC2 product proposed by amazon. Data storage is ensured by S3.

This paper is an extended version of our previous paper [3], presented at the 'IC-SOFT 2020' conference. The method improves by

- Replacing classical accessibility graphs by the Timed accessibility graphs proposed in [7].
- Using temporal logic TCTL in addition to CTL in order to respond to the real-time constraints.
- Updating the proposed cloud-based architecture to deal with the verification of reconfigurable real-time constraints.

The main objective of this paper is to propose a new formal verification method that improves the classical ones by controlling complexity. As a running example, a formal case study is provided to demonstrate the relevance of our contributions. The obtained results are compared with different works. The comparison shows that the verification is improved in terms of execution time (i.e., less complexity to perform systems formal verification).

The remainder of the paper is organized as follows. Section 2 presents some required concepts. The distributed formal verification is presented in Sect. 3. Section 4 presents the evaluation of the proposed method. Finally, Sect. 5 concludes this paper and gives an overview about our future work.

2 Background

In this section, we present basic concepts which are required to follow the rest of the paper.

2.1 Reconfigurable Timed Net Condition/Event System

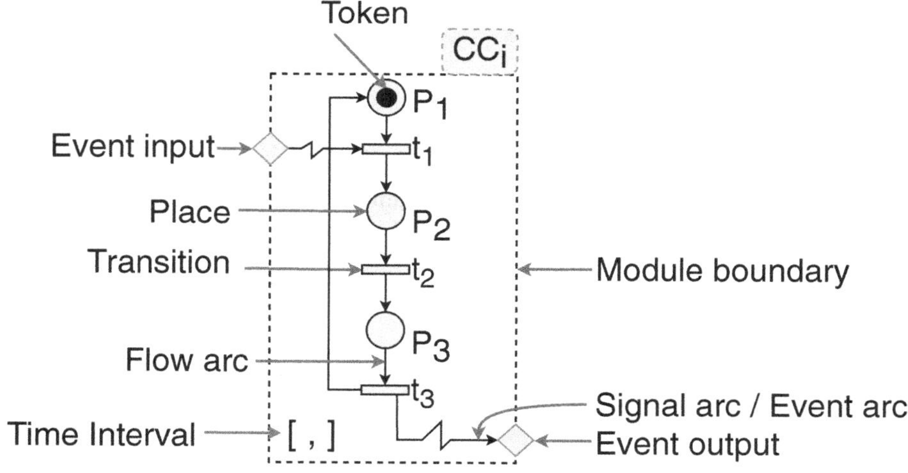

Fig. 1. Graphical model of a generic control component modeled by TNCES [3].

R-TNCES is a modeling formalism used to specify and verify reconfigurable Real Time Systems. R-TNCES is based on Petri nets and control components CCs. A control component (CC) is defined as a software unit. Control components are applied as a formal model of the controller of a physical process and are modeled by TNCES as shown in Fig. 1. Each CC resumes the physical process in three actions: Activation, working and termination. An R-TNCES RTN is defined in [20] as a couple $RTN = (B, R)$, where R is the control module and B is the behavior module. B is a union of multi TNCES-based CC modules, represented by

$$B = (P; T; F; W; CN; EN; DC; V; Z_0)$$

where,

a) P (resp, T) is a superset of places (resp, transitions),
b) F is a superset of flow arcs,
c) W: $(P \times T) \cup (T \times P) \rightarrow \{0, 1\}$ maps a weight to a flow arc, $W(x, y) > 0$ if $(x, y) \in F$, and $W(x, y) = 0$ otherwise, where $x, y \in P \cup T$,
d) CN (resp, EN) is a superset of condition signals (resp, event signals),
e) DC is a superset of time constraints on input arcs of transitions,
f) $V : T \rightarrow \wedge, \vee$ maps an event-processing mode for every transition;
g) $Z_0 = (M_0, D_0)$, where M_0 is the initial marking, and D_0 is the initial clock position.

R is a set of reconfiguration functions $R = \{r_1, ..., r_n\}$. r is structured as follow: $r = (Cond, s, x)$ such that:

1. $Cond \rightarrow$ {true, false} is the pre-condition of r, which means specific external instructions, gusty component failures, or the arrival of certain states.
2. s: $TN(^*r) \rightarrow TN(r^*)$ such that $TN(^*r)$(resp. $TN(r^*)$) be the original (resp. target) TNCES before (resp. after) r application is the structure modification instruction.
3. x: $last_{state}(TN(^*r)) \rightarrow initial_{state}(r^*)$ is the state processing function, where $last_{state}(TN(^*r))$ (resp. $initial_{state}(TN(r^*))$) is the last (resp. the initial) state of $TN(^*r)$ (resp. $TN(r^*)$).

2.2 Timed Accessibility Graph

Timed accessibility graphs is an extension on accessibility graphs proposed in [7], during model-checking it allows us to control verification complexity thank its time property. Timed accessibility graph (TAG) of a TNCES TNS is a structure tAG given by

$$tAG(St, Ed, S_O)$$

where,

- St denotes the set of reachable states;
- Ed: $St \rightarrow St$ denotes the set of edges that defines state-transitions such that each edge is labeled by the executed step;
- s_0 denotes the initial state.

A state $s \in St$ is a structure given by

$$State(M_p, Pclocks, D)$$

where,

- M_p is the set of marked places;
- $Pclockst$ s is a vector of integers representing places clock positions;
- D is the delay of the state which denotes the minimal number of time units after which at least one step becomes enabled.

2.3 Computation Tree Logic CTL

Computational tree logic CTL is a temporal logic for branching-time based on propositional logic used by [1] for model checking. CTL can describe the context and branching of the system state, it models system evaluation as a tree-like structure where each state can evolve in several ways (i.e., specify behavior systems from an assigned state in which the formula is evaluated by taking paths). CTL has a two-stage syntax where formulae in CTL are classified into state and path formulae. The former is formed according to the following grammar:

$$\Phi ::= true|AP|\Phi_1 \wedge \Phi_2|\Phi_1 \vee \Phi_2|\neg\Phi|E\varphi|A\varphi$$

While path formulae which express temporal properties of paths are formed according to the following grammar:

$$\varphi ::= X\Phi|F\Phi|G\Phi|\Phi_1 U \Phi_2$$

where Φ, Φ_1 and Φ_2 are state formulae. AP is the set of atomic propositions. The CTL syntax include several operators for describing temporal properties of systems: A (for all paths), E (there is a path), X(at the next state), F (in future), G (always) and U (until).

Definition 1. *Equivalence of CTL Formulae: CTL formulae σ_1 and σ_2 (over AP) are called equivalent, denoted $\sigma_1 \equiv \sigma_2$ whenever they are semantically identical. Therefore, $\sigma_1 \equiv \sigma_2$ if $Sat(\sigma_1) = Sat(\sigma_2)$ for all transition systems TS over AP such that $Sat(\sigma) = \{s \in S|s \models \sigma\}$. Table 1 presents an important set of equivalences rules (expansion and distributive laws).*

Table 1. Some equivalence rules for CTL.

Expansion laws
$EG\phi \equiv \phi \wedge EXEG\phi$
$AF\phi \equiv \phi \vee AXAF\phi$
$EF\phi \equiv \phi \vee EXEF\phi$
$A[\phi U \psi] \equiv \psi \vee (\phi \wedge AXA[\phi U \psi])$
$E[\phi U \psi] \equiv \psi \vee (\phi \wedge EXE[\phi U \psi])$
Distributive laws
$AG(\sigma_1 \wedge \sigma_2) \equiv AG\sigma_1 \wedge AG\sigma_2$
$EF(\sigma_1 \vee \sigma_2) \equiv EF\sigma_1 \vee EF\sigma_2$

2.4 Infrastructure as a Service IaaS

Cloud computing is an increasingly popular paradigm for ubiquitous, convenient, on-demand network access to a shared pool of configurable computing resources. In practice, cloud service providers tend to offer services that can be grouped into three categories as follows:

(i) software as a service,
(ii) platform as a service, and
(iii) infrastructure as a service presented in Fig. 2.

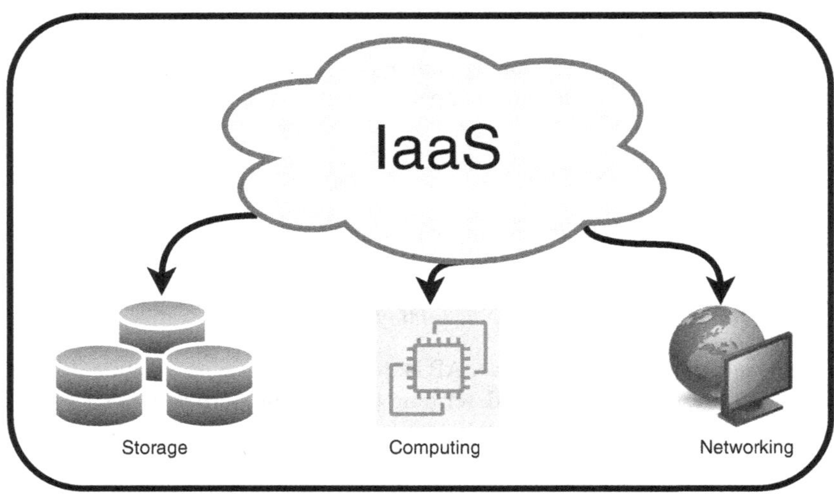

Fig. 2. Infrastructure as a Service.

IaaS is defined by [8] as web service that provides provision processing, storage, networks, administrative services needed to store applications and a platform for running applications [8]. It is designed to make web-scale cloud computing easier for developers. Amazon Web Services Elastic Compute Cloud (EC2) and Secure Storage Service (S3) are examples of IaaS offerings as shown in Fig. 2.

3 Distributed Cloud Based Formal Verification

We present in this section the proposed distributed cloud-based formal verification of R-TNCESs.

3.1 Motivation

R-TNCES is an expressive formalism, which allows considering different aspects of Reconfigurable real-time systems (time, probability, reconfigurability and concurrency) [9]. The correctness of systems modeled by R-TNCES can be ensured by formal verification. However, such a formalism makes the verification process complex, due to the combinatorial growth of the state space according to the model size, and due to the high number and complexity of the properties that the designer wants to verify. Thus, we aim to make model checking more efficient by reducing the time validation of properties to be verified. Therefore, we propose a new method for R-TNCES verification, which facilitates both generation and analysis of state space. To ensure our objective, we implement different tasks that can be presented in two parts as follows:

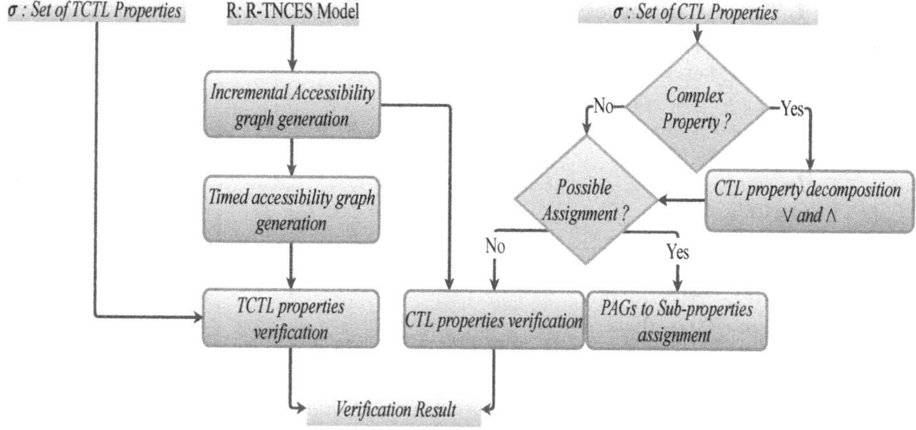

Fig. 3. Global idea for the formal verification according to the distributed cloud based verification.

- *Part 1*: CTL properties verification:
  a) Incremental state space generation, which is to construct the state space by part,
  b) the complex properties are decomposed to simple or less complex ones, then
  c) if possible, we assign a partial graph to the property to be verified.
  d) Finally, we proceed to CTL properties verification.
- *Part 2*: TCTL properties verification:
  a) Timed state space generation, which is generated from accessibility graphs computed during part 1, then
  b) we proceed to TCTL properties verification.

Figure 3 presents scheduling of the presented tasks.

3.2 Formalization

In this section, we present formal verification steps according to the distributed cloud-based formal verification of R-TNCESs.

Incremental State Space Generation. Incremental state space generation consists of generating accessibility graphs by part, while preserving models semantics. Let $RTN(R, B)$ be an R-TNCES model, this task consists in two steps:

(i) Basic accessibility graph generation BAG, which consists of generating accessibility graphs for each $CC_i \in TNCES_j$ where, $i \in 0 \ldots NumberCC(TNCES_j)$ and $j \in 0 \ldots NumberTN(B)$. This step is implemented in Algorithm 1. It takes an R-TNCESs as input and proceed to BAGs generation through several function including $Generate\_State\_Space(CC)$ which, take a CC modeled by TNCES and return its accessibility graph using SESA tool [15].

Algorithm 1. Timed Basic accessibility generation.

```
Input: RTN: R-TNCES; TN_0: TNCES;
Output: S_TBAG: Set of elementary accessibility graphs;
for int i = 0 to | ∑TN | do
    for each CC ∈ TN do
        if ( !Tagged (CC)) then
            Insert(S_BAG, Generate_State_Space(CC));
            tag(CC);
        end
    end
    for each BAG ∈ S_BAG do
        if ( !Tagged (BAG)) then
            Insert(S_BAG, Generate_TBAG(BAG));
            tag(BAG);
        end
    end
end
return S_TBAG
```

Algorithm 2. Accessibility graph construction.

```
Input: S_TBAG: Set of Times basic accessibility graphs ; ∑CChain: Set of Cchains;
Output: S_AG: Set Accessibility graphs;
for int i = 0 to | ∑CChain | do
    AG ← TBAG_{CC_i^0};
    for int j = 0 to | ∑CC_i | do
        AG ← Compose(AG, TBAG_{CC_i^j});
    end
    Insert(S_AG, AG)
end
return S_AG
```

(ii) Basic Timed Accessibility Graph BTAG Generation from a Graph BAG, which consists on generating a new graphs that consider time properties from another graph, we adopt the algorithm proposed in [7] to proceed to the TBAGs generation as shown in Fig. 4

(iii) Partial accessibility graphs (PAGs) composition: This step is implemented in Algorithm 2. It consists of composing pair of graphs computed during the first step (BAGs) and throughout iterations of the second step (PAGs), mainly by using the function $Compose(AG, AG)$ that takes two graphs and composes them and returns a new composed graph.

Complex CTL Properties Decomposition. We assume that properties that contain the operators ($\wedge$) or ($\vee$) are complex. Two kinds of complex properties are distinguished as follows:

- Decomposable: The operators ($\wedge$) or ($\vee$) are not linked to factors (State operators or path quantifiers). This kind of properties are directly splited into a set of sub-properties (e.g., $\Phi = P_1 \wedge P_2$ gives $\sigma_1 = P_1$ and $\sigma_2 = P_2$) (Fig. 5).

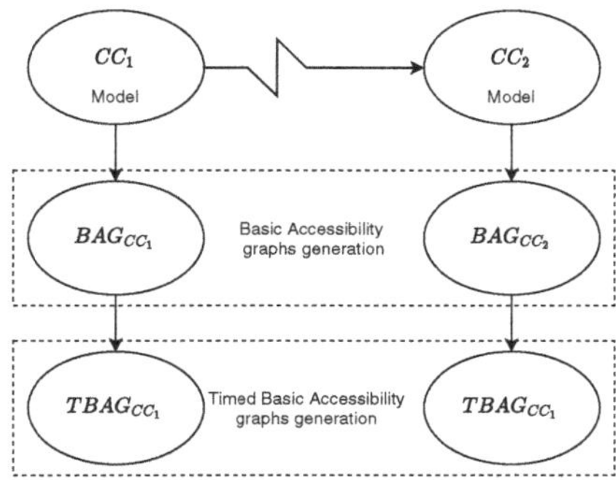

Fig. 4. Timed Basic accessibility graph generation.

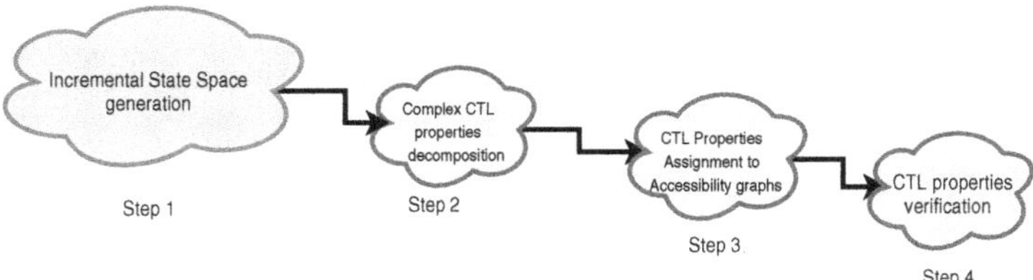

Fig. 5. First step of reconfigurable real time systems verification.

- Non-decomposable: The operators $(\wedge)$ or $(\vee)$ are linked to factors. For this kind of properties, we firstly applied expansion or distribution laws and then re-check if they are decomposable or not (Fig. 6).

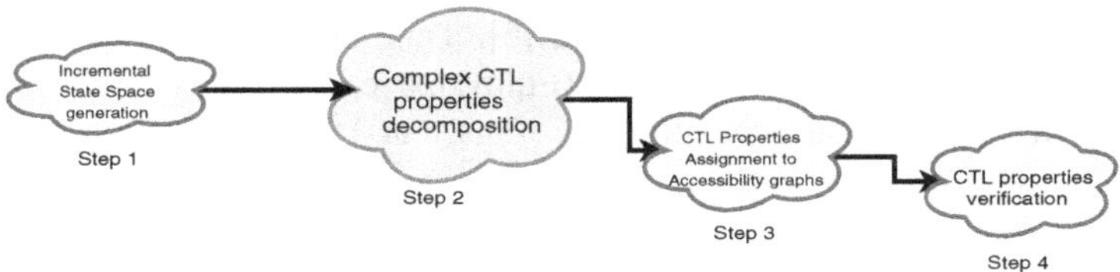

Fig. 6. Second step of reconfigurable real time systems verification.

Figure 7 shows the majors steps of complex CTL properties decomposition task.

CTL Properties Assignment to PAGs. We assign to each property one or several state spaces computed during incremental state space generation. The assignment is done based on two criteria:

(i) Path quantifier and state operators, and
(ii) places concerned by the property such that we assign the smallest state space that contains the concerned places.

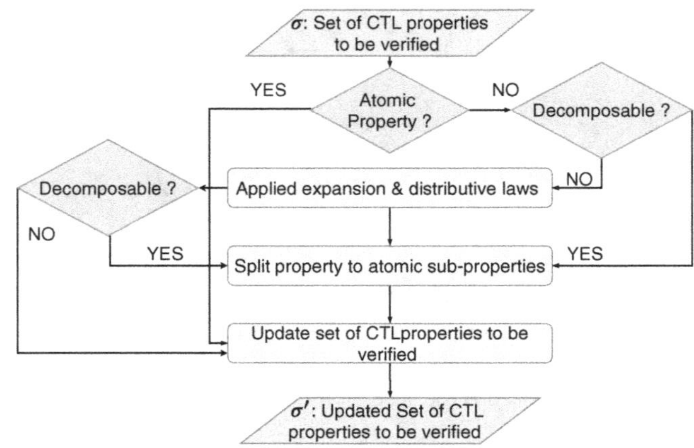

Fig. 7. Complex CTL properties decomposition.

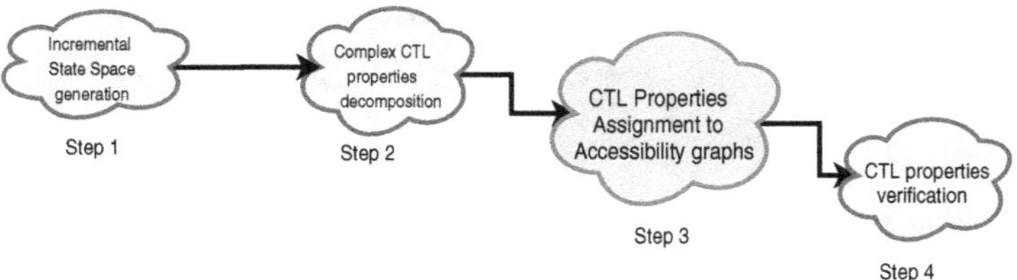

Fig. 8. Third step of reconfigurable real time systems verification.

CTL Properties Verification. In short-term we integrate CTL properties verification method inspired from methods proposed in [5]. This method consider relationships which exist among properties to be verified (Equivalence, dominance and composition) and processes the verification in parallel way (Figs. 8 and 9).

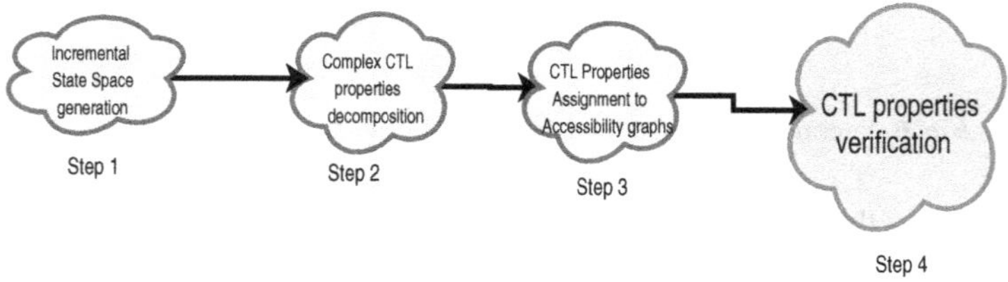

Fig. 9. Fourth step of reconfigurable real time systems verification.

3.3 Distributed Architecture for Formal Verification

In this subsection, we present the proposed distributed cloud-based architectures shown in Fig. 10. The idea that motivates the development of this architecture is to increase

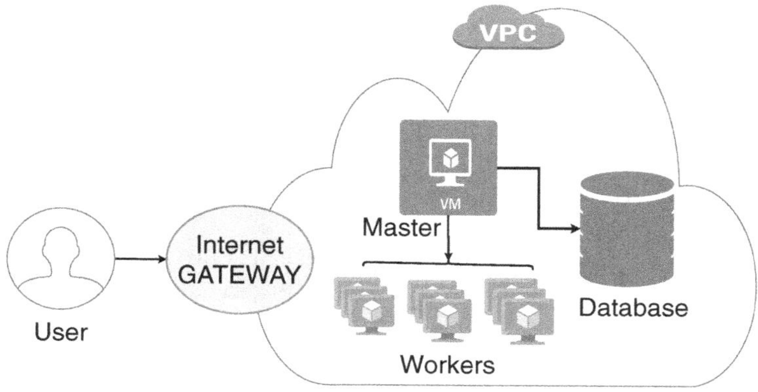

Fig. 10. Distributed cloud-based architecture.

computation power and storage availability. It is composed of computational and storage resources. To develop the architecture shown in Fig. 10, we use IaaS to allocate the following resources:

- Computation resources: which represent the master that coordinates the executed tasks, and the workers that execute the presented tasks above.
- Storage resources: represents the allocated cloud database that stores accessibility graphs computed during verification.

3.4 Reconfigurable Real-Time System Verification in a Distributed Cloud-Based Architecture

The Reconfigurable real-time system verification is performed on the proposed architecture as follow

- $Master$: has the coordinator role it:
  - Receives the verification request;
  - Sends to each worker the task to perform (Accessibility graph generation, Properties decomposition and assignment, and CTL or TCTL properties verification);
  - Stores and retrieves data from storage unit.
- $workers$: perform different tasks received from the Master and return the results.

Note that the TCTL properties are considered as non-decomposable, thus the Master distributes them to the works for parallel verification by considering the time constraints.

4 Experimentation

In this section, to validate and demonstrate the gain of our proposed contributions, we use a formal case study.

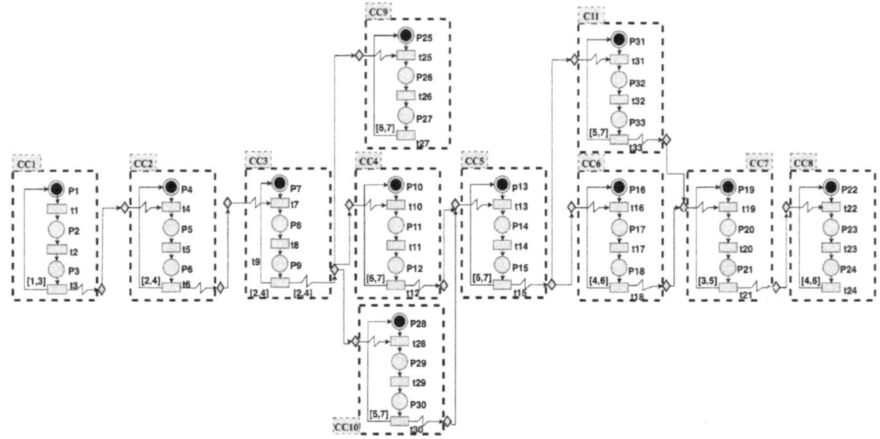

Fig. 11. Behavior model with three configurations process.

4.1 Case Study

To demonstrate the performance and the gain of the proposed contribution, we use R-TNCES formalism to model a sequential system S_{01}, used in the original conference paper [3], which is denoted by $RTN_{S_{01}}(B_{S_{01}}, R_{S_{01}})$. S_{01} is composed of 11 physical processes modeled by 11 CCs. The behavior module of the system ($B_{S_{01}}$) is modeled graphically as shown in Fig. 11. This model covers three configurations (C_1, C_2, C_3). It is assumed that every configuration has one control chain (C_{Chain_i}) as follows.

- C_{Chain_1}: CC_1, CC_2, CC_3, CC_9.
- C_{Chain_2}: $CC_1, CC_2, CC_3, CC_4, CC_5, CC_{11}, CC_7, CC_8$.
- C_{Chain_3}: $CC_1, CC_2, CC_3, CC_{10}, CC_5, CC_6, CC_7, CC_8$.

This behavior module can be reconfigured automatically and timely between the three configurations ($C_i, i = 1, ..., 3$), according to the environment changes or to the user requirements. $RTN_{S_{01}}$ can apply six different reconfiguration scenarios according to the control module $R_{S_{01}}$, which are described as follows: $R_{S_{01}} = (C_1, C_2); (C_1, C_3);(C_2, C_1); (C_2, C_3); (C_3, C_1); (C_3, C_2)$.

4.2 Application

In this section, we present the application of the formal verification of $RTN_{S_{01}}$ according to the cloud-based formal verification.

Incremental State Space Generation. In order to generates $RTN_{S_{01}}$ accessibility graph $AG_{RTN_{S_{01}}}$, we apply Algorithms 1 and 2. First, we generates accessibility graphs for each physical process, which are denoted by ($TBAG_i$, $i =_{1,...,11}$). Then, we proceed to successive pair graphs compositions until we constitute $AG_{RTN_{S_{01}}}$. Table 2

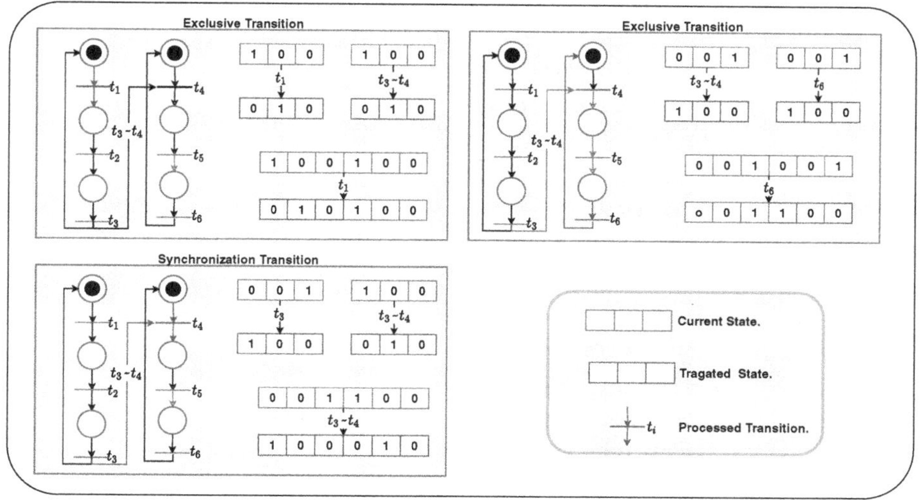

Fig. 12. Example of accessibility graphs composition according to the transition type.

Table 2. Incremental state space generation [3].

R-TNCES model	Control chains	PAGs
RTN_{S01}	$CChain_1$	$(CC_1, CC_2); (CC_1, CC_2, CC_3); (CC_1, CC_2, CC_3, CC_9)$
	$CChain_2$	(CC_1, CC_2, CC_3, CC_4), $(CC_1, CC_2, CC_3, CC_4, CC_5)$, $(CC_1, CC_2, CC_3, CC_4, CC_5, CC_{11})$, $(CC_1, CC_2, CC_3, CC_4, CC_5, CC_{11}, CC_7)$, $(CC_1, CC_2, CC_3, CC_4, CC_5, CC_{11}, CC_7, CC_8)$
	$CChain_3$	$(CC_1, CC_2, CC_3, CC_{10})$, $(CC_1, CC_2, CC_3, CC_{10}, CC_5)$, $(CC_1, CC_2, CC_3, CC_{10}, CC_5, CC_6)$, $(CC_1, CC_2, CC_3, CC_4, CC_5, CC_6, CC_7)$, $(CC_1, CC_2, CC_3, CC_4, CC_5, CC_6, CC_7, CC_8)$

shows PAGs computed during the first step of the system verification. Note that each computed PAG is stored in the cloud database. Moreover, Fig. 12 shows an example of a pair graphs composition.

Decomposition of CTL Properties. In order to validate the basic behavior of the system and to guarantee that system model satisfies the good requirements, we must ensure the CTL functional properties. In particular, to ensure: a) The safety, the system allows only one process to be executed at any time, i.e., no activation of two CCs from two different configurations at the same time, b) the liveness, whenever any process wants to change the configuration, it will eventually be allowed to do so, and c) the non-blocking, any active CC is eventually ended. Table 3 presents the above mentioned properties specified by CTL.

Table 3. Set of CTL properties to be verified [3].

σ: Set of CTL Properties
P_1: $EF(p_3)$, P_2: $AF(p_9)$,
P_3: $AF(p_{15})$, P_4: $AF(p_{21})$,
P_5: $AF(p_{24})$, P_6: $AF(p_{17})$,
P_7: $AF(p_{32})$, P_8: $AF(p_{35})$
P_9: $EF(p_{12} \wedge EG(p_{24}))$,
P_{11}: $EG(p_{12} \wedge EGp_{35}))$,
P_{12}: $EG(p_{12} \wedge EG(p_{33}))$,
P_{13}: $\neg EF(p_{27} \wedge EG(p_{24}))$,
P_{14}: $EF(p_{12}) \wedge EF(p_{18})$,
P_{15}: $AF(p_{12}) \wedge EG(p_{33}) \wedge EG(p_{21}) \wedge AF(p_{24})$,
P_{16}: $AF(p_{12}) \wedge EG(p_{33}) \wedge EG(p_{21}) \wedge AF(p_{24})$

Table 4. CTL properties decomposition and assignment [3].

σ: Set of CTL properties	Decomposition	Assignment
P_1: $EF(p_3)$, P_2: $AF(p_9)$, P_3: $AF(p_{15})$, P_4: $AF(p_{21})$, P_5: $AF(p_{24})$, P_6: $AF(p_{17})$, P_7: $AF(p_{32})$, P_8: $AF(p_{35})$	Non-decomposable	P_1: $TBAG_1$, P_2: CC_1, CC_2, CC_3, P_3: $CC_1, ..., CC_5$, P_4: $CC_1, ..., CC_7$, P_5: $CC_1, ..., CC_8$, P_6: $CC, ..., CC_6$, P_7: $CC, ..., CC_{11}$
P_9: $EF(p_{12} \wedge EG(p_{24}))$, P_{12}: $EG(p_{12} \wedge EG(p_{33}))$, P_{13}: $\neg EF(p_{27} \wedge EG(p_{24}))$,	Non-decomposable	P_9: $CC_1, ..., CC_8$, P_{12}: $CC_1, ..., CC_{11}$, P_{13}: $CC_1, ..., CC_8$
P_{14}: $EF(p_{12}) \wedge EF(p_{18})$	P'_{14}: $EF(p_{12})$ P''_{14}: $EF(p_{18})$	P'_{14}: $CC_1, ..., CC_4$ P''_{14}: $CC_1, ..., CC_6$
P_{15}: $AF((p_{12}) \wedge EG((p_{33})) \wedge EG(p_{21})) \wedge AF(p_{24})$	P'_{15}: $AF(p_{12})$ P''_{15}: $EG((p_{33}) \wedge EG(p_{21}))$ P'''_{15}: $AF(p_{24}$	P'_{15}: $CC_1, ..., CC_4$, P''_{15}: $CC_1, ..., CC_7$, P'''_{15}: $CC_1, ..., CC_8$
P_{16}: $AF(p_{12}) \wedge EG(p_{33}) \wedge EG(p_{21}) \wedge AF(p_{24})$	P'_{16}: $AF(P_{12})$ P''_{16}: $\neg AF(p_{30})$	P'_{16}: $CC_1, ..., CC_4$, P''_{16}: $CC_1, ..., CC_{10}$

Assignment of CTL Properties to PAGs. We apply the possible decomposition to the CTL properties in σ, then we assign each property to be verified to the correspondent accessibility graph (BAG or PAG). The results are shown in Table 4.

CTL and TCTL Properties Verification. CTL properties are distributed according to their assignment one by one on workers by the Master, then workers proceed to their verification using the SESA tool [15]. Where, TCTL properties are non-decomposable thus their distribution depends on time constraints. Table 5 shows a set of TCTL properties. The order of verification of the mentioned properties is: $P_1, P_2 > P_3, P_4, P_6 > P_7 > P_5$.

Table 5. TCTL properties to be verified.

$\sigma_{F_{MPS}}$: Set of TCTL properties
P_1: $EF[1,3]p_3 = 1$,
P_2: $EF[10,18]p_9 = 1$,
P_3: $EF[10,28]p_{12} = 1$,
P_4: $EF[9,41]p_{18} = 1$,
P_5: $EF[26,43]p_{24} = 1$,
P_6: $EF[10,18]p_{27} = 1$,
P_7: $EF[20,42]p_{33} = 1$,

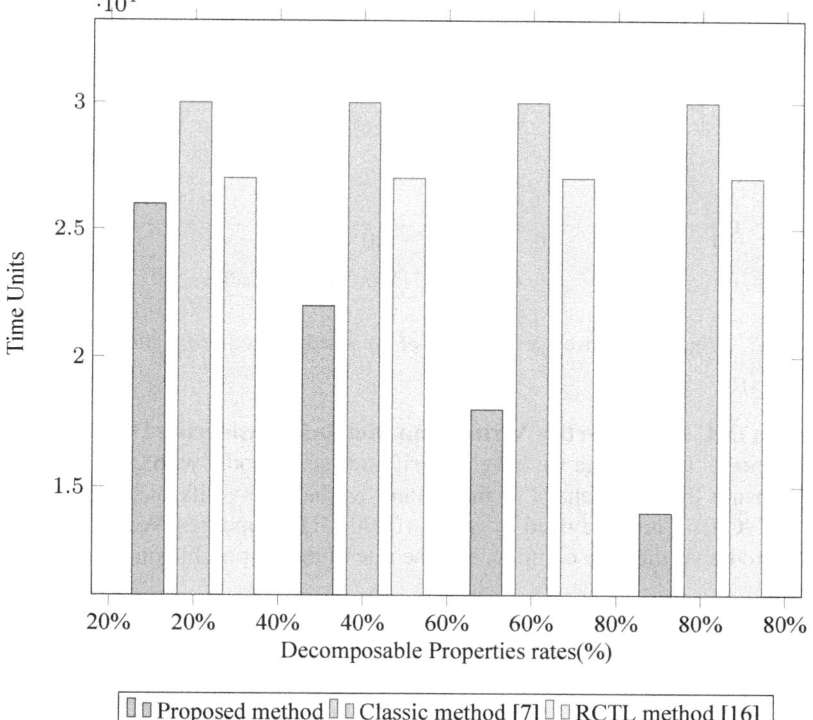

Fig. 13. Classic methods VS Proposed method.

4.3 Evaluation

In this subsubsection, the evaluation of the proposed method is presented considering two factors: The decomposable rate and the complex CTL properties rate.

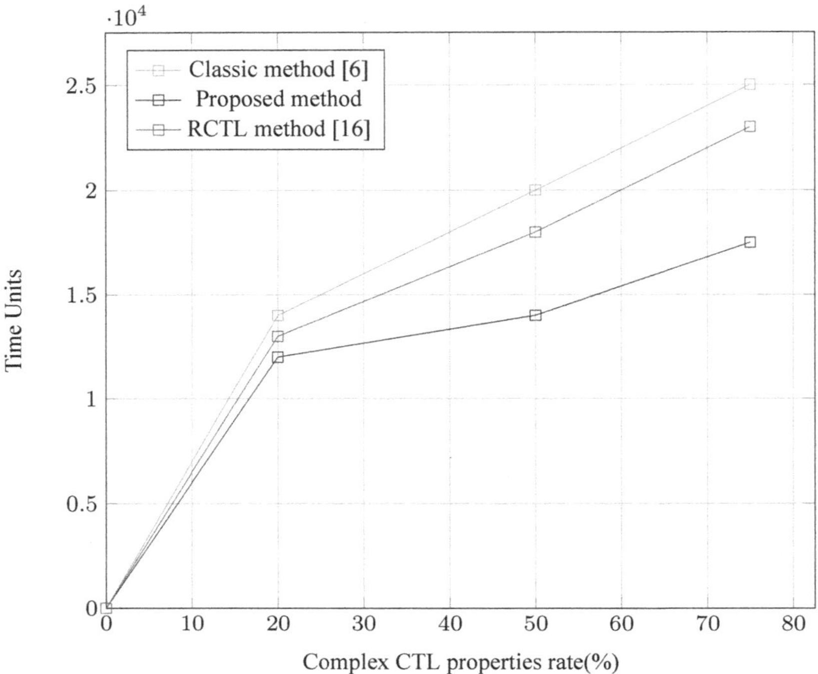

Fig. 14. Improved performance of proposed method verification.

Evaluation of CTL Properties Verification Method Considering Different Decomposable Ratex. Let assume we have to verify a system model with 2500 TNCESs. In order to ensure the well-behave of the system we have to verify at least 4 properties for each TNCES. Thus, we need to verify 10000 CTL properties. We assume that the properties to be verified are complex and the rate of decomposable one can be:

(i) Low in $0, 20\%$,
(ii) $Medium$ in $20, 60\%$, or
(iii) $High$ when more than 60%.

The results show in Fig. 13 that the gain increases proportionally to decomposable properties rate. Thus, the gain is clearly shown when similarity rate is 'High'. This is explained by the fact that, when properties are decomposed their verification is less complex [4].

Evaluation of CTL Properties Verification Method Considering Complex CTL Properties Rate. Figure 14 we can observe an important gain when performing parallel verification thanks to the proposed architecture. This gain is explained by the fact that the proposed architecture allows us to reduce considerably times execution by

(i) Avoiding redundant calculation,
(ii) Avoiding wait time execution,
(iii) Performing several properties verification at the same time.

5 Conclusion

This work deals with the formal verification of reconfigurable real-time systems modeled by R-TNCES using CTL and TCTL specifications. In this paper, we present a cloud-based solution for the formal verification problem. A distributed cloud-based architecture is developed with two hierarchical levels (Master and worker) where, data storage is ensured by Amazon Simple Storage S3 (Murty, 2008)). It allows us to increase computational power, data availability, and to perform parallel execution. The proposed method aims to improve state space analysis by using a hybrid distributed cloud-based architecture for computation tasks. Developed architecture is composed of:

1. A local workstation, where simple computation tasks are executed. First, a classification algorithm is applied in order to distinguish between simple and composed properties. Then, we compute a matrix relationships that mention any eventual relationship between each couple of properties. Finally, we generate a parallelization tree that we explore to extract a suitable execution order for each property to be verified.
2. A virtual workstation, where complex tasks are computed. Virtual machines use SESA tool to perform CTL properties verification and stores results in the shared memory.

We introduce the modularity and the timed concept to the generated state spaces which allow us to execute the generation step in a parallel way via several workers (virtual machines) and to deal with time constraints. We detect the complex CTL properties and decompose them into several simple or less complex properties, then proceed to their verification via workers using the SESA tool [15]. The TCTL properties are them verified following the order established by the master according to the time constraints. Incremental Timed state space generation and the decomposition of CTL properties allow us to run a targeted verification, which is less complex and more efficient in terms of execution time. This work opens several perspectives; first, we plan to apply our approach in the verification of real-case with complex properties to check the functional and the temporal specifications. Then, automatize the detection of complex properties by using the IA thanks to ontologies. Also, we plan to introduce a deep learning method to detect similar behavior of systems, which will allow us to reduces complexity during verification. Besides, To apply our methodology in the verification process of many research fields in (i) smart systems like smart grids, (ii) robotics, (iii) vehicular technologies, and other more evaluations of the proposed contributions.

References

1. Baier, C., Katoen, J.P.: Principles of Model Checking. MIT Press, Cambridge (2008)
2. Camilli, M., Bellettini, C., Capra, L., Monga, M.: CTL model checking in the cloud using mapreduce. In: 2014 16th International Symposium on Symbolic and Numeric Algorithms for Scientific Computing (SYNASC), pp. 333–340. IEEE (2014)
3. Choucha, C.E., Ramdani, M., Khalgui, M., Kahloul, L.: On decomposing formal verification of CTL-based properties on IaaS cloud environment. In: Proceedings of the 15th International Conference on Software Technologies, Volume 1: ICSOFT, pp. 544–551. INSTICC, SciTePress (2020). https://doi.org/10.5220/0009972605440551
4. Choucha, C.E., Salem, M.B., Khalgui, M., Kahloul, L., Ougouti, N.S.: On the improvement of R-TNCESs verification using distributed cloud-based architecture. In: Proceedings of the 15th International Conference on Software Technologies, Volume 1: ICSOFT, pp. 339–349. INSTICC, SciTePress (2020). https://doi.org/10.5220/0009836103390349
5. Choucha, C.E., Ougouti, N.S., Khalgui, M., Kahloul., L.: R-TNCES verification: distributed state space analysis performed in a cloud-based architecture. In: Proceedings of the the 33rd Annual European Simulation and Modelling Conference, pp. 96–101. ETI, EUROSIS (2019)
6. Hafidi, Y., Kahloul, L., Khalgui, M., Li, Z., Alnowibet, K., Qu, T.: On methodology for the verification of reconfigurable timed net condition/event systems. IEEE Trans. Syst. Man Cybern. Syst. **99**, 1–15 (2018)
7. Hafidi, Y., Kahloul, L., Khalgui, M., Ramdani, M.: New method to reduce verification time of reconfigurable real-time systems using R-TNCESs formalism. In: Damiani, E., Spanoudakis, G., Maciaszek, L.A. (eds.) ENASE 2019. CCIS, vol. 1172, pp. 246–266. Springer, Cham (2020). https://doi.org/10.1007/978-3-030-40223-5_12
8. Hayes, B.: Cloud computing. Commun. ACM **51**(7), 9–11 (2008)
9. Housseyni, W., Mosbahi, O., Khalgui, M., Li, Z., Yin, L., Chetto, M.: Multiagent architecture for distributed adaptive scheduling of reconfigurable real-time tasks with energy harvesting constraints. IEEE Access **6**, 2068–2084 (2017)
10. Järvensivu, M., Saari, K., Jämsä-Jounela, S.L.: Intelligent control system of an industrial lime kiln process. Control. Eng. Pract. **9**(6), 589–606 (2001)
11. Khalgui, M., Hanisch, H.M.: Reconfiguration protocol for multi-agent control software architectures. IEEE Trans. Syst. Man Cybern. Part C (Appl. Rev.) **41**(1), 70–80 (2011)
12. Khalgui, M., Mosbahi, O., Li, Z., Hanisch, H.M.: Reconfiguration of distributed embedded-control systems. IEEE/ASME Trans. Mechatron. **16**(4), 684–694 (2011)
13. Koubâa, A., Qureshi, B., Sriti, M.F., Javed, Y., Tovar, E.: A service-oriented cloud-based management system for the internet-of-drones. In: 2017 IEEE International Conference on Autonomous Robot Systems and Competitions (ICARSC), pp. 329–335. IEEE (2017)
14. Padberg, J., Kahloul, L.: Overview of reconfigurable Petri nets. In: Heckel, R., Taentzer, G. (eds.) Graph Transformation, Specifications, and Nets. LNCS, vol. 10800, pp. 201–222. Springer, Cham (2018). https://doi.org/10.1007/978-3-319-75396-6_11
15. Patil, S., Vyatkin, V., Sorouri, M.: Formal verification of intelligent mechatronic systems with decentralized control logic. In: Proceedings of 2012 IEEE 17th International Conference on Emerging Technologies & Factory Automation (ETFA 2012), pp. 1–7. IEEE (2012)
16. Ramdani, M., Kahloul, L., Khalgui, M., Li, Z., Zhou, M.: RCTL: new temporal logic for improved formal verification of reconfigurable discrete-event systems. IEEE Trans. Autom. Sci. Eng. 1–14 (2020). https://doi.org/10.1109/TASE.2020.3006435
17. Ramdani, M., Kahloul, L., Khalgui, M.: Automatic properties classification approach for guiding the verification of complex reconfigurable systems. In: ICSOFT, pp. 625–632 (2018)
18. Zhang, J., et al.: R-TNCES: a novel formalism for reconfigurable discrete event control systems. IEEE Trans. Syst. Man Cybern. Syst. **43**(4), 757–772 (2013)

19. Zhang, J., et al.: Modeling and verification of reconfigurable and energy-efficient manufacturing systems. Discret. Dyn. Nat. Soc. **2015** (2015)
20. Zhang, J., Khalgui, M., Li, Z., Mosbahi, O., Al-Ahmari, A.M.: R-TNCES: a novel formalism for reconfigurable discrete event control systems. IEEE Trans. Syst. Man Cybern. Syst. **43**(4), 757–772 (2013)

A Genetic Algorithm with Tournament Selection for Automated Testing of Satellite On-board Image Processing

Ulrike Witteck[1(✉)], Denis Grießbach[1(✉)], and Paula Herber[2(✉)]

[1] Institute of Optical Sensor Systems, German Aerospace Center (DLR), Berlin-Adlershof, Germany
{ulrike.witteck,denis.griessbach}@dlr.de

[2] Embedded Systems Group, University of Münster, Münster, Germany
paula.herber@uni-muenster.de

Abstract. In the satellite domain, on-board image processing technologies are subject to extremely strict requirements with respect to reliability and accuracy in hard real-time. In this paper, we address the problem of automatically selecting test cases from a huge input domain that are specifically tailored to provoke mission-critical behavior of satellite on-board image processing applications. Due to the large input domain of such applications, it is infeasible to exhaustively execute all possible test cases. Moreover, the high number of input parameters and complex computations make it difficult to find specific test cases that cause mission-critical behavior. To overcome this problem, we define a test approach that is based on a genetic algorithm combined with input parameter partitioning. We partition the input parameters into equivalence classes to automatically generate a reduced search space with complete coverage of the input domain. Based on the reduced search space, we run a genetic algorithm to automatically select test cases that provoke worst case execution times and inaccurate results of the satellite on-board image processing application. For this purpose, we define a two-criteria fitness function and evaluate two different selection methods with a case study from the satellite domain. We show the efficiency of our test approach on experimental results from the Fine Guidance System of the ESA medium-class mission PLATO.

Keywords: Image processing · Software testing · Genetic algorithms

1 Introduction

Several on-board image processing applications in the satellite domain are subject to extremely strict requirements especially with regard to reliability and mathematical accuracy in hard real-time. Therefore, it is important to test such applications extensively. However, their huge input domain makes manual testing error-prone and time-consuming. Executing all possible test cases is impossible.

M. van Sinderen et al. (Eds.): ICSOFT 2020, CCIS 1447, pp. 134–157, 2021.
https://doi.org/10.1007/978-3-030-83007-6_7

Due to this problem, we are looking for a test approach that automatically and systematically generates test cases for testing satellite on-board image processing applications. However, the automated test generation for such applications poses two major challenges: first, a huge amount of possible test cases because of a large number of input parameters that make a systematic and efficient coverage of the whole input domain infeasible. Second, due to complex algorithmic computations it is difficult to select test cases with a high probability to provoke mission-critical behavior. That are scenarios where, for example, the real-time behavior of the system or the delivered mathematical accuracy does not meet specified requirements. Such scenarios may cause system failures, damages, or unexpected behavior during mission lifetime.

In [3,7,8,14–16], the authors investigate various real-time embedded systems with huge input domains and complex functional behavior. However, the presented approaches are not designed to search for test cases provoking real-time critical behavior and scenarios where the mathematical accuracy of the application gets critically low at the same time.

In this paper, we present an approach to automatically generate test cases that provoke mission-critical behavior using a genetic algorithm. It is based on the master thesis of the first author [17] and is an extended version of our test approach presented in [20]. The key idea of our approach presented in [20] is twofold: first, we apply an existing test partitioning approach [19] to automatically generate a test set that is complete with respect to multidimensional coverage criteria but provides a significantly smaller search space than the full combination of all possible input scenarios. Second, we propose a genetic algorithm that automatically searches for test cases that provoke mission-critical behavior within this reduced search space, namely test cases that provoke long execution times and mathematically inaccurate results.

Compared to [20], this paper makes the following contributions:

- We provide a concise summary of our test partitioning approach [19], and give more details on its integration into our genetic test approach to reduce the search space.
- We extend our genetic algorithm with a new selection method, namely tournament selection.
- We show with experimental results from the PLAnetary Transits and Oscillation of stars (PLATO) mission that tournament selection provokes test cases with much longer execution times and much smaller accuracy than the previously used stochastic universal sampling method.
- We identify and discuss the equivalence classes of the most mission-critical test cases for our case study, and draw conclusions about the sources and causes of mission-critical behavior.

We investigate the efficiency of our test approach using the Fine Guidance System (FGS) algorithm of the European Space Agency (ESA) mission PLATO as a case study. The FGS calculates high-precision attitude data of the spacecraft by comparing tracked star positions in image frames taken on-board with known star positions from a star catalog. The experimental results demonstrate the efficiency of the genetic approach with regard to the automated search of specific test cases tailored for robustness testing.

This paper is structured as follows: Sect. 2 describes the concept of partition testing and genetic algorithms in general as well as gives an introduction of the PLATO mission and the PLATO FGS algorithm. Section 3 outlines related work on the use of genetic algorithms for test case generation. Section 4 presents our genetic algorithm. First, it presents the automated generation of a reduced search space by means of equivalence classes and multidimensional coverage criteria. Then, it provides our description of the algorithm components. Thereafter, it gives an overview of our automated test case generation approach. Our implementation and experimental results are presented in Sect. 5. Finally, Sect. 6 provides a summary of the main results and gives an outlook on future work.

2 Preliminaries

In this section, we introduce the concept of equivalence class partition testing and genetic algorithms in general. Moreover, we give an overview of the PLATO mission as well as its mission-critical FGS algorithm.

2.1 Equivalence Class Partition Testing

Large input or output domains of applications often lead to a huge amount of possible test cases. That makes testing inefficient and time-consuming. It is therefore preferable to examine only as many test cases as necessary to satisfy specified test criteria. However, the selection of specific test cases from a huge input or output domain is a major problem when testing applications [19].

A possible solution to this problem is equivalence class partition testing. The approach partitions the input or output domain in disjoint sub-domains, the equivalence classes. That means equivalence classes represent subsets of parameter values that completely covers the input or output domain. The test approach assumes that all elements in one class provoke the same system behavior according to a given specification. Hence, it is sufficient to test only a few test cases of each equivalence class to cover the whole input or output domain. The selection of test cases from equivalence classes can be performed using various criteria, e.g. border values, special values, or randomly selected test cases [19].

Equivalence class partition testing removes redundant test cases but completely covers the whole input or output domain. Thus, it makes testing more efficient and less time-consuming compared to exhaustive testing [19].

2.2 Genetic Algorithms

Manual test case selection for embedded software tests is often error-prone and inefficient. Especially, a large number of input parameter combinations makes manual testing expensive. A solution to this problem is a genetic algorithm designed to automatically search for test cases specifically tailored to provoke erroneous behavior, i.e. the violation of given system requirements. Thus, the test case design becomes an optimization problem: the genetic algorithm searches for parameter combinations in the input domain that satisfy given test criteria [20].

In general, a genetic algorithm is a search-based method that solves complex optimization problems. Utilizing a cost function the approach evaluates automatically generated optimization parameters with respect to predefined test criteria. It rapidly provides high-quality solutions to a problem. It is therefore able to efficiently solve a search problem [1,12,20].

Genetic algorithms are inspired by the concept of biological evolution. Solutions to a problem experience evolutionary mechanisms like selection, mutation, and recombination. In terms of genetic algorithms, solutions to a problem are treated as individuals composed of a specified number of genes. In each generation, the genetic algorithm creates a population of individuals from previously generated individuals. This is done until a population satisfies a certain criterion. The survival probability of an individual, e.g. the probability to select an individual into the next generation, depends on its fitness value. The fitness value measures the quality of an individual with respect to specified criteria. The genetic algorithm calculates the fitness value for each individual by means of the cost function. The selection strategy affects the convergence of the genetic algorithm. A common problem is that the algorithm provides a locally optimal solution because of too high convergence. On the other hand, if the convergence is too low solutions do not evolve. To preserve diversity in the population, the genetic algorithm generates new individuals by applying crossover and mutation mechanisms. The goal of crossover is to generate a better population by exchanging genes from fitter individuals. The mutation mechanism preserves the diversity of genes by inserting new genes into the population [5,9,12,20].

Genetic algorithms provide the advantage to run on parallel processors. Moreover, they are able to solve different complex, computation-intensive problems, with many possible solutions in a wide search-space. They also allow to automatically search in a huge input domain for optimal test data that provoke a specified behavior of the software application [1,5,9,20].

2.3 Case Study: PLATO Mission

PLATO is an ESA mission in the long-term space scientific program "cosmic vision". The main goal of the PLATO mission is to find and characterize Earth-like exoplanets orbiting in the habitable zone of solar-type stars.

The scientific objective is achieved by long uninterrupted ultra-high precision photometric monitoring of large samples of bright stars. This requires a very large Field of View (FoV) as well as a low noise level. The novelty of the mission is its multi-camera approach to achieve a high pupil size and the required FoV. 24 normal cameras monitor stars fainter than magnitude 8 at a cycle time of 25 s. In addition, two fast cameras observe stars brighter than magnitude 8 at a cycle time of 2.5 s. The cameras are equipped with four Charge Coupled Devices (CCDs) in the focal plane, each with 4510×4510 pixels. Each fast camera is connected to a data processing unit that runs the FGS algorithm. The algorithm calculates attitude data with an accuracy of milliarcseconds from the acquired CCD image data.

In each cycle, the FGS reads a 6×6 pixel sub-image for each guide star from a full CCD-image. Guide stars are predefined stars in a star catalog that satisfy given criteria. A linear center of mass calculation estimates the initial centroid position in each sub-image. Subsequently, the FGS algorithm refines each centroid using a Gaussian Point Spread Function (PSF) observation model. The PSF describes the distribution of starlight over CCD pixels. Based on measured pixel intensities, the algorithm determines the PSF model including centroid position, intensity, image background, and PSF-width. To refine these parameters, the FGS algorithm applies a non-linear least square fitting method.

The quality of the centroid calculation depends on the input star signal and its distribution over several pixels. If the star signal in a pixel is little interfered by noise and the Signal-to-Noise Ratio (SNR) is high, the star information is usable. At least 5 linear independent observations are necessary to estimate the 5 parameters of the observation model. The distribution of the star signal over pixels depends on the star position on the Focal Plane Assembly (FPA), the sub-pixel position, the magnitude, and the PSF shape. If the star signal in the image pixels is not sufficiently good, then the centroid estimation is less accurate or the algorithm does not converge or converges late [19].

After calculating the centroid parameters of each star, the FGS algorithm transforms the pixel coordinates of the calculated centroid position into a star direction vector. The algorithm calculates the attitude data by means of the QUaternion ESTimator (QUEST) algorithm from at least two star directions and its corresponding reference vectors from a given star catalog [6]. The QUEST algorithm also measures the validity of the input data by means of the scalar TASTE test [13]. If at least one input star is misidentified, the TASTE value is high [6]. In our test approach, we use the value as a qualitative measure of the mathematical accuracy of the FGS algorithm and denote it as quality index [20].

The input of the FGS algorithm is a combination of stars. Since the star parameters of a single star affect the performance and accuracy of the centroid calculation, the performance and accuracy of the FGS algorithm also depend on the combination of input stars. The calculated attitude data is unusable if the FGS result is incorrect or the delivery is too late. In this case, all captured science data cannot be further processed and the mission is lost [20]. Hence, the FGS is regarded as mission-critical component, which therefore requires an extensive test procedure [11].

3 Related Work

Various papers present automated software test approaches that are based on genetic algorithms. In [7,14–16], the authors used genetic algorithms to automatically generate test data for structural-oriented tests, like control flow testing and data flow testing as well as for function-oriented tests, for example examining the temporal behavior of an application [20].

In [15], the authors present a genetic algorithm for structural testing. Their algorithm uses data flow dependencies of a program to automatically optimize test data. The study shows that genetic algorithms are feasible to automatically generate test data that achieve high coverage of variable definition and reference paths in the program code. Further, the study shows that data generated by the genetic algorithm achieves higher coverage of the program flow graph in fewer generations compared to data generated by random testing. However, we look for a test approach that does not depend on the internal system structure [20].

Sthamer et al. [14], present an evolutionary approach to investigate the temporal behavior of embedded systems. Their approach automatically searches for input situations where the system under test violates specified timing constraints. For this purpose, they defined a fitness function based on the execution time. As a case study, the authors used an engine control system. The experiments demonstrate that the evolutionary approach generates test data that detect errors in the timing behavior of systems with large input domain and strict timing constraints. The study shows that the evolutionary approach is applicable to different test goals as well as for testing systems of various application fields. However, our goal is to consider temporal behavior as well as mathematical accuracy of image processing applications for various input values. Therefore, we define a fitness function that includes additional metrics to evaluate the individuals [20].

All of these approaches show that genetic algorithms improve the software test efficiency. The studies confirm that genetic algorithms are suitable to automatically generate test cases that satisfy special test criteria from a large input domain. However, to reach optimal results it is important to adapt the fitness function to the specific problem [20].

4 Genetic Test Approach

Many satellite on-board image processing applications require a high number of different input parameters and perform complex algorithmic computations. This makes it hard to systematically and efficiently capture the input domain to find test cases that are tailored to provoke real-time critical behavior or scenarios where the mathematical accuracy gets critically low. But, we need such test cases to verify compliance of the satellite on-board image processing application with strict requirements in reliability and mathematical accuracy in hard real-time.

To overcome this problem, we define a test approach based on a genetic algorithm that automatically searches for test cases that increase the robustness of a satellite on-board image processing application. Our key idea is a novel two-criteria fitness function that is specifically tailored for the satellite domain. In this paper, we updated our genetic algorithm with a new selection method, namely tournament selection, to increase the selection pressure.

Figure 1 gives an overview of our proposed approach. As the figure depicts, the input of our genetic algorithm (see Sect. 4.3) is a parameter specification to configure it and an automated generated, reduced test set with complete coverage on the input domain.

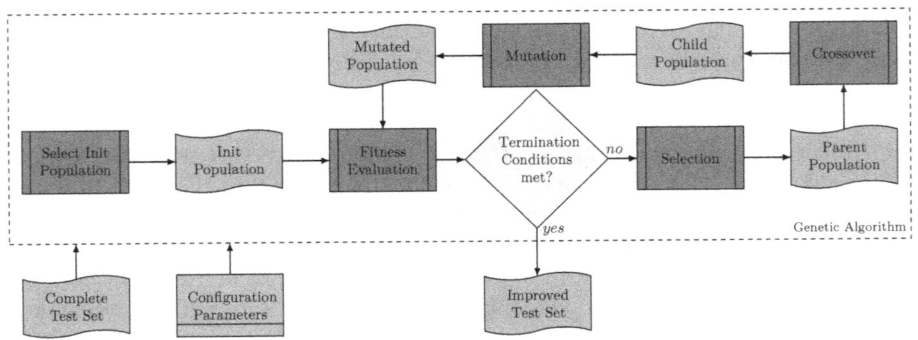

Fig. 1. Overview of the automated test case generation approach [20].

We generate the complete test set by means of an equivalence class partitioning approach for on-board satellite image processing applications presented in [19]. In this paper, we present our equivalence class definitions for the FGS input parameters as well as our multidimensional coverage criteria to systematically select only one representative input from each equivalence class combination. Our genetic algorithm selects test cases from the complete test set and evaluates them according to their fitness values. It iteratively evolves promising test cases using evolutionary mechanisms, namely selection, crossover, and mutation. As a result, it delivers test cases that satisfy given test criteria.

4.1 Assumptions and Limitations

In this paper, we consider systems whose inputs are objects in an image. In our case study, the observed objects are stars uniformly distributed in the image [6]. We take four star parameters into account that affect run time and mathematical accuracy of the FGS algorithm: position in the image, magnitude, sub-pixel position, and PSF shape. Performance and mathematical accuracy of the FGS algorithm also depend on the number and distribution of preselected guide stars. Previous experiments have shown that 30 input stars provide sufficiently good results. Therefore, we define a combination of 30 stars as a test case.

Moreover, we specify that a test set consists of several test stars. A test star covers a special combination of equivalence classes. We denote a test set as complete if it reaches full coverage on the input domain with respect to the coverage criteria presented in Sect. 4.2. Thus the set includes one star for each equivalence class combination.

In our test approach, we use the TASTE-value as a qualitative measure of the mathematical accuracy of the FGS algorithm. Hence, a low quality index corresponds to high accuracy of the FGS algorithm [20].

4.2 Automated Search Space Reduction

A distinctive feature of satellite on-board image processing algorithms is their large input domain. That makes the search space of the genetic algorithm incredibly high. Our key idea is to use a reduced test set with complete coverage on the input domain as search space for our genetic algorithm. To automatically generate such a test set, we use the partitioning approach given in [19].

We define equivalence classes for input parameters that mainly affects the distribution of the star signal over pixels and thus have an impact on the mathematical accuracy and execution time of the FGS algorithm. We define the set of input parameters I as input domain. The parameter set contains of position on the FPA $\mathcal{P}$, star magnitude $\mathcal{M}$, sub-pixel position $\mathcal{E}$ as well as PSF shape $\mathcal{G}$.

In the following, we present our equivalence class definitions of the input parameters and our multidimensional coverage criteria. Subsequently, we explain the automated generation of a reduced test set that is complete with respect to our multidimensional coverage criteria.

Position on the FPA. Due to optical aberrations of the telescope, the PSF shape of a star is wider at the FPA border regions than close to the center. A small PSF leads to a low number of pixels with a high SNR, if the other input parameters provide sufficient good, constant values. In case of a wide PSF, more pixels contain a signal but the SNR is low. However, both cases can be sufficient for an accurate parameter estimation [19]. As described in [19] we partition the FPA in circular ring areas as shown in Fig. 2. The rectangles present the full CCDs of the fast camera. The circular ring sectors represent the equivalence classes of parameter $\mathcal{P}$. The tester defines the initial radius r_0 and the angle θ_0 of the circular vectors.

More formally, we partition the parameter $\mathcal{P}$ into equivalence classes $P_{(r_i,\theta_j)}$. Each class $P_{(r_i,\theta_j)}$ corresponds to a circular ring sector of the FPA with inner radius r_{i-1} and outer radius r_i as well as right polar angle θ_{j-1} and left polar angle θ_j.

$$\mathcal{P} = P_{(r_0,\theta_0)} \cup P_{(r_0,\theta_1)} \cup ... \cup P_{(r_0,\theta_m)} \cup ... \cup P_{(r_n,\theta_m)} \tag{1}$$

n is the number of radius borders and m is the number of polar angle borders.

Let S denote the set of available stars. A star $s \in S$ is a representative of equivalence class $P_{(r_i,\theta_j)}$ if following condition holds:

$$r_{i-1} \leq p(s) < r_i, \text{ with } p(s) = \sqrt{{x_s}^2 + {y_s}^2} \tag{2}$$

and

$$\theta_{j-1} \leq t(s) < \theta_j, \text{ with } t(s) = \arctan \frac{x_s}{y_s} \tag{3}$$

where (x_s, y_s) is the position of star s on the FPA, $p(s)$ is the star distance to the FPA center and $t(s)$ is the polar angle of star s [19].

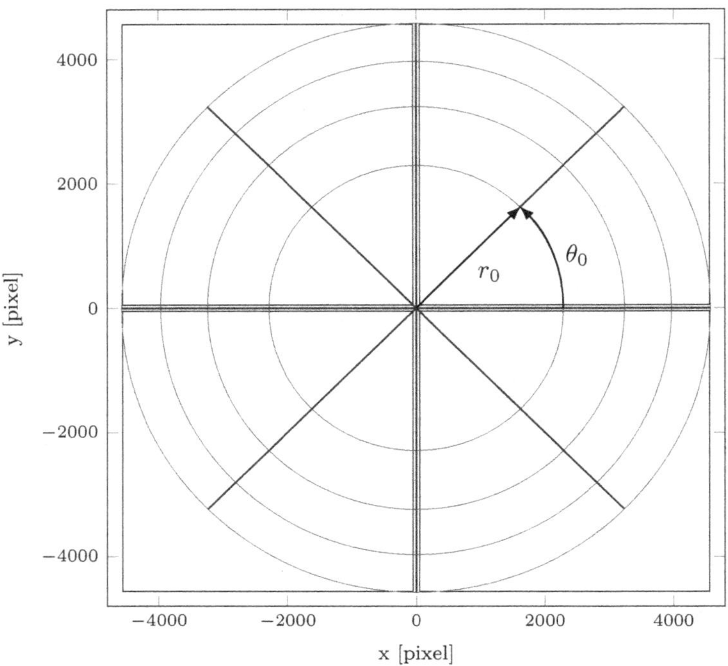

Fig. 2. FPA equivalence class example [19].

Position in the Pixel. Besides the star position on the FPA, the sub-pixel position of the star also affects the SNR in a pixel. Most star information is accumulated only in few pixels with high SNR if the star centroid is positioned in the pixel center. If the star centroid is positioned in a pixel corner or near a pixel border then the star information is distributed more evenly over several pixels. Therefore, more pixels have an adequate SNR. The other pixels in the image have a low SNR. But due to movement of the telescope, the centroid may move to neighbor pixels and causes variations in the pixel illumination and the apparent centroid position. Hence, we partition the pixels into 4 equally sized areas as shown in Fig. 3. Areas with the same pattern represent one equivalence class.

We define equivalence classes E_i with $i = 0...3$ of input parameter $\mathcal{E}$ such that

$$\mathcal{E} = E_0 \cup E_1 \cup ... \cup E_3. \tag{4}$$

For the definition of the equivalence classes, we specify the lower left corner l and the upper right corner u of the central pixel area by

$$l = (\frac{a}{2} - \frac{b}{2}, \frac{a}{2} - \frac{b}{2}) \text{ and } u = (\frac{a}{2} + \frac{b}{2}, \frac{a}{2} + \frac{b}{2}). \tag{5}$$

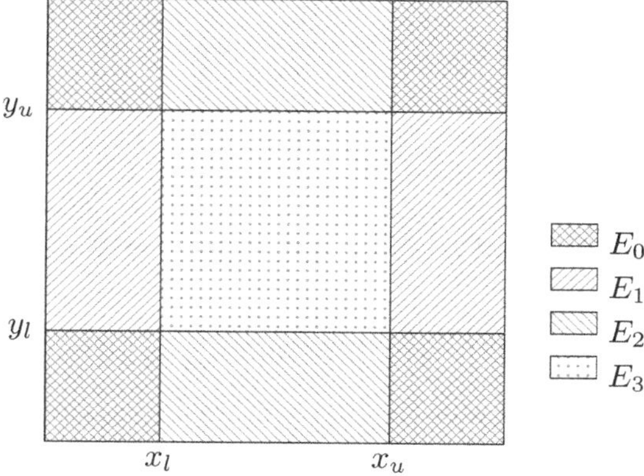

Fig. 3. Sub-pixel equivalence class example [19].

a is the pixel size and b is the width of the central pixel area. The last value depends on the ratio r of the central pixel area to the complete pixel. The tester specifies this ratio. A star is a representative of an equivalence class if it satisfies the corresponding condition.

$$\begin{aligned}
&E_0 : (0 \leq e_x(s) < x_l \ \vee \ x_u \leq e_x(s) < a) \wedge \ (0 \leq e_y(s) < y_l \ \vee \ y_u \leq e_y(s) < a) \\
&E_1 : (0 \leq e_x(s) < x_l \ \vee \ x_u \leq e_x(s) < a) \wedge \ y_l \leq e_y(s) < y_u \\
&E_2 : x_l \leq e_x(s) < x_u \ \wedge \ (0 \leq e_y(s) < y_l \ \vee \ y_u \leq e_y(s) < a) \\
&E_3 : x_l \leq e_x(s) < x_u \ \wedge \ y_l \leq e_y(s) < y_u
\end{aligned} \tag{6}$$

$e_x(s)$ and $e_y(s)$ return the x-coordinate and y-coordinate of star s in the pixel respectively [19].

Magnitude. The measured star flux (photo-electrons per second) affects the pixel illumination. That is the accumulated number of photo-electrons in a pixel. The star flux is non-linear to the star magnitude. A low magnitude corresponds to a high number of photo-electrons. That leads to a higher SNR per pixel.

A useful partitioning of the magnitude values into equivalence classes is not obvious. Hence, we partition the flux value range into equidistant parts that represent the equivalence classes. Figure 4 illustrates our partitioning idea.

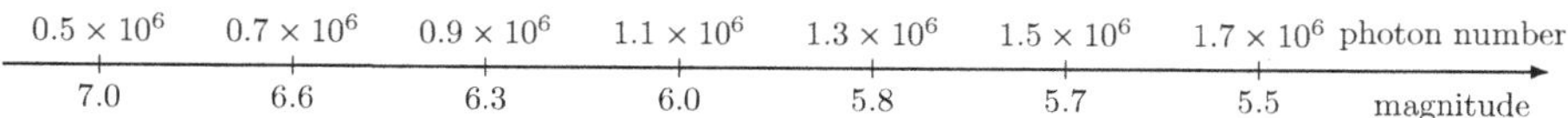

Fig. 4. Magnitude equivalence class example [19].

To compute the upper limit of a sub-range, we define Eq. (7).

$$F_{m_j} = F_{7.0} + j\frac{F_{5.5} - F_{7.0}}{I_{\mathcal{M}}} \tag{7}$$

F_{m_j} is the flux of a star with magnitude m_j and $j = 1...I_{\mathcal{M}}$ represents the j-th equivalence class of parameter $\mathcal{M}$. $F_{5.5}$ and $F_{7.0}$ correspond to the numbers of photons for magnitude 5.5 and 7.0. For each flux limit we calculate the magnitude value using Eq. (8).

$$m = -2.5\ log\left(\frac{F_m}{F_0 TQA}\right) \tag{8}$$

Thus we partition the parameter $\mathcal{M}$ into equivalence classes M_l.

$$\mathcal{M} = M_{l_1} \cup ... \cup M_{l_j} \cup ... \cup M_{5.5} \tag{9}$$

with $l_j \in \mathbb{R}$ and $5.5 \leq l_j < 7.0$. Each equivalence class M_{l_j} is a magnitude sub-range with upper limit l_j. Each star s is a representative of equivalence class M_{l_j} if it satisfies the condition in Eq. (10).

$$l_{j-1} \leq m(s) < l_j \tag{10}$$

where $m(s)$ denotes the observed magnitude of star s. The tester specifies the number of equivalence classes $I_{\mathcal{M}} \in \mathbb{N}$ of the parameter $\mathcal{M}$ [18].

PSF Shape. The accuracy of the centroid calculation also depends on the PSF shape. In the best case scenario, the shape is a symmetric Gaussian-PSF. Then, the observation model perfectly fits the star. Therefore, the accuracy of the centroid calculation is high. However, in reality, the PSF shape is non-Gaussian. In that case, the observation model is less accurate and movements lead to stronger variations in the expected centroid positions [18].

Thus, we partition the input parameter $\mathcal{G}$ in two equivalence classes G_G and G_{NG} since two PSF shapes are distinctive. If a star has a Gaussian-PSF shape it is in class G_G otherwise it is in class G_{NG} [19]. In this paper, we only consider more realistic stars with non-Gaussian PSF shape.

Multidimensional Coverage Criteria. While individual parameter values might lead to an accurate estimation in short time, a combination of parameters may change the quality of the results. To measure the coverage of a test set with respect to input parameter combinations we define multidimensional coverage criteria on the input domain $I = \{\mathcal{P}, \mathcal{M}, \mathcal{E}, \mathcal{G}\}$.

The individual coverage of an input parameter denotes the ratio of equivalence classes that are covered by at least one test star from a given test set to the number of equivalence classes of this input parameter. Equations (11) to (14) define the individual coverage for the input parameters $\mathcal{P}, \mathcal{M}$, $\mathcal{E}$ and $\mathcal{G}$ respectively.

$$C_{\mathcal{P}} = \frac{\#\ covered\ elements\ of\ \mathcal{P}}{|\mathcal{P}|} \tag{11}$$

$$C_{\mathcal{M}} = \frac{\#\ covered\ elements\ of\ \mathcal{M}}{|\mathcal{M}|} \tag{12}$$

$$C_{\mathcal{E}} = \frac{\#\ covered\ elements\ of\ \mathcal{E}}{|\mathcal{E}|} \tag{13}$$

$$C_{\mathcal{G}} = \frac{\#\ covered\ elements\ of\ \mathcal{G}}{|\mathcal{G}|} \tag{14}$$

The Cartesian product of the equivalence classes of the input parameters $\mathcal{P}$, $\mathcal{M}$, $\mathcal{E}$ and $\mathcal{G}$ is the coverage domain for our multidimensional coverage criteria. Hence, an input combination is a tuple of equivalence classes (P_i, M_j, E_k, G_l), where $P_i \in \mathcal{P}$, $M_j \in \mathcal{M}$, $E_k \in \mathcal{E}$ and $G_l \in \mathcal{G}$ [18]. Furthermore, tuple of parameter values $((p,t), m, e, g) \in (P_i, M_j, E_k, G_l)$ represents a test star. The following example clarifies these definitions.

Example 1. $\big((1969.4, 322.5), 6.5, (0.3, 0.2), G\big) \in (P_{(3239,360)} \times M_{6.6} \times E_2 \times G_{NG})$ The test star is a representative of FPA area with outer radius 2687 and outer polar angle 225°. The star belongs to equivalence class $M_{6.6}$ because its magnitude value is between 6.3 and 6.6. The star center is located in the lower-middle pixel sub-area. That corresponds to the vertical pixel areas and therefore to equivalence class E_2. The star is part of equivalence class G_{NG}, because it has a non-Gaussian-PSF shape.

Our multidimensional coverage criterion is fully satisfied if the test stars in a test set cover all possible input combinations at least once. In contrast to [19], we only consider realistic stars with non-Gaussian PSF shape. Hence, the number of required covered input combinations for complete coverage in this paper is $|\mathcal{P} \times \mathcal{M} \times \mathcal{E}|$. In the following, we denote a test set that completely covers the input domain with respect to our multidimensional coverage criteria as a complete test set. The multidimensional coverage C results from the ratio of input combinations covered by at least one test star to the total number of input combinations [19].

$$C = \frac{\#\ covered\ input\ combinations}{|\mathcal{P} \times \mathcal{M} \times \mathcal{E}|} \tag{15}$$

Automated Test Set Generation. Our test set generation algorithm uses the previous definitions to automatically and systematically generate a reduced test set that completely covers the input domain of the satellite on-board image processing application according to our multidimensional coverage criteria. First, the algorithm calculates the equivalence class borders for each input parameter based on the tester specifications. Subsequently, it assigns each test star of a given test set to the corresponding equivalence classes of each input parameter. For each equivalence class, combination only one test star is used. Thus, the algorithm removes redundant test stars from the test set.

Based on Eqs. (11) to (15) the algorithm computes the individual coverage of each input parameter and the multidimensional coverage. The algorithm uses the coverage values to assess a given test set with respect to its coverage on the input domain of the satellite on-board image processing application. Moreover, the algorithm systematically generates test stars for equivalence class combinations that are not covered. In this way, it efficiently inserts missing but relevant test stars. If the given test set is empty, the algorithm generates a new test set that completely satisfies the multidimensional coverage criteria.

The generation algorithm automatically increases the multidimensional coverage and therefore the error detection capability of the given test set. As a result, we get a complete but reasonably small test set [19]. We use this automated generated test set as search space of our genetic algorithm. The following sections describe the genetic approach in more detail.

4.3 Genetic Algorithm

The goal of our genetic algorithm is to automatically search for test cases in an automated generated test set that provoke mission-critical behavior with respect to run time and mathematical accuracy. In the following, we describe the components and strategies of our genetic approach.

Individual Representation. In terms of our genetic algorithm, a test case represents an individual with 30 genes, analogous to a test case with 30 stars. Our individual representation is based on the equivalence class definitions described in Sect. 4.2. We define a gene as a tuple of equivalence class identifiers (i_P, i_M, i_E, i_G) where P defines the position of the star in the image, M the magnitude of the star, E the sub-pixel position, and G the PSF shape [20]. Figure 5 illustrates the individual representation of an example individual.

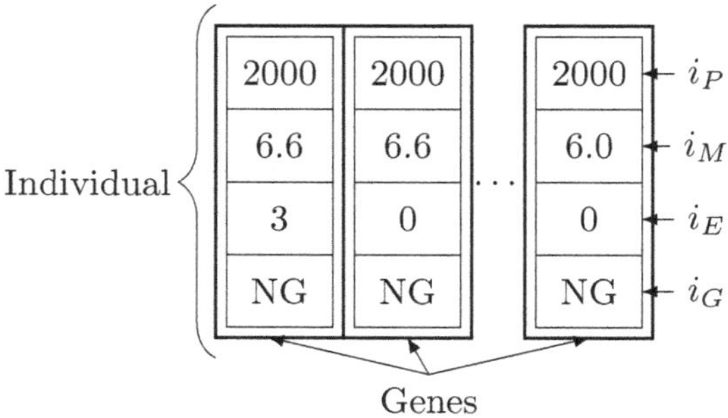

Fig. 5. Individual representation.

Initial Population. As search space, our genetic algorithm uses the automated generated test set that is complete with respect to our multidimensional coverage criteria. The generation procedure is presented in Sect. 4.2.

For each individual, the genetic algorithm randomly selects 30 stars from its search space. Each selected star in an individual covers a different combination of equivalence classes. This prevents that in the end an individual contains the same star 30 times. The genetic algorithm generates individuals until the required population size specified by the tester is reached [20].

Fitness Function. By means of a fitness function, the genetic algorithm calculates a fitness value for each individual to evaluate its suitability to survive.

In Eq. (16), we define a two-criteria fitness function that depends on execution time and quality index of the FGS execution. To capture a trade-off between both parameters and to define the impact of the parameters on the new generation, we apply the weighted sum with weighting factors w_{time} and w_{taste}.

$$\begin{aligned} fitness(c) &= f_{time}(c) \cdot w_{time} + f_{taste}(c) \cdot w_{taste}, \\ \text{with } f_{time}(c) &= \frac{time}{a_{time}},\ f_{taste}(c) = \frac{taste}{a_{taste}}, \\ 0 \leq w_{time}, w_{taste} &\leq 1 \text{ and } w_{time} + w_{taste} = 1 \end{aligned} \tag{16}$$

$fitness(c)$ provides the fitness of an individual c. Individuals that cause long execution times and a high quality index, i.e. a low accuracy, have a high fitness value. $f_{time}(c)$ calculates the fitness value of an individual c with respect to the FGS execution time. $f_{taste}(c)$ calculates the fitness value of an individual c with respect to the quality index. Since both metrics have different magnitudes, we normalize the values using reference values before combining them in the fitness function. The tester defines both reference value a_{time} and a_{taste} for example as average of execution times or quality values measured by random testing.

Input: population, w_{time}, w_{taste}, a_{time}, a_{taste}
Output: fitTime, fitTaste

maximalFit = 0;
foreach *individual* $\in$ *population* **do**
  time, taste = FGS(individual);
  fitValue = $\frac{time}{a_{time}} \cdot w_{time} + \frac{taste}{a_{taste}} \cdot w_{taste}$;
  if *fitValue* > *maximalFit* **then**
    maximalFit = fitValue;
    fitTime = time;
    fitTaste = taste;
  end
  individual.fit = fitValue;
end

Algorithm 1. Fitness evaluation.

Algorithm 1 describes the evaluation process of our genetic algorithm. The algorithm sends each individual in the population as input to the FGS algorithm and calculates its fitness value by means of our fitness function. Algorithm 1 also provides the longest execution time *fitTime* and worst quality index *fitTaste* of the current population [20].

Selection. In [20], we used the stochastic universal sampling method as selection mechanism for our genetic algorithm. Since the fitness values of individuals are very tight, the selection probability of each individual is nearly the same. That means the selection pressure is very low and individuals with low fitness value are selected into the next generation. To increase the selection pressure we replace the selection mechanism with the efficient tournament selection method.

The genetic algorithm selects k individuals with replacement from the current population and selects the individual with the highest fitness value to the new population. This step is repeated until the new population reaches the specified population size. k is the tournament size and is defined by the tester. In this way, the tester is able to adapt the selection pressure. A low tournament size leads to a low selection pressure while a large tournament size causes a high selection pressure [4]. Algorithm 2 describes the steps of the tournament selection.

```
Input: currentPopulation, popsize, k
Output: selectedPopulation
selectedPopulation ← ∅;
for i ← 1 to popsize do
    bestFitness = 0;
    bestIndividual ← 0;
    for j ← 1 to k do
        tournamentIndividual ← getRandomIndividual(currentPopulation);
        if bestFitness < tournamentIndividual.fitness then
            bestIndividual ← tournamentIndividual;
            bestFitness = tournamentIndividual.fitness;
        end
    end
    selectedPopulation ← selectedPopulation ∪ bestIndividual;
end
```

Algorithm 2. Tournament selection.

Crossover. Our genetic algorithm performs the parameterized uniform crossover strategy to insert new individuals [5, p. 89]. The crossover mechanism randomly chooses two not yet selected individuals as parents from the population. For every single gene of the parents, the genetic algorithm decides according to the crossover probability p_c whether the genes are exchanged or not. Because an individual should not contain a test star twice, the genes do not cross if one of them is already contained in its target individual.

The genetic algorithm applies the crossover operator to each individual pair in the population. As a result, the crossover mechanism returns a child population containing new individuals. We define that the tester specifies the crossover probability p_c [20].

Mutation. The mutation process decides according to a mutation probability p_m for each gene of each individual in the population whether the gene mutates or not. In case the gene mutates, the genetic algorithm randomly selects a new star from its search space, which is not contained in the individual, as a gene. Depending on the mutation probability p_m, the mutation function preserves the diversity in the population or inserts minimal changes to find test cases that locally provoke critical behavior [5]. The tester specifies the mutation probability p_m. As a result, the mutation process returns a mutated population [20].

Termination Condition. The genetic algorithm terminates if it reaches a defined number of generations, the best solution has not improved in the last n generations [2], or the FGS algorithm execution time exceeds a specific value. The tester defines these criteria [20]. There is no termination condition with respect to the quality index since no PLATO requirements exist for this measure.

4.4 Automated Test Generation

The goal of our proposed test approach is to find star combinations that provoke long execution times as well as inaccurate results of the satellite on-board image processing application. We automatically generate a reduced search space for the genetic algorithm that is complete with respect to our multidimensional coverage criteria presented in Sect. 4.2. For the search space generation, we apply the partitioning test approach presented in [19]. The generated test set contains one star per equivalence class combination of the parameters. Without using stars having unrealistic Gaussian-PFS shape, this results in approximately 7.7×10^{-53} possible combinations of 30 stars as FGS input. Testing all possible combinations is still infeasible. Hence, our key idea is a genetic algorithm that is specifically tailored to find particular test cases in a large input domain.

Algorithm 3 gives an overview of the structure of our defined genetic algorithm using the components described in Sect. 4.3. The complete test set *TS*, which is significantly reduced by the partitioning approach, is the search space of our genetic algorithm. The algorithm creates the initial population by randomly selecting stars from its test set until the population size *popSize* is reached. Using our two-criteria fitness function, the algorithm calculates the fitness value for each individual based on the execution time and quality index delivered by the FGS algorithm. By specifying the parameter weights w_{time} and w_{taste}, the tester is flexible to define the test goal.

Based on the fitness values, our genetic algorithm selects the fittest individuals from each tournament with k individuals into a new population. On the newly selected population, Algorithm 3 performs the crossover by means of the parameterized uniform crossover strategy. The crossover function generates new individuals by mixing genes of selected individuals according to the crossover probability p_c. Subsequently, the genetic algorithm applies the mutation operator to the newly generated child population. Our genetic algorithm iteratively

Input: TS, popSize, w_{time}, w_{taste}, a_{time}, a_{taste}, p_c, p_m, T, maxTime, k
Output: P

P ← ∅;
t = fitTime = fitTaste = 0;
P ← getInitialPopulation(popSize);
popFit, fitTime, fitTaste ← evaluation(w_{time}, w_{taste}, a_{time}, a_{taste});
while $t < T$ **and** $fitTime < maxTime$ **do**
    P ← selection(k);
    P ← crossover(p_c);
    P ← mutation(p_m);
    popFit, fitTime, fitTaste ← evaluation(w_{time}, w_{taste}, a_{time}, a_{taste});
    t++;
end

Algorithm 3. Genetic algorithm.

evolves individuals until it reaches a predefined maximum number of generations T or the achieved maximum execution time of a generation exceeds a specified maximum execution time $maxTime$. Algorithm 3 provides a population P of individuals that provoke the longest execution times and lowest mathematical accuracies of the satellite on-board image processing algorithm.

Using the genetic algorithm, our test approach improves an already reduced test set to efficiently provoke worst-case execution time and inaccurate results of the FGS algorithm. If the test detects violations of the requirements, the FGS algorithm has to be corrected and tested again [20].

5 Evaluation

We have implemented our test approach to investigate its efficiency to generate specific test cases that provoke mission-critical behavior for satellite on-board image processing applications. We used the FGS algorithm of the PLATO mission as a case study.

Our objective is to evaluate our approach for the development and test of the FGS algorithm implementation. In particular, we test execution time and mathematical accuracy of the algorithm under realistic hardware conditions. For that purpose, we run the FGS algorithm on a GR-XC6S FPGA development board [10] running at 50 MHz.

In our experiments, we have used a complete test set that covers all equivalence class combinations defined in Sect. 4.2 as search space of the genetic algorithm. We have used the following start parameters to calculate the equivalence classes of the FGS input parameters $\mathcal{P}$, $\mathcal{M}$, $\mathcal{E}$, and $\mathcal{G}$ as described in Sect. 4.2:

- Initial radius r_0 of FPA partitioning: 2290 pixel
- Initial polar angle θ_0 of FPA partitioning: 45°
- Number of magnitude sub-ranges: 6
- Ratio r of central sub-area to pixel area: 0.25

As a result, we get 32 equivalence classes of parameter $\mathcal{P}$, 6 equivalence classes for parameter $\mathcal{M}$, and 4 equivalence classes for input parameter $\mathcal{E}$. Since Gaussian-PSF stars are unrealistic, we eliminate them from the test set. This significantly reduces the number of possible star combinations to 7.7×10^{-53} to cover the whole input domain of the FGS algorithm. We generate a complete test set by means of the partitioning approach presented in [19]. Our test application randomly selects star combinations from this test set and sends picture sequences of 1000 times steps for each star to the development board, where the FGS algorithm calculates the attitude data. As a result, the test application receives execution time and quality index for each time step and averages them over all time steps. Based on these values, our genetic algorithm calculates the fitness value of the executed star combination.

Table 1. Genetic algorithm configuration.

Population size	20
Number of genes	30
Max execution time [ms]	300
a_{time} [ms]	3.5
a_{taste}	5.5×10^{-10}
p_c	0.5
p_m	0.06
Maximum generation number	100
Tournament size	7

In this paper, we updated the configuration specified in [20]. Table 1 lists all parameters that we used for the configuration of our genetic algorithm. In contrast to [20], we have taken the standard deviation of the maximum execution times and quality indexes from previous experiments as reference values a_{time} and a_{taste} respectively. Moreover, we increased the maximum generation number to 100 since the results in [20] indicates that fitter individuals will be found if the maximum number of generations is increased. Due to our updated selection method, the configuration includes a new parameter to define the tournament size for each selection process. We set this value to 7. As stated in [4], tournament sizes of 2, 4 or 7 individuals are often used. However, for our problem a tournament size of 7 provides the best results.

Similar to [20], we have set the population size to 20 due to time reasons. Further, we have set the maximum execution time of the FGS algorithm to 300 ms according to PLATO requirements. There are no termination conditions with respect to the quality index as no PLATO requirement exists for this measure. We have performed 10 independent runs of each experiment and averaged the results since genetic algorithms involve randomness due to the random selection of the initial population as well as the crossover and mutation process.

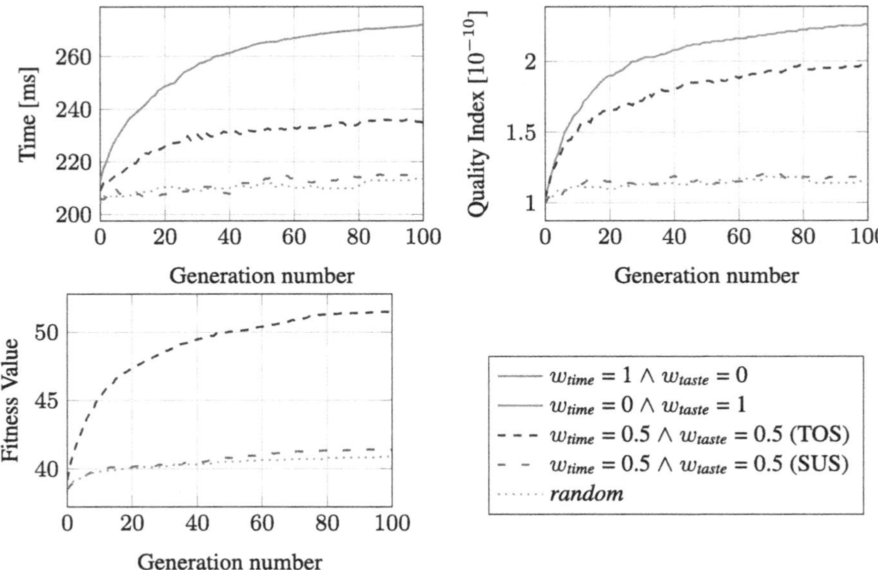

Fig. 6. Experimental results.

In the first two experiments, our genetic algorithm optimizes solutions for one fitness criteria: either execution time or quality index. For that, we have set the respective weighting factor w_{time} or w_{taste} to 1 and the other to 0. Thus, the calculated fitness value corresponds to the execution time or quality index respectively. The fitness values of both experiments are shown in Fig. 6 by the solid lines. The upper left part of Fig. 6 presents the average of the highest execution time per generation over 10 runs. As the figure shows, the execution times do not violate the PLATO timing requirement. The upper right part shows the average of the highest quality index per generation over 10 runs. Both diagrams show that the execution time as well as the quality index already increase significantly in the first 20 generations. However, both diagrams indicate that higher execution times and quality indexes will be found if the number of generations would be increased for both experiments.

In a third experiment, we have set w_{time} and w_{taste} to 0.5 each to investigate the capability of our genetic algorithm provoking a long execution time and a high quality index at the same time. The corresponding execution time and quality index are shown in the upper parts of Fig. 6 by the dashed lines. As the figure shows, the execution times do not violate the timing requirement. The execution time and quality index slightly decrease in some generations in favor of a lower accuracy or higher execution time respectively. That is possible because an individual with a short execution time may be fitter compared to another individual with a longer execution time, because of a much higher quality index.

The resulting evolution of the averaged fitness values per generation is shown in the lower part of Fig. 6 by the dashed line. Like in the first experiments, the fitness value significantly increases in the first 20 generations. However, the fitness value continues to increase over all generations.

Figure 6 compares the resulting fitness values of the genetic algorithm using the tournament selection (TOS), indicated by the dashed line, with the fitness values generated using the stochastic universal sampling (SUS) selection method, indicated by the loosely dashed line. In both experiments, we set the weighting factors w_{time} and w_{taste} to 0.5. Compared to the results reached with the stochastic universal sampling selection method that is used in [20], we reach much higher execution times, quality indexes as well as fitness values using the tournament selection method. Moreover, with tournament selection, the fitness values increase significantly faster in the first generations compared to stochastic universal sampling selection. Thus, fewer generations are needed to select better individuals. With the stochastic universal sampling method, the selection pressure is too low. The individuals have nearly the same fitness value. Therefore, all individuals are selected with almost equal probability into the new population. Using the tournament selection method the tester is able to adapt the selection pressure to the specific problem by selecting the tournament size. A larger tournament size leads to higher selection pressure. As Fig. 6 shows, a higher selection pressure leads to higher execution time, quality index, and fitness value.

We have compared our experimental results with random testing. For that, we have randomly selected combinations of 30 stars from our complete test set. Figure 6 shows the measured execution times, quality index, and fitness value of the random test by the dotted lines. The results are averaged over 10 runs. We have calculated the fitness values using our fitness function with w_{time} and w_{taste} equals 0.5. Per generation, the maximum fitness values are selected from 20 random test cases. Figure 6 shows, the maximum fitness value reached by random testing is lower compared to the genetic algorithm using the tournament selection method or the stochastic universal sampling selection method. This demonstrates that our genetic algorithm is more capable to find a higher execution time and higher quality index (i.e. lower mathematical accuracy) executing fewer test cases compared to random testing [20].

We also evaluate in which equivalence classes the fittest individuals of each run from our third experiment end up. The left part of Fig. 7 illustrates the standard deviation of the number of stars per radius. The figure depicts that stars near the FPA center are more likely to provoke worst case execution time and high quality indexes of the FGS algorithm. The right part of Fig. 7 shows the standard deviation of the number of stars per polar angle. Four circular ring sectors stand out where many stars end up. In these areas, stars may be more affected by optical aberrations of the telescope.

Considering the radius and the polar angle all equivalence classes of parameter $\mathcal{P}$ with maximum radius r_0 as well as all equivalence classes with left polar angle 45, 90, 225, and 270 provide test stars that are able to provoke mission critical behavior of the FGS algorithm.

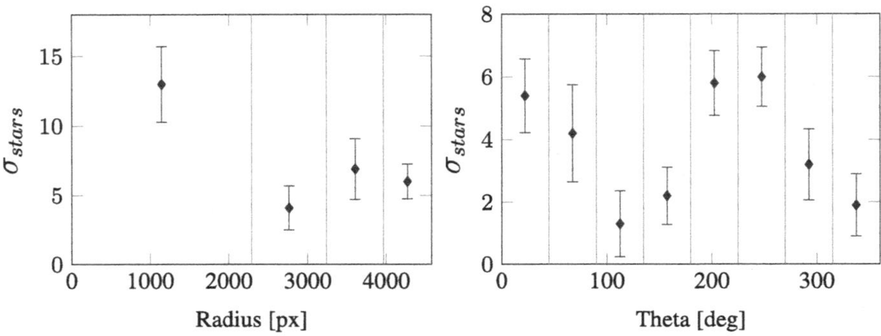

Fig. 7. Selected test stars per FPA radius and FPA polar angle.

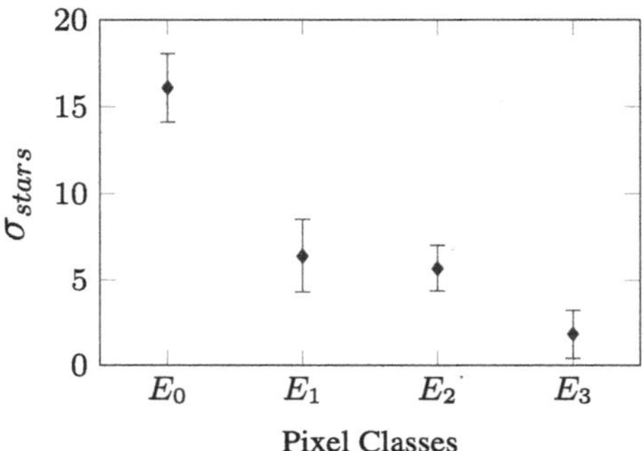

Fig. 8. Selected test stars per pixel class.

Regarding the pixel position, most stars fall into the pixel corner class E_0, as Fig. 8 demonstrates. Due to the movement of the telescope, stars in the corner area are more likely to move to neighboring pixels than stars located in the center class. Due to the movement, the pixel illumination and the apparent star position varies. That leads to inaccurate centroid calculations. In this case, more iterations are needed to refine the centroid position of a star, which means the execution time increases, and the mathematical accuracy decreases. As Fig. 8 shows, stars in the pixel center, i.e. E_3, are less suited to provoke the intended behavior of the FGS algorithm since the accuracy of these stars is less affected by movements.

Figure 9 depicts the standard deviation of the number of stars per magnitude class. The figure shows fittest individuals are bright stars, i.e. stars with low magnitude. That means stars in equivalence classes $M_{5.5}$ and $M_{5.7}$ are suitable to provoke mission critical behavior of the FGS algorithm.

Regarding the combination of the parameters, the experiment demonstrates that stars with low magnitude, located near the FPA center in the circular ring sectors with upper angle 90, 135, 225, or 270 and with its centroid located in

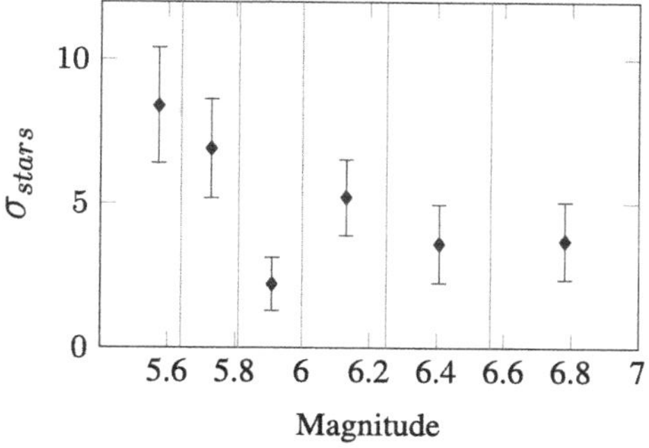

Fig. 9. Selected test stars per magnitude.

a pixel corner are most suited to provoke long execution times and inaccurate mathematical results of the FGS algorithm. However, we need further investigations to rule out the possibility of a systematic error, e.g. stars are shifted on the FPA by an offset, in the test data. Nevertheless, the experiment shows that our genetic algorithm is capable to efficiently find equivalence class combinations that provide test cases suitable to provoke long execution times and mathematical inaccurate results of the FGS algorithm.

Note that our genetic algorithm automatically provides test sets that have high execution times and quality indexes in a few generations. Hence, it improves the efficiency of the software testing process. However, it will never examine all possible 7.7×10^{-53} star combinations. Therefore, we can not rule out if there are other combinations that provoke longer execution times or higher quality indexes. But it increases the confidence in the robustness of the satellite on-board image processing application [20].

6 Conclusion

Due to complex computations performed by satellite on-board image processing applications, it is difficult to find test cases that provoke mission-critical behavior in a huge input domain. In this paper, we have presented a genetic algorithm that automatically finds test cases that provoke real-time critical behavior or scenarios where the mathematical accuracy gets critically low.

We first reduce the number of required test cases by using the partitioning test approach proposed in [19]. In this paper, we summarize the definition of equivalence classes for each input parameter to remove redundant test cases from a given test set as well as the definition of multidimensional coverage criteria to insert missing but relevant test cases. By means of the partitioning approach, we get a reasonably small test set that completely covers the whole input domain.

We have defined the complete test set as search space of our genetic algorithm. This makes the search faster since the search space is significantly smaller than the full combination of all possible input scenarios. Moreover, we have defined a two-criteria fitness function that is based on execution time and mathematical accuracy of a given satellite on-board image processing application. Using that function our genetic algorithm automatically steers the search to test cases that provoke long execution times or inaccurate results or both. The tester is able to specify which criterion has more impact on the fitness value of a test case.

Using the selection method presented in [20], the individuals do not evolve because of too low selection pressure. In this paper, we changed the selection method of our genetic algorithm to tournament selection to increase the selection pressure. Moreover, using the updated selection method the tester is able to adapt the selection pressure by changing the tournament size. Additionally, the tester specifies the input parameters of the genetic algorithm, for example, population size, termination conditions, etc. This makes our genetic algorithm flexible and adaptable to different test goals and various on-board image processing applications.

To demonstrate the efficiency of our genetic approach, we have investigated the capability of the algorithm to automatically find test cases that support robustness testing of a given satellite on-board image processing application. As a case study, we used the FGS algorithm as an application with high criticality for the PLATO mission. In our experiments, the updated genetic algorithm automatically evolves test cases with higher execution times and lower mathematical accuracy of the FGS algorithm compared to the genetic algorithm presented in [20] as well as random testing. The experiments demonstrate that our genetic algorithm finds equivalence class combinations that provide more suitable test cases than others.

In this paper, we have considered the TASTE value as a qualitative measure of mathematical accuracy. To investigate the accuracy of the application more precisely, we plan to consider errors of the results, e.g. angle errors for each axis, as criteria for the mathematical accuracy. Further, we have evaluated our approach by means of a single satellite on-board image processing application. Since our approach is flexible, the useability for other applications, e.g. blob feature extraction in the robotics domain, can be investigated [20].

References

1. Alander, J.T., Mantere, T.: Automatic software testing by genetic algorithm optimization, a case study. In: Proceedings of the 1st International Workshop on Soft Computing Applied to Software Engineering, pp. 1–9 (1999)
2. Bhandari, D., Murthy, C., Pal, S.K.: Variance as a stopping criterion for genetic algorithms with elitist model. Fund. Inform. **120**(2), 145–164 (2012)
3. Bringmann, E., Krämer, A.: Systematic testing of the continuous behavior of automotive systems. In: International Workshop on Software Engineering for Automotive Systems, pp. 13–20. ACM (2006)
4. Fang, Y., Li, J.: A review of tournament selection in genetic programming. In: Cai, Z., Hu, C., Kang, Z., Liu, Y. (eds.) International Symposium on Intelligence Computation and Applications. LNCS, vol. 6382, pp. 181–192. Springer, Heidelberg (2010). https://doi.org/10.1007/978-3-642-16493-4_19

5. Gerdes, I., Klawonn, F., Kruse, R.: Evolutionäre Algorithmen: Genetische Algorithmen - Strategien und Optimierungsverfahren - Beispielanwendungen. vieweg, 1 edn. (2004)
6. Grießbach, D.: Fine guidance system performance report. Technical report. PLATO-DLR-PL-RP-0003, DLR (2020)
7. Hänsel, J., Rose, D., Herber, P., Glesner, S.: An evolutionary algorithm for the generation of timed test traces for embedded real-time systems. In: International Conference on Software Testing, Verification and Validation (ICST), pp. 170–179. IEEE Computer Society (2011)
8. Huang, W., Peleska, J.: Complete model-based equivalence class testing. Int. J. Softw. Tools Technol. Transf. **18**(3), 265–283 (2016)
9. Girgis, M.R.: Automatic test data generation for data flow testing using a genetic algorithm. J. Univ. Comput. Sci. **11**(6), 898–915 (2005)
10. Pender Electronic Design GmbH: Gr-xc6s-product_sheet (2011)
11. Pertenais, M.: Instrument technical requirement document. Technical report. PLATO-DLR-PL-RS-0001, DLR (2019)
12. Sharma, A., Patani, R., Aggarwal, A.: Software testing using genetic algorithms. Int. J. Comput. Sci. Eng. Surv. **7**(2), 21–33 (2016). https://doi.org/10.5121/ijcses.2016.7203
13. Shuster, M.D.: The taste test. Adv. Astronaut. Sci. **132** (2008)
14. Sthamer, H., Baresel, A., Wegener, J.: Evolutionary testing of embedded systems. In: Proceedings of the 14th International Internet & Software Quality Week (QW 2001), pp. 1–34 (2001)
15. Varshney, S., Mehrotra, M.: Automated software test data generation for data flow dependencies using genetic algorithm. Int. J. **4**(2), 472–479 (2014)
16. Wegener, J., Mueller, F.: A comparison of static analysis and evolutionary testing for the verification of timing constraints. Real-Time Syst. **21**(3), 241–268 (2001)
17. Witteck, U.: Automated test generation for satellite on-board image processing. Master thesis. TU Berlin (2018)
18. Witteck, U., Grießbach, D., Herber, P.: Test input partitioning for automated testing of satellite on-board image processing algorithms. In: Proceedings of the 14th International Conference on Software Technologies - Volume 1: ICSOFT, pp. 15–26. INSTICC, SciTePress (2019). https://doi.org/10.5220/0007807400150026
19. Witteck, U., Grießbach, D., Herber, P.: Equivalence class definition for automated testing of satellite on-board image processing. In: van Sinderen, M., Maciaszek, L. (eds.) Software Technologies. ICSOFT 2019. Communications in Computer and Information Science, vol. 1250, pp. 3–25. Springer, Cham (2020). https://doi.org/10.1007/978-3-030-52991-8_1
20. Witteck, U., Grießbach, D., Herber, P.: A genetic algorithm for automated test generation for satellite on-board image processing applications. In: Proceedings of the 15th International Conference on Software Technologies - Volume 1: ICSOFT, pp. 128–135. INSTICC, SciTePress (2020). https://doi.org/10.5220/0009821101280135

Model-Based Threat Modeling for Cyber-Physical Systems: A Computer-Aided Approach

Monika Maidl[1](✉), Gerhard Münz[1], Stefan Seltzsam[1], Marvin Wagner[2], Roman Wirtz[2], and Maritta Heisel[2]

[1] Siemens AG, Otto-Hahn-Ring 6, 81739 Munich, Germany
{monika.maidl,muenz.gerhard,stefan.seltzsam}@siemens.com
[2] University of Duisburg-Essen, Duisburg, Germany
{marvin.wagner,roman.wirtz,maritta.heisel}@uni-due.de

Abstract. Harming the security of a Cyber-Physical System (CPS) can lead to substantial damage and endanger for life because such a system includes many devices that interact with the physical world. Following the principle of security-by-design, the consideration of security should take place as early as possible during software development. However, the current state of the art often lacks systematic documentation of possible threats, and the identification of all relevant threats is not a trivial task.

In previous work, we presented a taxonomy of relevant attack actions for CPSs. The distinguishing feature of the taxonomy is its two-dimensional structure. We map typical attack actions to the attack surface. The attack surface is described by the component's interfaces which can be misused by attackers to gain access to a component, thus potentially harming the security of the system. On top of this taxonomy, we described an example of an attack action catalog. The application of our taxonomy and the attack action catalog still requires manual effort from practitioners, e.g. when looking up relevant attack actions.

Therefore, we developed a tool based on our taxonomy which we present in the present paper. In a first step, we formalized our taxonomy in form of a metamodel. Each threat model is an instance of that metamodel. The metamodel reflects the way in which the taxonomy links attack actions with parts of the system. Furthermore, we created a graphical editor that assists practitioners in creating the threat model. Based on the taxonomy's metamodel and attack action catalogs, the tool pre-filters relevant attack actions and allows to systematically document them in the threat model. Our tool provides different views on the threat model, thus helping to focus on the relevant aspects for a specific task.

Keywords: Security threats · Threat modeling · Attack actions · Taxonomy · Catalog · Tool-support

M. van Sinderen et al. (Eds.): ICSOFT 2020, CCIS 1447, pp. 158–183, 2021.
https://doi.org/10.1007/978-3-030-83007-6_8

1 Introduction

Cyber-Physical Systems (CPSs) are running in many places, especially in critical infrastructures. These systems interact with the physical world, e.g. by monitoring values measured with sensors. The recent development in the context of the Internet-of-Things leads to increasing use of CPSs, also into private homes. Usually, a CPS is composed of different components that communicate with each other via interfaces. Due to their connected nature and their dissemination, CPSs are often subject to attacks. Therefore, it is essential to design critical systems with adequate security measures in place, following security standards like IEC 62443 [9].

The term *threat modeling* summarizes methods that deal with identifying and documenting incidents that may have an impact on the system's security.

Shostack [17] defines the term as follows: "Threat modeling is the use of abstractions to aid in thinking about risks." Uzunov and Fernández [20] give an alternative definition: "Threat modeling is a process that can be used to analyze potential attacks or threats, and can also be supported by threat libraries or attack taxonomies."

The knowledge about such threats can be captured in so-called threat libraries which exist for many types of systems. Security engineers can look up relevant threats and document them for their concrete system. However, these libraries often do not follow a common structure for the different threat descriptions.

A well-known taxonomy for security is STRIDE [11]. STRIDE provides six categories for typical threat categories. The disadvantage of the taxonomy is its generic nature, i.e. the categories are not mapped to specific elements of the system. Therefore, the application of STRIDE requires high expertise from security engineers.

In previous work, we presented a two-dimensional taxonomy that addresses the disadvantage of STRIDE by mapping typical attack actions to the attack surface [13]. The first dimension of this taxonomy is similar to STRIDE since it denotes The new approach is to combine this attack action dimension with a second dimension: The second dimension, which we call the attack surface dimension, consists of the system elements that constitute the attack surface of the system. It is described by the elements that allow some interaction, i.e. the component's interfaces. Attackers may perform malicious actions at these points, thus leading to harm to the system's security. The taxonomy allows creating catalogs of typical attack actions to CPSs. Practitioners can use these catalogs to look up relevant attack actions for the system they analyze.

Although our taxonomy and the attack action catalogs assist practitioners in identifying relevant threats, manual effort is still required, e.g. when documenting the identified threats. To support practitioners in systematically identifying and documenting relevant threats to the system, we developed a tool based on our taxonomy following a model-based approach. We first formalize the taxonomy and its dependencies to the system model by developing a metamodel. For the attack surface, we make use of our metamodel for CPS which we presented in

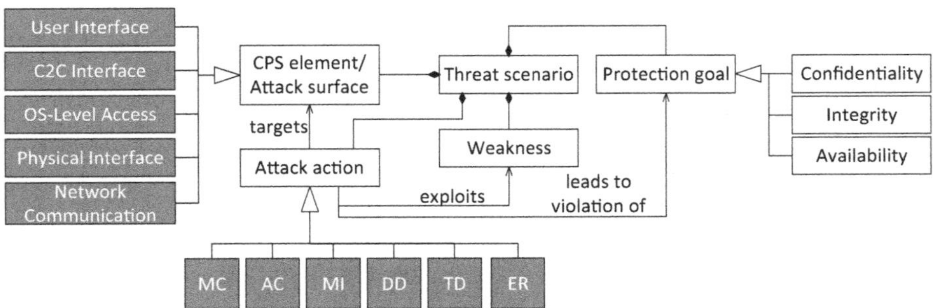

Fig. 1. Threat modeling terminology [13].

previous work [14]. Our metamodel includes the elements of a threat model, i.e. a systematic listing of threats to a system. The focus of our metamodel is to show the dependencies between the aspects of threats and different elements of the system, thereby reflecting the relation between the two dimensions of the taxonomy. To instantiate the metamodel, i.e. to create a threat model for a previously modelled system, we provide a graphical editor. The editor allows to systematically analyze the system, and it pre-filters relevant attack actions based on the provided interfaces. Furthermore, it is possible to embed attack action catalogs into the editor, thus ensuring flexibility for different development projects. To help practitioners in focusing on relevant aspects, our editor provides different views on the model.

The remainder of the paper is structured as follows: In Sect. 2, we describe the terminology which we use in this paper. In Sect. 3, we describe the taxonomy for which we present our tool support in this paper. It is followed by its formalization in form of our metamodel in Sect. 4. Section 5.1 explains how catalogs can be structured with our taxonomy, and we provide an example of a catalog. Our graphical editor to create a threat model is described in Sect. 6. We discuss related work in Sect. 7 and conclude the paper with a summary of our contributions and an outlook on future work in Sect. 8.

2 Terminology

The terminology in the context of threat modeling varies between different standards and publications. To have a common understanding for this paper, we provide an overview of the used terminology in Fig. 1.

The output of threat modeling is a list of *Threat scenarios*. Each threat scenario consists of the following elements: an *Attack action*, a *CPS element* as part of the *Attack surface*, a *Weakness*, and a *Protection goal*. As protection goals, we consider the CIA triad *Confidentiality*, *Integrity*, and *Availability*.

The threat scenario describes how an attack action leads to the violation of a protection goal by exploiting a weakness. The attack action targets an element of the attack surface of the CPS, i.e. an interface or network communication.

In some cases, a sequence of attack actions are required for the violation of protection goals, and these are described as part of the threat scenarios.

For illustration, we describe the example of a threat scenario: An attacker, pretending to be a legitimate device of the CPS, sends manipulated configuration (attack action) to an embedded component that is accessible via a C2C interface. As a result, the configuration of the control program is changed (violating the protection goal 'integrity of configuration'), and the embedded component behaves in an unintended way.

The goal of threat modeling is to consider all relevant attack actions against the CPS. To support this, we use categories of attack surface elements and attack action types. The elements marked in gray provides an overview of the categories which we use for our taxonomy (see Sect. 3). The attack surface denotes the first dimension, and the attack action types are the second dimension.

3 Two-Dimensional Taxonomy

In the following, we describe our two-dimensional taxonomy. We provide a two-dimensional taxonomy of attack actions for the scope of CPSs. Section 5.1 later exemplifies the usage of the taxonomy by describing a catalog of attack actions.

We first describe the two dimensions and show how we combine them for our taxonomy. Finally, we compare the taxonomy with existing ones, i.e. STRIDE [11] and CAPEC [15].

3.1 Attack Surface Dimension

The first dimension lists the parts of a system that form the attack surface, i.e. those points of a system at which an attack action may be performed. The *elements of the attack surface* depend on the type of system, and reflect the technical scope and level of detail typically considered in threat modeling. In this work, a CPS is viewed as a set of different types of components like embedded devices and hosts (workstations and servers) that are running standard operating systems and domain-specific applications and services. The components communicate through a combination of network protocols. In previous work, we proposed a metamodel for CPSs which is intended to be used as a basis of security analysis and specifies the elements of the attack surface of a CPS [14]. These elements form the attack surface dimension, and in the following, we explain them in detail.

The primary parts of an attack surface are the interfaces of the system components, as interfaces are the parts of the system that are open for interaction. Corresponding to the scope and level of detail considered in this paper, the various interfaces related to operating systems are covered by one abstract attack surface element, and the same holds for network communication.

User Interface. User interfaces are designed to let human users interact with the system. User interfaces can be realized in different ways, e.g. as a graphical user interface of an application running on the local computer, as a web-based user interface accessed over the network via a web browser, or as a human-machine interface realized with an embedded device. Apart from interfaces for regular users of the CPS, user interfaces for administration purposes need to be covered as well. User interfaces are usually associated with user accounts to implement user identification, authentication, and authorization.

Component-to-Component (C2C) Interface. These interfaces are similar to user interfaces but are designed to allow interaction between components instead of humans. Typically, an application running on a system component calls a service that runs on another component according to some protocol. C2C interfaces implement protocols and may include authentication and authorization. Typically, the protocol used by some C2C interface is utilizing standard network services that are implemented as part of the operating system. Interfaces (e.g. APIs) that exist internally in a component without being accessible by other components are not considered as C2C interfaces but considered as part of OS level access.

OS Level Access. There are various possible ways of how an attacker can interact with the operating system of a component. This includes local APIs and files, as well as the installation and modification of software, and network services that are implemented as part of the operating system. We use the element OS level access to represent the range of actual OS interfaces. This corresponds to the typical scope and level of detail of security analyses for CPSs, where the interfaces of the operating system are not modeled in all detail.

Physical Interface. These interfaces require physical access or physical proximity to the component to interact with the system. This is often relevant for CPSs with components that are widely deployed across sites. Included are interfaces used to communicate with the component, such as serial ports, USB port, local diagnosis or management interfaces, and near-field communication, e.g. Bluetooth. Other kinds of physical interactions are covered as well, such as manipulating the hardware and removing a hard drive.

Network Communication. User interfaces and C2C interfaces may involve network communication between different components of the CPS, using a protocol. Communication takes place over a potentially complex network infrastructure composed of network cables and network devices like routers and firewalls. We use Network Communication as an element of the attack surface that subsumes all possibilities to attack the communication between components of the CPS. An attacker could e.g. perform wiretapping at an accessible LAN port, or hack into a network device to disturb the communication. This abstraction corresponds to the typical scope and level of detail of the design of CPSs, which builds on an existing network infrastructure such as the Internet or production networks.

3.2 Attack Action Type Dimension

Attack actions are a central part of threat scenarios, as shown in Sect. 2, and describe the action an attacker takes at the attack surface of the system. Hence it is straightforward to use types of attack actions as a dimension of our taxonomy. Actual attack actions are often creative ways to interact with the system in an unintended way, and hence the known attack actions are very heterogeneous. Therefore it is not straightforward to find suitable types. We devised the following guiding principles for the development of our attack action types.

1. Focus on actions that an attacker performs at some location of the attack surface.
2. Strictly differentiate between attack actions and harm. As detailed in Sect. 3.5, after the identification of a relevant attack action for a CPS, it is a separate step to analyze whether a protection goal can be violated by that attack action.
3. Common attack actions should be assignable to one of the attack action types in a straightforward way. As a reference for common attack actions, we use the list compiled from industrial projects, as well as external sources [5]. Coverage of 'esoteric'attack actions has less priority.
4. Keep it simple: For good usability, the list of attack action types should not be too long, and easy to grasp.

As the next step, we considered existing taxonomies, in particular STRIDE and the taxonomy-level of CAPEC. To meet the guiding principles, we performed some adaptations. Section 3.4 contains a detailed comparison of the attack action types with the taxonomies of STRIDE and CAPEC, showing the adaptations.

The following list presents the attack action types, which form the attack action type dimension of our taxonomy. We argue for each case that the first two principles are fulfilled.

MC. Misuse credentials: Attacker obtains the authentication credentials for the account of a legitimate user and uses these to get access.
Note that this type covers all attack actions that relate to passwords, e.g. actions like obtaining passwords by social engineering, or guessing the password. Such attacks are very common indeed. Login interfaces are part of the attack surface. And as misuse of a password is not in itself harmful, the second principle is also observed.

AC. Exploit weakness of access control: Attacker circumvents or breaks access control and gets access.
This type covers the actions of attackers who are confronted with some form of access control. Access control is located at places where interaction with users or other components is expected, and hence the first principle is fulfilled. The second principle is observed by the same argument as for MC. One could argue that credentials are part of access control, but we decided to single out the misuse of credentials as a separate type, as AC is about exploiting (usually technical) weaknesses, while MC is about misusing legitimate credentials.

MI. Submit malicious input: Attacker enters or sends malicious data or commands.
This type comprises many common attack actions, in particular many actions against Web applications like SQL-injection. The first principle is fulfilled since interfaces that take input are open for interaction and hence are part of the attack surface. The second principle is fulfilled as it requires separate considerations to determine harm that might be caused by malicious input.

DD. Disclose data: Attacker reads or sniffs data.
This type comprises attack actions where an attacker can easily read data at the attack surface, e.g. by sniffing clear-text protocols. So the first principle is observed. Concerning the second principle, note that this type stands for various actions in which data is read at a place directly accessible to the attacker. Whether such reading results in harm, by violating the protection goal of confidentiality, is a different (although in this case fairly easy) consideration: Determining whether the data that can be read is sensitive.

TD. Tamper data: Attacker manipulates data.
This type is similar to the type DD. The difference is that this type covers attacks where data is manipulated at the attack surface.

ER. Exhaust resources: Attacker uses up limited, shared resources needed by the system.
This type covers attack actions that exploit the use of shared resources, e.g. CPU, memory, or network bandwidth. The attack surface for these actions is some form of access to the shared resource, e.g. the possibility to run applications on the operating system, or the possibility to send traffic in a network. So the first principle is fulfilled. Concerning the second principle, like in the two previous cases, it might be easy to determine the harm that follows from the exhaustion of a shared resource, but this attack action type focuses on the ways how to perform the exhaustion.

The example attack action catalog in Tables 4 and 5 shows that the third principle is met, by mapping a range of common attack actions to our attack action types.

3.3 Two-Dimensional Taxonomy

As the attack action types of Sect. 3.2 stand for attack actions at the attack surface, it is a natural step to relate the attack action types with the attack surface elements of Sect. 3.1. Table 1 shows the mapping, where the statements in each field express the relation. In most cases, the statements are straightforward, while some statements clarify the relevant aspects of the attack surface. Furthermore, some attack actions are not relevant for certain elements of the attack surface, resulting in empty fields in the table.

The two-dimensional taxonomy helps to systematically cover attack actions for the attack surface of a system.

We provide some explanations for the statements in the table: The attack action types DD and TD are considered for user and C2C interfaces. By design,

Table 1. Two-dimensional taxonomy [13].

	User interface	C2C interface	OS level access	Physical interface	Network comm.
MC	Attacker misuses credential to authenticate to the user interface	Attacker misuses credential to authenticate to the C2C-interface	Attacker misuses credential to obtain access to the operating system	Attacker misuses credential to obtain access to physical interface	
AC	Attacker exploits weakness in the access control of the user interface	Attacker exploits weakness in the access control of the C2C interface	Attacker exploits weakness in the access control of the operating system	Attacker exploits weakness in the access control of the physical interface	
MI	Attacker enters malicious input at the user interface	Attacker sends malicious input to the C2C interface	Attacker sends malicious input to some OS level interface	Attacker enters malicious input at the physical interface	
DD			Attacker reads data out of memory	Attacker reads data via physical interface	Attacker sniffs network communication
TD			Attacker manipulates data stored in memory	Attacker manipulates data via physical interface	Attacker manipulates network communication
ER			Attacker exhausts resources of the operating system		Attacker exhausts network resources

these interfaces display data and provide functionality for editing. Using this functionality is not an attack action. If the access to a user or C2C interface is meant to be restricted, then the attack action types MC and AC apply and cover possible ways an attacker can get access despite the access protection.

The last row of Table 1 shows that the attack action type ER is only considered for OS level access and network access. Only at these elements of the attack surface, an attacker has direct access to limited resources, like CPU, memory, or network bandwidth. In contrast, user interfaces, C2C interfaces, and physical interfaces do not provide direct access to resources. Malformed input to these interfaces that causes the receiving component to crash, e.g. due to overload, is covered by the type MI.

The column for OS level access reflects the fact that this element of the attack surface comprises various interfaces of the operating system. For MC, the user accounts of the operating system are in focus. The attack action type AC refers to the various access control mechanisms of the operating system, e.g. privilege of processes and file permissions. It comprises attacks to exploit weaknesses in these mechanisms, e.g. to obtain higher privileges. Malicious input (MI) can

Table 2. Mapping of taxonomy categories - STRIDE [13].

Category	Description	MC	AC	MI	DD	TD	ER
Spoofing of user identity	Impersonating something or someone else.	✓	✓				
Tampering with data	Modifying data or code					✓	
Repudiation	Denying to have performed an action						
Information disclosure	Exposing information to someone not authorized to see it				✓		
Denial of service	Deny or degrade service to users			✓			✓
Elevation of privilege	Gain capabilities without proper authorization		✓	✓			

take the form of malware that exploits vulnerabilities in the operating system. Malicious input may originate from a user with OS level access who is tricked into downloading and executing malware. Another path of malicious input is specially crafted packets sent to a network service of the operating system.

For network communication, as explained in Subsect. 3.1, the scope and level of detail applied in the design of a CPS usually does not include the network infrastructure. Hence, threat modeling for a CPS focuses on attack actions against the network communication between components. These attack actions are disclosing (DD), tampering (TD), and exhausting resource (ER). The attack action types MC, AC, and MI are not relevant as the network communication does not process credentials, does not implement access control, and does not handle inputs. These tasks are performed by the protocol stack of the corresponding user or C2C interface.

3.4 Comparison with Other Taxonomies

In a systematic literature review on threat analysis of software systems performed by Tuma et al. [19], five methodologies make use of some sort of knowledge base, are applicable to the architectural or design level, and take the architectural design as input. Three of them use STRIDE [7,8,17] as taxonomy, the remaining two refer to CAPEC [2,3]. As our taxonomy also provides a knowledge base and is supposed to be used in the same context of threat analysis, this section provides a detailed comparison with STRIDE and CAPEC.

STRIDE. STRIDE [11] is a well-known categorization model for threats against computer systems. It has been developed by Microsoft and is integrated in the

Microsoft Threat Modeling Tool[1]. STRIDE is a mnemonic for six threat categories: *Spoofing*, *Tampering*, *Repudiation*, *Information disclosure*, *Denial of service*, and *Elevation of privilege.*

We found that some of the STRIDE categories refer to the impact of a successful attack (e.g. denial of service) rather than to the actual action an attacker performs. To avoid confusion, our taxonomy clearly focuses on attack actions that describe what an attacker does. The impact of an attack action can be assessed in a subsequent step by determining the violated protection goals.

Table 2 shows how the STRIDE categories can be mapped to our attack action types. As can be seen, the STRIDE categories *Tampering* and *Information disclosure* are directly related to the attack action types TD and DD. *Spoofing* can be achieved by misusing credentials of existing accounts (MC), or by exploiting an access control weakness (AC). *Denial of service* is typically caused by malicious input (MI), such as a specially crafted packet leading to a segmentation fault, or by exhausting limited resources (ER), e.g. with a flooding attack. Malicious input (MI) as well as bypassing access control (AC) can lead to *Elevation of privilege.*

We did not map the STRIDE category *Repudiation* to any of our attack actions types. This is because we see repudiation as violation of a protection goal (i.e. non-repudiation), not an attack action. In fact, various attack actions can be used with the goal to repudiate an action, such as tampering log files. But our types focus on the action of the attacker rather than the goal of the action.

The main extension of our attack action types compared to STRIDE is the attack action type MI, which includes all kinds of injection attacks, such as SQL injection, code injection through exploitation of a buffer overflow vulnerability, infection of a system with malware etc. In STRIDE, these attacks do not have an explicit category but can only be categorized indirectly by the harm they cause (e.g. denial of service).

STRIDE itself does not include an attack surface dimension. The Microsoft Threat Modeling Tool allows us to associate STRIDE categories with elements of a Data Flow Diagram (DFD), which contains processes, data stores, external interactors, and data flows between them. However, the combination of STRIDE categories and DFD elements is not used to provide a better understanding of a STRIDE category for a DFD element. More importantly, DFDs do not reflect the different parts of the attack surface of a system. So the combination of STRIDE with DFDs lacks the possibility to create a catalog of relevant attack actions for each attack surface element, similar to the ones in Tables 4 and 5.

CAPEC. The Common Attack Pattern Enumeration and Classification (CAPEC) [15], maintained by MITRE[2], provides a catalog of attack patterns.

[1] Microsoft Threat Modeling Tool (last access: May 25, 2021): https://www.microsoft.com/en-us/securityengineering/sdl/threatmodeling.

[2] MITRE: https://www.mitre.org/ (last access: May 18, 2021).

Table 3. Mapping of taxonomy categories - CAPEC [13].

Mechanism of attack	Description	MC	AC	MI	DD	TD	ER
Engage in deceptive interactions	Spoofing and social engineering	✓	✓	✓			
Abuse existing functionality	Manipulation of data or system behavior by misusing system functionality		✓	✓		✓	✓
Manipulate data structures	Manipulation of data by exploiting a system vulnerability			✓		✓	
Manipulate system resources	Manipulation of shared resources			✓		✓	
Inject unexpected items	Manipulation of system behavior through malicious input			✓			
Employ probabilistic techniques	Fuzzing and bruteforcing		✓	✓			
Manipulate timing and state	Exploitation of concurrency issues (e.g. race condition)			✓		✓	
Collect and analyze information	Theft of information			✓	✓		
Subvert access control	Exploitation of access control weakness		✓				

In CAPEC version 3.2, attack patterns are classified according to two different schemes. The first scheme is called *domains of attack* and assigns attack patterns to the categories *Software*, *Hardware*, *Communications*, *Supply chain*, *Social engineering*, and *Physical security*. These categories refer to the type of weakness that is exploited, such as a software vulnerability, a weak physical control, or an unaware user. We found that CAPEC attack patterns in the domain *Communications* largely correspond to the attack actions associated to our attack surface element *Network Communication*. Similarly, most attack patterns belonging to *Hardware* and *Physical security* are related to the attack actions of the attack surface element *Physical Interface*. For the other domains, however, we did not find any clear correlation with the different elements of the attack surface.

The second CAPEC classification scheme is called *mechanisms of attack* and refers to general attacking techniques, which is similar to the attack action dimension of our taxonomy. Table 3 shows a mapping of our attack action types to CAPEC mechanisms of attack. Attack patterns belonging to the mechanism *Engage in deceptive interactions* range from attacks targeting user credentials and clickjacking to DLL injection and DNS spoofing. In our taxonomy, these attacks are separated into the attack action types MC, AC, and MI. Similarly, *Abuse of existing functionality* covers a broad spectrum of attack patterns that, in our taxonomy, belong to different attack action types. As can be seen, the attack mechanisms *Manipulate data structures*, *Manipulate system resources*, and *Manipulate timing and state* are related to the attack action types MI and TD. These two types distinguish between attacks sending malicious input to a system interface, and attacks tampering data (e.g. configuration files) directly, whereas the three CAPEC mechanisms differentiate between types of manipulated data and resources. The mechanism *Employ probabilistic techniques* includes password brute-forcing, which relates to the exploitation of an access control weakness (AC), and fuzzing attacks, which corresponds to sending potentially malicious input to an interface (MI). *Collect and analyze information* subsumes active and passive information gathering techniques, belonging to the attack action types MI and DD, respectively.

All in all, we can state that CAPEC's approach to classify attack patterns into mechanisms of attacks has some similarities to the attack action dimension of our taxonomy. The attack surface dimension of our taxonomy, however, is not reflected in CAPEC. Some CAPEC domains of attack are slightly related to specific attack surface elements, but in general, CAPEC domains of attack refer to types of exploited weaknesses. As a consequence, CAPEC lacks the possibility to easily query attack patterns that are relevant for a specific attack surface element of a CPS.

3.5 Using the Taxonomy for Threat Modeling

In the process of threat modeling, our taxonomy helps to obtain a list of threat scenarios as described in Sect. 2. The elements of the attack surface that need to be considered can be directly extracted from the design of the CPS. In the first step of threat modeling, for each of these elements and each relevant attack action type, attack actions are looked up from the catalog.

Once an attack action is found to be relevant, the next step is to analyze whether the attack action could lead to the violation of a protection goal of the CPS. This is an essential step of threat modeling, in which know-how about the architecture of the system is combined with a thorough understanding of the protection goals for the data and functionalities of the system. If a path to the violation of a protection goal has been found, a threat scenario is documented. The threat scenario is completed by describing the weakness of the CPS that is exploited by the attack action. Usually, the attack action is directly associated with a weakness, so this step is not challenging. For example, the infection with malware is exploiting unpatched vulnerabilities, while a brute force attack on a password is exploiting weak passwords. In fact, it would be a natural extension of an attack action catalog to link the attack actions to related weaknesses and hints for security measures. For example, enforcing a strong password policy is a security measure to protect against brute forcing.

After threat modeling has been completed, the weaknesses are used as a basis to select (additional) security measures for the CPS.

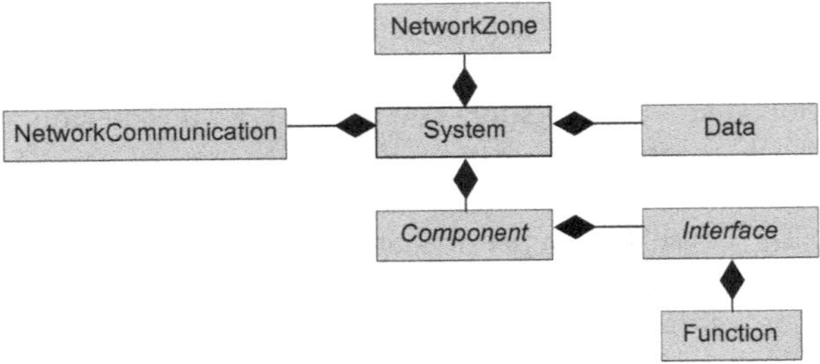

Fig. 2. Relevant artifacts of the system's metamodel.

We point out some aspects of using the taxonomy with an example: A component has several user interfaces and C2C interfaces. The relevant attack action types, namely MC, AC, and MI, are analyzed for each of these interfaces. This helps to identify weaknesses in the design of access control for these interfaces, and weaknesses in the processing of inputs. The component also has several physical interfaces, and the need to adequately protect each of them may have been overlooked during design. Going through the attack action types helps to identify the critical gaps. Furthermore, the component runs a standard operating system that needs to be securely configured and hardened. The attack action types allow the architect to understand which parts of the OS need particular protection, e.g. by encrypting files, disabling unneeded network services, or implementing other hardening measures. For each of the network communications of the CPS, the attack action types DD, TD, and ER are analyzed, and as a result, the architect might decide to use another protocol or a secure channel for a protocol.

4 Metamodel

As a first step towards tool support, we formalize our taxonomy and the relations. Based on the *Eclipse Modeling Framework (EMF)* [18], we create a metamodel for this purpose. The notation of metamodels EMF is similar to UML class diagrams. For better readability and space reasons, we have decomposed the metamodel into four sub-metamodels *System*, *ThreatModel*, *ThreatScenarioListing*, *ProtectionGoal*. The gray elements in the metamodels are taken from our CPS system model [14]. Classes with a cursive name are abstract classes. The focus of our metamodel is on the dependencies between the aspects of threats and the different elements of the system, thereby reflecting the relation between the two dimensions of the taxonomy as presented in Sect. 3.

4.1 CPS Metamodel

We use the metamodel for cyber-physical systems (CPS) from our previous work [14] as a starting point. It contains the elements of the attack surface, i.e. the interfaces and network communication. In the present paper, we focus on the

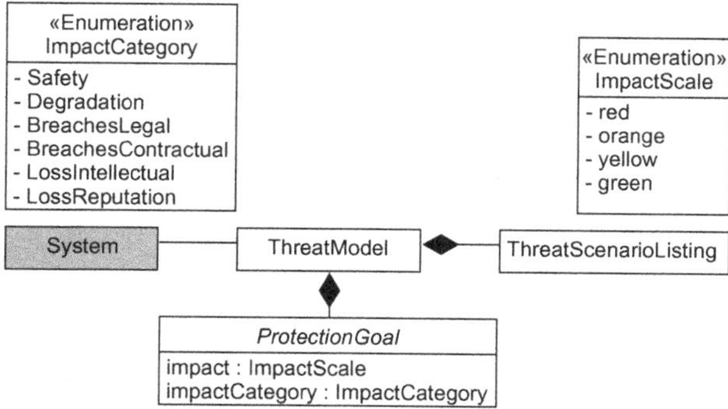

Fig. 3. Metamodel of *ThreatModel*.

crucial parts of the CPS metamodel that are important for the implementation of the taxonomy. Figure 2 shows this compact version. The *System* class is the root element of the sub-metamodel. It contains four other classes: (i) *NetworkZone* representing network zones in a CPS, (ii) *Component* which can be further refined to specific types, e.g. a host, (iii) *NetworkCommunication* representing the communication between two components, and (iv) *Data* (represents data which is processed in a CPS). A component has a set of *Interfaces*. These interfaces offers some functionalities (class *Function*) to other components. Later on, we map attack actions to the different interface types (see Sect. 3.1). Our editor uses this information for filtering relevant attack actions (see Table 1).

4.2 Threat Model

The second sub-metamodel, which is shown in Fig. 3, shows how the other three sub-metamodels are linked. The root element is the *ThreatModel* which has an association to the system. This way, the threat model can make references to the elements of the system, and the automatic mapping of attack actions to the interfaces can be used. A threat model consists of *ThreatRiskAnalysis*s and *ProtectionGoal*s, both of which are further refined in the next sub-sections.

A protection goal has two attributes. First, there is the attribute *impact* of the type *ImpactScale*. This attribute expresses how severe a violation of the protection goal would be. We use an enumeration for the *ImpactScale*. This enumeration has four literals *red*, *orange*, *yellow*, and *green*. Red means a high impact and green means a low impact. Orange and yellow are between them. Orange means a higher impact than yellow.

The second attribute is *impactCategory* which has the type *ImpactCategory* in form of an enumeration. It has the six literals *Safety*, *Degradation*, *BreachesLegal*, *BreachesContractual*, *LossIntellectual*, and *LossReputation*. The impact category describes what kind the impact has to the system. We use these six categories because they are the most common ones.

4.3 Protection Goals

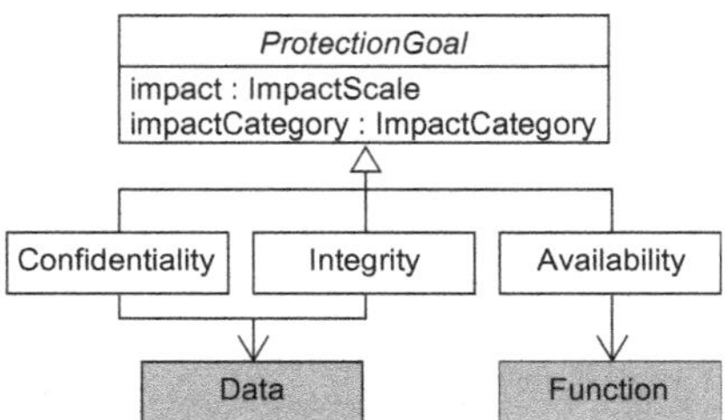

Fig. 4. Metamodel of *ProtectionGoal*.

Figure 4 shows the third sub-metamodel. The class *ProtectionGoal* is an abstract class. It has the three specializations *Confidentiality*, *Integrity*, and *Availability* which are equal to the CIA triad. Confidentiality and integrity have an association to some data processed by the System. This way, the metamodel provides the possibility to document which data shall be protected. The metamodel for CPS as presented in [14] includes the relation of data to components and network communications, i.e. where data is stored and transferred. Availability has an association to a function of the System. An interface of a component offers some functions (see Fig. 2). Thus, an availability goal denotes that the availability of a function shall be preserved.

4.4 Threat Scenario Listing

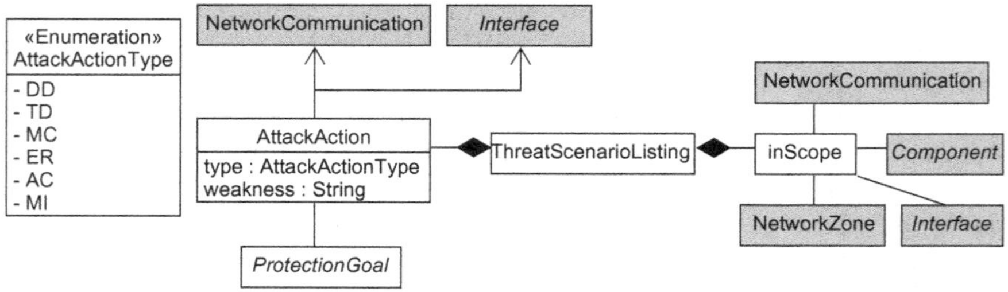

Fig. 5. Metamodel of *ThreatScenarioListing*.

Figure 5 shows the last sub-metamodel. The *ThreatScenarioListing* is part of a threat model. A threat model can have multiple threat scenario listings for different perspectives. Each analysis consists of *inScope*-classes and a set of *AttackActions*. *inScope* has the purpose to express that a part of a system (*NetworkCommunication*, *Component*, *Interface*, or *NetworkZone*) is in scope for that analysis. So, not each element has to be in scope, and it can be filtered what shall be analyzed. Attack actions are also part of a threat scenario listing. Each attack action has the attribute *type* which has the type *AttackActionType* which is an enumeration and has six literals DD, TD, MC, ER, AC, and MI. These are the abbreviations of attack actions as shown in Table 1. They form the second dimension of our taxonomy. Furthermore, there is the attribute *weakness* that documents the weakness exploited by the attack action. The associations from an attack action to a *NetworkCommunication* and an *Interface* are to express that an attack action is performed at this element of the attack surface. They form the other dimension of the taxonomy. Between an attack action and a protection goal, there is another association to express that this action harms the protection goal.

5 Attack Action Catalog

In the following, we describe how attack action catalogs can be structured with the help of our taxonomy which we presented in Sect. 3. Furthermore, we present an example of such a catalog.

5.1 Structuring Attack Action Catalogs with the Taxonomy

While Table 1 helps to focus on relevant attack action types for a certain interface, architects and software developers find it hard to identify specific attack actions based on abstract attack action types: They need an understanding of actual attack actions rather than abstract categories. There are many threat and attack catalogs that contain actual attack actions, but it is hard to find relevant entries, especially for people without a deep security background.

We propose to use our two-dimensional taxonomy to structure catalogs of specific attack actions. This means that each specific attack action is assigned to an attack action type and an element of the attack surface. In that way, the (typically large) set of attack action is clustered into 20 subsets in a way that is meaningful for threat modeling. Practitioners can find the relevant attack actions efficiently by looking into the appropriate field of the structured catalog. Hence the catalog provides a useful way to make security knowledge about attacks available during threat modeling.

5.2 Example Catalog

In Tables 4 and 5, we provide an example catalog of attack actions against CPSs, structured according to our taxonomy. The catalog captures the range of attacks that have been considered in security analyzes for CPSs over many years in industrial projects, and also reflects the results of penetration tests and real world incidents. Besides, the catalog was compared and extended with external resources, e.g. from the *Bundesamt für Sicherheit in der Informationsbranche* [5], as well as academic sources like [20]. The catalog is not aiming for completeness.

Instead, the aim is to cover the most relevant cases and include attacks that exploit typical weaknesses in standard IT technology. To cover attacks that are specific to domain-related technology (e.g. embedded devices, sensors) or attacks to specific components like network devices, the catalog can be augmented.

In Table 4, we show the mapping of the attack actions *Misuse Credentials (MC)*, *Exploit Weakness of Access Control (AC)*, and *Submit Malicious Input (MI)*. For each of the attack actions, we provide examples in the context of a specific interface type or a network communication. An empty cell denotes that the attack action is not relevant for the corresponding attack surface element.

In Table 5, we show the second part of the example catalog. It contains the attack actions *Disclose Data (DD)*, *Tamper Data (TD)*, and *Exhaust Resources (ER)*.

Attack actions and their relevance are changing over time, so it is important to emphasize that such a catalog has to be continuously updated. Furthermore, it is possible to use the taxonomy to create a catalog for a specific context, e.g. for critical infrastructures. To do so, the examples can be refined with more details.

5.3 Further Benefits

The example catalog of Sect. 5.1 illustrates the structuring of attack actions according to the two-dimensional taxonomy. In this section, we discuss further ways to use taxonomy-based catalogs in the context of threat modeling.

Specific Catalogs for Types of Components. A CPS consists of heterogeneous components like controllers, network devices, and standard IT components. By providing a separate catalog for each type of component, attack actions that are specific to the technologies of that component type can be listed and provided to practitioners. Such catalogs could either complete or replace a generic catalog.

Reusing Threat Modeling Results. In practice, often a certain type of CPS is used as a blueprint for industrial projects. After performing threat modeling for that type of CPS, the knowledge generated by that process of threat modeling can be captured in the form of a specific attack action catalog. More precisely, the entries in the generic catalog(s) can be replaced by more specific and relevant attacks for the blueprint. In that way, it is possible to make knowledge reusable for future projects.

Using Catalogs in Tooling for Threat Modeling. The benefits of taxonomy-based catalogs are significantly increased by automation: We have developed a prototype for a tool, and are in the piloting phase. Our tool guides practitioners through the process of threat modeling and presents relevant attack action types when the practitioner is working in a certain part of the system.

Table 4. Attack action catalog for CPSs Part 1 [13].

	User Interface	C2C Interface	OS Level Access	Physical Interface	Network Comm.
MC	– Phishing to obtain a user's password – Brute force attack on weak password – Setting password through weak password recovery mechanism	– Extract default or hard-coded passwords – Brute force attack on weak passwords – Misuse fake MAC or IP address to authenticate	– Misuse of temporary or default password – Brute-force attack to guess password of OS account – Misuse of shared password (e.g. shared between sites)	– Social engineering to obtain password to server management consoles or BIOS	
AC	– Misuse of client-side authentication or authorization – Access via debugging interface – Misuse of direct object references e.g. in URLs – Session hijacking	– Misuse of client-side authentication or authorization – Security downgrade through algorithm negotiation – Misuse of excessively granted privileges	– Bypass of kiosk mode – Misuse of open network service (e.g. Telnet, VNC) – Misuse of (unnecessarily) high privileges in OS – Misuse of unlocked user session	– Access through server management consoles or BIOS – Re-boot with different OS from CD or USB – Access through unprotected near-field communication protocol – Misuse of hardware interfaces (UART, JTAG) – Misuse of shut-down button	
MI	– Cross-site scripting – SQL-injection – Malware infection of component through malicious payload	– Fuzzing attack – Malware infection of component through malicious payload – Crash due to overload	– Trick OS-user to install or run malware – Network packet exploiting vulnerability in network protocol implementation of the OS, e.g. ping-of-death	– Malware infection of component through infected USB stick	

Table 5. Attack action catalog for CPSs Part 2 [13].

	User Interface	C2C Interface	OS Level Access	Physical Interface	Network Comm.
DD			– Read sensitive data from files or Windows registry, e.g. passwords, operational data – Read data from process memory by causing a core dump	– Steal media, i.e. SD card, USB stick, or hard disk – Install keylogger – Take a covert look at a display – Read data through hardware interfaces (UART, JTAG)	– Read clear text protocols, e.g. HTTP, FTP – Sniff data sent over unprotected WLAN
TD			– Manipulate data in files or databases – Manipulate configuration or software	– Change data on removable media	– Manipulate or replay message – Man-in-the-middle attack
ER			– (Malicious) application uses up CPU or memory		– Flooding the network – Occupy wireless interfaces with a jammer

6 Tool-Support

We use a model-based approach for our tool based on two frameworks. The first framework is EMF [18] (see Sect. 4) and the second framework is called Sirius[3].

6.1 Sirius

Sirius allows you to create your own eclipse graphical modeling workbench and diagrams. It builds on EMF and the *Acceleo Query Language (AQL)*[4]. AQL is a specification language similar to the *Object Constraint Language (OCL)*[5]. AQL expressions are used to interact with the model, e.g. to manipulate model instances or to query data from the model. Sirius has some built-in graphical elements, for example text fields, nodes, and containers. Diagrams can be specified in a hierarchical tree structure. The diagrams provide a user-friendly view of model instances.

6.2 Workflow of Our Tool

The metamodels of Sect. 4 provide the fundamentals for the Sirius editors. We implemented two editors for different purposes, each having several diagrams. The first editor enables the user to model a CPS with different components, interfaces, communications, and data. That editor builds on our previous work [14]. Therefore, we do not further discuss it in this paper. However, the CPS editor is essential for the second editor, which uses our taxonomy from Sect. 3. We provide a simple example to show how our editor works. Figure 6 shows a CPS which is modeled with our editor. There is the component *Host 1* with a user interface (small box), which can be accessed remotely from a *User Browser* via a network communication with the *https* protocol.

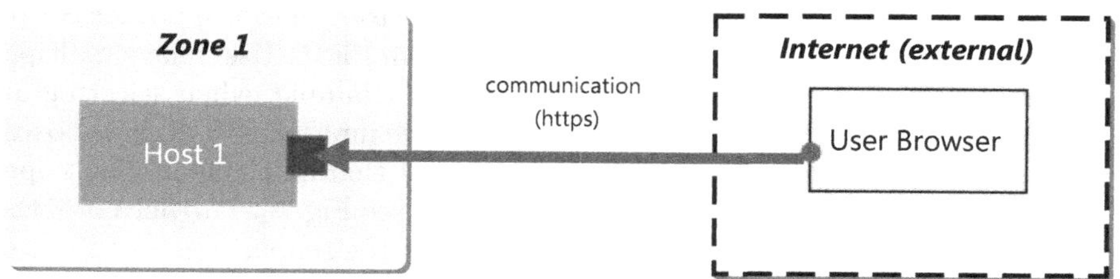

Fig. 6. Example of a CPS.

[3] https://www.eclipse.org/sirius/.
[4] https://www.eclipse.org/acceleo/documentation/.
[5] https://www.omg.org/spec/OCL/2.4/PDF.

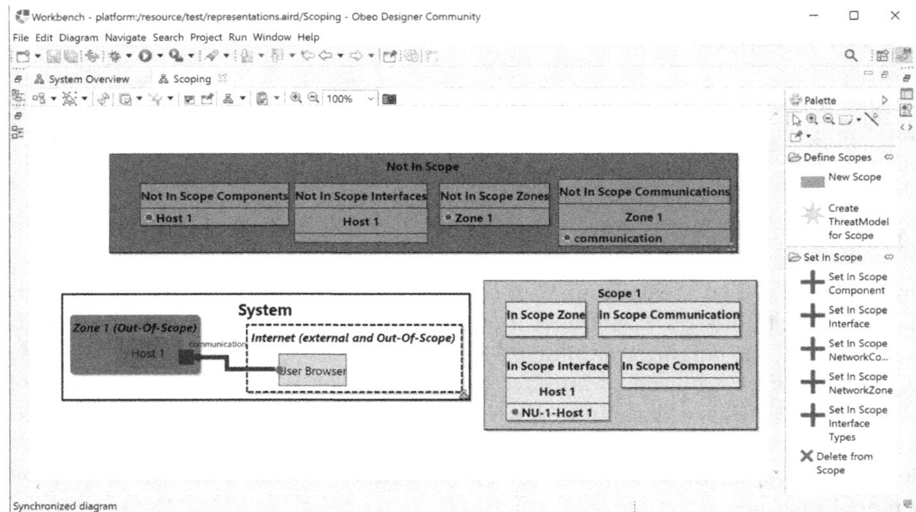

Fig. 7. Scoping.

Scoping. The first step is shown in Fig. 7. Its purpose is to set the focus for the threat analysis. The user can obtain some information from that diagram. First, there is a graphical representation of the CPS which is extracted from the CPS model. The box entitled *Not in scope* denotes the CPS elements that are not in scope. The box *Scope 1* contains the elements that are in scope for the analysis. It is possible to define different scopes within a model, each of them focusing on different elements.

The palette on the right side provides different tools for users to create or manipulate the model. The graphical representation and the *Not in Scope* container have only an informative use, i.e. they only extract some information from the model and present it to the user.

A new scope, e.g. *Scope 1*, can be created with the tool *New Scope*. Each Scope is an instance of the class *ThreatScenarioListing* from Fig. 5. Users have multiple dialogs to set elements of the system in scope. For example, when selecting an interface to be in scope, they get a list of all available interfaces. Via checkboxes, it is possible to select the desired ones. To document that an element is in scope, we instantiate the class *inScope* of the metamodel (see Fig. 5). Furthermore, the corresponding element is shown in the green box of the scope.

Analysis. The second step is the core part of threat modeling, i.e. the identification and documentation of the attack actions. This step is supported by our taxonomy from Sect. 3. For all interfaces that are specfied to be in scope, the user is guided to identify and document attack actions with the dialog shown in Fig. 8. For each documented attack action, a class *AttackAction* from Fig. 5 will be instantiated. Our tool filters relevant attack actions according to the

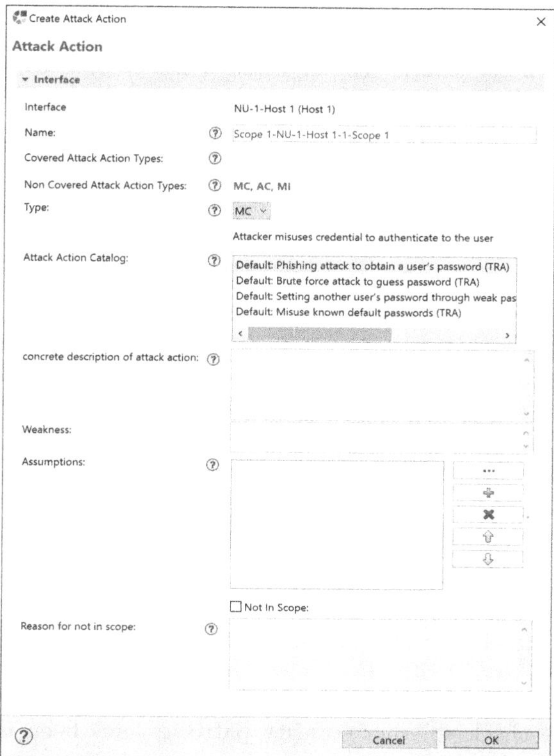

Fig. 8. Dialog to document attack actions.

taxonomy, and presents the examples contained in the catalog to the user. Furthermore, the user dialog informes the user about which attack action types have already covered for the given interface, thereby showing the progress of coverage. Using the provided text fields, users can describe the attack action more precisely, give a weakness, and assign assumptions, Alternatively, if there are reasons why an attack action type is not in scope for that interface, users document that reason in the dialog.

To filter relevant attack actions, we use following AQL expression as shown Listing 1. It realizes the mapping of our taxonomy given Tables 2 and 3.

```
if (element.oclIsTypeOf(system::C2CInterface)
  or element.oclIsTypeOf(system::NetworkUserInterface)
  or element.oclIsTypeOf(system::LocalUserInterface))
then
  threats::AttackActionType.eLiterals→select(a|a.name='MC' or
      a.name='AC' or a.name='MI')
else if (element.oclIsTypeOf(system::PhysicalInterface))
then
  threats::AttackActionType.eLiterals→select(a|a.name='AC' or
      a.name='DD' or a.name='MI' or a.name='TD')
else if (element.oclIsTypeOf(system::OSLevelInterface))
```

```
then
  threats::AttackActionType.eLiterals→select(a|a.name='MC' or
      a.name='TD' or a.name='DD' or a.name='ER' or a.name='MP' or
      a.name='AC')
else
  threats::AttackActionType.eLiterals→select(a|a.name='AC' or
      a.name='MI' or a.name='TD' or a.name='DD' or a.name='ER')
endif endif endif
```

Listing 1. AQL expression for filtering relevant attack action types.

element is the CPS's element for which attack actions shall be identified, i.e. an interface or network communication. With the expression, we check which type *element* is and select the corresponding attack action types for it. Afterward, users can choose one of them and document it in the model.

7 Related Work

Almorsy et al. [2] introduced a new architecture software security analysis. They use OCL to formalize system architectural security attack scenarios and security metrics. Since our approach is model-based (cf. Sect. 3.1), our proposed taxonomy can be formalized in a similar way.

The paper by Halkidis et al. [8] evaluates the protection that selected security patterns of Blakley and Heath [4] offer against attacks. As attack categories, the authors make use of STRIDE. The analyzed system is annotated with stereotypes in order to check whether security patterns have been used sufficiently. This approach of using stereotypes can be compared with our interface types, e.g. there is a stereotype *ApplicationEntryPoint* that corresponds to our user interface. The difference to our taxonomy is that the annotations are not associated with attack actions, but are associated with security patterns.

Uzunov and Fernández [20] introduce system elements (called decomposition layers) to describe threat patterns. The system elements are similar to our attack surface elements, e.g. the decomposition layer 'User interaction'corresponds to a user interface. In contrast to our work, the authors do not use the system elements for structuring the threat patterns.

CAPEC (cf. Sect. 3.4) is often used as a comprehensive repository for attack descriptions rather than as a taxonomy. An example is Adams et al. [1], where CAPEC is used as source to identify relevant attacks, by using machine learning and natural language processing. Another example is the approach of [12] to leverage the CAPEC repository for finding relevant attacks, based on problem patterns, solution patterns, and context patterns.

Xiong and Lagerström performed a literature review on threat modeling [21]. This literature review lists many papers on threat modeling approaches that are based on (semi-)formal methods for representing threats, like game theory, Petri nets, Dolev-Yao threat model, PrT nets, Hidden Markov models, Byzantine model, flow model, and others. The usage of taxonomies in these approaches is different to our use. The taxonomy does not represent threats, but provides a structure for knowledge databases. Other papers covered in that literature review describe the use of threat modeling in a specific domain.

There are numerous risk management processes, e.g. CORAS [6], that require a detailed identification of threat scenarios. CORAS has its own modeling language and provides guidelines on how the method can be carried out. The method is model-based and has tool-support. The identification of threat scenarios is often performed in brainstorming sessions which does not necessarily follow a systematic procedure. Our taxonomy can be used as an input for those sessions to create CORAS diagrams.

Shevchenko et al. [16] evaluates methods for threat modeling of cyber-physical systems. They list twelve methods and rate them according to 5 criteria. The usage of an attack action catalog is no criteria. Some of the methods can be enhanced with an attack action catalog.

Khan et al. [10] apply STRIDE-based threat modeling to cyber-physical systems and apply their adapted method on a real world example. They state 10 possible threat consequences (TC) as an example. The authors use data flow diagrams (DFD) to model a cyber-physical system and link the DFD elements to TCs. The method of the paper is on a high level and our taxonomy can be applied after their method.

Currently, our taxonomy only allows us to analyze a system with regard to security. The LINDDUN methodology of Deng et al. [7] introduces privacy threat categories which have been derived from STRIDE. The relation of STRIDE to privacy may help to transfer our taxonomy into the privacy context, as well.

8 Conclusion

After having presented a two-dimensional taxonomy in previous work, we presented our tool support in the present paper. We first presented a metamodel that formalizes the taxonomy and the dependencies to the system model's elements, i.e. the attack surface. Based on that metamodel, we developed a graphical editor that filters relevant attack actions and that allows documenting the threat model systematically. To provide flexibility, the tool provides functionalities to import different attack action catalog. The current piloting of the tool and the taxonomy in the industrial context promises good results. Further feedback from practitioners will continuously be integrated into the tool.

Currently, our taxonomy, the attack action catalogs, and the tool are limited to the domain of CPS. The transfer to other domains requires us to adapt the first dimension, i.e. to define the elements of attack surfaces in other domains. Currently, we are working on system models for cloud-based systems which shall be used as input for security analyses, too. The new attack surface can be derived from that model, which makes it easy to adopt our taxonomy for cloud-based systems. Concerning attack action types, first experiments have shown that the types used in this paper are also suitable in the domain of cloud applications.

Another important aspect will be the consideration of other software qualities such as privacy. LINDDDUN [7] will be a good starting point for this adoption since it brings STRIDE to the context of privacy. Another important topic would be to identify overlaps between different qualities. For example, the protection goal of confidentiality is relevant for both security and privacy. The same countermeasures can therefore be applied to improve both qualities.

About our tool, we plan to add more catalogs to it and to make these catalogs publicly available via the Internet. Other practitioners and research may contribute to this resource with their own catalogs.

References

1. Adams, S.C., Carter, B.T., Fleming, C.H., Beling, P.A.: Selecting system specific cybersecurity attack patterns using topic modeling. In: 17th IEEE International Conference on Trust, Security and Privacy in Computing and Communications/12th IEEE International Conference on Big Data Science and Engineering, TrustCom/BigDataSE 2018, New York, NY, USA, 1–3 August 2018, pp. 490–497 (2018). https://doi.org/10.1109/TrustCom/BigDataSE.2018.00076
2. Almorsy, M., Grundy, J., Ibrahim, A.S.: Automated software architecture security risk analysis using formalized signatures. In: 35th International Conference on Software Engineering, ICSE 2013, San Francisco, CA, USA, 18–26 May 2013, pp. 662–671 (2013). https://doi.org/10.1109/ICSE.2013.6606612
3. Berger, B.J., Sohr, K., Koschke, R.: Automatically extracting threats from extended data flow diagrams. In: Caballero, J., Bodden, E., Athanasopoulos, E. (eds.) Proceedings of the Engineering Secure Software and Systems - 8th International Symposium, ESSoS 2016, London, UK, 6–8 April 2016, pp. 56–71. Springer, Cham (2016). https://doi.org/10.1007/978-3-319-30806-7_4
4. Blakley, B., Heath, C.: The open group security forum: security design patterns. Technical guide. TheOpen Group (2004)
5. BSI: Industrial control system security - top 10 threats and countermeasures 2016. Bsi-cs 005e—version 1.20 of 08/01/2016, federal office for information security (BSI) (2016). https://www.allianz-fuer-cybersicherheit.de/ACS/DE/_/downloads/BSI-CS_005E.pdf?__blob=publicationFile&v=3
6. Dahl, H., Hogganvik, I., Stølen, K.: Structured semantics for the CORAS security risk modelling language. In: Proceedings of 2nd International Workshop on Interoperability solutions on Trust, Security, Policies and QoS for Enhanced Enterprise Systems (IS-TSPQ'07) (2007)
7. Deng, M., Wuyts, K., Scandariato, R., Preneel, B., Joosen, W.: A privacy threat analysis framework: supporting the elicitation and fulfillment of privacy requirements. Requir. Eng. **16**(1), 3–32 (2011). https://doi.org/10.1007/s00766-010-0115-7
8. Halkidis, S.T., Tsantalis, N., Chatzigeorgiou, A., Stephanides, G.: Architectural risk analysis of software systems based on security patterns. IEEE Trans. Dependable Secur. Comput. **5**(3), 129–142 (2008). https://doi.org/10.1109/TDSC.2007.70240
9. IEC 62443: Industrial communication networks - network and system security - security for industrial automation and control systems. In: International Standard, International Electrotechnical Commission (IEC) (2013–2018)
10. Khan, R., McLaughlin, K., Laverty, D., Sezer, S.: Stride-based threat modeling for cyber-physical systems. In: 2017 IEEE PES Innovative Smart Grid Technologies Conference Europe (ISGT-Europe), pp. 1–6. IEEE (2017)

11. Kohnfelder, L., Grag, P.: The threats to our products. Technical report. Microsoft Co-oporation (2009). https://adam.shostack.org/microsoft/The-Threats-To-Our-Products.docx
12. Li, T., Paja, E., Mylopoulos, J., Horkoff, J., Beckers, K.: Security attack analysis using attack patterns. In: 2016 IEEE Tenth International Conference on Research Challenges in Information Science (RCIS), pp. 1–13 (2016). https://doi.org/10.1109/RCIS.2016.7549303
13. Maidl, M., Münz, G., Seltzsam, S., Wagner, M., Wirtz, R., Heisel, M.: Threat modeling for cyber-physical systems: a two-dimensional taxonomy approach for structuring attack actions. In: van Sinderen, M., Fill, H., Maciaszek, L.A. (eds.) Proceedings of the 15th International Conference on Software Technologies, ICSOFT 2020, Lieusaint, Paris, France, 7–9 July 2020, pp. 160–171. ScitePress (2020). https://doi.org/10.5220/0009829901600171
14. Maidl, M., Wirtz, R., Zhao, T., Heisel, M., Wagner, M.: Pattern-based modeling of cyber-physical systems for analyzing security. In: Proceedings of the 24th European Conference on Pattern Languages of Programs. EuroPLop 2019, pp. 23:1–23:10. ACM, New York, NY, USA (2019). https://doi.org/10.1145/3361149.3361172. https://doi.acm.org/10.1145/3361149.3361172
15. MITRE: Common Attack Pattern Enumeration and Classification (CAPEC). https://capec.mitre.org (2019)
16. Shevchenko, N., Frye, B.R., Woody, C.: Threat modeling for cyber-physical system-of-systems: methods evaluation. Carnegie Mellon University Software Engineering Institute. Technical report (2018)
17. Shostack, A.: Threat Modeling - Designing for Security, 1st edn. Wiley, Hoboken (2014)
18. Steinberg, D., Budinsky, F., Paternostro, M., Merks, E.: EMF: Eclipse Modeling Framework 2.0, 2nd edn. Addison-Wesley Professional, Boston (2009)
19. Tuma, K., Calikli, G., Scandariatoa, R.: Threat analysis of software systems: a systematic literature review. J. Syst. Softw. **144**, 275–294 (2018)
20. Uzunov, A.V., Fernández, E.B.: An extensible pattern-based library and taxonomy of security threats for distributed systems. Comput. Stand. Interfaces **36**(4), 734–747 (2014)
21. Xiong, W., Lagerström, R.: Threat modeling - a systematic literature review. Comput. Secur. **84**, 53–69 (2019). https://doi.org/10.1016/j.cose.2019.03.010

A Machine Learning Based Methodology for Web Systems Codeless Testing with Selenium

Phuc Nguyen and Stephane Maag(✉)

Télécom SudParis, Samovar, Institut Polytechnique de Paris, 19 Place Marguerite Perey, 91120 Palaiseau, Cedex, France
stephane.maag@telecom-sudparis.eu

Abstract. Web system testing is a crucial software development cycle. However, though there are real needs for testing these complex systems, it often requires specific skills in testing and/or technical programming. Moreover, the lifecycles of web systems are today very dynamic. They are often modified, updated, integrating new data, links, widgets, etc. Therefore, the testing processes and scripts for these systems have to be modified as well which can be very costly in terms of time and resources. Based on that context, this paper aims at reducing these prerequisites and constraints for tester in proposing a codeless testing automation framework. Our approach is based on Selenium and a machine learning technique to propose generic testing scripts that can be automatically tuned to the tested use cases. Experiments are provided leading to relevant results demonstrating the success of our methodology.

Keywords: Codeless web testing · Automation testing · Selenium · Machine learning · SVM

1 Introduction

Web system testing is a crucial software development cycle. In an era where a single software bug can cause massive financial losses, quality assurance testing is paramount for any software product. It is a stage where the errors and issues still present in the system should be discovered and fixed. Besides, this can be a costly process [14,25]. Resources (including time and people) are spent to prepare the test case scenarios and to execute them. Its cost is estimated to be between 40% and 80% of the total cost of development [16]. While automated testing methods appear to take over the role of the human tester, the issues of reliability and the capability of the testing method still need to be resolved. For example, testing all the functionalities implemented in the web page services can be a real pain. For that purpose, there are tools to ease automate some of this pain away. One of the most used way to deal with it, especially due to its efficiency, is using a browser automation system like Selenium [10] in order to run specific tests on installed browsers and return results, raising potential failures in browsers as they crop up.

M. van Sinderen et al. (Eds.): ICSOFT 2020, CCIS 1447, pp. 184–202, 2021.
https://doi.org/10.1007/978-3-030-83007-6_9

Nevertheless, processing with automated testing tools such as Selenium [10] still raises concerns. Since tests are repetitive and require a lot of maintenance, a small change or modification in the content of a webpage may cause a test fail (e.g., adding a '-' or changing a text in a page [22]). This is a real challenge for industrial and researchers who study and propose approaches to deal with this problematic. One current popular domain is about "Codeless Functional Test Automation" or "Machine Learning/Artificial Intelligence (ML/AI) in test automation". The objective is to process the machines figuring out how to automate the software/web service product under test. The machine can detect or predict the changes and adopt those changes to the suitable test cases. Codeless testing provides the testers a way to efficiently reduce the cost of test automation creation, test execution, and maintenance. In our work, we examine on Selenium and the benefits of using machine learning in automated web application testing. The motivation is to utilize the selenium framework in the world of automated testing and define a novel machine learning approach for codeless testing which can enable to test multiple web services without using any code. This paper is an extension of our previous publication [22] in which we herein present an extended use case focused on the Form in a web service. This studied use case is more complex than the previous one. For that reason, our methodology has been extended as well in particular in the use of the machine learning technique. New experiments, that needed much more computing resources, are performed and the results are discussed.

Therefore, the main contributions of our paper are:

- we propose a "codeless testing" framework based on the Selenium toolkit and support vector machine,
- we integrating our novel use case in our defined framework and implementing generic test cases to test the submit of Form within multiple web pages,
- we perform several experiments and obtain results that illustrate the success of our approach. We demonstrate that our method helps in decreasing implementation and maintenance costs of automated tests.

Finally, our paper is organised in six sections. Section 2 presents the basis of our approach whose Selenium and the codeless testing concept. Section 3 defines, presents and details our ML-based web testing framework. In the Sect. 4, we perform our experiments and discuss our interesting results. The state of art is then presented in Sect. 5 while we conclude and propose perspectives in Sect. 6.

2 Preliminaries

2.1 The Selenium Framework

Selenium [10] is a suite of automation testing tools which allows the testers run the tests directly on the target browser, drive the interactions on the required web page and rerun them without any manual input. Selenium has become very popular among testers because of the various advantages it offers. With its advent in 2004, Selenium made the life of automation testers easier and is now a favorite tool for many automation testers. Selenium was invented with the introduction of a basic tool named as "JavaScriptTestRunner", by Jason Huggins at ThoughtWorks to test their internal Time and Expenses application. Now it has gained popularity among software testers and developers as an open-source portable automation testing framework. Nowadays, Selenium is currently used in production in many large companies as Netflix, Google, HubSpot, Fitbit, and more. According to [3,5], there are 42,159 companies that use Selenium, taking 26.83% market share in software testing tool (see Fig. 2 and Fig. 1).

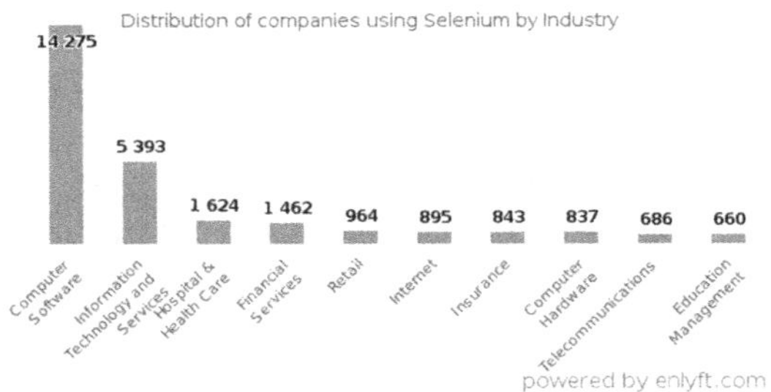

Fig. 1. Selenium used by company area.

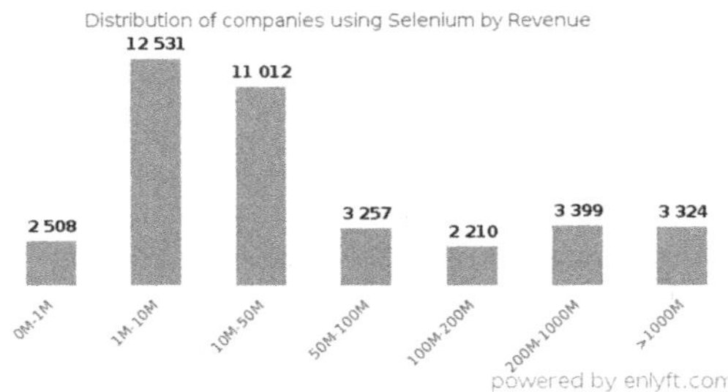

Fig. 2. Selenium used by company revenue.

The primary reason behind such overwhelming popularity of Selenium is that it is open source. This not only helps keep the costs in check but also ensures that companies are using a tool that will get continually updated. Other reasons include the multi-dimensional flexibility that it offers in terms of scripting languages, operating systems, browsers, and integration with other tools. This widens the scale of reach and test coverage, enabling enterprises to deliver a web application that is highly reliable and functional. Selenium test scripts can be written in Java, Python, C#, PHP, Ruby, Perl and .Net. This allows a large number of testers to easily use it without any language barriers. It can be carried out on Windows, MacOS, and Linux, using any browsers out of Mozilla Firefox, Internet Explorer, Chrome, Safari, and Opera. This enables a thorough cross browser compatibility testing with strong environment support.

Selenium suite includes three major components (Fig. 3), each tool has the different approach for automation testing. The testers or developers can choose tools out of it depending upon the testing requirement.

- *Selenium IDE*
  Selenium IDE, earlier known as Selenium recorder, is a tool used to record, edit, debug and replay functional tests. Selenium IDE is implemented as an extension to the Chrome browser and add-on in Firefox browser. With Selenium IDE plugin, the testers can do simple record-and-playback of interactions with the browser, they can also export tests in any of the supported programming languages like Ruby, Java, PHP, Javascript, etc.
- *Selenium Grid*
  Selenium Grid allows the testers to run parallel automated tests on multiple machines and browsers at the same time. The main function of this tool is to save time. If the test suite is large, the testers can use Selenium Grid to reduce the time running. Considering how scripts normally run slow on a browser, using performance-improving techniques such as parallel testing can help with the problem. Testers can also use it to test one application in different browsers in parallel, when one machine is running Firefox, the other – Chrome, and so on. Testers can also create different configurations with Grid, combining different versions of browsers and operating systems. Needless to say that when used in large production environments, Grid is a huge time-saver.
- *Selenium Webdriver*
  Selenium Webdriver (which is also known as Selenium 2.0 or 3.0 currently version) is an enhanced version of Selenium RC and the most used tool. Selenium Webdriver is by far the most important component of Selenium Suite. It provides a programming interface to create and execute automation scripts. It accepts commands via client API and sends them to browsers. Selenium WebDriver allows testers to choose a programming language of their choice to create test scripts. Test scripts are written in order to identify web elements on web pages and then desired actions are performed on those elements. Selenium Webdriver currently supports most popular browsers (Chrome, Firefox, Opera, etc.). Every browser has different drivers to run tests. In our "codeless testing framework", we use Selenium Webdriver to conduct the automated tests on multiple popular web browsers.

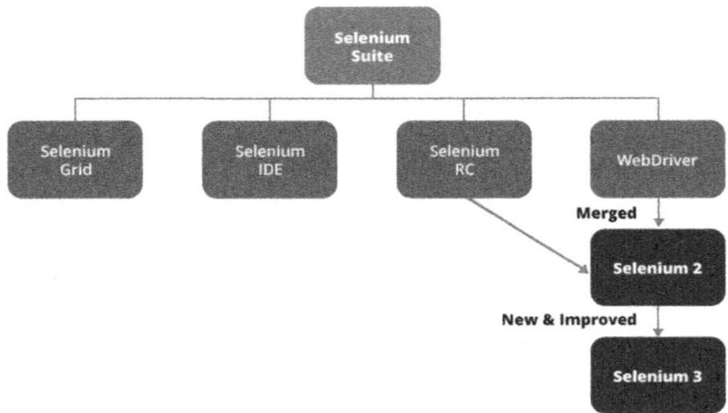

Fig. 3. Selenium suite components.

2.2 Codeless Testing

Although those advantages listed above, Selenium still has its cons. The most challenge of using Selenium in automation testing is steep learning curve. Testers require high technical skills to accurately design and maintain test automation. Maintenance including modification and updating Selenium test code in an efficient way is a very common problem in automated test. The impact of the changes occur in the web under test could suffer during its development. Change or modification from web User Interface (UI) or from its structure to its elements or its attributes will make the whole test suites collapse. Nowadays, one of automated testing trends - *Codeless Testing* was introduced to resolve those problems.

Codeless Testing for web services refers to the methodology which use a generic test case to test multiple websites. This approach allows any tester without deep programming knowledge to perform tests. Organizations started adapting tools and approaches to simplify test automation and empower team members who lacked sophisticated programming skills [19]. "Codeless" tools were originally meant to help the tester avoid the hours of programming that are usually necessary to get the most out of testing logic. While their objective was to address programming complexity, most tools in the market adapted a no-code approach by avoiding the code, but not really addressing the logical complexity in testing. A common misconception is that codeless test automation tools should completely avoid code. We believe this is actually a disservice, as very soon users will start hitting roadblocks. Testing requirements are typically as vast as application development. It is hard to believe that all testing requirements could be addressed with some canned, pre-packaged solution. Some level of logic development flexibility is required, but in a way so that the user does not get bogged down by the syntactical complexities. Note that, though the name codeless testing, but it does not mean it is completely code free. While a tester can generate most of the tests code free, certain tests may still need some coding. Testers can use codeless testing for keeping up with the deployment needs.

3 An ML-Based Web Testing Framework

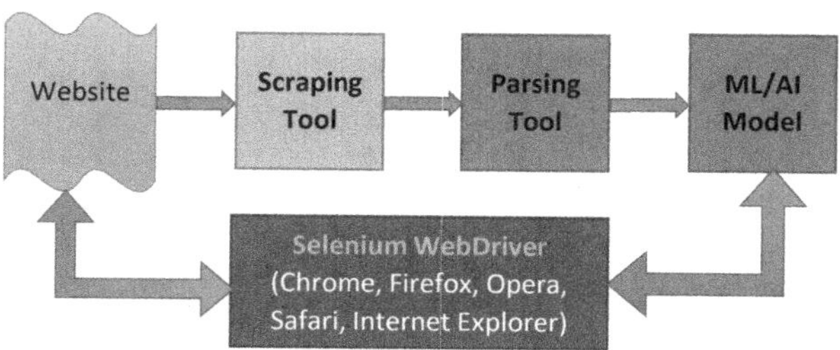

Fig. 4. The architecture of codeless testing framework.

The architecture overview of our codeless testing framework is illustrated in Fig. 4, defined in [22]. As mentioned in the previous sections, our framework is combined Selenium and Machine Learning algorithm, it is composed by four main components.

- **Selenium Webdriver Component.**
  This is the major module, plays a role as an engine to drive the browser for automating website and for testing. As referring in Fig. 2, Selenium Webdriver [11] (or Selenium 2.0) is the core module in our testing framework. Selenium WebDriver plays as a browser automation framework that accepts commands and sends them to a browser. It is implemented through a browser-specific driver. It controls the browser by directly communicating with it. The flexibility that Selenium Webdriver provides is almost unmatched in the test automation world.
- **Scraping Data Component.**
  This scraping tool was implemented in Python. We utilize BeautifulSoup [2] as a web scraping library to pull data out of DOM in HTML or XML format.
- **Processing Data Component.**
  This component has a role to process the data after pulling from HTML DOM file, it will clean and extract the useful data, then transform the clean data to the next stage for training.
- **SVM Model.**
  An machine learning model to recognise or predict the search element pattern which appeared in HTML data of testing website.

3.1 Scraping and Processing Web Data

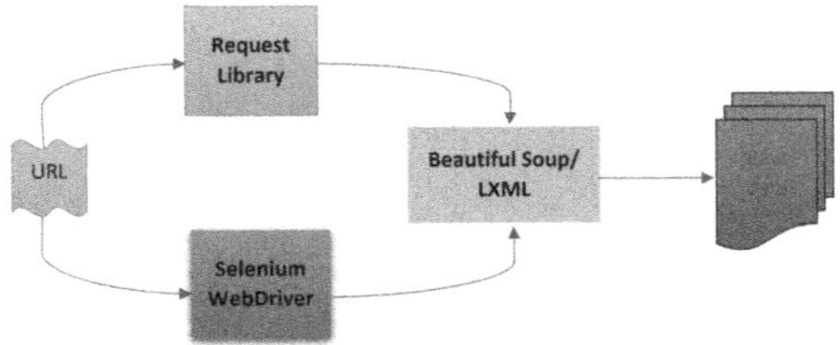

Fig. 5. The structure of scraping tool.

The general architecture of scraping tool is showed in Fig. 5 [22]. The main target of scraping tool is exactly as its name - to collect HTML data and their position in the DOM tree from the website which is driven by Selenium Webdriver. We use both Selenium Webdriver and Request library to send a HTTP request to the URL of the webpage we want to access. We discover that some websites with heavy render JavaScript will not response to the request module. Also, some website can detect the request is done automated (not by human browsing) by their tool, it will deny to establish the connection. Selenium Webdriver works fine with almost major of websites, however the speed is recorded as very slow since Selenium needs to open the real browsers to perform tasks. Moreover, using different browsers (Chrome, Firefox, Opera, etc.) will have different behaviours of navigation website. For example, some website are optimized for Chrome but not Firefox or vice versa, or some website are completely crashed on Microsoft Edge browser. Therefore, we use both modules Selenium Webdriver and Request library [9] to ensure that our scraping tool can adapt with most of websites to collect at most as data it can. First, using request library for speed up the test, if request fail, then Selenium Webdriver will do its job. Moreover, each website has its different DOM structure, thousands of websites will have thousands of DOM structures, therefore it's a challenge process to automate retrieve the data from multiple of websites concurrently. However, our scraping tool able to scrape and collect variety of websites. For summary, our scraping tool follows two tasks:

1. Query the website using requests or Selenium WebDriver and return its HTML content.
2. Using BeautifulSoup [2] and LXML [8] libraries to go through the HTML structure of each website, parse HTML content and extract the useful data.

3.2 Support Vector Machines (SVM) Model

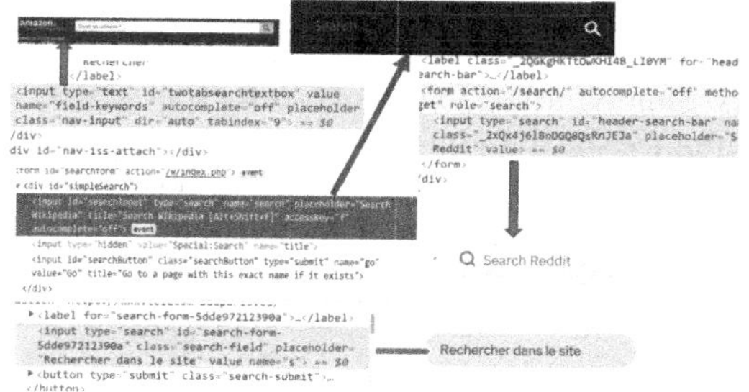

Fig. 6. SVM model detects search box pattern.

According to [12], Support Vector Machines (SVM) are supervised learning models with associated learning algorithms that analyze data used for classification and regression analysis. In addition to performing linear classification, SVMs can efficiently perform a non-linear classification using what is called the kernel trick, implicitly mapping their inputs into high-dimensional feature spaces. To adapt with the changing of website is very challenging task in web testing taking into account the fact that web HTML elements are keep changing dynamically in both structure and attribute value. In our proposed framework, the objective of SVM model is to recognize the pattern of web elements corresponding to search box in each website as illustrated in the Fig. 6 of [22]. Specifically, the SVM model will learn the HTML structure of each website, in case of any modification in term of element web, the SVM model will find the similar pattern of HTML web and adjust its model according to the changes (Fig. 6). For the next testing, if the website is changed, the SVM model will detect its changes and "guide" the Selenium code to adapt automatically with it. In this case, the test code will not be broken and can be reused. More specific, the goal of the SVM is to train a model that assigns new unseen web element into a particular category. It achieves this by creating a linear partition of the feature space into two categories. In each website, structured data is extracted for each HTML element, they have to be turned into proper feature vectors. We use SVM model to recognize the feature importance of each web element corresponding to its density and apply in the feature importance property of our model. We have tried many features and preprocessing steps as part of our cross-validation routine, and we kept the ones yielding best performance and moved them in the final model. Feature importance gives a score for each feature attribute, the higher of the score, the more important or more relevant of the feature is. Therefore, the weight for each element attribute is assigned according to its frequency and informative ranking.

3.3 Data Collection and Analysis

In order to have the dataset for our training SVM model, we need to gather the large amount of data. By using the scraping tool described in section A, we are successful to retrieve the data from the list of 5000 websites provided by [7]. This data contains one millions URLs on top ranking of Alexa [1]. Our tool can scrape any website has the search functionality, it will pull down the web elements corresponding to the search box. Since the collected raw data is undesired format, unorganized, and extremely large. Therefore in further steps, we need to use the processing tool to enhance the data quality. The main steps for preprocessing data are formatting, cleaning. Data cleaning is applied to remove messy data, duplicate data and manage missing values. Formatting is required to ensure that all variables within the same attribute are consistently written. Once structured data is extracted for each HTML element, they have to be turned into proper feature vectors.

4 Experimental Studies

Testing Method.
To test our "codeless testing" framework, our experiences focus on two functionalities of websites: **"search-functionality"** and **"contact-functionality"**.

1. Search - Functionality.
First, let follow the scenario: if the users want to use Google to search for the term "Codeless Testing", normally they will open their favourite browser, let say Chrome to navigate to the website of Google. After the official site of Google page fully loaded, the users need to locate the search box, then type the search term "Codeless Testing". All of this manual steps performed by human can be completely replaced those steps by our codeless testing framework. By analyzing the multiple search activities on various websites, we can group the search scenario in three cases:

- *Case 1 (Traditional search)*: we call it traditional because the search box is appeared directly in the website interface, the user can easily locate it and enter the search query. We studied that 80–90% search websites are designed in this case 1. For example: google, youtube, yahoo, amazon, etc., (Fig. 7).

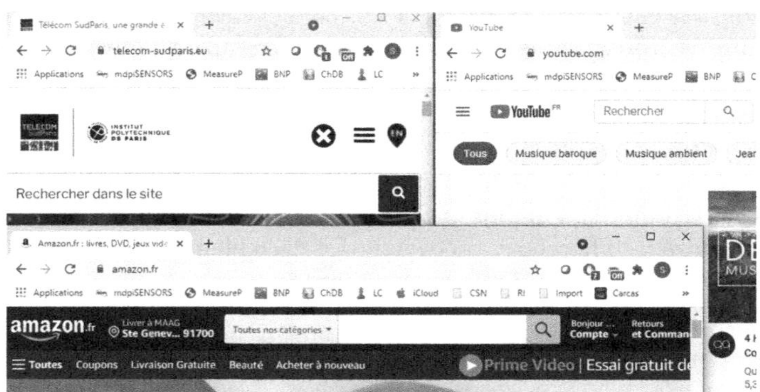

Fig. 7. Case 1 search type: traditional search.

- *Case 2 (Hidden bar search)*: The search bar is hidden, the users are required extra step by clicking the search button to activate/open the search bar. Once the search bar appears, the user can enter their search phase as normal (Fig. 8).

Fig. 8. Case 2 search type: hidden search box.

- *Case 3 (Pattern/Condition Search)*: the websites have many filters/criteria for search, the users must select the right criteria to proceed. For instance, some hotel or housing websites only allow users to select the special search key in their pattern database (region, type of house, size of house, prize, room,...). Or in particular website only allow the users to perform the search on specify content provided in their database, if the users type random search query, or the query is not corresponding to their form, there will be nothing to return (Fig. 9).

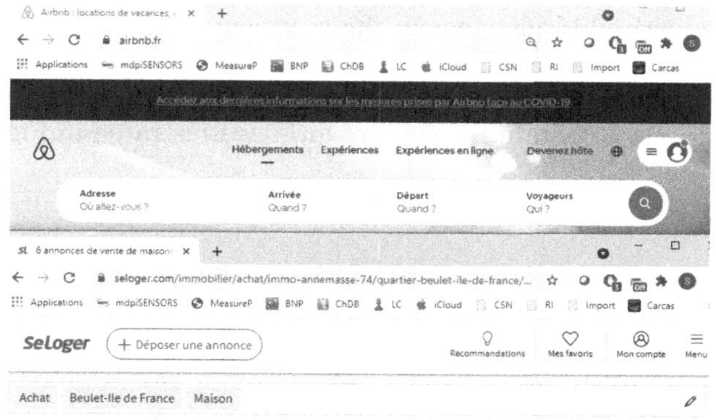

Fig. 9. Case 3 search type: filters/criteria search.

Test Scenario for Search Functionality
In order to test the search functionality in website, we defined three verdicts in our generic test case: *pass, fail, error.*

- The test is considers as *pass* when a browser is fully load the website, the "search term" is entered in the search box, the website must return the answer corresponding to the "search term".
- Browser must be able to load full website and be navigated to the search box, if website is not loaded $\Longrightarrow$ *fail.*
- If any website does not contain a search box or does not have the search functionality in their services $\Longrightarrow$ *error.*
- When entering "search term" in the search box $\Longrightarrow$ "search term" must be appeared inside the search box, if it is not appeared $\Longrightarrow$ *fail.*
- Search box must accept any type of query as string for input (number, text, special characters...).
- If there is condition/limit/boundary/criteria for input search (case 3 as described above) $\Longrightarrow$ not consider in our test case $\Longrightarrow$ *error.*
- If a website requires more than a step rather than type search term (case 3) $\Longrightarrow$ *error.*
- Website must return the result for the search term $\Longrightarrow$ "no result found or nothing found" is still consider as a *pass* case

2. Contact - Functionality.
For further verifying the efficiency of our framework, we decided to use our codeless framework to test an additional functionality of web service: the functionality of contact page. According to [4], a contact page is a common web page on a website for visitors to contact the organization or individual providing the website. The contact page typically contains one or more of the following items: an email address, telephone number, links to social media of the owner's website, and a contact form for a text message or inquiry. The contact form can be a set of input boxes to collect the feedback or the request from users. In our experiment, we assume that the user will have these behaviours when using this contact services: the user will surf to the contact web page, he will fill his information (name, email address...), then write his questions in the comment box, after that he will send that message to the website. If the message is sent correctly, we consider this is the *pass* case, otherwise the verdict will be *fail*, we also define the verdict is *error* if the website does not contain the contact form as illustrated in Fig. 10.

4.1 Experiments Setup

In the experiment phase, we test our framework on the dataset.

Project Tools
In order to run the experiment, we setup our computer environment as below:

- Python 3.6.8
- Dependencies: Keras/Tensorflow, scikit-learn: core platform to analyse/process data and training SVM model

- Libraries: Selenium, Request HTTP, Beautiful Soup, LXML
- Jupyter Notebook App: online web-base platform to visualize the data

Fig. 10. The general contact form of website.

Testbed

- OS: x86-64 Microsoft Windows 10 Pro, version 10.0.18363, Build 18363
- Processor: Intel© Core^{TM} i7-7500U CPU @ 2.70 GHz × 2
- Memory: 16 GB
- SSD: 512 GB
- Dataset:
  - Metadata: 1.3 Mb in csv format. 1000 rows × 7 columns
  - Training set: 70% metadata in npy format (numpy array)
  - Test set: 20% metadata in npy format (numpy array)
- Browsers: (Table 1)

Table 1. Browser version [22].

Chrome	78.0.3904.70 (Official Build) (64-bit)
Firefox	70.0 (64-bit)
Opera	76.0.3809.132
Internet Explorer	11.418.18362
Microsoft Edge	44.18362.387.0 Build 18362

4.2 Results and Discussions

Automation Testing Against Multiple Web Sites. To evaluate the efficiency of our framework, we conducted the test using *a generic test case* against

Table 2. Testing **search-functionality** against 1000 web sites [22].

	Pass	Fail	Error
Chrome	48%	18%	34%
Firefox	57%	16%	27%
Opera	47%	12%	41%
Internet Explorer	9%	19%	72%
Microsoft Edge	17%	19%	64%

Table 3. Testing **contact-functionality** against 1000 web sites.

	Pass	Fail	Error
Chrome	14%	12%	74%
Firefox	17%	15%	68%
Opera	16%	15%	69%
Internet Explorer	7%	17%	76%
Microsoft Edge	13%	13%	74%

on 1000 websites chosen randomly on the list of Alexa described in Sect. 5, the results are showed in Table 2 and Table 3 following.

The percentage of result getting *error* is high does not imply that our framework is defective. It happened due to the fact that we did the test on 1000 websites chosen randomly. Therefore, there are plenty of websites that do not have the search functionality an contact functionality. Moreover, we observed that most modern websites nowadays, the designers has replaced the contact page with the FAQ page following a direct interaction by a chat-bot, meanwhile the user can have the instant reply by a virtual robot. This case is not in our context of experimental, therefore we obtained most of the results are *error* verdict.

Through Table 2 and Table 3, we can see that Internet Explorer and Microsoft Edge perform the worst. It make senses since Microsoft has stopped support for Internet Explorer. Microsoft Edge is replaced as the main and fast browser in Windows. However, the Selenium Webdriver for Microsoft Edge is not fully supported and still under development. We encountered that Internet Explorer and Microsoft Edge will crash if testing more than 20 websites concurrently. Through the experience result for automation testing the search functionality showed in Fig. 11, Firefox performs the best in term of *pass* case but it is after Chrome when dealing with the *error* case. Chrome is the best browser can handle *error*. We experienced that Chrome is a good choice when testing the websites which are rendered heavily with JavaScript, while Firefox still suffers for those sites. Opera is fairly good in our test. We were also surprise with the performance of Opera consider that it is not as popular as Chrome and Firefox.

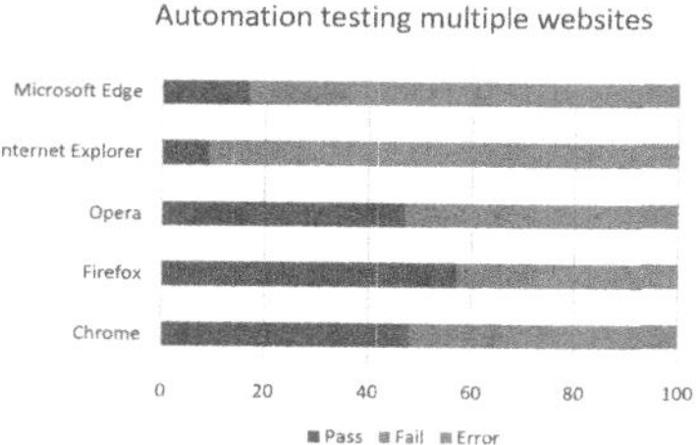

Fig. 11. Automation testing against multiple web sites [22].

Testing with Extension (add-On). During our experiment, we encountered that our test will be interrupted if there is pop-up suddenly appearing during the test. The pop-up can be any type (advertisement, data privacy, etc.) but the most appearance is the pop up which requires to accept the term and privacy when browsing website as seen in Fig. 10. Without clicking the accept button, there is no way to browse the website further. Considering that the test is running automated under Selenium code, there is no interference by manual hand to click the accept button. Therefore, the test mostly will be broken if facing with pop up. In order to solve this problem, we must add the blocking pop-up extension to the browser. This has the trade-off, adding extension allows to test pop-up websites, but in return, the speed of test will be very slow. The reason is, adding extension is done in Selenium code, therefore, every time running test, the webdriver will add automated the extension in the browser again. Therefore, the performance will be slow down (Fig. 12).

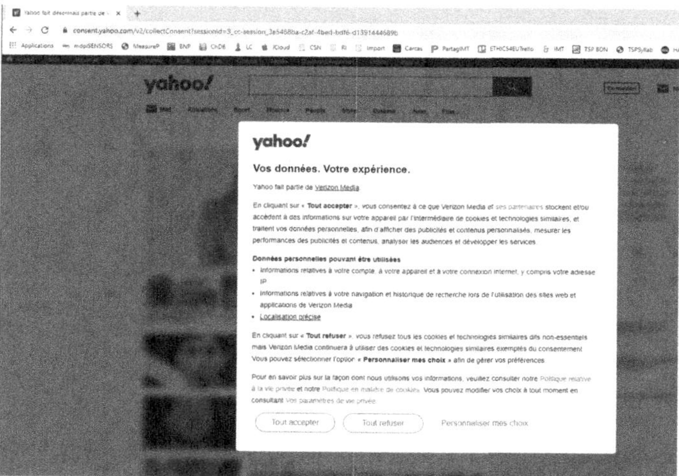

Fig. 12. Pop-up blocks the browser in Yahoo site.

For the experiment, we chose two extensions below due to their efficiency in blocking pop up, there are more than 10 millions users using those extensions:

- *Ublock* [13]: is a free and open-source, cross-platform browser extension for content-filtering, including ad-blocking.
- *I dont care about cookie* [6]: This browser extension removes cookie warnings from almost all websites and saves thousands of unnecessary clicks.

Since the above extensions are only full supported for Chrome and Firefox, therefore in this experiment, I only run the test on two those browsers. The test was run on randomly 20 websites concurrently on each browser in two modes: with extension and without extension. The Table 3 and Table 4 illustrate our results.

Through Table 4, we can see that using extension to block the popup is very effective during the test. It help to enhance the pass case and reduce the fail case. However, the speed to run the test with add-on is very slow, mostly double time comparing with the test without add-on as shown in Fig. 13. We also note that Firefox is more efficient in Chrome in term of time performance in both cases: with and without extension as illustrated in Fig. 13.

Table 4. Verdict result when testing with/without extension [22].

	With extension			Without extension		
	Pass	Fail	Error	Pass	Fail	Error
Chrome	12	2	6	9	5	6
Firefox	11	3	6	9	5	6

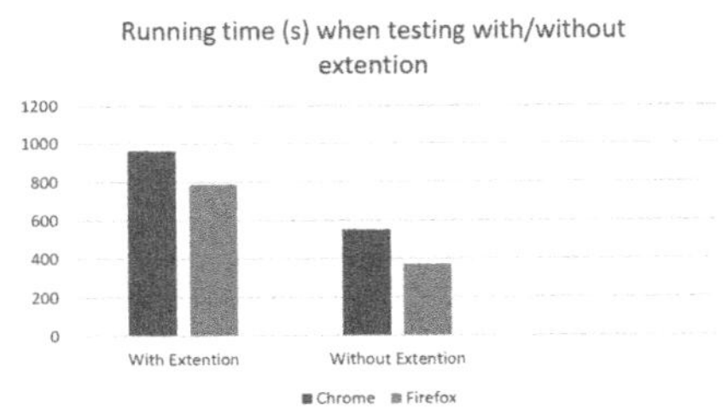

Fig. 13. Browser with extension testing [22].

Cross Browsers Testing. Through the experiment in Sect. 7.1, we have seen that Firefox is the most efficient browser in our framework, Chrome and Opera perform fairly good. Internet Explorer and Microsoft Edge are the least efficient browsers. In order to compare the speed performance of those five browsers. We chose randomly 10 websites and run those same websites on each browser, then measure the running time. We chose only 10 websites because Internet Explorer

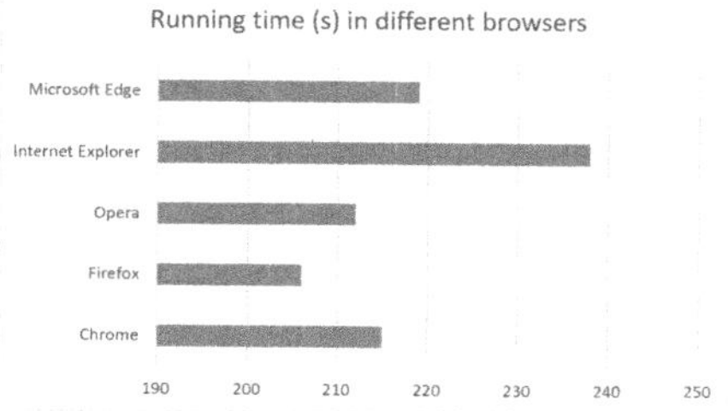

Fig. 14. Cross browsers testing [22].

and Microsoft Edge will crash if running large number of websites at the same time.

As seen in Fig. 14, Firefox is the fastest browser during the test. Internet Explorer performs the worst since it has been abandoned from Microsoft a time ago. Note that, the result was shown in Fig. 14 is for reference only. Depending on the websites and network, each browser will have the different behaviours. This mean, in some contexts, Chrome is faster than Firefox or Opera. This is due to the fact that there are websites designed or optimized for a specific browser. For example, when searching on Google site, if the browser is Chrome the website may present "richer" content – something more dynamic and styled which may have a heavy reliance on Javascript and CSS.

Precision of Codeless Framework in Testing. In this section, we demonstrates the performance of our codeless framework by evaluate the model via its precision rate. We used five most popular browsers to test 50 specific websites on both case: search-functionality and contact-functionality. By using one generic test case, we conducted the test on 50 fixed websites (not random websites) to verify the accuracy of three verdict: *pass, fail, error.*

Table 5. Precision rates.

	Precision (Search-Functionality)	Precision (Contact-Functionality)
Chrome	93%	66%
Firefox	94%	68%
Opera	90%	65%
Microsoft Explorer	82%	54%
Microsoft Edge	88%	64%

As shown in Table 5, our codeless framework archives the high precision rate when testing search-functionality on three browsers: Chrome, Firefox, Opera.

This results thank to the full supporting and integration of selenium driver for those three web browsers, while Microsoft Explorer and Microsoft Edge are not in this case. In compare with search-functionality, the precision rate of contact-functionality is less. This happened due to the fact that most modern websites have wider variety of contact form, our training model has limit data to be adapted with this changes. In general, the result in Table 5 confirms our proposed method: combining machine learning technique with selenium, a generic test case can be adapted to test multiple websites, this will help the tester in reducing time and effort to maintain the test code.

5 State of the Art

There are several recent papers in the literature proposing automation testing methods based on machine learning techniques [15,18,20,21,24]. However, none of them has proposed a novel of codeless for web service testing. Moreover, in the market area, many start-up companies with several tools have entered the market recently, all with the promise of solving the coding skill conundrum. There is a lot of buzz about no-code or low-code concepts, and companies such as Salesforce promote plug-and-play offerings. Some testing tools such as Testcraft, TestSigma, Ranorex, Tricentis, Leapwork, etc. advertise that they can provide this option by building a user-friendly UI on top of the code layer and also enabling switching between two modes. They promote that testers can still write scripts and receive detailed feedback but skip the coding part. However, when it comes to test automation, we believe there is an issue with how “codeless” is being interpreted. The majority of these tools are trivializing the real-world complexity of testing. Although automation testing techniques have been studied for years by industrial and researchers [17], codeless testing is a rather novel discipline. Despite the above mentioned tools, there are very few papers or initiatives dedicated to codeless testing. We may cite the very recent patent [23] in which the Rapid Automation First-pass Testing (RAFT) framework is depicted. However, whether in the proposed tools or the few published methodologies descriptions, the details are not provided. In our paper, we present a generic framework allowing to focus on codeless testing integrating ML technique.

6 Conclusion and Perspectives

Herein, we have proposed a novel framework for testing websites using “codeless testing automation”. Our main purposes is to ease the functional testing of web systems to human testers without specific skills in testing or programming language. Besides, our approach deals to testing websites in a generic way that is dynamically adaptable to any data changes into the scraped pages. By that way, we aim at reducing time and effort to change or modify test code. Selenium has been used. For defining our approach, we did use a machine learning technique (SVM) to recognize the feature importance of each web element corresponding to its density and apply in the feature importance property of our model. We successfully evaluated our approach on a new use case that consists to validate the correct function of submitting a contact form through a specific web page. The experiments as well as the results show that our framework can be efficient to perform the automation testing with most of standard websites by using the generic test case without rewriting the test code.

As perspectives, we aim at tackling more complex use cases. In our current paper and our previous publication [22], some relevant use cases have been processed. Though they provide complexities, they are related to specific data that can be considered as static (presence of fields). In the future, we will study how to test websites with dynamic data (eventually provided by database). Furthermore, we are currently tackling how to accelerate the codeless testing automation by processing Selenium Grid through virtualized environment. Finally, we will expand our approach to other ML techniques such as neural ones.

References

1. Alexa top website ranking. https://www.alexa.com/topsites/countries/FR
2. Beautiful soup documentation. https://www.crummy.com/software/BeautifulSoup/bs4/do
3. Companies using selenium. https://enlyft.com/tech/products/selenium
4. Contact page. https://en.wikipedia.org/wiki/Contact$_$page
5. Enlyft. https://enlyft.com/tech/products/selenium
6. Idontcareaboutcookie blocking popup extention. https://www.i-dont-care-about-cookies.eu/
7. List of top one million website on alexa ranking
8. Lxml toolkit. https://lxml.de/
9. Request library. https://pypi.org/project/requests/2.7.0/
10. Selenium automates browsers. https://selenium.dev/
11. Selenium webdriver document. https://selenium-python.readthedocs.io/locating-elements.html
12. Support vector machine. https://en.wikipedia.org/wiki/Support-vector_machine
13. Ublock blocking popup extension. https://github.com/gorhill/uBlock
14. Ameur-Boulifa, R., Cavalli, A.R., Maag, S.: Verifying complex software control systems from test objectives: application to the ETCS system. In: Proceedings of the 14th International Conference on Software Technologies, ICSOFT 2019, Prague, Czech Republic, 26–28 July 2019, pp. 397–406 (2019). https://doi.org/10.5220/0007918203970406
15. Rosenfeld, A., Kardashov, O., Zang, O.: Automation of android applications functional testing using machine learning activities classification. In: IEEE/ACM 5th International Conference on Mobile Software Engineering and Systems (MOBILESoft) (2018)
16. Eldh, S., Hansson, H., Punnekkat, S., Pettersson, A., Sundmark, D.: A framework for comparing efficiency, effectiveness and applicability of software testing techniques. In: Testing: Academic and Industrial Conference - Practice And Research Techniques, TAIC PART 2006, Proceedings, pp. 169–170 (2006)
17. Fewster, M., Graham, D.: Software Test Automation. Addison-Wesley Reading, Boston (1999)

18. Joshi, N.: Survey of rapid software testing using machine learning. Int. J. Trend Res. Dev. **3**, 91–93 (2016)
19. Lalanne, F., Cavalli, A.R., Maag, S.: Quality of experience as a selection criterion for web services. In: Yétongnon, K., Chbeir, R., Dipanda, A., Gallo, L. (eds.) Eighth International Conference on Signal Image Technology and Internet Based Systems, SITIS 2012, Sorrento, Naples, Italy, 25–29 November, pp. 519–526. IEEE Computer Society (2012)
20. Li, J.J., Ulrich, A., Bai, X., Bertolino, A.: Advances in test automation for software with special focus on artificial intelligence and machine learning. Softw. Qual. J. **28**(1), 245–248 (2019). https://doi.org/10.1007/s11219-019-09472-3
21. Nguyen, D.M., Do, H.N., Huynh, Q.T., Vo, D.T., Ha, N.H.: Shinobi: a novel approach for context-driven testing (CDT) using heuristics and machine learning for web applications: an analysis of chemosensory afferents and the projection pattern in the central nervous system. In: Duong, T., Vo, N.S. (eds.) Industrial Networks and Intelligent Systems, INISCOM 2018, Lecture Notes of the Institute for Computer Sciences, Social Informatics and Telecommunications Engineering, vol. 257, pp. 86–102. Springer, Cham (2018). https://doi.org/10.1007/978-3-030-05873-9_8
22. Nguyen, D.P., Maag, S.: Codeless web testing using selenium and machine learning. In: van Sinderen, M., Fill, H., Maciaszek, L.A. (eds.) Proceedings of the 15th International Conference on Software Technologies, ICSOFT 2020, Lieusaint, Paris, France, 7–9 July 2020, pp. 51–60. ScitePress (2020). https://doi.org/10.5220/0009885400510060
23. Patel, A., Arkadyev, A., Sharma, R., Liang, R., Kota, S.B.: Rapid automation first-pass testing framework, uS Patent App. 16/207,618 (2020)
24. Bhojan, R.J., Vivekanandan, K., Ramyachitra, D., Ganesan, S.: A machine learning based approach for detecting non-deterministic tests and its analysis in mobile application testing. Int. J. Adv. Res. Comput. Sci. **9**, 1–5 (2019)
25. Shariff, S.M., Li, H., Bezemer, C.P., Hassan, A.E., Nguyen, T.H., Flora, P.: Improving the testing efficiency of selenium-based load tests. In: 2019 IEEE/ACM 14th International Workshop on Automation of Software Test (AST), pp. 14–20. IEEE (2019)

Multilevel Readability Interpretation Against Software Properties: A Data-Centric Approach

Thomas Karanikiotis, Michail D. Papamichail(✉), and Andreas L. Symeonidis

Electrical and Computer Engineering Department, Aristotle University of Thessaloniki, Intelligent Systems & Software Engineering Labgroup, Information Processing Laboratory, Thessaloniki, Greece
{thomas.karanikiotis,mpapamic}@issel.ee.auth.gr, asymeon@eng.auth.gr

Abstract. Given the wide adoption of the agile software development paradigm, where efficient collaboration as well as effective maintenance are of utmost importance, the need to produce readable source code is evident. To that end, several research efforts aspire to assess the extent to which a software component is readable. Several metrics and evaluation criteria have been proposed; however, they are mostly empirical or rely on experts who are responsible for determining the ground truth and/or set custom thresholds, leading to results that are context-dependent and subjective. In this work, we employ a large set of static analysis metrics along with various coding violations towards interpreting readability as perceived by developers. Unlike already existing approaches, we refrain from using experts and we provide a fully automated and extendible methodology built upon data residing in online code hosting facilities. We perform static analysis at two levels (method and class) and construct a benchmark dataset that includes more than one million methods and classes covering diverse development scenarios. After performing clustering based on source code size, we employ Support Vector Regression in order to interpret the extent to which a software component is readable against the source code properties: cohesion, inheritance, complexity, coupling, and documentation. The evaluation of our methodology indicates that our models effectively interpret readability as perceived by developers against the above mentioned source code properties.

Keywords: Developer-perceived readability · Readability interpretation · Size-based clustering · Support vector regression

1 Introduction

The term *readability* can be described as "the ease of a reader to understand a written text". In the case of standard text (literature, news, post, etc.) this definition is straight forward; however from a software engineering point of view and in specific when we refer to source code, *readability* is a complex concept linked to several factors beyond the understanding of the specifics of each programming language. These factors are the comprehension of the purpose, the control flow, and the functionality that the source

M. van Sinderen et al. (Eds.): ICSOFT 2020, CCIS 1447, pp. 203–226, 2021.
https://doi.org/10.1007/978-3-030-83007-6_10

code serves, aggregated at the level of code block, method, class, component and/or system.

The vital importance of readability as a software quality attribute is more than evident considering the fact that according to several studies, reading code is one of the most time and effort-consuming tasks while maintaining software [15, 17]. This is also reflected in the definition of ISO/IEC 25010:2011 [7], which suggests that readability can be used as a measure to define the extent to which a software component is maintainable. This fact makes no surprise as readability is crucial for maintainability-related tasks like fixing bugs as well as evolving the source code so as to cover future requirements (both functional and non-functional). On top of the above, according to Knight and Myers, checking for readability issues has a positive impact in several quality attributes such as portability, maintainability, and reusability and should thus constitute a special part of the software inspection procedure [9]. Finally, given the reuse-oriented software development paradigm which has become state-of-the-practice, the need to produce readable software is even more prominent.

Given the importance of readability, several research efforts are directed towards assessing the extent to which software components are readable [1, 3, 13, 18] using static analysis metrics, such as the widely used Halstead metrics [6]. Upon building readability evaluation models, these approaches are in essence effective, however they exhibit certain inherent weaknesses. At first, the majority of the proposed approaches relies on quality experts who are responsible for defining the readability degree of each software component under evaluation and/or determining the appropriate thresholds of metrics that result in the desirable readability degree. In addition, given that expert-aided evaluation is both time and resources consuming, the used datasets are often small and thus cover only limited development scenarios. All the above lead to subjective evaluation, which is also depicted in the absence of a certain standardization in terms of defining the factors that influence readability (this absence is reflected in readability-related features that are usually selected intuitively and are based on the authors expertise in certain use cases). Finally, providing a single readability score without actionable recommendations regarding the certain axes that need improvement makes it difficult for developers to perform targeted audits.

In this work, we aspire to overcome the aforementioned limitations by proposing a data-driven readability interpretation methodology applicable at both method and class levels. To that end, we employ data residing in online code hosting facilities (i.e. GitHub) in order to build a fully-automated and interpretable readability evaluation methodology that expresses the extent to which a software component (method or class) is readable as perceived by developers. In order to accomplish that, we extend our previous work [8], where we proposed a generic methodology for readability interpretation at method level. Here, upon performing static analysis in more that 1 million methods and classes included in the most popular and reused GitHub Java projects, we define a readability score at both method and class levels based on the compliance of the respective component with the widely accepted code writing practices as reflected in the number of identified violations. In order to cover various assessment scenarios, we employ clustering for segmenting our dataset into coherent groups that share similar (within cluster) characteristics. Subsequently, for each cluster, we employ Support

Vector Regression and build models that enable a comprehensive and interpretable evaluation of the readability degree on five axes, each corresponding to a primary source code property: *cohesion*, *inheritance*, *complexity*, *coupling*, and *documentation*.

Summarizing, the advances of this work with respect to our previous paper [8] are the following:

- The extension of the previous models that evaluate readability on a method level and on three independent axes, in order to also measure readability on a class level, based on primary source code properties, *cohesion* and *inheritance* and on the aggregation of the methods readability scores.
- The formulation of our ground truth, aggregating the coding violations based not only on their severity, but also on the frequency with which they appear on the training corpus.
- The creation of a web application[1] for the demonstration of our methodology on a set of projects.

The rest of this paper is organized as follows. Section 2 provides background information on static analysis metrics and reviews current approaches on readability estimation, while Sect. 3 describes our benchmark dataset and designs a scoring mechanism for the readability degree of source code components. The developed models are discussed in Sect. 4, while Sect. 5 evaluates the efficiency of our readability interpretation methodology against different axes. Finally, Sect. 6 presents the web application built to apply our approach, while Sects. 7 and 8 conclude the paper and provide insight for further research.

2 Related Work

The recent needs of an effective software development process that assures the expectations of the end-users have made the assessment of software quality necessity, while the adoption of agile software development procedures has changed the focus of the research community towards maintainability, as it is a crucial factor for software health and evolution. Readability has always been highly related to maintainability and, thus, a lot of research approaches aspire to evaluate the readability of a given code or propose fixes that could improve the code comprehensibility. Despite the fact that many research approaches have been proposed for various purposes, such as an editor that could help the developer improve the code readability [14], it has been proven that these approaches usually fail to quantify the readability of a software component and, thus, measure the quality improvements [11]. Therefore, there is a high need of a system that could evaluate readability as perceived by the community of developers and measure its improvements in practice.

The first step towards the evaluation of software readability was made by Buse *et al.* [1]. The authors built a system that could evaluate the readability of a given code and classify it as "more readable" or "less readable", using metrics related to the structure, the documentation and the logical complexity of the code. The metrics were selected in

[1] https://readability-evaluator.netlify.app/.

an expert-based logic from the authors, who, upon evaluation, proved that only the first 8 principal components contain almost 95% of the total variability.

The work of Buse *et al.* inspired a lot of subsequent approaches. Dorn [3] uses mainly structural and visual perception features, aspiring to quantify features that improve visual readability. The evaluation was based on 5,000 human participants and concluded that it can achieve almost 2.3 times better results than any other approach. On the other hand, Posnett *et al.* [13] extended the approach made by Buse *et al.* , adding the size of the given code into the model that quantifies readability, due to the size dependency the rest of the features appear to have. In the same approach, the importance of the Halstead's V [6] was identified, as it contains high explanatory power. These approaches formed the basis for a study [10], which aspired to quantify the readability of open source projects over time and proved that they usually achieve quite high readability scores, even after a lot of changes.

Scalabrino *et al.* [18] proposed the use of textual features as a crucial improvement of the previous approaches. In order to support their suggestion, the authors conducted an empirical study. Their model was based both on textual and structural features, such as the number of terms coexisting both in identifiers and in comments, comments readability and the number of full-word identifiers. The study concluded that this model can easily outperform the previous approaches, indicating that the textual features can also contain valuable information. In their next work [19], the authors aspired to extend the previous model by adding new textual features, while for the empirical study more than 5,000 people were recruited. The new results proved that the addition of the new textual features improved the model's accuracy, outperforming the current state-of-the-art models, while a correlation between better readability models and FindBug warnings was established. Contrary to the previous approaches, Choi *et al.* [2] were only based on structural features to build a model that could quantify code readability. The authors created a tool, named *Instant R. Gauge*, which was able to achieve more than 70% accuracy on human-annotated data.

Last but not least, Fakhoury *et al.* [5] examined the performance of the related approaches on readability evaluation, conducting a study about readability commits and the respective code improvements. The results showed that the readability models proposed in the bibliography are not able to detect and quantify the readability improvements introduced by the readability commits.

In this work, in an attempt to overcome the limitations depicted in the observations made by Fakhoury, we propose a generic data-driven methodology for evaluating readability both at method and class level. Using data residing in online code hosting facilities, we formulate our ground truth based on commonly accepted coding practices and aspire to evaluate the readability of a software component, as it is perceived by the developers, refraining from the use of experts. In an effort to provide interpretable results, we made use of Support Vector Regression models to analyze the quality of the source code and evaluate the readability of a software class or method on three independent axes, each corresponding to a primary code property.

3 Readability as Perceived by Developers

3.1 Benchmark Dataset

In an effort to define readability as perceived by developers, our primary design choice is harnessing the deluge of the available data residing in online code hosting facilities so as to formulate a ground truth that expresses the extent to which a software component is readable. In an effort to cover various evaluation scenarios, we perform analysis at both method and class levels. In specific, our dataset contains more than 1 million methods and classes included in the most popular (as reflected in the number of GitHub stars) and reused (as reflected in the number of GitHub forks) GitHub Java projects. We perform static analysis in order to compute two types of information: a) a large set of static analysis metrics that quantify six major source code properties: *cohesion*, *inheritance*, *complexity*, *coupling*, *documentation*, and *size*, and b) the identification of various coding violations regarding widely accepted code writing practices. Given their scope and impact, these violations are categorized into eight categories (Best Practices, Documentation, Design, Code Style, Error Prone, Performance, Multithreading, and Security) and three levels of severity (Minor, Major, and Critical). Upon selecting only the violations that are related to readability and in an effort to maintain the purity of our ground truth, we eliminate the violations that fall into the categories of *Performance*, *Multithreading*, and *Security*.

Table 1. Dataset statistics.

Metric	*Value*
Number of GitHub projects	330
Number of classes	172,065
Number of methods	1,002,990
Number of static analysis metrics	27
Number of code properties	6
Number of coding violations	193
Number of violations categories	5
Lines of code analyzed	9,359,380

Certain statistics regarding the benchmark dataset are given in Table 1, while Table 2 presents the calculated static analysis metrics along with their associated property. It is worth noting that the metrics referring to cohesion and inheritance are only applicable at class level. The static analysis metrics were calculated using the SourceMeter [20] tool, while the identification of coding violations was performed using the PMD tool [12].

The aforementioned tables have been altered from the respective ones in [8], in order to incorporate also the necessary data and source code metrics for the evaluation of readability in class level.

Table 2. Overview of the computed static analysis metrics.

Code property	Metric name	Metric description
Cohesion	LCOM5	Lack of cohesion in methods
Complexity	NL	Nesting level
	WMC	Weighted methods per class
	HDIF	Halstead difficulty
	HEFF	Halstead effort
	HNDB	Halstead number of delivered bugs
	HPL	Halstead program length
	HPV	Program vocabulary
	HTRP	Time required to program
	HVOL	Volume
	McCC	McCabe's cyclomatic complexity
	MI	Maintainability index
Coupling	NII	Number of incoming invocations
	NOI	Number of outgoing invocations
Inheritance	DIT	Depth of inheritance tree
	NOA	Number of ancestors
	NOC	Number of children
	NOD	Number of descendants
	NOP	Number of parents
Documentation	CD	Comment density
	CLOC	Comment lines of code
	DLOC	Documentation lines of code
	TCD	Total comment density
	TCLOC	Total comment lines of code
Size	LOC	Lines of code
	LLOC	Logical lines of code
	NOS	Number of statements

3.2 Clustering Based on Size

Given that our benchmark dataset includes more than 1 million methods and classes that exhibit high diversity both in terms of size and scope, our first step involves applying clustering techniques so as to split the code components in a set of cohesive clusters that share similar characteristics. This design choice originates from the fact that in practice, methods and classes of different size usually serve different functionalities or follow different architectures. For instance, methods with a small number of lines of code (<5) are mainly used as setters/getters or specific utilities (read data from files, middleware functions etc.), while larger ones mainly provide more advanced functionality. The same applies for classes, as size can be used as a measure of the number of functionalities they serve. As a result, from a static analysis metrics perspective, they should be handled accordingly.

Figure 1 presents the histogram (logarithmic scale) of the lines of code regarding the analyzed components. Figure 1(a) refers to methods, while Fig. 1(b) refers to classes. Given the distributions, it is obvious that the dataset covers a wide range of development scenarios.

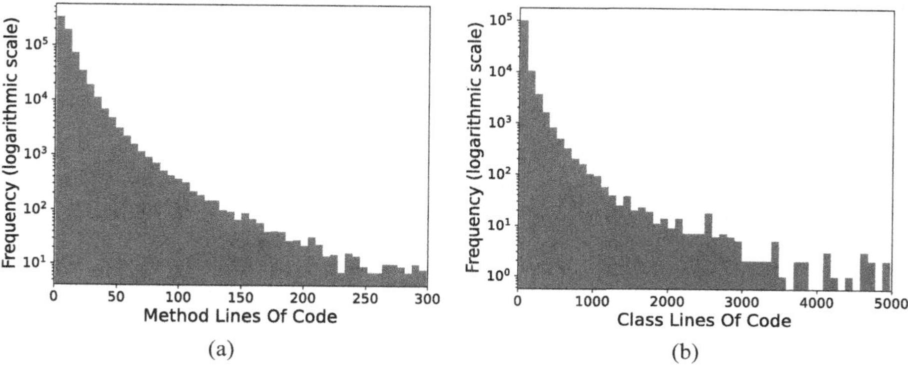

Fig. 1. Distribution of lines of code at (a) class and (b) package level.

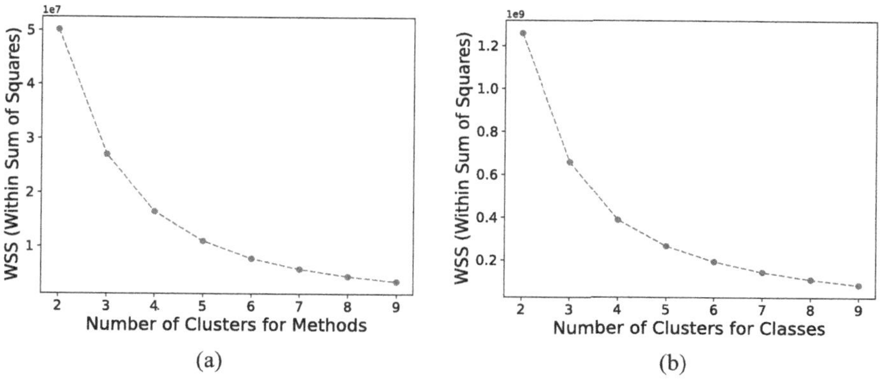

Fig. 2. Overview of cohesion for different clusterings at (a) method and (b) class level.

Upon examining the data and in an effort to eliminate any introduced bias from the high frequency of setters/getters and methods that provide no functionality (empty methods), our first step involves removing the methods that have less than 3 lines of code combined with minimal complexity as reflected in the values of McCabe Cyclomatic Complexity ($\leq$1). These methods correspond to 29.43% of the dataset (295,204 methods). Similarly, for the case of classes, we eliminate those that appear to have less than 10 lines of code and only one method. These classes correspond to 30.56% of the dataset (52,582 classes).

Our next step involves applying clustering using the k-Means algorithm. During this process and in order to identify the optimal number of clusters, we calculated the cohesion as expressed by the within sum of squares regarding different clusterings. Figure 2 illustrates the calculated cohesion for the cases where the number of clusters varies from 2 to 8. Figure 2(a) depicts the analysis results at method level, while Fig. 1(b) refers to classes. Given the provided results, we selected five as the optimal number of clusters for both cases.

Table 3. Overview of the formulated clusters.

Cluster	Methods			Classes		
	Number of methods	LOC Range	Mean silhouette	Number of classes	LOC Range	Mean silhouette
#1	481,399 (70.0%)	[1, 10]	0.76	98,563 (83.4%)	[11, 96]	0.79
#2	155,871 (22.7%)	[11, 24]	0.47	15,566 (13.2%)	[97, 294]	0.49
#3	40, 571 (5.9%)	[25, 51]	0.49	3, 258 (2.7%)	[295, 744]	0.58
#4	8, 417 (1.2%)	[52, 112]	0.49	647 (0.5%)	[745, 1868]	0.53
#5	1, 262 (0.2%)	>112	0.47	126 (0.1%)	>1868	0.55

The formulated clusters are presented in Table 3. For assessing the results of the clustering procedure, we used mean silhouette value [16] which combines the criteria of both cohesion and separation and is given by the following equations as they were originally presented in [8]:

$$s(i) = \frac{b(i) - a(i)}{max\{a(i), b(i)\}} \tag{1}$$

$$a(i) = \frac{1}{|C_i| - 1} \sum_{j \in C_i, i \neq j} d(i, j) \tag{2}$$

$$b(i) = min \frac{1}{|C_i|} \sum_{j \in C_k, k \neq i} d(i, j) \tag{3}$$

In the above equations $a(i)$ refers to the mean euclidean distance between i and all other data points in the same cluster, where $d(i, j)$ is the euclidean distance between data points i and j in the cluster C_i. On the other hand, $b(i)$ represents the smallest mean euclidean distance of i to all points in any other cluster, of which i is not a member. As shown in Table 3, the mean silhouette value regarding the five formulated clusters at method level ranges from 0.47 to 0.76, while at class level it ranges from 0.49 to 0.79. Finally, the mean silhouette values for the whole clustering at method and class level are 0.68 and 0.73, respectively.

Finally, in an effort to refrain from having clusters that exhibit high similarities in terms of the behaviour of the static analysis metrics and thus facilitate the modelling procedure, we merge clusters #2 and #3 into one cluster that represents the cluster of *medium size methods* (and *medium size classes*) and clusters #4 and #5 into one that represents the cluster of *large size methods* (and *large size classes*). These two clusters along with cluster #1 that represents *small size methods* (and *small size classes*) are going to be used during modelling.

3.3 Defining Ground Truth

After having constructed our final clusters at both levels, each corresponding to a different size category, the next step involves the formulation of the readability score which will be used as the information basis for building our readability evaluation models. To that end, we use the number of identified violations as our information basis upon which we compute the readability score for each source code component (method or class) that reflects the extend to which it is readable. The number of identified violations represents the compliance of the source code with widely accepted coding practices which create a common ground between developers and thus are crucial for determining the ease of a developer to read and comprehend a code fragment; in other words its readability.

Given that each violation affects the source code in a different manner along with the fact that based on their impact, violations are categorized into three severity degrees (*Minor*, *Major*, and *Critical*), one could argue that these severity degrees could be used as weights for calculating a total number of identified violations for a certain component. Although this strategy appears to be reasonable from a quality perspective, it assumes that all violations of a certain severity (e.g. the "Minor" ones) have the same impact, which is not always the case, especially considering the fact that this category includes more than 70 different violations. In an effort to overcome this limitation and given that our methodology is data-driven, we evaluate the significance of each violation based on its occurrence frequency in the benchmark dataset. The higher the occurrence frequency of a certain violation, the lower the significance. Given the aforementioned strategy, we resort in computing the significance (weight) for each violation using the following equation:

$$w(viol) = log(\frac{Max_{ViolFreq}}{freq(viol) + 1}) \tag{4}$$

In the above equation, $Max_{ViolFreq}$ refers to the highest occurrence frequency among all violations, while $freq(viol)$ refers to the occurrence frequency of the respective violation. The term +1 is used in order to eliminate the cases where a certain violation has zero occurrences and thus its weight would be infinite. Finally, given that the occurrence frequency among violations exhibits very high differences which do not necessarily reflect the actual difference in their significance, we use logarithm as a smoothing factor.

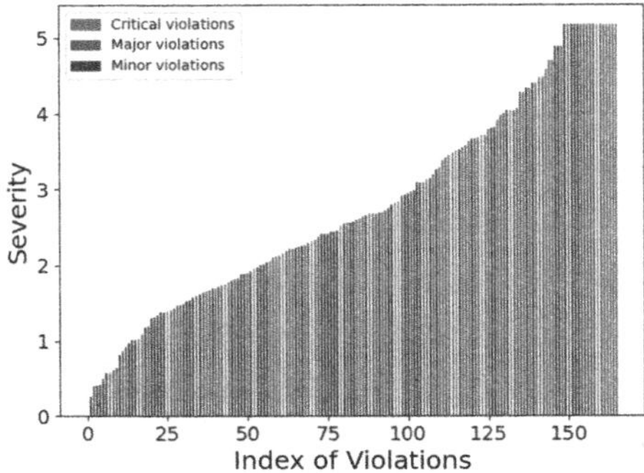

Fig. 3. Overview of the calculated weighs for all violations. (Color figure online)

Figure 3 depicts the calculated weights for all identified violations. Each bar refers to a certain violation, while the color ranges based on its categorization into the three aforementioned severity levels (Blue for "Minor", Green for "Major" and Red for "Critical"). As shown in the figure, in many cases the typical categorization differs from the calculated significance based on the analysis results originating from the benchmark dataset.

Having computed the weights for all violations, the readability score for a certain component is based on the following equations:

$$IdentifiedViolations(i) = \sum_{viol=1}^{K} w(viol) * freq(viol) \quad (5)$$

$$ViolPerLoc(i) = \frac{IdentifiedViolations(i)}{LLOC(i)} \quad (6)$$

$$R_{Score}(i) = 1 - Normed\{ViolPerLoc(i)\} \quad (7)$$

In the above equations, $IdentifiedViolations(i)$ refers to the calculated number of identified violations of the $i - th$ component (method or class), while $w(viol)$ and $freq(viol)$ represent the weight and the occurrence frequency of a certain violation. $ViolPerLoc(i)$ refers to the number of identified violations per Lines of Code regarding the $i - th$ component included in the dataset, while $LLOC(i)$ refers to the number of logical lines of code. Finally, $R_{Score}(i)$ refers to the reusability score for a certain component which is calculated as the normalized values of $ViolPerLoc(i)$ in the range $[0, 1]$. It should be noted that Eqs. 6 and 7 are used exactly like Eqs. 4 and 6 in [8], while we altered the calculation of the identified violations (Eq. 5), in order to incorporate the impact of each violation.

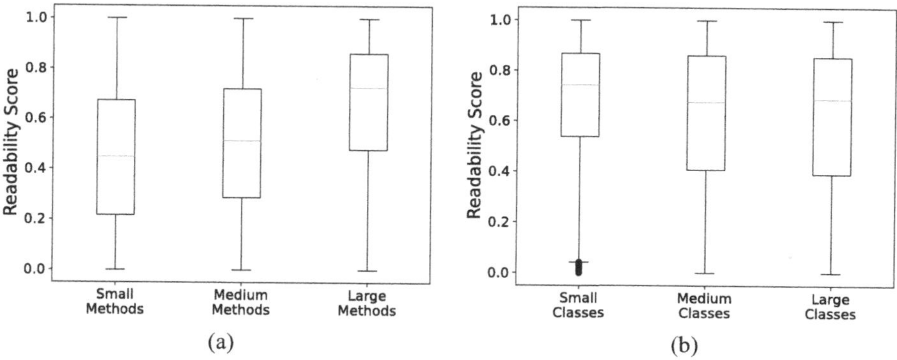

Fig. 4. Overview of the distribution of the readability scores at (a) method and (b) class level.

Figure 4 depicts the boxplots of the readability scores for the three formulated clusters at both method (Fig. 4(a)) and class levels (Fig. 4(b)). Given the boxplots in both levels, it is obvious that in all clusters, the majority of the scores is distributed among a large interval and thus covers a wide range of evaluation scenarios. In the case of methods, the cluster of "small methods" appears to have the highest range, which makes no surprise given that it contains almost 70% of the dataset and thus contains methods that exhibit significant differences in terms of adopting certain coding practices. Finally, it is worth noting that the "large methods" cluster appears to have the highest mean readability score. Although this may be surprising, it is logical from a software engineering point of view given that our dataset originates from the "best" GitHub Java projects as reflected in their adoption by the community of developers. These projects have hundreds of contributors and thus need to comply with certain code writing practices in order to ensure efficient collaboration, especially in the more complex parts of the source code.

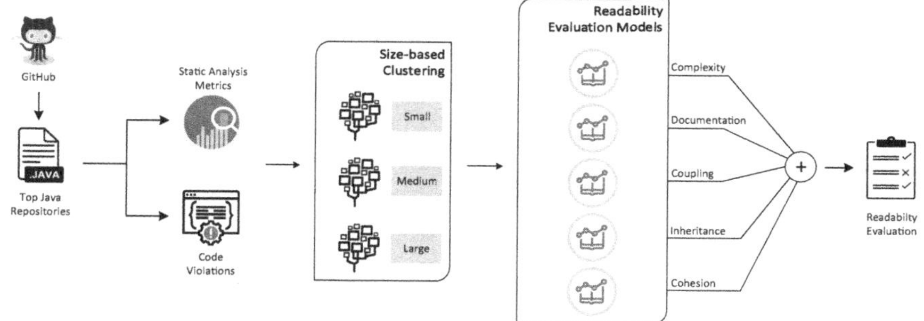

Fig. 5. Overview of readability evaluation system.

4 System Design

In this section we design our readability interpretation system (shown in Fig. 5) applicable at both method and class levels based on the values of a large set of static analysis metrics that quantify five major source code properties; *cohesion*, *inheritance*, *complexity*, *coupling*, and *documentation*.

4.1 Data Preprocessing

The preprocessing stage is used to examine the set of available metrics, detecting the overlays between them, in order to reduce the dimensions of the dataset and form the final set of metrics that will be used in our model. Specifically, we compute the pairwise correlations among all metrics to eliminate metrics that appear to be interdependent. Figure 6 illustrates the heatmap with the results of the correlation analysis at method level, while Fig. 7 at class level.

Given the heatmap for the case of methods, we can easily notice the high correlations between metrics that belong to the same category (e.g. *Complexity*, *Coupling* and *Documentation*), while metrics between different categories appear to have lower correlations. From a software quality point of view, the results seem quite reasonable. For instance, a method with high *Halstead Effort* (*HEFF*) has a high probability to also exhibit high *Halstead Time Required to Program* (*HTRP*) (with a correlation value of 1), while there is no clue about the *Number of Incoming Invocations* (*NII*) or the *Number of Outgoing Invocations* (*NOI*)(with a correlation value of 0.00027 and 0.16 respectively). In the case of classes and given that cohesion is only quantified by the metric LCOM5, the heatmap illustrates the correlation of the metrics that refer to inheritance.

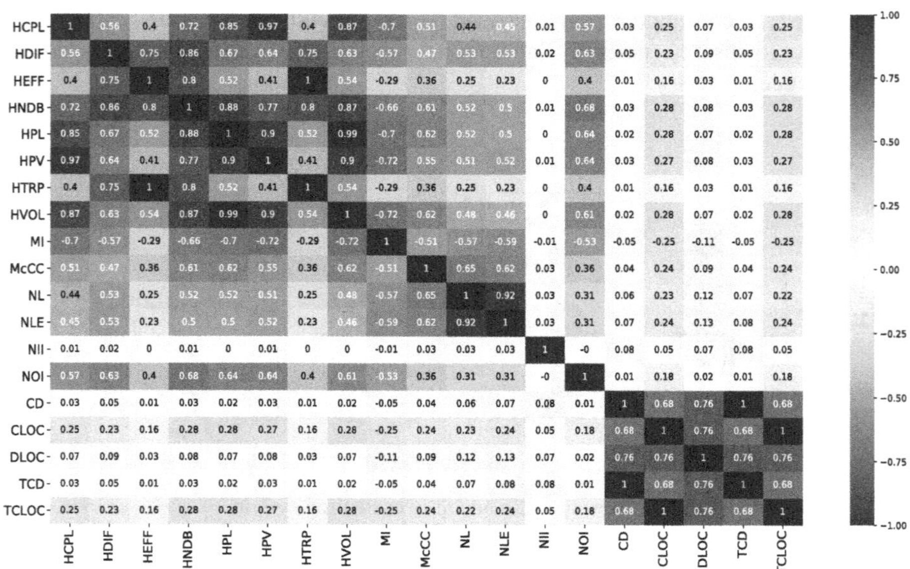

Fig. 6. Heatmap representation of correlation analysis at method level.

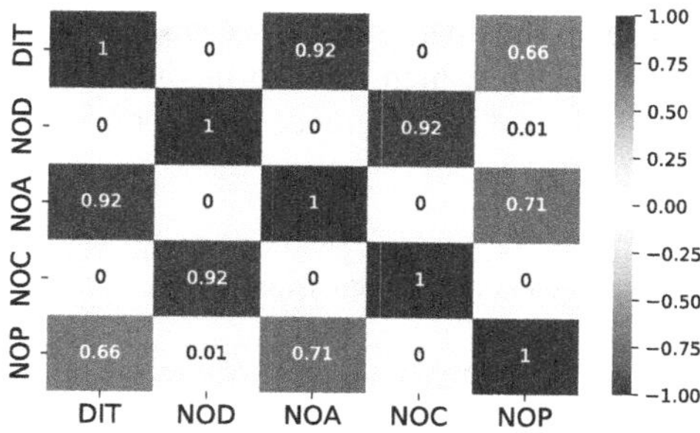

Fig. 7. Heatmap representation of correlation analysis at class level.

Table 4. The final metrics used in our model.

Code property	Level	Metrics
Complexity	Method	NL, HDIF, HPV, McCC, MI
Coupling	Method	NII, NOI
Documentation	Method	CD, CLOC, DLOC
Cohesion	Class	LCOM5
Inheritance	Class	DIT, NOP, NOC

The correlation analysis showed that a lot of metrics coming from the same category are highly correlated. For each metric category, upon examining the highly correlated metrics and keeping one metric for each of these groups, the final dataset consists of the metrics depicted in Table 4, as noted from [8].

4.2 Model Construction

As already mentioned, in the case of methods, we calculate one readability score per each metric category, i.e. the readability score concerning the *Complexity* metrics, the *Coupling* metrics and the *Documentation* metrics, evaluates the readability of each method from the perception of each axis separately. These three values are then aggregated to form the final readability score of the source code. As for the classes, we follow a similar approach as we calculate one readability score for each one of the categories *Inheritance* and *Cohesion*. Given the hierarchical structure of the source code in object-oriented programming, the third readability evaluation axis for a certain class originates from the already calculated readability score regarding its methods.

For the evaluation of the readability score of one method upon each metrics category, a well-known regression model was used, the Support Vector Regression (SVR) model [4]. Our methodology involves creating for each size cluster one SVR model that evaluates each code property. As a result, we resort in nine independent SVR models for the case of methods (three for each cluster) that evaluate *Complexity*, the *Coupling*, and *Documentation*, while in the case of classes we have six that evaluate *Cohesion* and *Inheritance*. The target of each model is the respective readability score as described in the previous section. The various parameters of each model are depicted in Tables 5 (originally created in [8]) and 6, which refer to methods and classes, respectively. g stands for gamma parameter, tol for tolerance as stopping criterion and C for the regularization parameter.

Table 5. The parameters of the regression models at method level.

Cluster	Category	g	tol	C
Small	Complexity	0.001	0.001	256
	Coupling	0.001	0.0001	256
	Documentation	0.001	0.01	256
Medium	Complexity	0.01	0.1	256
	Coupling	0.01	0.01	256
	Documentation	0.001	0.01	64
Large	Complexity	0.001	0.01	32
	Coupling	0.2	0.1	64
	Documentation	0.15	0.001	256

Table 6. The parameters of the regression models at class level.

Cluster	Category	g	tol	C
Small	Cohesion	0.001	0.001	256
	Inheritance	0.1	0.0001	256
Medium	Cohesion	0.001	0.001	1
	Inheritance	0.2	0.01	64
Large	Cohesion	0.001	0.1	64
	Inheritance	0.7	0.0001	256

As for the training process of each constructed model, we follow a 80/20 training-testing split, while we validate the performance of each model by using 10-fold cross-validation. Tables 7 and 8 present the training and testing errors for each trained model after performing cross-validation applicable at method and class level, respectively. The results in Table 7 are slightly different from the respective ones in [8], due to the different set of projects used.

At method level and for a certain cluster, the output of each one of the three models represents the readability score of the method regarding the respective property. The final readability score of the method is simply calculated by a weighted average of the three scores, where the weights are based on the number of metrics included in each property. As already mentioned in the preprocessing stage, 5 metrics are included in

Table 7. The cross-validation errors of the regression models at method level.

Cluster	Category	Training		Testing	
		MAE	MS	MAE	MSE
Small	Complexity	20.24%	6.53%	20.37%	6.55%
	Coupling	22.73%	7.41%	22.90%	7.53%
	Documentation	23.46%	7.69%	23.60%	7.76%
Medium	Complexity	18.23%	5.34%	21.02%	7.39%
	Coupling	21.95%	6.77%	22.17%	6.88%
	Documentation	21.84%	6.74%	22.06%	6.88%
Large	Complexity	16.84%	4.87%	21.55%	7.44%
	Coupling	19.29%	6.33%	21.42%	7.48%
	Documentation	19.15%	6.21%	22.84%	8.75%

Table 8. The cross-validation errors of the regression models at class level.

Cluster	Category	Training		Testing	
		MAE	MSE	MAE	MSE
Small	Cohesion	18.70%	5.78%	18.50%	5.61%
	Inheritance	18.53%	5.70%	18.49%	5.64%
Medium	Cohesion	23.36%	8.04%	23.38%	8.05%
	Inheritance	22.93%	7.86%	23.65%	8.29%
Large	Cohesion	22.49%	7.49%	26.60%	10.02%
	Inheritance	21.05%	6.96%	26.95%	10.20%

Complexity and 2 metrics are included in *Coupling*, while *Documentation* involves 3 metrics. Thus, the final aggregation function is depicted in the following equation:

$$RS_{method} = 0.5 \cdot S_{cmplx} + 0.2 \cdot S_{cpl} + 0.3 \cdot S_{doc} \tag{8}$$

where RS_{method} is the final readability score of the method, S_{cmplx} is the readability score regarding *Complexity*, S_{cpl} the readability score regarding *Coupling* and S_{doc} the readability score regarding the *Documentation*. Regarding classes, we follow the same strategy for evaluating the code properties, while the third axis originates from the calculated readability score regarding its methods. Thus the final aggregation function at class level is the following:

$$RS_{class} = 0.2 \cdot S_{coh} + 0.6 \cdot S_{inh} + 0.2 \cdot S_{methods} \tag{9}$$

where RS_{class} is the final readability score of the class, S_{coh} is the readability score regarding *Cohesion*, S_{inh} the readability score regarding *Inheritance* and $S_{methods}$ the mean readability score of the methods included in the class.

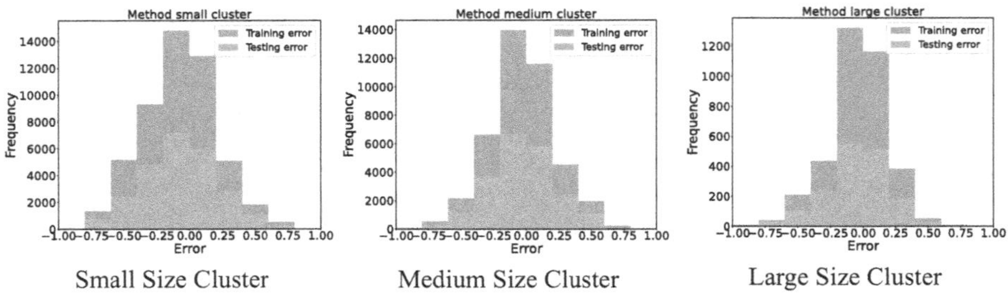

Fig. 8. Error histograms of all size clusters at method level.

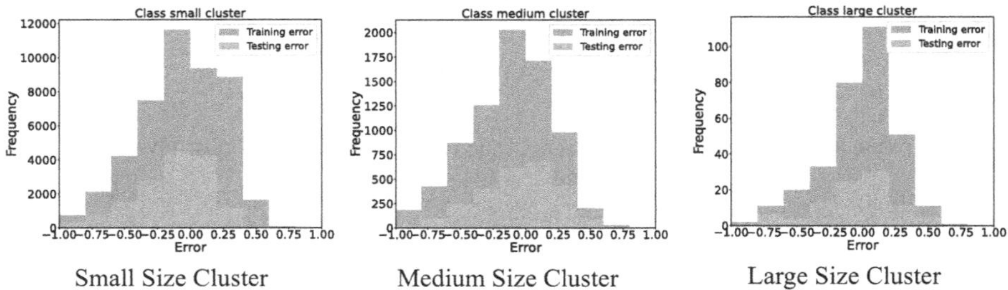

Fig. 9. Error histograms of all size clusters at class level.

Finally, in an effort to evaluate the efficiency of our models, we calculate the errors of the training and testing. Figure 8 illustrates the training and testing histograms for all size clusters at method level, while Fig. 9 depicts the respective error histograms at class level. At both levels, the models seem to be trained effectively, as the training and testing errors are low and lie mostly around 0. At the same time, the distributions of the two errors are quite similar and the differences are minimal, indicating that the models avoided overfitting.

5 Evaluation

In this section we evaluate our constructed methodology for estimating software readability in a set of diverse axes. At first, in an effort to evaluate the effectiveness and efficiency of our system, we apply our methodology on a set of diverse projects that exhibit different characteristics. As for the second axis and towards assessing whether the calculated readability scores are reasonable from a quality perspective, we perform manual inspection on the values of the static analysis metrics regrading methods and classes that received both low and high readability scores. Finally, in an attempt to evaluate the effectiveness of our approach in practice, we harness the readability evaluation results in order to improve the readability degree of a certain Java method.

5.1 Readability Estimation Evaluation

Table 9. The readability score interpretation on evaluation repositories.

Repo	Num. of methods	Num. of classes	Total LOC	Method level		Class level	
				Actual	Predicted	Actual	Predicted
#1	5,847	1,925	48,371	41.15%	45.81%	72.75%	65.83%
#2	3,034	493	19,207	49.74%	46.16%	65.18%	61.21%
#3	985	136	9,787	45.84%	40.62	69.54%	62.09%
#4	94	16	671	39.74%	49.12%	56.75%	60.73%

In the first step towards assessing the validity of our system, we evaluate its efficiency based on the readability scores computed for four randomly selected repositories (around 10K methods and 80K Lines of Code) that exhibit significant differences in terms of size (number of methods and total lines of code) and scope. Table 9 presents certain statistics regarding the size and the readability evaluation for the examined repositories. In specific, the table contains the number of methods and classes as well as the lines of code along with the mean values regarding the actual and the predicted overall readability scores at both levels. In addition, in an effort to further examine the readability interpretation results against the evaluated source code properties, Fig. 10 illustrates the percentage of the methods that received low, medium and high readability scores. Low score refers to values below 0.33 (or 33%), medium refers to values in the interval $(0.33, 0.66]$, while high refers to scores above 0.7 (or 70%).

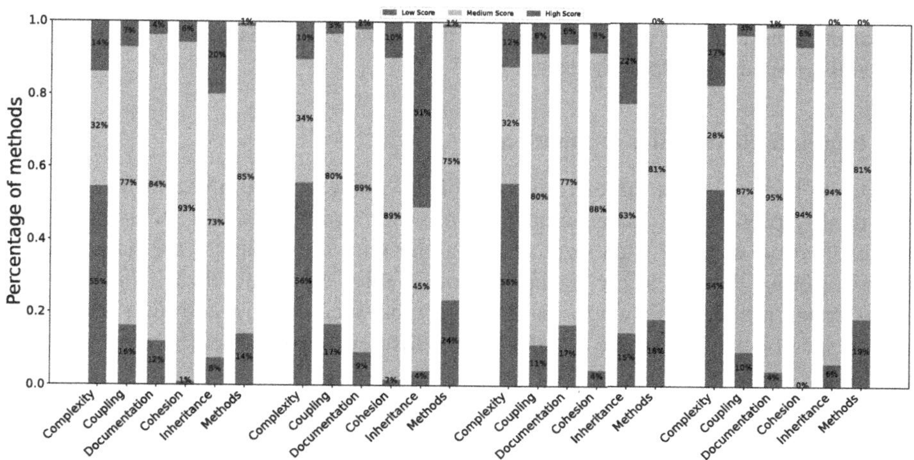

Fig. 10. Percentage of scores per category.

According to the provided results, it is obvious that the overall predicted readability score, which occurs as an aggregation of the respective scores for the three source code properties, aligns with the one computed using the number of identified violations. In the case of classes, the difference between the actual and the predicted score lies in the interval $[3\%, 5\%]$ in most cases, while in the case of classes this difference lies in the interval $[4\%, 7\%]$. The highest difference in the case of methods appears in the smallest repository. Upon manually examining its methods, we identified several methods which are outliers from a static analysis metrics point of view (empty methods). These methods were given a very high score and thus the mean predicted score appears to be positively biased. In addition, given the mean values of the readability score for the examined properties, according to which the mean score in all cases lies in the interval $[40\%, 60\%]$, one may conclude that our models do not exhibit bias towards making predictions around a certain value. This is also reflected in the distribution of the scores as illustrated in Fig. 10.

Upon further examining the calculated readability scores in terms of decomposing the final score into the three different axes under evaluation and in an effort to assess whether the calculated scores are logical from a quality perspective, we examined the variance of the scores for each respective property. The results at method level showed that the scores regarding documentation exhibit the lowest variance, while the ones regarding complexity appear to have the highest variance. This makes no surprise given that the way of documenting source code in a certain project depends on the design choices made by the main contributors that drive the development process and thus refers to the project as a whole. As a result, the within-project variance of the documentation scores are expected to be low. This is reflected in the percentage of methods receiving low, medium, and high values regarding the four examined projects. On the other hand, complexity and coupling are properties that fully depend on the provided functionality and thus methods with different scope and target may exhibit high differences. This is also reflected in the percentage of methods receiving different readability evaluation, where in the cases of coupling and complexity this percentage is almost evenly distributed in all four projects.

5.2 Example Readability Estimation

In order to further assess the effectiveness of our models and evaluate it from a software quality perspective, we examined the methods and classes that received high or low readability score for each size cluster, along with the values of the related static analysis metrics that led to the predicted score. Table 10 presents these values regarding six different methods (two for each cluster) that received low and high readability score, respectively, while Table 11 refers to six different classes selected using the same criteria.

As for the methods of low size, it is obvious that the method that received low readability score appears to have no documentation as reflected in the zero value of the Comments Density (CD) metric. On top of that and given the number of outgoing invocations (11), it appears to be highly coupled as it calls eleven other methods during its execution. As a result, the low readability score is logical from a quality perspective. The same applies for the method which received high score given that it appears

Table 10. Overview of the static analysis metrics per property for methods with different quality scores.

Metric name	Small size cluster		Medium size cluster		Large size cluster	
	High score (85.52%)	Low score (20.58%)	High score (83.71%)	Low score (18.95%)	High score (87.43%)	Low score (12.37%)
NL	0	1	2	3	1	4
HDIF	7	18	20.62	33.09	5.67	46.31
HPV	18	36	30	69	74	195
McCC	1	1	3	6	1	226
MI	114.7	102.6	100.75	80.71	73.84	−17.41
NII	0	0	1	2	0	1
NOI	1	11	2	6	4	13
CD	0.36	0.29	0.34	0.07	0.11	0.006
CLOC	4	0	8	2	10	2
DLOC	4	0	8	0	5	0

Table 11. Overview of the static analysis metrics per property for methods with different quality scores.

Metric name	Small size cluster		Medium size cluster		Large size cluster	
	High score (88.36%)	Low score (17.73%)	High score (85.2%)	Low score (19.60%)	High score (80.01%)	Low score (5.12%)
LCOM5	0	3	1	7	1	17
DIT	1	1	2	2	1	3
NOP	1	1	2	1	1	4
NOC	0	0	1	22	4	6

to exhibit almost no coupling and has an average documentation level. It is worth noting that both methods exhibit high scores in terms of complexity. As for the classes that belong to the small size cluster, the one receiving low score appears to have low cohesion as it could be split int 3 cohesive classes (based on the value of LCOM5).

As for the methods of medium size, it is obvious that the method that received low readability score appears to be more complex and coupled than the one that received high score as reflected in the values of McCabe Cyclomatic Complexity (McCC) and Nesting Level (NL), as well as in the number of incoming and outgoing invocations. In addition, the method which received a low score exhibits significantly higher volume as reflected in the value of Halstead Program Volume (HPV), which is calculated from the number of distinct and total operations and operands. Similar to the case of the classes that belong to the small cluster, the medium-size class that received low score appears lack both in terms of cohesion and inheritance as compared to the one that received high score. These differences are obvious given the values of the metrics LCOM5 and NOC.

The same conclusions are drawn, while inspecting the computed values of the static analysis metrics of the methods and classes included in the large size cluster. At method level, it is worth noting that as size increases, the impact of complexity into the readability degree becomes even more evident. This is reflected in the high difference in the values of Maintainability Index (MI) between the two methods of the large size cluster. At class level the same applies for the cohesion. Given all the above, the readability evaluation in all twelve cases (six methods and six classes) appears to be logical and can be explained by the values of the static analysis metrics.

5.3 Application of Readability Enhancement in Practice

Further assessing the effectiveness of our readability evaluation system in terms of providing actionable recommendations that can be used in practice during development, we resort to the exploration of a certain use-case where we harness the results of our system towards improving the readability degree of a certain method.

```
private static void updateDb(boolean isForceUpdate) {
    if (isUpdateReady) {
        if (isForceUpdate) {
            if (isSynchCompleted) {
                updateDbMain(true);
                updateBackupDb(true);
            } else {
                updateDbMain(false);
                updateBackupDb(true);
            }
        } else {
            updateCache(!isCacheEnabled);
        }
    }
}
```

Fig. 11. Initial version of method.

Figure 11 presents the initial source code of the method under evaluation. This method is responsible for updating a certain database along with the backup database and works in two different modes. The first mode refers to the case when the variable *ForceUpdate* is true and involves updating the main database along with the backup database, while the second refers to the case when the variable *ForceUpdate* is false and involves only updating cache. At this point, it is worth noting that no update operation should be performed in the main database in cases when *isUpdateReady* is false or synchronization is not complete (*isSynchCompleted* is false). Upon evaluating the respective method using our trained models the overall readability score is 0.428 (or 42.8%), while the scores for the three properties were as follows: 0.637 (or 63.7%) for the Complexity, 0.472 (or 47.2%) for the Coupling, and 0.052 (or 5.2%) for the Documentation. Given these results, it is obvious that our method lacks proper documentation, while at the same time we can see that there is a relatively large nesting level as reflected in the NL value which is 3.

We try to optimize our method in two directions. At first, we add detailed documentation explaining the different control flow paths in order to improve the comprehensibility of the code. Our second audit targets reducing complexity by refactoring the navigation to the different available control flow paths and thus improve clarity. Figure 12 presents the optimized version of the source code, which originates from the aforementioned audits. Upon evaluating the optimized version, the overall readability score is

```
/**
 * Update mainDB, backupDB, and cache
 */
private static void updateDb(boolean isForceUpdate) {

    // Do nothing in case the update is not ready
    if (!isUpdateReady){
        return;
    }

    // Update cache in case of non forced update
    if (!isForceUpdate) {
        updateCache(!isCacheEnabled);
        return;
    }

    // General Update Pipeline (Backup and Main DB)
    updateBackupDb(true);
    updateDbMain(isSynchCompleted ? true : false);
}
```

Fig. 12. Final version of method.

0.80 (or 80%), while the scores regarding the three properties were as follows: 0.833 (or 83.3%) for the Complexity, 0.472 (or 47.2%) for the Coupling, and 0.963 (or 96.3%) for the Documentation. As given by the comparison of the two code fragments, which are functionally equal, the performed audits had a significant impact on the readability degree, which is reflected in the scores. Finally, given that the two code fragments have the same number of incoming and outgoing invocations, the score regarding the coupling property remains the same. Finally, there is still room for improvement by splitting the method into multiple methods each being responsible for a certain task. In that way, we can also improve coupling.

6 Readability Evaluation Web Application

In an effort to test our readability interpretation methodology in practice, we developed a prototype service[2] that is deployed as a web application. Figure 13 illustrates the web interface, where users are able to overview the readability interpretation results (right part of the screen) along with the source code of the respective component (left part of the screen) regarding several evaluation scenarios that took place in the context of this paper. On top of that and using the interactive editor, users will be able to use the trained models for evaluating their source code components and get actionable feedback towards improving the readability of their code.

[2] https://readability-evaluator.netlify.app/.

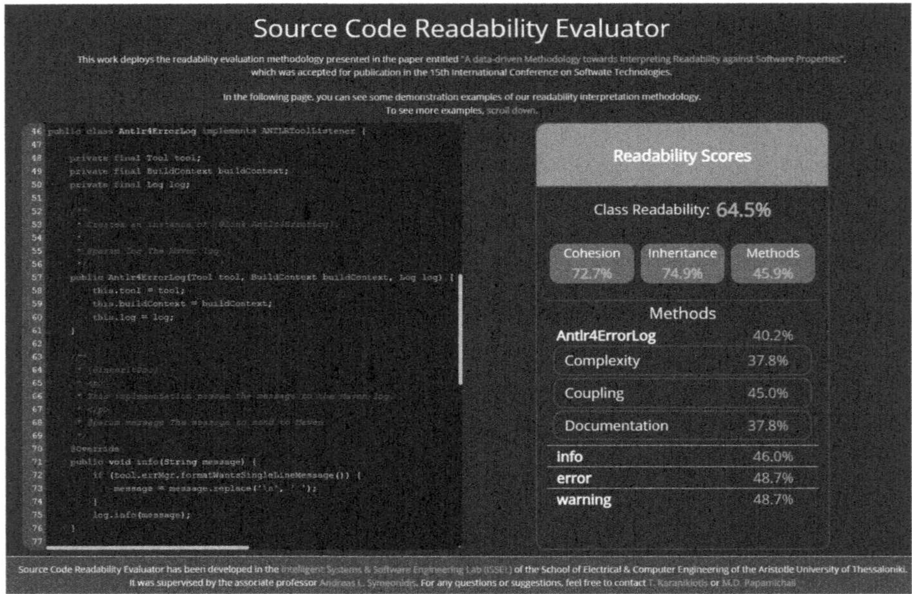

Fig. 13. Overview of the interface of the Source Code Readability Evaluator.

7 Threats to Validity

Our approach towards readability evaluation interpretation seems to achieve high internal validity, as it has already been proved from the evaluation. The limitations and threats to the external validity of our approach span along the following axes: a) limitations imposed by the definition of our ground truth, and b) the selection of our benchmark dataset.

Our design choice to quantify readability based on the compliance of the source code with widely accepted coding practices as reflected in the number of identified violations originates from the fact that the primary target of coding violations is to set up a common ground between the development community in terms of following certain code writing guidelines. Apart from preventing the occurrence of various types of errors (already known and documented), this common ground is crucial for improving the understandability of the source code and thus influences readability. Furthermore, given that we interpret readability as perceived by developers, our benchmark dataset is built upon harnessing crowdsourcing information regarding the popularity and the degree of reuse for a large number of GitHub Java projects. This information reflects the high adoption of the selected projects among the community of developers and thus was considered appropriate towards formulating our benchmark dataset. Of course, our methodology can be applied as-is using a different benchmark dataset that covers the individual needs of specific evaluation scenarios.

8 Conclusions and Future Work

In this work, we proposed a multilevel readability evaluation methodology, that can interpret readability as perceived by developers in an automated way, based on a large set of static analysis metrics and coding violations. Our methodology can express the extent to which a software class or method is readable in a way that a developer can easily comprehend. Upon assessing the performance of our approach on a set of diverse axes, our system is proven to be effective in evaluating readability on various axes, both for class and method components, which correspond to primary source code properties. Upon attempting to evaluate the effectiveness of our methodology also in providing actionable and applicable recommendations towards audits that can enhance the readability degree of the project under evaluation, our system can be a valuable tool for developers.

Future work relies on several directions. At first, we can expand our dataset by adding additional projects with different characteristics and thus improve the ability of our models to generalize. Finally, the design of our target variable can be further investigated for the incorporation of additional metrics other than violations.

References

1. Buse, R., Weimer, W.: Learning a metric for code readability. IEEE Trans. Softw. Eng. **36**, 546–558 (2010). https://doi.org/10.1109/TSE.2009.70
2. Choi, S., Kim, S., Kim, J., Park, S.: Metric and tool support for instant feedback of source code readability. Tech. Gaz. **27**(1), 221–228 (2020). https://doi.org/10.17559/tv-20181030091239
3. Dorn, J.: A general software readability model. Master Thesis, University of Virginia, Department of Computer Science (2012)
4. Drucker, H., Burges, C.J.C., Kaufman, L., Smola, A.J., Vapnik, V.: Support vector regression machines. In: Mozer, M.C., Jordan, M.I., Petsche, T. (eds.) Advances in Neural Information Processing Systems 9, pp. 155–161. MIT Press (1997). http://papers.nips.cc/paper/1238-support-vector-regression-machines.pdf
5. Fakhoury, S., Roy, D., Hassan, S.A., Arnaoudova, V.: Improving source code readability: theory and practice. In: Proceedings of the 27th International Conference on Program Comprehension, ICPC 2019, pp. 2–12. IEEE Press (2019). https://doi.org/10.1109/ICPC.2019.00014
6. Halstead, M.H.: Elements of software science (Operating and programming systems series). Elsevier Science Inc., USA (1977)
7. ISO: ISO/IEC 25010 (2020). https://iso25000.com/index.php/en/iso-25000-standards/iso-25010. Accessed 20 March 2020
8. Karanikiotis, T., Papamichail, M., Gonidelis, I., Karatza, D., Symeonidis, A.: A data-driven methodology towards interpreting readability against software properties. In: ICSOFT, pp. 61–72 (2020). https://doi.org/10.5220/0009891000610072
9. Knight, J.C., Myers, E.A.: An improved inspection technique. Commun. ACM **36**(11), 50–61 (1993)
10. Mannan, U.A., Ahmed, I., Sarma, A.: Towards understanding code readability and its impact on design quality, pp. 18–21 (2018). https://doi.org/10.1145/3283812.3283820
11. Pantiuchina, J., Lanza, M., Bavota, G.: Improving code: The (mis) perception of quality metrics, pp. 80–91 (2018). https://doi.org/10.1109/ICSME.2018.00017

12. PMD tool (2020). https://pmd.github.io. Accessed March 2020
13. Posnett, D., Hindle, A., Devanbu, P.: A simpler model of software readability. In: Proceedings of the 8th Working Conference on Mining Software Repositories, MSR 2011, pp. 73–82. Association for Computing Machinery, New York (2011). https://doi.org/10.1145/1985441.1985454
14. Prabhu, R., Phutane, N., Dhar, S., Doiphode, S.: Dynamic formatting of source code in editors. In: 2017 International Conference on Innovations in Information, Embedded and Communication Systems (ICIIECS), pp. 1–6 (2017). https://doi.org/10.1109/ICIIECS.2017.8276008
15. Raymond, D.R.: Reading source code. In: Proceedings of the 1991 Conference on Centre for Advanced Studies on Collaborative Research, pp. 3–16 (1991)
16. Rousseeuw, P.J.: Silhouettes: a graphical aid to the interpretation and validation of cluster analysis. J. Comput. Appl. Math. **20**, 53–65 (1987). https://doi.org/10.1016/0377-0427(87)90125-7
17. Rugaber, S.: The use of domain knowledge in program understanding. Ann. Softw. Eng. **9**, 143–192 (2000). https://doi.org/10.1023/A:1018976708691
18. Scalabrino, S., Linares-Vásquez, M., Poshyvanyk, D., Oliveto, R.: Improving code readability models with textual features. In: 2016 IEEE 24th International Conference on Program Comprehension (ICPC), pp. 1–10 (2016). https://doi.org/10.1109/ICPC.2016.7503707
19. Scalabrino, S., Linares-Vásquez, M., Oliveto, R., Poshyvanyk, D.: A comprehensive model for code readability. J. Softw. Evol. Process **30**(6), e1958 (2018)
20. SourceMeter static analysis tool (2020). https://www.sourcemeter.com/. Accessed March 2020

Efficient Verification of Reconfigurable Discrete-Event System Using Isabelle/HOL Theorem Prover and Hadoop

Sohaib Soualah[1,4](✉), Yousra Hafidi[1,2,4](✉), Mohamed Khalgui[1](✉), Allaoua Chaoui[3](✉), and Laid Kahloul[2](✉)

[1] LISI Laboratory, National Institute of Applied Sciences and Technology, University of Carthage, 1080 Tunis, Tunisia

[2] LINFI Laboratory, Computer Science Department, Biskra University, Biskra, Algeria

[3] MISC Laboratory, Faculty of NTIC, University Constantine 2, Abdelhamid Mehri, Constantine, Algeria

[4] University of Tunis El Manar, Tunis, Tunisia

Abstract. This paper deals with the modelling and verification of reconfigurable discrete event systems using model driven engineering Hadoop. Hadoop is therefore a platform for establishing a dialogue between several machines. Its objectives are to solve the main problems of Hard disk size and of computing powers limitations. Isabelle/HOL is an interactive/automated theorem prover that combines the functional programming paradigm with high order logic (HOL), which makes it efficient for developing solid formalizations. In this paper, we are interested in reconfigurable discrete event systems, which we formalise using Isabelle/HOL. The proposed method consists of formalising a reconfigurable discrete event system with Isabelle/HOL, using Hadoop, we apply the distributed verification to perform an efficient verification of systems. The reason of this choice consists in the fact that theorem proving deals with the verification of infinite systems while model checking deals with finite systems and suffers from the well known state space explosion problem. Furthermore, thanks to Hadoop it can apply the distributed verification, which means more reduction in verification time. We implement the contributions of this paper using Hadoop platform and Isabelle tool. Finally, we illustrate the proposed method through FESTO MPS case study.

Keywords: Reconfigurable discrete-event systems · Hadoop · Formal verification · Theorem prover · Isabelle/HOL

1 Introduction

The development of systems in the industry is improved productivity, but will have the challenge of safety. The development of safe systems is considered as an

M. van Sinderen et al. (Eds.): ICSOFT 2020, CCIS 1447, pp. 227–241, 2021.
https://doi.org/10.1007/978-3-030-83007-6_11

important task because any failure can be critical according to a domain (e.g., air and railway traffic control [9], manufacturing systems [10], real time systems and intelligent control systems [10]). Many researchers are working in this context, which give as result new types of systems. One of this system is Reconfigurable discrete event systems (RDESs) are characterized by their discrete nature and their structures change over time. An RDES is defined as a hardware or software automation system capable of modifying its internal structure to answer the compromise exibility vs performance [7], which means guarantee performance by giving response to customer's needs. Two types of reconfigurations: static and dynamic [16]. The static reconfigurations is applied offline before running the system. The dynamic reconfigurations is applied automatically at run-time without any interruption. The latter can be executed: (1) manually by users, (2) automatically by agents (robot, machine, schedule, etc.), and (3) in a hybrid way which is the combination of the two types. In the last few years, there has been a growing interest from researchers in the safety of reconfigurable discrete event systems, they are following many verification approaches [7].

To deal with the safety of reconfigurable discrete event systems, many existing works have been proposed in this perspective of safety, adopt formal verification to check the hardware and software of systems, which give as result new formalisms and improved verification methods. Formal verification is a technique to check system properties and requires mathematical experiences and skills. Model checking [2] is one of the most used solutions to validate systems, such as manufacturing systems [10], telecommunication systems [4], and transport networks [3]. It presents an automatic verification technique to check functional properties. Model-checking uses mathematical methods to verify if a property is satisfied in a given system model. If the property is violated, a counter example of the system execution is provided. Some researchers have improved the verification using model checking.

Recently, several related works on formal verification methods, using model-checking [2], are used to validate the safety of reconfigurable discrete event systems.

The work reported in [6] presents a new methodology for formal verification of reconfigurable discrete event control systems (RDECSs), where is based on the checking of reconfiguration scenarios (inter-verification) and also the checking of the internal behavior of each configuration (intra-verification). The required properties of the system are specified using the computation tree logic (CTL) and verified using model checking. Authors in [5] propose an extension to the IEC 61499 [12] standard called Reconfigurable Function Block, encapsulating several reconfiguration scenarios in one function block. In order to verify the system and to evaluate its performance, authors model it using a class of Petri nets called GR-TNCES [11]. After that, PRISM is used as a model checker to verify the safety of each reconfiguration scenario of the system. In [17], authors propose a new extension of TNCES formalism named reconfigurable net condition/event systems (R-TNCESs). This last allows to deal with reconfiguration and time properties with modular specification in the same formalism.

We find that all those works presented above are important for the verification task of RDESs. However, there is some negligence regarding analysed properties. Actually, the complexity of model checking depends on two parameters: the size of the model, and the number of properties to be verified. For instance, Bounded Model Checking (BMC) is based on a reduction of model checking to satisfiability formulae [8]. Therefore, the large increase in the system state space that produces the well known "state explosion problem". Thus, our ability to do model checking depends on our ability to deal with a large model of the system and the number of the properties. In addition, the verification task in this all works is applicted in one machine, which means the time of verification is significant. On the contrary, if the verification task is distributed over several machines. For several years now, the world of computing has entered an era in which the main problem is no longer how to acquire data but rather how to manage the enormous amount of data that we are able to acquire. Managing such large amounts of data poses problems. One of these problems is how to organize and treat for this data: a single machine does not have the power to perform sufficiently fast treats on the data. The solution to these problems is to use several machines: by sharing their hard drive, the machines from a much larger storage group, and sharing their processor (and/or graphics card), the machines form a much more efficient computing group. This is where Hadoop intervenes, to bring context, tools and conventions in order to quickly set up such a cluster, store data and run programs in a distributed way. A cluster is a set of computers connected to each other by a network and able to organize themselves to distribute the load (computing or storage). Each computer in this cluster is called a node. We use, in this work theorem proving Isabelle/HOL for the formalization and verification of RDESs, it is characterized by the use of high-order logic powerful expression language. Using such a theorem proving has several advantages [15]. First, it gives a certificate to formal proof when it succeeds. Second, when the verification of the given property fails, it generates a counterexample as a proof to the formula negation, instead of a sequence of states or trees labeled with states, as in traditional model checkers. Thanks to Hadoop [13], it can apply the distributed verification, which means more reduction time. This paper presents the following contributions:

In this paper, we are interested in reconfigurable discrete event systems, which we formalise using Isabelle/HOL. The proposed method consists of formalising a reconfigurable discrete event system with Isabelle/HOL, using Hadoop, we apply the distributed verification to perform an efficient verification of systems.

- In this paper, we use the results of our previous work [15] for formalising RDESs.
- In order to reduce verification time, we use Hadoop for efficient verification.

The difference between our previous work presented in [15] and our current work is:

In previous work [15], the main idea is to analyse the properties of the system after defining relations between them. Thus, we can later reduce their number according to these relations. In the current work, we distribute the properties of the system in several machines after that we do the verification. Thus, we can later reduce the verification time. Consequently, we aim to reduce the execution time of the verification task. To this end, we first formalise RDES with Isabelle/HOL using our previous work [15] and we propose a new verification method, which allows us to distribute the properties of the system in several machines. According to distribution of properties, we will do the verification for this properties in each machine. We can summarise our work as follows: 1) Formalise a reconfigurable discrete event system with Isabelle/HOL. 2) Distributed verification in order to reduce verification time. A formal case study is presented to illustrate the feasibility of our proposed contributions. Results show that the proposed contributions reduce the verification time by distributing of properties to be verified for the reconfigurable discrete event system. The remainder of the paper is organized as follows. Section 2 presents a background about Isabelle/HOL theorem prover, FESTO Modular Production System, and Hadoop. Section 3 involves details and the formalisation of our proposed method. Section 3 illustrates the performance evaluation of the suggested approach. Finally, Sect. 2 concludes the paper and highlights some perspectives of the work.

2 Background

In this section, we present details about Isabelle/HOL theorem proving, FESTO Modular Production System, and Hadoop.

2.1 Isabelle/HOL Theorem Proving

Isabelle/HOL is a theorem prover based totally on the aggregate of the functional programming paradigm with high order logic (HOL), which makes it efficient for developing solid formalizations. [14]. Using Isabelle/HOL, we can formalize a system and prove its properties (i.e., formalize systems, formulating lemmas and theorems on them) [1]. Isabelle/HOL has a high degree of credibility for created proofs because it allows us to prove every step, and consequently the complete proof is correct. Isabelle has a number of methods, to describe data structures. In the following, we show the main Isabelle concepts used in this paper.

- The theory: The main concept enveloping all elements used to write a program in Isabelle/HOL.
- Types bool, nat and list: These are the most important predefined types. Although the lists are already predefined, and can define their own type.
- Types synonym: Synonym types are abbreviations for existing types.
- Function: In most cases, defining a recursive function is as simple as other definitions.
- Record: A record in Isabelle is an element enveloping more than one type, to define another type.
- Lemma: is used to prove a function or properties.

2.2 FESTO Modular Production System

The FESTO modular production system is taken as a as running example in this paper. Festo MPS consists of three stations: Distribution, Testing and Processing Station. Figure 1, shows ten physical units composing this situation. The Distribution station is formed of a pneumatic feeder and a converter which transmits cylindrical workpieces from a stock to the Test station. The Test Station is composed of a detector, a tester and an elevator. It performs tests on workpieces for height, type of material and color. Workpieces that satisfy these tests are transmitted to the Processing Station, which is composed of a rotating disk, a drill machine and a control machine. The rotating disk is composed of locations to contain and transport workpieces from the input position, to the drilling position, to the control position and finally to the output position. We assume in this paper that FESTO performs in different production modes by using two drilling machines $Driller_1$ and $Driller_2$, as follows:

- *light*1 production mode ($L1$): (respectively light 2 production mode ($L2$)): Only $Driller1$ (respectively Driller2) describes the system behavior in which work-pieces are drilled by machine $Driller_i$ (i in 1 ... 2).
- *Medium* production mode (M): $Driller_1$ or $Driller_2$ are activated but used sequentially to drill workpieces (i.e., $Driller_1$ or $Driller_2$ works).
- *High* production mode (H): $Driller_1$ and $Driller_2$ are activated and used simultaneously to drill two pieces in the same time.

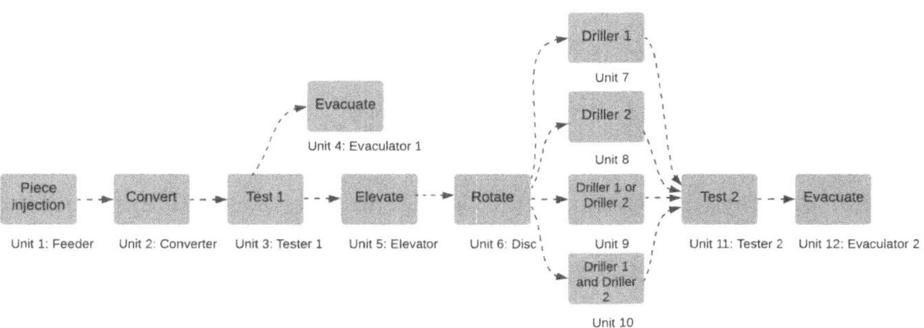

Fig. 1. The behavior module of the system [15].

In Fig. 2 we depict the possible reconfiguration modes considered in our paper. The system reconfigures in order to avoid any problem caused by a physical fault (i.e., when $Driller_1$ or $Driller_2$ breakdown) or to answer user requirements. The reconfiguration behavior of the studied system loses its usefulness when both machines $Driller_1$ and $Driller_2$ are broken. In the last case, the system totaly stops.

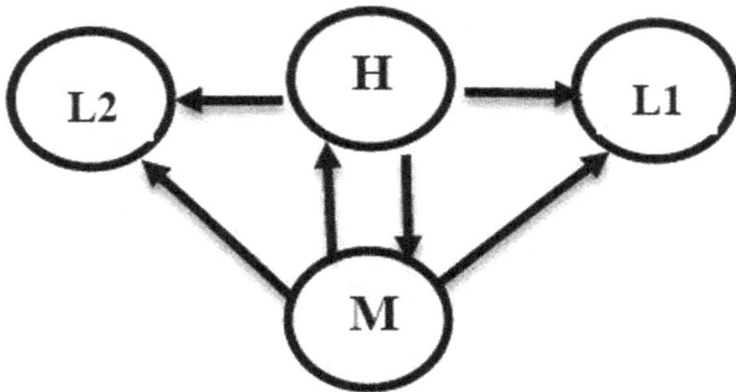

Fig. 2. FESTO possible reconfiguration mode [15].

2.3 Hadoop

Hadoop [13] is therefore a platform for establishing a dialogue between several machines in a cluster. Its objectives are to solve the main problems of handling large amounts of data. Hard disk size limitation and limitation of computing powers is tow problems. To solve these problems, Hadoop is structured into two main layers:

- HDFS: Hadoop File system, a virtual file system that stores multiple machines in a cluster
- Hadoop MapReduce: a Java software framework for developing distributed executable programs using the MapReduce algorithm developed by Google.

A MapReduce job consists of several phases:

- 1. Preprocessing of input data.
- 2. Split: separation of the data into treatable blocks and formatted as (key, value).
- 3. Map: application of the map function on all pairs (key, value) formed from the input data, this produces other pairs (key, value) in the output,
- 4. Shuffle & Sort: redistribution of data so that the pairs produced by Map with the same keys are on the same machines,
- 5. Reduce: aggregation of pairs with the same key to obtain the final result.

Example. We have a text file toto.txt and we need to count the occurrence of each word in the text:

- Preprocessing of input data, e.g.: possible decompression of the file.
- Split: separates data into treatable blocks and formatted as (key, value), (nb-line, line).
- Map: application of the map function on all pairs (offset, line) formed from the input data, it produces other pairs (word, 1) in output.
- Shuffle & Sort: redistribution of data so that the pairs produced by Map with the same keys are on the same machines

- Reduce: aggregation of pairs with the same key to obtain the final result (word, nb-occurrences).

Figure 3 depicts the overall MapReduce word count process.

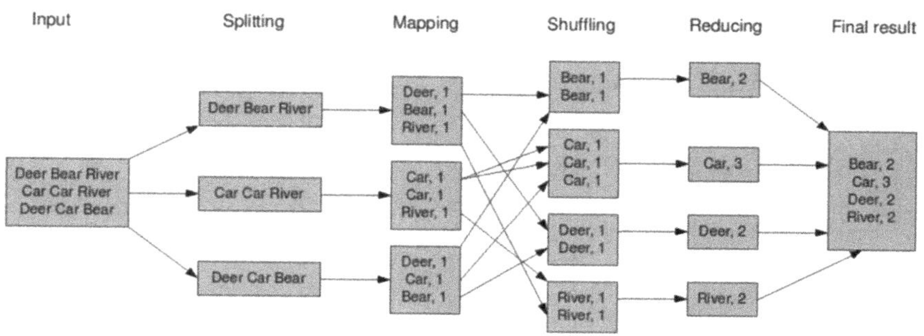

Fig. 3. The job MapReduce word count.

3 Efficient RDES Verification Using Isabelle/HOL and Hadoop

RDES is a complex system. Therefore, the verification of RDES is a difficult task. The time of verification depends on the size of the system and the number of properties to be verified. We propose in this paper a new method for the distributed verification of RDES with Isabelle/HOL and Hadoop. We aim to reduce the execution time of verification by distributing the number of properties to be verified. The improvement of verification time is obtained by using several machines to do the verification at the same time. Figure 4 presents an overview of our proposed contributions, after formalize an RDES with Isabelle/HOL starts by distributing the properties on several machines then do the verification.

3.1 Formalisation of RDES in Isabelle/HOL

Based on our previous work [15], a RDES consists of: a set of reconfiguration rules that it uses to pass from a configuration to another. A configuration is a stable situation that has a certain duration in which a system performs an activity, i.e., system's components are in a specific communication with each other.

Definition 1: A RDES is a structure defined as follows:
$RDES = (B, RR)$ where: B is the behaviour and RR reconfiguration rules of the system.

Definition 2: RDES Behavior. The behaviour of a system B is the union of m configurations, represented as follows:

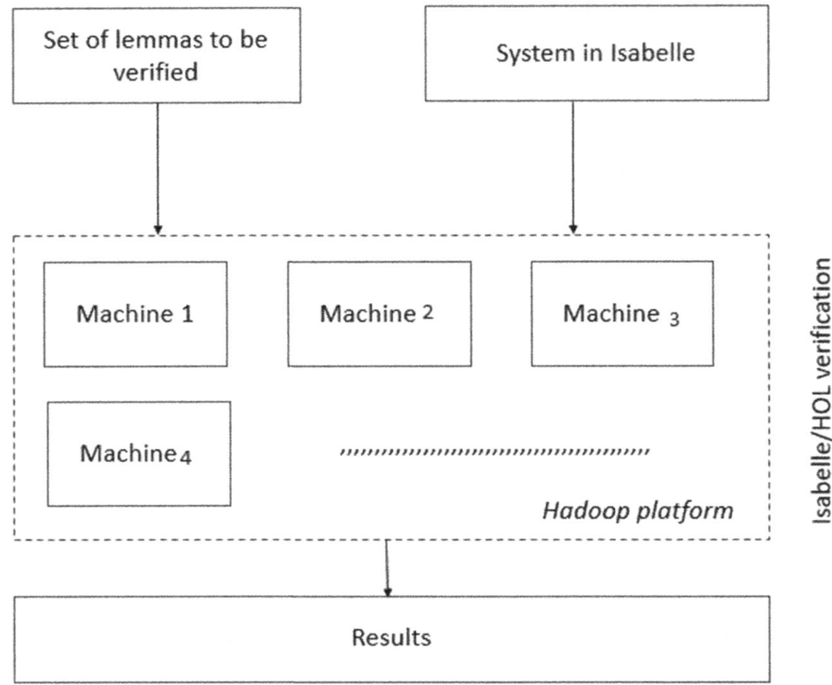

Fig. 4. Overview of our method.

$B = Conf_0, Conf_1, Conf_2, ..., Conf_i, ...Conf_m$ Where: (1) $conf_0$ is the initial configuration, (2) $Conf_i$ represented by the following tuple:

$Conf_i = (U, L)$ Where: (1) U: the set of units, (2) L: the set of links between units.

Definition 3: RDES Reconfigurations Rules. The reconfigurations rules of a system RR is a set of transformations between configurations. $RR = \{r_i,...,r_m\}$ allowing automatic transformations between configurations. A reconfiguration rule of a RDES r_i $(Conf, Conf')$ is a structure changing the system from a configuration $Conf$ to another one $Conf'$ defined as follows:

$r_i\ (Conf, Conf' isastructurechangingthesystem) = (Condition, Operation, S-Conf, D-Conf\ )$, where: (1) $Condition \in \{True, False\}$: the pr-condition of r_i,

(2) $Operation$ is including the addition/removal of units and links from a source $Conf_i$, to obtain a target $Conf_j$ configuration,

(3) $S - Conf$ denotes the configuration $Conf_i$ before the application of r_i

and (4) $D - Conf$ denotes the target configuration $Conf_j$ after the reconfiguration rule r_i is applied. The reconfiguration rule r_i for the transformation from a $Conf_i$ to another $Conf_j$ configuration, when we apply a reconfiguration scenario. If $Condition = True$, r_i is executable, otherwise it cannot be executed.

The transformation from $Conf_i$ to $Conf_j$. Figure 5 shows RDES formalization in Isabelle/HOL.

```
record UNIT=
Uname:: "string"
state :: "bool"
record Arc=
Aname:: "string"
S unit :: "UNIT"
D unit :: "UNIT"
record SC=
SCname::"string"
allUnit::"UNIT list"
allArc:: "Arc list"
record RR=
RRname::"string"
Pre_Conf ::" SC"
Next_Conf ::" SC"
c:: "string"
Op:: "string"
record Isa System=
Sname:: "string"
RRs::" RR list"
SCs::" SC list"
```

Fig. 5. Isabelle formalisation Isa_System.

3.2 Distributed Verification Using Hadoop

The challenge in the reconfigurable systems verification process is the reduction of verification time. We propose in this section our distributed verification. The goal of such a step is to minimise the verification time by using several machines running simultaneously. The main idea of this step is based on distributing the number of properties to be verified over machines do the verification at the same time.

Formalisation. Before introducing the new suggested method, we present the general schema of proofs in the Isabelle/HOL as a *lemma*. A *lemma* consists of: 1) name is the name of proof, 2) formula is the property to be verified, and 3) proof goal a proof goal is the suitable result. Figure 6 presents the global schema of the proof. Let us denote by P a proof written in the Isabelle/HOL, by f a formula of P and by C_i a configuration of the system where i in $1..n$. The next

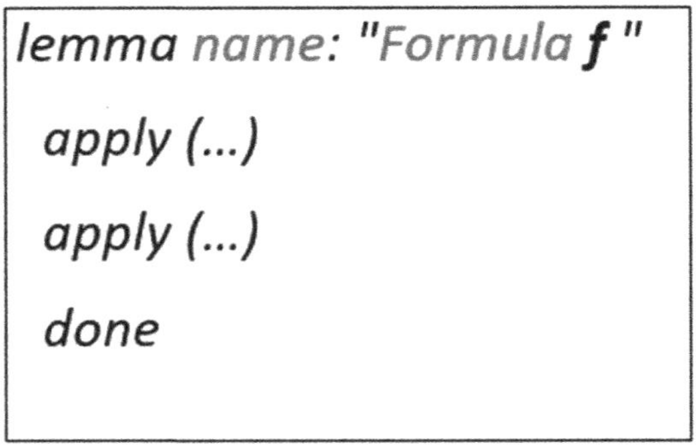

```
lemma name: "Formula f "
  apply (...)
  apply (...)
  done
```

Fig. 6. The Global schema of proof.

step after generating the RDES system in Isabelle/HOL consists of improving the verification. To this end, we adopt MapReduce technique to get a distributed verification. MapReduce has two main tasks: Map and Reduce, where Blocks of data (properties) distributed across different machines are processed by Map tasks in parallel. A results are aggregated in Reducers. The data exchanged between Map and Reduce are pairs (key, value):

- A key: it is any type of data: integer, text. . .
- A value: it is any type of data.

In our case the pairs (key, value) are represented: $(C_i,\ P_j)$. Mapper, Reducer, and its job in the next subsections we show in detail.

Mapper. The Map function receives an input pair and can produce any number of output pairs. The pairs in and out are (key, value). Map tasks each process a pair and produce 0...n pairs. The same keys and/or values may be produced. Hadoop launches a Map instance for each line of each data file to be processed. Each instance processes the assigned line and produces output pairs. Figure 7 depicts the Map function.

Reducer. The Reduce function receives a list of input pairs. These are the pairs produced by the Map instances. Reduce can produce any number of pairs in the output, but usually exactly one. Entry pairs processed by an instance of Reduce

```
Map (configuration input_key, propertie input_values) :
        Boolean res =Verifier( input_key, input_values):
            Send-Intermediate (input_key, res);
```

Fig. 7. The Map function.

all have the same key. Hadoop runs an instance of Reduce for each different key that Map instances have generated, and only provides them with pairs with the same key. That's what aggregates the values. In general, Reduce must process values, in our case a process is the verification step. Figure 8 depicts the Reduce function.

```
Reduce (configuration key, Iterator intermediate_values):
        Boolean result;
      foreach v in intermediate_values:
              result and =  v ;
      Send (key, Boolean( result ));
```

Fig. 8. The Reduce function.

A MapReduce Job

- 1. Preprocessing of input data.
- 2. Split: separation of the data into treatable blocks and formatted as (key, value).
- 3. Map: application of the map function on all pairs (key, value) formed from the input data, this produces other pairs (key, value) in the output,
- 4. Shuffle & Sort: redistribution of data so that the pairs produced by Map with the same keys are on the same machines,
- 5. Reduce: aggregation of pairs with the same key to obtain the final result.

Running Example. In this section, we apply the proposed approach to the RDES in order to illustrate our contribution. For the production system FESTO as running example Table 1. The important properties to be verified in the system are safety, liveness, and deadlock-free. In this example, the concerned safety property is validated when at most one units is active in the state (i.e., impossible to activate two units in two different configurations at the same time). The liveness and the non-blocking properties are verified if any request to change a configuration is satisfied after a finite time. To validate the system, we investigate

Table 1. Isabelle proofs.

$lemmal1$:" ((getUnit ($Unit1$))) " by (simp add: $Unit1\_def$)
$lemmal2$:"((getUnit ($Unit7$)) ∨ (getSUnit ($Unit8$)))" by (simp add: $Unit7\_def, Unit8\_def$)
$lemmal3$: " (getUnit ($Unit9$))" by (simp add: $Unit9\_def$)
$lemmal4$: " (getUnit ($Unit2$)) "by (simp add: $Unit2\_def$)
$lemmal5$: " (getUnit ($Unit9$))" by (simp add:$Unit9\_def$)
$lemmal6$: " (getUnit ($Unit2$)) " by (simp add: $Unit2\_def$)
$lemmal7$:"((getUnit ($Unit9$)) → (getUnit($Unit8$) ∨ (getUnit ($Unit7$)))) " by (simp add: Unit9_def)
$lemmal8$: "((getUnit ($Unit8$) ∨ (getUnit($Unit7$)) → (getUnit ($Unit9$))))" by (simp add:$Unit8\_def$, $Unit7\_def, Unit9\_def$)
$lemmal9$: "(getSUnit ($Unit5$)) " by (simp add: $Unit5\_def$)
$lemmal10$: " ((getUnit ($Unit8$)) ∧ (getUnit ($Unit7$))) → (getUnit ($Unit9$)) " by (simp add: $Unit8\_def$, $Unit7_def, Unit9\_def$)
$lemmal11$: " ((getUnit (Unit1)) → getUnit ($Unit10$)))" by (simp add: $Unit1\_def, Unit10\_def$)

that every configuration respects its activation conditions. Some details of our formal verification (i.e., Proofs in the Isabelle/HOL) are shown in Table 1.

A MapReduce job for our example:

- 1. Preprocessing of input data
- 2. Split: In Table 2 shows the separation of the data in pairs (C_i, P_j), where i in $1..n$, and j in $1..m$.
- 3. Map: Application of the map function is presented above on all pairs (C_i, P_j) formed from the input data, this produces other pairs (C_i, *bool*) in output as shown in Table 3, where *bool* Boolean represent the verification result of P_j of input pairs (C_i, P_j).
- 4. Shuffle & Sort: The system sorts/groups the pairs according to the key (C_i), in a list [(C_i, [$bool_1$,$bool_2$, ...]), ...] as shown in Table 4.
- 5. Reduce: For each group of data with the same key (C_i) is called the reduce function is shown in Table for the aggregation of values with the same key (C_i) to obtain the final result ((C_i), ($bool_1 \wedge bool_2 \wedge ...$)), as shown in Table 5.

Table 2. The Input pairs of map.

(C_1, L_1), (C_1, L_2) (C_1, L_7), (C_1, L_3), (C_1, L_4)
(C_2, L_5), (C_2, L_8), (C_1, L_9)
(C_3, L_10), (C_3, L_6), (C_3, L_11)

Table 3. The output of Map.

$(C_1, true)$, $(C_1, true)$, $(C_1, true)$ $(C_1, true)$, $(C_1, true)$
$(C_2, true)$, $(C_2, true)$, $(C_1, true)$
$(C_3, true)$, $(C_3, true)$, $(C_3, true)$

Table 4. The system groups the pairs.

$(C_1, [true, true, true, true, true])$
$(C_2, [true, true, true])$
$(C_3, [true, true, true])$

Table 5. The output of Reduce.

$(C_1, (true \wedge true \wedge true \wedge true \wedge true)) = (C_1, true)$
$(C_2, (true \wedge true \wedge true)) = (C_2, true)$
$(C_3, (true \wedge true \wedge true)) = (C_3, true)$

4 Performance Evaluation

Figure 9 shows two curves corresponding to the verification process with and without using our proposed method. The values of the abscises axis correspond to the number of properties when the system runs two times. The ordinate axis correspond to the verification time. The curve in blue corresponds to the verification without the proposed method. The curve in red corresponds to the distributed verification using proposed method. It is important to note that the verification time decreases gradually when we use the proposed method. The reduction in the verification time is followed by a distribution in the number of properties.

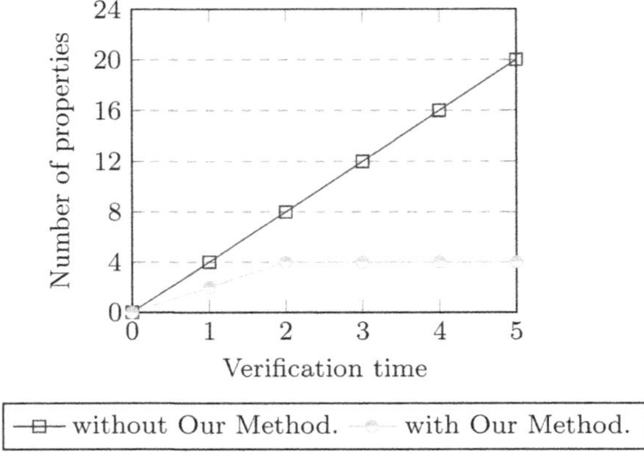

Fig. 9. Comparison between verification process with and without using the proposed algorithm.

5 Conclusion

This paper deals with the modeling and verification of reconfigurable discrete event systems using Hadoop and Isabelle/Hol theorem prover. The proposed improvement exploits the MapReduce technique for distribution of proofs. Instead of layer by layer verification, the proposed method uses more than machine to reduce verification time. Our method is divided into two steps, step: 1) we formalize the system in Isabelle/HOL. Step: 2) the second step is applying the distributed verification, it serves to distribute the properties to be verified over machines., which greatly reduces verification time. In a future work, we plan to implement an automatic middleware on ISABELLE allowing to generate the system automatically. We plan also to deal the correctness of the generated result itself.

References

1. Ali, T., Nauman, M., Alam, M.: An accessible formal specification of the UML and OCL meta-model in Isabelle/HOL. In: 2007 IEEE International Multitopic Conference, pp. 1–6. IEEE (2007)
2. Clarke, E.M., Henzinger, T.A., Veith, H., Bloem, R.: Handbook of Model Checking, vol. 10. Springer, Heidelberg (2018). https://doi.org/10.1007/978-3-319-10575-8
3. Dotoli, M., Epicoco, N., Falagario, M., Cavone, G.: A timed petri nets model for performance evaluation of intermodal freight transport terminals. IEEE Trans. Autom. Sci. Eng. **13**(2), 842–857 (2016)
4. Girault, C., Valk, R.: Petri Nets for Systems Engineering: A Guide to Modeling, Verification, and Applications. Springer, Heidelberg (2013). https://doi.org/10.1007/978-3-662-05324-9
5. Guellouz, S., Benzina, A., Khalgui, M., Frey, G.: Reconfigurable function blocks: extension to the standard IEC 61499. In: 2016 IEEE/ACS 13th International Conference of Computer Systems and Applications (AICCSA), pp. 1–8. IEEE (2016)

6. Hafidi, Y., Kahloul, L., Khalgui, M., Li, Z., Alnowibet, K., Qu, T.: On methodology for the verification of reconfigurable timed net condition/event systems. IEEE Trans. Syst. Man Cybern.: Syst. **50**, 3577–3591 (2018)
7. Hafidi, Y., Kahloul, L., Khalgui, M., Ramdani, M.: New method to reduce verification time of reconfigurable real-time systems using R-TNCESs formalism. In: Damiani, E., Spanoudakis, G., Maciaszek, L.A. (eds.) ENASE 2019. CCIS, vol. 1172, pp. 246–266. Springer, Cham (2020). https://doi.org/10.1007/978-3-030-40223-5_12
8. Jiang, Y., Liu, J., Dowek, G., Ji, K.: SCTL: towards combining model checking and proof checking. arXiv preprint arXiv:1606.08668 (2016)
9. Khalgui, M., Mosbahi, O., Hanisch, H.M., Li, Z.: Retracted article: a multi-agent architectural solution for coherent distributed reconfigurations of function blocks. J. Intell. Manuf. **23**(6), 2531–2549 (2012). https://doi.org/10.1007/s10845-011-0556-y
10. Khalgui, M., Mosbahi, O., Li, Z., Hanisch, H.M.: Reconfiguration of distributed embedded-control systems. IEEE/ASME Trans. Mechatron. **16**(4), 684–694 (2010)
11. Khlifi, O., Mosbahi, O., Khalgui, M., Frey, G.: GR-TNCES: new extensions of R-TNCES for modelling and verification of flexible systems under energy and memory constraints. In: 2015 10th International Joint Conference on Software Technologies (ICSOFT), vol. 1, pp. 1–8. IEEE (2015)
12. Lewis, R.: Modelling control systems using IEC 61499: Applying function blocks to distributed systems. No. 59, IET (2001)
13. Lin, J., Dyer, C.: Data-intensive text processing with MapReduce. Synth. Lect. Human Lang. Technol. **3**(1), 1–177 (2010)
14. Meghzili, S., Chaoui, A., Strecker, M., Kerkouche, E.: On the verification of UML state machine diagrams to colored petri nets transformation using Isabelle/HOL. In: 2017 IEEE International Conference on Information Reuse and Integration (IRI), pp. 419–426. IEEE (2017)
15. Soualah, S., Hafidi, Y., Khalgui, M., Chaoui, A., Kahloul, L.: Formalization and verification of reconfigurable discrete-event system using model driven engineering and Isabelle/HOL. In: Proceedings of the 15th International Conference on Software Technologies: ICSOFT, pp. 250–259 (2020)
16. Zhang, J., Frey, G., Al-Ahmari, A., Qu, T., Wu, N., Li, Z.: Analysis and control of dynamic reconfiguration processes of manufacturing systems. IEEE Access **6**, 28028–28040 (2017)
17. Zhang, J., Khalgui, M., Li, Z., Mosbahi, O., Al-Ahmari, A.M.: R-TNCES: a novel formalism for reconfigurable discrete event control systems. IEEE Trans. Syst. Man Cybern.: Syst. **43**(4), 757–772 (2013)

A Method for the Joint Analysis of Numerical and Textual IT-System Data to Predict Critical System States

Patrick Kubiak[1(✉)], Stefan Rass[2], Martin Pinzger[2], and Stephan Schneider[3]

[1] Volkswagen Financial Services AG, Brunswick, Germany
patrick.kubiak@vwfs.com
[2] Alpen-Adria-University, Klagenfurt, Austria
{stefan.rass,martin.pinzger}@aau.at
[3] University of Applied Sciences Kiel, Kiel, Germany
stephan.schneider@fh-kiel.de

Abstract. We present a method for the joint analysis of textual and numerical IT-system data usable to predict possibly critical system states. Towards a comparative discussion culminating in a justified model and method choice, we apply logistic regression, random forest and neural networks to the prediction of critical system states. Our models consume a set of different monitoring performance metrics and log file events. To ease the analysis of IT-systems, our models judge the future system state using one binary outcome variable for the system state's criticality as "alarm" or "no alarm". Moreover, we use feature importance measures to give IT-operators guidance on which system parameters, i.e., features, to consider primarily when responding to an alarm. We evaluate our models using different configurations, including (among others) the demanded lead time window for incident response, and a set of common performance measures. This paper is an extension to previous work that adds details on how to jointly process textual and numerical data.

Keywords: Machine learning · IT-operations · AIOps

1 Introduction

One of the major challenges for IT-operations departments is to manage a complex and heterogeneous IT-infrastructure landscape. This situation results in a heterogeneous toolbox of monitoring systems as well as a large number of different IT-system parameters that IT-operators have to monitor. Commonly, each monitoring system has its own set of rules to notify IT-operators in any case a system state turns from regular operation into a critical state. In some instances, such rules come as isolated thresholds for each IT-system parameter of interest, whose excess or undercut generates notifications, i.e., alarms. Furthermore, IT-systems store necessary information to judge the system state in different data sources having a non-compatible kind of format, i.e., numerical monitoring data and textual log file data. In this paper, we present a novel method to combine

M. van Sinderen et al. (Eds.): ICSOFT 2020, CCIS 1447, pp. 242–261, 2021.
https://doi.org/10.1007/978-3-030-83007-6_12

data from these two major data sources of IT-operations departments usable for *machine learning* (ML) models. We aim to use such a combined data set to i) judge the system state using one binary outcome instead of a set of different isolated alarms; ii) predict incoming critical system states using an experimental setup for data acquisition and iii) analyze the influence of monitoring metrics and log file events on the system state using a single ML model. We give a detailed procedure to transform textual log file data into a suitable format to be usable with numeric monitoring data for a joint analysis and predictive inference. Furthermore, we apply a set of classification methods, i.e., *logistic regression* (LogReg), *random forest* (RF) and *neural networks* (NN), on this data set to achieve i) and ii), and for a comparative study of the three methods. We evaluate the prediction quality of our models using a set of common diagnostic metrics. For iii), we use RF importance measures, i.e., *mean decrease in accuracy* (MDA) and *mean decrease in Gini* (MDG), to explain the reasons why each model did or did not raise an alarm. Hence, we use feature importance measures as a tool to analyze the influence of each monitoring metric and log file event as triggers for (critical) changes of the system state.

This paper will answer following research questions (RQ):

1. **RQ1:** How can we join numeric and textual IT-system data to be usable in a single ML model?
2. **RQ2:** How accurate are different models to predict the system state in the form of a binary classification problem?
3. **RQ3:** Which features do have the biggest influence on the system state and can be considered as most promising triggers, i.e., root causes, for changes?

We start with a related work section to demarcate this paper from previous work. In Sect. 3, we present a short description of our experimental setup that is similar to the configuration of our previous paper [1]. The focus of this paper is a detailed description of the data preparation process, which was necessary to "unify" data of heterogeneous types (textual and numeric) and out of multiple sources, as presented in Sect. 4. We extended our experiments using other ML methods as presented in Sect. 5. Furthermore, we used a diverse set of evaluation metrics and changed the approach to evaluate the relevance of features on the binary outcome that classifies the overall system state as normal or critical. Previous work [1] suggested a relatively simple importance measure by taking a relative count of how often a feature appeared as significant in a model (a decision tree), relative to all cases (technically, a conditional probability for the feature to appear or not appear in the prediction model). This work adopts the more popular concept of importance measures of the relative count of appearance (conditional probability of feature significance) is agnostic of the level of appearance in the tree. This extended work allows us a more detailed evaluation of our models and more informative results as presented in Sect. 6. We close our work with new findings related to threats of validity in Sect. 7 and a conclusion in Sect. 8.

2 Related Work

The IT-operations domain is a predestined field for ML researchers since it generates a huge amount of data, which often exceeds human analysis capabilities. Most ML models in the literature focus either on numerical or textual data and leave possible advantages of a joint analysis unexplored. However, the literature offers a vast lot different papers related to this domain, which enable practitioners to maximize the availability of IT-systems due to automation, issue prevention, easier problem determination and faster troubleshooting [2]. We can achieve such advancements using processual recommendations [3, 4], e.g., ITIL, or ML methods that accelerate the understanding of data and improve its potential as valuable resource for organizations. We consider *symptoms monitoring* and *detected error reporting* as main monitoring mechanisms for our work. Symptoms refer to as side-effects in case of abnormal behavior of IT-systems while errors occur when things go wrong and the system state differs to the expected system state [5]. Errors are undetected until monitoring systems or system users observe any differences in the system state. Symptom monitoring is the standard mechanism to permanently check if any threshold violations of runtime metrics, e.g., CPU utilization, occurred [5]. Detected errors are typically protocolled in log files that are an extensive collection of all system events. On monitoring data, different researchers applied, among others, regression methods [6, 7] or classification methods [8–10]. Often, we prefer to transform log file data into sequences of log file events beforehand. Thus, corresponding ML methods consume event-driven input data and allow us to apply event pattern mining [11–14] or event summarization methods [15, 16]. Among others, one approach discovers whether there is correlation between the system load intensity, recorded by monitoring agents, and the occurrence of computational intensive log file events [17]. Nevertheless, the analysis of both data sources in a complementary manner has not be exhaustively explored yet. We recommend two surveys [5, 18] to interested readers to get a more comprehensive selection of available ML methods in the IT-operations domain. Furthermore, we proposed a method selection guide for practitioners in dependency of the type of data and the application in an earlier work [2].

3 Experimental Setup for Data Acquisition

For data acquisition, we used an experimental concept for an automated load and performance test scenario to simulate real-life user interactivities on a small-scale digital twin of a real-life IT-system environment [1]. This IT-system resembles a productive system without being one and allows us to fully control and manipulate the systems behavior as requested. Since the IT-system is a training environment and mainly used for occasional (and non-periodically happening) user trainings, there was no continuous system load on it. Therefore, we developed test scripts to emulate regular system load, such as client transactions sent to the system, and load peaks. Here, we used *VuGen* (link) and scheduled the test scripts using *LoadRunner Enterprise* (link), which both are software products of *Micro Focus*. This step was necessary to generate the required lot of anomalies in short time, which we would otherwise have to collect over long periods (possibly months to years) on a productive system. The major advantage of this setup is to produce any sort of behavior to generate data for model training that satisfies our requirements best, e.g., a balanced data set. In particular, such an experimental setup allowed us to trigger rare events and anomalies of diverse kinds to the amount and extent required [1]. Thus, we consider artificially generated system load intensity based on real transactions of an industrial IT-system to obtain the data to evaluate our method and models.

3.1 Application Architecture and Implementation

The IT-system of our choice is a *Java* web application. The *contract management system* (CMS) is an on premise cloud application hosted at our data center running on an *OpenStack* environment. Figure 1 presents the architecture of the CMS.

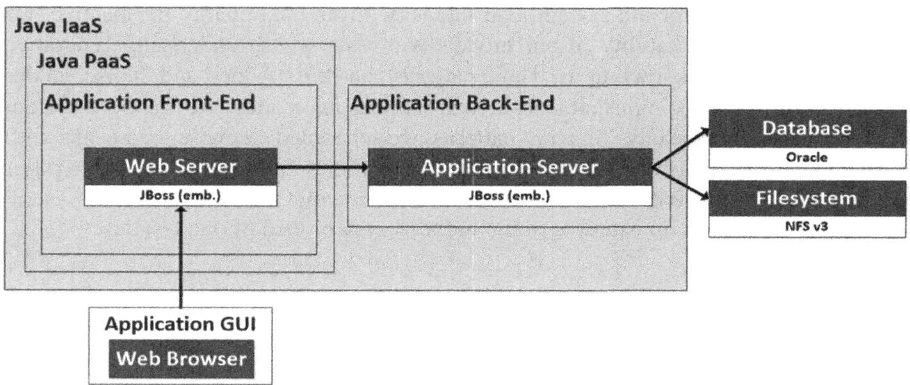

Fig. 1. Architecture of the CMS [1]

We use a *platform as a service* (PaaS) as frontend component of the CMS and an *infrastructure as a* service (IaaS) as backend component of the CMS. Both components run on *Linux RHEL 7.x* operating system but use different application runtime frameworks. The PaaS uses *WildFly* (link) while the IaaS uses *JBoss EAP* (link). However, both components generate own log file data with a varying structure. For the collection of the monitoring metrics, we used *DX Application Performance Management* (link) on both components. Table 1 presents the sizing of the PaaS and IaaS components.

Table 1. Sizing of the PaaS and IaaS

	PaaS	IaaS
CPU	4 x Intel Xeon CPU E5-2680 v4 @ 2.40 GHz	8 x Intel Xeon CPU E5-2680 v4 @ 2.40 GHz
Memory	8 GB	8 GB
Disk space	4 GB	20 GB

Section 3.3 presents a description of obtained log file messages and monitoring metrics, which then refer to as features of our predictive models.

3.2 Load and Performance Test Design

To generate necessary system load on our testbed, we triggered a varying number of *virtual users* (vUsers) on the system that act in the same way as human system users do. Hence, the vUsers call a set of system transactions, e.g., search for existing contracts in the database or create new contracts, and the CMS does not recognize any deviation to human users. The only difference depends on the scripted induction of the system load since the vUsers follow a predefined schedule and call system transactions without any breaks what human users naturally do. However, we designed a concept for a 10-day long experiment for data acquisition and let a varying number of simultaneous working vUsers be the trigger for the system load intensity. From data quality perspective, we aim to evaluate the suitability of our models with data whose underlying generative processes are entirely known to us. Thus, patterns can be explained and "noise" under normal conditions is distinguishable from load-induced anomalies. We produced system load for 8 h on each test day. To avoid patterns, we scheduled stepwise load peaks with a varying intensity to the CMS, which refer to as anomalies that we aim to predict. After each load peak, the system returned to a similar baseline that refers to as normal system state. Figure 2 presents an example of the induced system load of one test day.

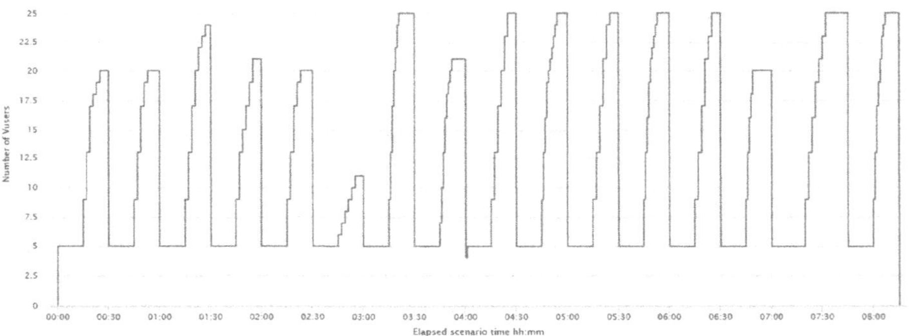

Fig. 2. System load of one test day

We triggered the changes of the system state in a 15-min interval to guarantee a balanced data set containing as much records for each system state as possible. We recognized a significantly negative influence on the accuracy of our models resulting from too imbalanced data in an earlier experiment. We used a rule-based approach for the data labeling related to the number of vUsers working on the system as presented in Sect. 4.4. Due to internal regulations of the enterprise, we had to limit our experimental setup to a maximum load intensity generated by $\leq$25 vUsers. This is one threat to validity and further discussed in Sect. 7.

3.3 Description of Monitoring Metrics and Log File Messages

The monitoring agents collected a set of groups of performance metrics, which consist of at least one but mostly of more metrics. For example, the CPU is a single measure while the agents collect measures for response times of over 50 different *JavaBeans*. Table 2 presents an overview of the collected groups of monitoring metrics.

Table 2. Collected groups of monitoring metrics [1]

Group of monitoring metrics	Description
Average response time (AR)	The average response time in ms of a JavaBean from the method call to the response
Memory pools (MP)	The dedicated part of the heap memory in bytes, which allocates memory for all instances and arrays at runtime
Concurrent invocations (CI)	The number of simultaneous calls of a JavaBean
CPU	The CPU utilization in %
% time spent in garbage collection (GC)	The percentage time within an interval, in which obsolete in-memory code is removed
Sockets (SO)	The number of available communication end points of the IT-system

From performance perspective, we can assume a critical system state if the IT-system meets at least one of the following conditions:

1. The values of the AR group of metrics increase significantly
2. The values of the AR and CI group of metrics increase at the same time
3. The value of the GC metric exceeds ≈25%
4. The values of the SO group of metrics range in the area of 0 over a longer period

For confidentiality reasons, we are unable to provide an overview of the exact log file messages and their meaning since inferences to the CMS are prohibited. Thus, Table 3 only presents an abstract overview of the log file messages grouped by their semantic meaning.

The total amount of different log file messages is 42 and all of them are error messages. We assume that errors are the most promising indicators to observe misbehavior on log file level. Therefore, we exclusively filtered out errors from the raw log file data and used them in our predictive models as described in Sect. 4.1.

4 Data Preparation

The core of our method is to unify textual and numerical IT-system data in one predictive model. In the following section, we describe necessary steps to transform the textual data in a numerical form joinable with the monitoring data. Afterwards, we applied a set of standard practices to analyze corresponding features in case of their predictive power and reduced the model complexity by removing features that did not satisfy the requirement of increasing the predictive ability.

Table 3. Overview of the log file messages

Description	Number of different Messages in the harvested logs	Component	
		PaaS	IaaS
Session data expired	12	X	X
Exception handling	8	X	X
Remote procedure call failed	5	X	X
Session timeout	2	X	X
Loading of language ID failed	1	X	
Generation of a new contract failed	1	X	
Database connection failed	1	X	
Error for some input string	1	X	
Top level exception	1	X	
Unexpected value	1		X
Some internal error	1		X
Failed to call a JavaBean	1		X
Some connection error	4		X
Invalid search request	1		X
Database error	1		X
Some missing parameter value	1		X

4.1 Extracting Error Event Sequences from Log Files

It is a common practice to transform raw log file data into event sequences since the analysis of structured log file events is much easier than exploring log file messages in the overall textual corpus, e.g., using appropriate forms of visualization. Furthermore, such log file event sequences allow us to apply different ML methods as described in Sect. 2. However, we focus on a timestamp-based structure of log file events in the form of an *event-occurrence-matrix* (EOM) as prerequisite for our method. Commonly, we can apply three different methods to obtain such a target structure from raw textual log file data: log parsers, classification or clustering methods. As described in Sect. 4.2, we applied clustering algorithms for this task since such methods identify clusters, i.e., log file events, in the data autonomously at the costs of accuracy (in comparison to log parser and classification methods). The major advantage is that clustering methods in this case offer a high degree of flexibility and may require less parameter tuning. We do not necessarily need deep knowledge about the log file structure, which is a requirement to develop specific (and possibly rigid) extractors, i.e., log parsers. Moreover, we avoid preparing any labeled training data as it is necessary to apply classification methods. However, log files contain a lot of information, which are not directly related to misbehavior and we want to train our models exclusively on conditions that lead to potential issues. Therefore, we filtered out error messages beforehand using *regular expressions*. We extracted 786,522 error messages out of approximately 95 million log file messages in total. Afterwards, we applied a set of *information retrieval* techniques to shrink the remaining error messages to text parts, which are necessary to generate the EOM. For example, we removed record specific data, e.g., unique identifiers (IDs), which may confuse clustering algorithms in the way that they may group error messages with same semantics into different clusters.

4.2 Numerical Representation and Clustering of Log File Messages

After we cleaned the texts in the log file data to the minimum extent required, we aim to transform the structure in the form of a timestamp-based EOM. A *document-term-matrix* (DTM) allows to convert text into numbers by counting the number of times each word, i.e., term, appears in the given document corpus. A DTM is a matrix, in which the element in row i and column j gives the number of appearance of term j (associated to the column) in the document i (associated to the row) and allows us to apply clustering methods on this – hereby numerical – representation of text [19]. For the clustering task, we applied the *Density-Based Spatial Clustering of Applications with Noise* (DBSCAN) algorithm [20]. In comparison to other clustering algorithms, e.g., *K-means*, the major advantage of DBSCAN is that it works without an a priori guess for the number of clusters. Given that we may hardly expect how many and what different kinds of messages will be in the logs to come, this is a crucial advantage. For the data in this work, we let a CMS generate logs for a period of 10 days. We explicitly refrain from manually digging into perhaps millions of rows in the raw log file to point out the applicability of the method with only least or no domain knowledge. In case that domain knowledge is available, refined results may be obtainable upon replacing DBSCAN by a more "pre-informed" clustering at this step. Nevertheless, in absence of specific domain knowledge, DBSCAN is a simple method to apply [1]. For our experiments, we took DBSCAN configured with $minPts = 4$ and $\varepsilon = 0.4$ after testing different configurations without considerable differences for the result. ε refers to as the radius and *minPts* refers to as the minimum number of points falling into the proximity of the cluster-center to reasonably call such an accumulation of points a "cluster". We obtained 28 clusters and 6 noise points for the PaaS logs and 14 clusters and 4 noise points for the IaaS logs. Unlike K-means or hierarchical clustering algorithms, DBSCAN does not force all observations into clusters. Hence, it has the ability to remove noise into separate noise clusters and prevents distorted clusters [21]. Now, we combine obtained cluster and timestamp information to generate the EOM having the structure of Table 4.

Each cluster then directly defines another indicator, i.e., feature x_i in the models; at each time t. Then, we can assign the error messages at this time to some cluster, corresponding to setting the variable $x_i = 1$ if error messages related to this cluster were found, i.e., they occurred, in the log, or $x_i = 0$ otherwise. Finally, the set of 0-1-valued variables $x_1, x_2, \ldots, x_{28}$ for the 28 clusters in the PaaS logs and $x_{29}, x_{30}, \ldots, x_{42}$ for the 14 clusters in the IaaS logs are the first part of the data set. Afterwards, we joined the EOM with the numeric monitoring data using the timestamp as primary key and obtained the final data set with 196 features.

Table 4. Event-occurrence-matrix

Timestamp	PaaS Event 1	...	PaaS Event 28	IaaS Event 1	...	IaaS Event 14
xx:xx:xx	1	...	0	0	...	1
xx:xx:xx	0	...	1	1	...	1

4.3 Feature Analysis and Dimension Reduction

A data set with 196 features is not easy to handle and may unnecessarily increase the complexity of our models. Therefore, we applied a set of standard practices to exclude features that do not improve the predictive power of the models. Removing such features results in a smaller data set that can significantly improve the efficiency and results of ML models [22]. Without any effort, we can directly remove 60 features. This features were constants having zero values due to the fact that the export of the monitoring data consists of each a column for all available JavaBeans regardless the CMS called corresponding JavaBeans within the 10 days or not. In other words, there were no measures for 60 monitoring metrics. To further decrease the dimensionality of the data set, we applied following statistical practices:

1. Remove features with low variance since they often suffer of little predictive information and have no positive influence to the skill of ML models [23]
2. Remove highly correlated features using a threshold of $\geq$0.9 [24] to judge the correlation as very strong
3. Remove outliers using the interquartile method [25]
4. Remove missing values using listwise deletion [26]

Step 2) may be optional in dependency of the applied ML methods. Strong correlation among features leads to the phenomenon of *multi-collinearity*. This can be troubling for some ML methods [23] and is a key problem for binary logistic regression [27], which is one of our choices for the prediction task. Finally, these steps reduced the number of features to 47 out of initial 196 features.

4.4 Data Labeling

For the labeling, we chose a deterministic approach based on the number of vUsers working simultaneously on the CMS since we assume the number of vUsers on the system as main trigger for the system load intensity. We added a column called "Alarm" that refers to as label of each record where $Alarm = 1$ denotes a critical system state and $Alarm = 0$ denotes a normal system state. We defined the following rules to label the data [1]:

1. Normal system state:$\geq$5 and $\leq$17 vUsers working on the CMS
2. Critical system state:$\geq$18 and $\leq$25 vUsers working on the CMS

Remark: it should be kept in mind that a deterministic labeling will generally produce data on which regression models may fail due to *separation*. Hence, a manual labeling or at least a manual check of a sample of the machine-generated labels is advisable, if regression models are to be evaluated. On the contrary, a divergence problem when fitting a regression model can in turn be an indicator of determinism and a pointer towards a trial with a deterministic (e.g., decision tree) model.

Internal regulations of the enterprise limited our experiments. We assume that a maximum of 25 vUser never really exhausted available resources of the CMS, i.e., the system was never overloaded or reached a serious critical system state. However, we deemed this experimental setup as suitable to get a first feeling in case of evaluating our method. Nevertheless, a critical discussion related to the limitations is part of Sect. 7 to ensure transparency to the readers.

5 Modeling and Evaluation

For the classification task, we applied three different ML methods: LogReg, RF and NN and evaluated their suitability using 16 different configuration cases and a set of common performance measures as described in the following sections. Our general prediction scheme is illustrated in Fig. 3. It visualizes the basic idea of our novel method for a joint analysis of time series data collected by monitoring agents and discrete event data.

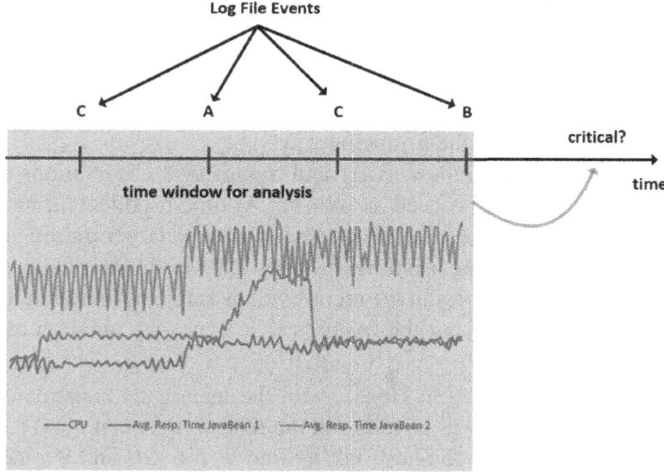

Fig. 3. General prediction scheme [1]

5.1 Choice of Classification Methods

Our initial choice for the classification task is LogReg since it is the de facto standard method for binary classification problems [28]. Moreover, it tells us - during the fitting

– if the dependent variable, i.e., alarm, has a deterministic dependence in question [1]. That is, either:

1. There is a stochastic element governing whether or not an alarm is raised, then the logistic model is a reasonable choice and the fitting of coefficients will converge
2. There is a deterministic process behind the alerts to occur, in which case the model fitting (a maximum likelihood optimization algorithm) will fail to converge, which is then the information that the logistic regression model is not a good choice.

In the case of 2), the LogReg tells us that we should rather fit a more "deterministic" model. In our previous work [1], we applied decision trees as our second choice since the LogReg in some cases failed to converge. We decided to rethink this decision since tree based models suffer of high variance and obtained results may be quite different in dependency of the randomly sampled data [29] in our evaluation design. Thus, we decided to use RF as alternative method, which reduces the variance of bagging as well as reduces the correlation between trees without increasing the variance too much [30]. Moreover, RF offers out-of-the-box analysis of the feature importance using the MDA and MDG measures, which enables us to identify features that are most likely relevant to judge the system state of the CMS. Additionally, we applied NN to complete the selection of candidates for the classification task since they are known to be powerful prediction methods and extend the evaluation of this work.

5.2 Configuration Cases

We want our models not only to classify the system state at current time t, we aim to predict incoming critical system states with a lead time window of t_{+1}, t_{+5}, t_{+10} and t_{+15} using historic records at t_{-1}, t_{-5}, t_{-10} and t_{-15}. Thus, we construct a set of 16 different cases, i.e., training data sets, in the following way [1]:

We denote the lead time window as Δt and the historic observations over a fixed time window as Δh. Now, we proceed as follows: At time t, collect all records within period $H = [t - \Delta h, t]$ and concatenate these records into a larger training data set that contains all data within this time window. In this way, we obtain a data set, in which each x_i occurs with multiple copies in the record. For example, if there fall three records into the past history, each carrying the features $x_1, \ldots, x_k$, we obtain a record with a feature set of $x_1^{(0)}, \ldots, x_k^{(0)}, x_1^{(1)}, \ldots, x_k^{(1)}$ and $x_1^{(2)}, \ldots, x_k^{(2)}$ where $x_i^{(j)}$ refers to as the i th feature at j timestamps prior to t. Hence, with the feature set constructed as above, $Alarm = 1$ if and only if there was an alarm in the records between t and $t + \Delta t$. Thus, we set $Alarm = 1$ if there was an alarm falling into $[t, t + \Delta t]$ and we instantiate the current record with historic observations collected from all records falling into the period $[t - \Delta h, t]$. Otherwise, we set $Alarm = 0$ since there has be no race condition occurred after t within Δt, which we aim to predict on the current system state and history. We consider following configurations for the evaluation of our models as presented in Table 5.

Each configuration case differs in its setting in case of Δt and Δh, which we both measure in minutes. We aim to identify whether a set of varying Δt and Δh influences the results in case of the prediction accuracy or the importance of the features and their

Table 5. Configuration cases [1]

Lead time (Δt)	Number of historic observations (Δh)			
	1	5	10	15
1	C1	C5	C9	C13
5	C2	C6	C10	C14
10	C3	C7	C11	C15
15	C4	C8	C12	C16

multiple copies to possibly identify somewhat like a prediction limit if the accuracy significantly decreases. Naturally, we would expect a larger retrospective window to increase the prediction accuracy, and likewise, the accuracy would be expected to deteriorate, the larger the forecasting window is made (i.e., the farer we attempt to look into the future). The second expectation turns out to be not the case.

5.3 Evaluation Design

The settings of the configuration cases allow us to test our models in case of a varying prediction horizon and history to identify whether there is an impact on the model results or not. Each of the cases (C1-16) represents a new data set, which we considered independently for training and test of our models. Thus, we fitted at least 16 models for each of the three classification methods. Furthermore, we fitted each model using a loop with 100 runs where we generate randomly sampled data for training and test in each of the runs. Unfortunately, we are unable to provide results for the NN for 100 runs but still present that their prediction quality seems to be similar to LogReg and RF after training and applying them once on all configuration cases. The reason is related to high computational time for evaluation of each case, repeating the evaluation 100 times for every method and running this experiment was considered as impractical. We evaluate the performance of our models using a set of common performance metrics, which we determine for every single run. These metrics are: *accuracy*, *precision*, *recall*, *F1-Score* and the *Matthews correlation coefficient* (MCC). Here, we follow a standard practice to evaluate our models on a broad range of performance metrics for a fair and honest evaluation. This practice is preferred over using a single metric that is being optimized (Zhang/Zhou 2014) as we only focused on the accuracy measure in our prior work. For all measures, we can consider the model quality as higher if the measures are higher with a maximum value of 1, which refers to as perfect classification. We remark that in the IT-operations domain we should give more attention to the recall than to the precision measure. This is because a miss, i.e., false negative, of predictive models in this area may cause expensive (tangible or intangible) damage, i.e., a service break, for organizations. Recall penalizes misses with high costs and is more reliable in this case. However, in each run, we additionally calculate the MDA and MDG measures to evaluate the importance of the features for the fitted RF. For evaluation of experimental studies, the popularity of both measures increases since both confirmed practical utility

[31] although there is a lack of clearance regarding their inner workings [31, 32]. We aim to use this information to identify the most promising indicators for the CMS turning into a critical system state. Moreover, we give practitioners, i.e., IT-operators, guidance at hand on which system parameters to focus on primarily if our models raise alarms to answer the "why" the system is turning into a critical state. For IT-operators, this is invaluable and can significantly ease the determination of root causes.

6 Results

Let us now present our results in case of the predictive quality along the set of performance measures and then present the analysis of the feature importance, which we exclusively obtained for the RF.

6.1 Performance Metrics

We start our evaluation with the results of the single run of the NN for all configuration cases as presented in Table 6.

Table 6. Results of the NN for a single run

Case	Accuracy	Precision	Recall	F1-score	MCC
1	0.97	0.96	0.98	0.97	0.94
2	0.93	0.93	0.93	0.93	0.86
3	0.94	0.88	0.95	0.92	0.87
4	0.95	0.94	0.90	0.92	0.88
5	0.99	1.00	0.99	0.99	0.98
6	0.99	0.99	0.99	0.99	0.97
7	0.99	0.99	0.98	0.98	0.97
8	0.98	0.96	0.98	0.97	0.96
9	1.00	1.00	1.00	1.00	1.00
10	0.97	0.98	0.97	0.96	0.93
11	0.97	0.96	0.95	0.95	0.93
12	0.99	0.98	0.98	0.98	0.97
13	0.99	0.96	1.00	0.98	0.96
14	0.98	0.97	0.98	0.97	0.95
15	0.98	0.97	0.98	0.98	0.95
16	0.99	0.99	0.98	0.98	0.97

For the single run, we obtained extremely high values for each performance measure for all configuration cases. During the model fitting and testing a set of different parametrizations for the NN, we obtained some interesting findings related to our experimental setup for data acquisition and the resulting data set(s). For each configuration case, we divided the data into training, test and validation data as it is common. We obtained high performance measures on the training as well as on the test and validation data. During model training, we recognized that the training loss steadily decreases while the validation loss steadily increases. Mostly, this indicates that the model suffers of overfitting. However, since our NN performed very good on training as well as on unseen test data, we assume that the model has a good generalization capability, which rules out overfitting as possible cause for the high performance metrics. The divergence of training and validation loss may indicate that the prediction results are high but not very confident. The reasons could be related to our deterministic approach for the labeling and the fact, that a maximum of 25 vUsers never really overloaded the CMS. Assuming that the feature values are too similar in both cases for records labeled with 1 or 0 may be a reason for the high prediction quality. In other words, the values do not vary enough for both labels and a clear allocation is missing. Further tests with different parametrization of the NN showed that NN with a low number of hidden layers, e.g., 1, and a low number of neurons, e.g., 2, counteracts the drift of the training and validation loss without a considerable decrease of the prediction quality. The losses differ more in case of deep NN having more hidden layers and a high number of neurons, e.g., 32, 64 or 128. In case of deep NN, we could counteract the increasing difference between the losses using a sigmoid hidden layer after a *rectified linear unit* (ReLu). Generally, the deep NN seem to perform better using sigmoid activation functions, e.g., *hyperbolic tangent function*, rather than using ReLu's. Thus, we assume that a set of <5 features is highly correlated with the binary target and the classification strongly depends on very few features. After analysis, we obtained that there is a considerable correlation between the target and the CPU and GC features (at least about 0.75). In the following, we present a selection of the obtained results for the LogReg and RF. We do this case wise and illustrate the results using boxplots. Figure 4 shows the performance for case 1 of LogReg and RF of 100 runs with in each randomly sampled training and test data.

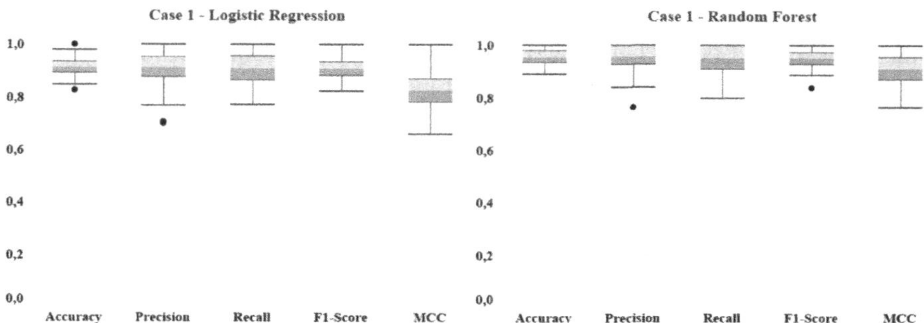

Fig. 4. Results of LogReg and RF for case 1 over 100 runs

We see that both classifier achieved good prediction quality within 100 runs but RF outperforms the LogReg in case of all performance metrics having median values of

0.96 (accuracy), 0.96 (precision), 0.95 (recall), 0.95 (F1-Score) and 0.91 (MCC) while the median values for LogReg are 0.91 (accuracy), 0.91 (precision), 0.91 (recall), 0.91 (F1-Score) and 0.83 (MCC). These results confirm the very good performance of the NN for the classification task on the data of the CMS. We remark that it is difficult to compare the results of a single run for NN and 100 runs for LogReg and RF but as a first impression, all of the three classification methods show a very strong predictive ability. The results of all remaining cases are similarly high without considerable differences. Thus, we summarize that a lead time window of 15 min has no apparent influence on the prediction accuracy. Due to our experimental setup, 15 min are the maximum horizon to forecast the system state of the CMS since we triggered changes of the system state every 15 min to the system as described in Sect. 3.2. This circumstance limits the forecasting horizon within our experiment for further analysis. However, we moreover investigated that an increasing number of past observations considered for analysis of cases with an identic lead time window significantly decreases the range of upper and lower quartiles and the whiskers. Thus, we obtained more stable results with less variation along the 100 runs. Figure 5 illustrates the results of case 13 of LogReg and RF.

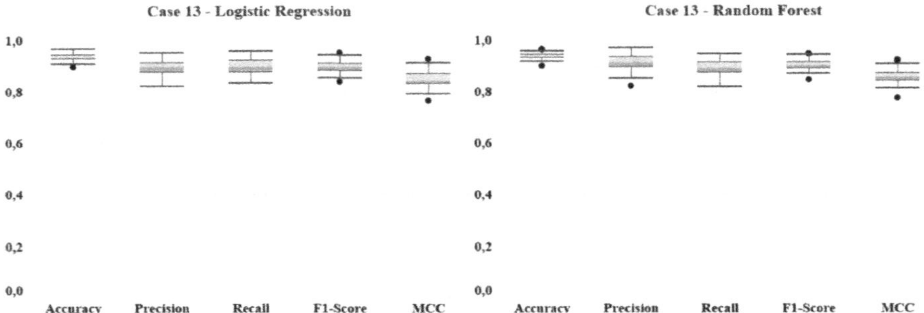

Fig. 5. Results of LogReg and RF for case 13 over 100 runs

For example, the quartiles of the recall measures of LogReg for case 1 are 0.96/0.86 and the whiskers are 1.00/0.77 while we obtained 0.92/0.88 for the quartiles and 0.96/0.83 for the whiskers of case 13. For RF, the recall measures of case 1 of the quartiles are 1.00/0.90 and the whiskers are 1.00/0.80 while for case 13, the quartiles are 0.91/0.87 and the whiskers are 0.95/0.82. This effect is consistently presents in all cases if the number of past observations increases and the lead time window remains unchanged. Summarized, we obtained (very) good prediction quality for LogReg, RF and NN and more stable, i.e., a less degree of variation, results if we consider more past observations to predict the system state with the same lead time window.

6.2 Feature Importance

To give IT-operators guidance about which features are most likely to be important for the judgement of the system state, we use MDA and MDG. The first one quantifies the feature importance by measuring the change of the prediction quality if the measures of the feature are randomly permuted, compared to the original observation. On the other hand, MDG is the sum of all decreases in Gini impurity to a given feature that the RF uses to form a split, normalized by the number of trees [33]. Similar to the performance measures, we calculated measures for MDA and MDG in each run and illustrate a selection of the results using boxplots. Figure 6 presents the results of MDG for case 1 that have a value of ≥5.

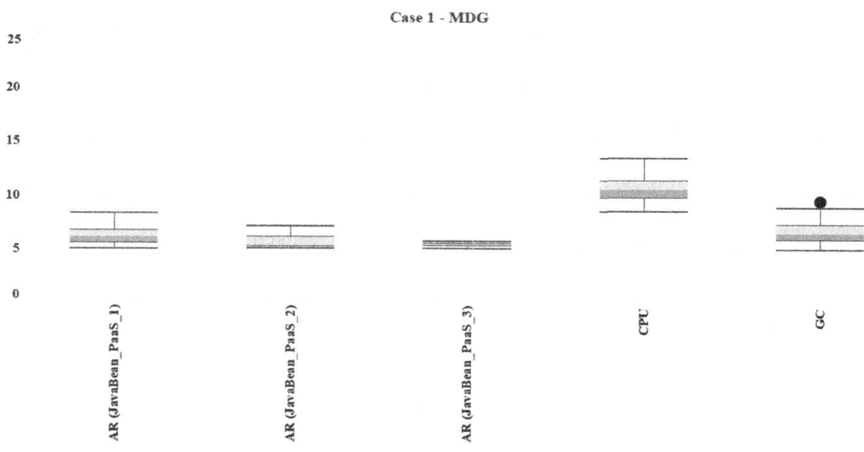

Fig. 6. MDG for case 1 over 100 runs

We see that MDG judges 5 features as important if the threshold is set to ≥5. These features are CPU, GC and three different features of the AR group of metrics, i.e., calls of JavaBeans. Using the same threshold for MDA, it judges 17 features in total as important. For the sake of space, Fig. 7 illustrates the results of the top-10 ranked features only.

We clearly see the overlap: all of the five features that MDG judged as important, MDA judges as important as well. Both measures show that the CPU utilization is the predominant feature. This impression confirms in case of the analysis of other configuration cases, which we but do not illustrate. For example, the increasing lead time window of case 4 increases the importance of the CPU up to a MDG median value of 66.83. MDA confirms this increase for case 4 having a median value of 31.92 for the CPU feature. Moreover, MDA judges the occurrence of an IaaS log file event as important for case 4, after all in 10 of the runs having a median value of 5.40. The importance of log file events is confirmed in several configuration cases, e.g., case 8 and 12, by MDA as well as MDG. Unfortunately, we are unable to derive any generic assumption for this effect since the importance of log file events occurs more likely sporadic. Nevertheless, it confirms the interplay of both types of IT-system data with the overall system state. Summarized, the CPU utilization is after analysis the most promising indicator for the system turning into critical in the most configuration cases having consistently MDA and MDG values of at least ≥5. Furthermore, the CPU utilization is the only feature that consistently shows to be important including its past observations, i.e., t_{-5} etc., for configurations considering multiple copies of the past observations in their data sets. This is consistent

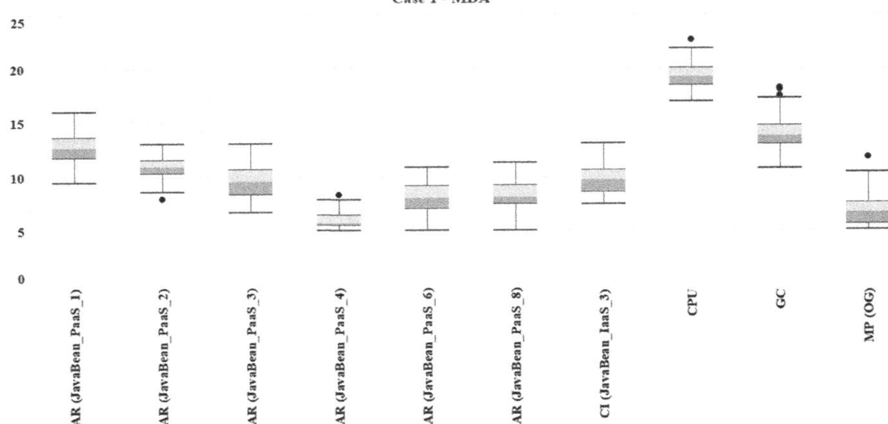

Fig. 7. MDA for case 1 over 100 runs (top-10 ranked features)

with our labeling approach based on the number of vUsers since each user very likely increases the CPU load. However, our results show that we moreover identified different AR, CI, MP or log file related features to be important in different configuration cases. We assume that these features would be difficult to investigate using domain knowledge only. IT-systems contain a high number of different system parameters and their impact to the system state may be hard to recognize without a statistical analysis. Thus, our method and models deliver advanced knowledge about the underlying IT-system and its inner workings related to the overall system state.

7 Threats to Validity

We acknowledge our experimental setup for data acquisition as main threat to construct validity and assume that the low load intensity on the CMS biased the evaluation of the predictive models. At the data-level, we identified that some of the measures of the features do not significantly differ independently whether the label is either 1 or 0. This is the result of:

1. A system state that probably never seriously endangered due to the maximum of 25 vUsers working on the CMS at the same time
2. An experimental and deterministic labeling on data that probably does not contain measures representing a real critical system state

We assume that our experimental setup for data acquisition is the main trigger for the conspicuous high performance metrics. Nevertheless, we addressed the threat of internal validity using an evaluation design with different configuration cases and 100 runs with randomly sampled data for training and test. Thus, at the algorithm-level we considered various parametrizations for our models, trained them on different data and tested them on unseen data to avoid phenomenon like overfitting to be the cause for the high prediction accuracy. Furthermore, we applied a set of different performance measures to ensure a fair and honest evaluation. In case of external validity, we propose a generalizable methodical approach for the joint analysis of textual and numerical IT-system data to predict the system state. However, the nature of ML methods is that they exclusively depend on the data used for the model fitting. Thus, our results are specific to the industrial IT-system used for data acquisition.

Despite all these threats and countermeasures, we emphasize that the main contribution of this work is the process and outline of steps that starts from heterogeneous data of incompatible type (numeric and textual), going through a data type unification for admissibility for statistical analysis, whose interpretation is presented with a discussion of potential pitfalls and possible conclusions. Thus, the threats to validity do not extend to the described method itself.

8 Conclusion and Future Work

We present a method to predict the overall state of IT-systems using a combination of heterogeneous data sources. Our method breaks down limitations of analyzing data with incompatible formats by compiling textual log file information and numeric data into a single prediction model. This method is designed towards explainability to identify root causes with help of statistical methods, which may ease the initiation of countermeasures to avoid system downtimes. We achieved following results:

1. **On RQ1:** We used a set of different data preparation processes to unify textual and numerical IT-system data in a single ML model. Our method requires a minimum degree of domain knowledge and is applicable to any IT-system (although data preparation processes always depend on the specific application and data) but is conceptually generalizable to incorporate domain knowledge if available.
2. **On RQ2:** We see that all models achieved high prediction quality even if the results of the NN seem to outperform LogReg and RF results. We admit that this impression may be biased since 100 runs on randomly sampled data to evaluate the NN were impractical due to the required computational time for training and testing.
3. **On RQ3:** The analysis of the feature importance points out the CPU utilization as most promising indicator to judge the system state. Thus, is should be considered as preferred root cause in case of alarms. It is also admitted that this result is to be taken specific for the experimental setup and may come out of different in other practical instances of systems. Nonetheless, the general reasoning behind this finding does apply to other settings than we described.

Our method and evaluation design allow us to analyze and to predict the overall system state using various available system parameters, covering a wide and diverse range of sources and formats. By analyzing the feature importance, we clearly see that monitoring metrics as well as log file events affect the system state and may be considered as root causes in different configuration cases. This analysis allows us to give IT-operators substantiated guidance on which system parameters to focus on in case of alarms. We believe that such a statistical analysis along all available system parameters accelerates the decision making of IT-operators. Moreover, we think that a detailed analysis would be hard to beat if we only consider domain knowledge and experience of the IT-operators although both are not negligible. Future work will complement the evaluation of our method by experts, i.e., monitoring architects and IT-operators. The expert evaluation will focus and the feasibility, utility and usability of our method in case of its practical applicability. Moreover, we will publish results of an empirical study that investigates the applicability of ML methods specific to the IT-operations area in general. Among others, this study will analyze the tradeoff between high accuracy vs. high explainability of ML models for prediction of IT incidents.

References

1. Kubiak, P., Rass, S., Pinzger, M.: IT-Application Behaviour Analysis: Predicting Critical System States on OpenStack using Monitoring Performance Data and Log Files, pp. 589–596. SCITEPRESS - Science and Technology Publications, Lieusaint - Paris (2020)
2. Kubiak, P., Rass, S.: An overview of data-driven techniques for IT-service-management. IEEE Access **6**, 63664–63688 (2018)
3. Hochstein, A., Tamm, G., Brenner, W.: Service-oriented IT management: benefit, cost and success factors. In: Proceedings of the 13th European Conference on Information Systems, Information Systems in a Rapidly Changing Economy, Regensburg, Germany (2005)
4. Potgieter, B.C., Botha, J.H., Lew, C.: Evidence that use of the ITIL framework is effective. In: Proceedings of the 8th Annual Conference of the National Advisory Committee on Computing Qualifications, Tauranga, New Zealand, pp. 160–167 (2005)
5. Salfner, F., Lenk, M., Malek, M.: A survey of online failure prediction methods. ACM Comput. Surv. (CSUR), **42**, 1–42 (2010)
6. Andrzejak, A., Silva, L.: Deterministic models of software aging and optimal rejuvenation schedules. In: 2007 10th IFIP/IEEE International Symposium on Integrated Network Management, pp 159–168. IEEE, Munich (2007)
7. Cheng, F.-T., Wu, S.-L., Tsai, P.-Y., et al.: Application cluster service scheme for near-zero-downtime services. In: Proceedings of the 2005 IEEE International Conference on Robotics and Automation, pp. 4062–4067. IEEE, Barcelona (2005)
8. Murray, J., Hughes, G., Kreutz-Delgado, K.: Hard drive failure prediction using non-parametric statistical methods. In: Proceedings of the ICANN/ICONIP (2003)
9. Kiciman, E., Fox, A.: Detecting application - level failures in component-based inernet services. IEEE Trans. Neural Netw. **16**, 1027–1041 (2005)
10. Shen, J., Wan, J., Lim, S.-J., Yu, L.: Random-forest-based failure prediction for hard disk drives. Int. J. Distrib. Sens. Netw. **14**, 155014771880648 (2018). https://doi.org/10.1177/1550147718806480
11. Zeng, C., Tang, L., Li, T., et al.: Mining temporal lag from fluctuating events for correlation and root cause analysis. In: Proceedings of the 10th International Conference on Network and Service Management (CNSM), Rio de Janeiro, Brazil (2014)
12. Kiran, R.U., Shang, H., Toyoda, M., Kitsuregawa, M.: Discovering recurring patterns in time series. In: Proceedings of the International Conference on Extending Database Technology, Brussels, Belgium (2015)
13. Kiyota, N., Shimamura, S., Hirata, K.: Extracting mutually dependent multisets. In: Yamamoto, A., Kida, T., Uno, T., Kuboyama, T. (eds.) DS 2017. LNCS (LNAI), vol. 10558, pp. 267–280. Springer, Cham (2017). https://doi.org/10.1007/978-3-319-67786-6_19

14. Zöller, M.-A., Baum, M., Huber, M.F.: Framework for mining event correlations and time lags in large event sequences. In: Proceedings of the IEEE 15th International Conference on Industrial Informatics (INDIN), Emden, Germany (2017)
15. Kiernan, J., Terzi, E.: Constructing comprehensive summaries of large event sequences. ACM Trans. Knowl. Discov. Data (TKDD) **3**, 1–31 (2009)
16. Jiang, Y., Perng, C.S., Li, T.: Natural event summarization. In: Proceedings of the 20th ACM International Conference on Information and Knowledge Management (2011)
17. Luo, C., Fu, Q., Lou, J.-G., et al.: Correlating events with time series for incident diagnosis. In: Proceedings of the 20th ACM SIGKDD International Conference on Knowledge Discovery and Data Mining, New York, NY, USA (2014)
18. Li, T., et al.: Data-driven techniques in computing system management. ACM Comput. Surv. **50**(3), 1–43 (2017). https://doi.org/10.1145/3092697
19. Imai, K.: Quantitative Social Science: An Introduction. Princeton University Press, Woodstock (2017)
20. Ester, M., Kriegel, H.-P., Sander, J., Xiaowei, X.: A density-based algorithm for discovering clusters in large spatial databases with noise. In: Proceedings of the Second International Conference on Knowledge Discovery and Data Mining (KDD'96), pp. 226–231 (1996)
21. Raschka, S., Mirjalili, V.: Machine Learning mit Python und Scikit-Learn und TensorFlow: das umfassende Praxis-Handbuch für Data Science, Deep Learning und Predictive Analytics, 2nd Edn. mitp, Frechen (2018)
22. Zhang, S., Zhang, C., Yang, Q.: Data preparation for data mining. Appl. Artif. Intell. **17**, 375–381 (2003). https://doi.org/10.1080/713827180
23. Kuhn, M., Johnson, K.: Feature Engineering and Selection: A Practical Approach for Predictive Models. CRC Press, Taylor & Francis Group, Boca Raton (2020)
24. Schober, P., Boer, C., Schwarte, L.A.: Correlation coefficients: appropriate use and interpretation. Anesth. Analg. **126**, 1763–1768 (2018)
25. Salgado, C.M., Azevedo, C., Proença, H., Vieira, S.: Noise versus outliers. In: Secondary Analysis of Electronic Health Records, pp. 163–183. Springer, Cham (2016). https://doi.org/10.1007/978-3-319-43742-2_14
26. Sauer, S.: Moderne Datenanalyse mit R: Daten einlesen, aufbereiten, visualisieren und modellieren. Springer, Wiesbaden (2018). https://doi.org/10.1007/978-3-658-21587-3
27. Senaviratna, N.A.M.R, Cooray, T.M.J.A.: Diagnosing multicollinearity of logistic regression model. In: AJPAS, pp. 1–9 (2019). https://doi.org/10.9734/ajpas/2019/v5i230132
28. Hosmer, D.W., Lemeshow, S.: Applied Logistic Regression, 2nd edn. Wiley, New York (2000)
29. James, G., Witten, D., Hastie, T., Tibshirani, R.: An introduction to statistical learning: with applications in R. Springer, New York (2013). https://doi.org/10.1007/978-1-4614-7138-7
30. Hastie, T., Tibshirani, R., Friedman, J.: The Elements of Statistical Learning: Data Mining, Inference, and Prediction, 2nd edn. Springer, New York (2009). https://doi.org/10.1007/978-0-387-84858-7
31. Louppe, G., Wehenkel, L., Sutera, A., Geurts, P.: Understanding variable importances in forests of randomized trees. In: Proceedings of the 26th International Conference on Neural Information Processing Systems (2013)
32. Genuer, R., Poggi, J.-M., Tuleau-Malot, C.: Variable selection using random forests. Pattern Recogn. Lett. **31**, 2225–2236 (2010)
33. Calle, M.L., Urrea, V.: Letter to the editor: stability of random forest importance measures. Brief. Bioinform. **12**, 86–89 (2011). https://doi.org/10.1093/bib/bbq011

Author Index

Printed in the United States
by Baker & Taylor Publisher Services